THE OUTER FRINGE

Faculty Benefits Other Than Annuities and Insurance

A special study for the Commission on Faculty and
Staff Benefits of the Association of American Colleges
directed by Mark H. Ingraham of the University of Wisconsin
with the collaboration of Francis P. King of the
Teachers Insurance and Annuity Association

THE
OUTER
FRINGE

Faculty Benefits Other
Than Annuities and Insurance

MARK H. INGRAHAM

with the collaboration of
FRANCIS P. KING

THE UNIVERSITY OF WISCONSIN PRESS
MADISON AND MILWAUKEE, 1965

Published by
The University of Wisconsin Press
Madison and Milwaukee
Mailing address: P.O. Box 1379, Madison, Wisconsin 53701

Printed in the United States of America
by North Central Publishing Company, St. Paul, Minnesota

Library of Congress Catalog Card Number 65-13503

PREFACE

LIKE the genera of insects, the range of faculty benefits is multivarious. Perhaps, after salary, the most important benefits are retirement plans and insurance provisions. The study of these by Greenough and King has been an invaluable source of information.

However, there are a large number of other programs of faculty benefits used by institutions of higher education in this country and many have believed that a factual report concerning their use, as well as an analysis of their relative worth and the conditions that lead to their success, would be of value.

Under the sponsorship of the Commission on Faculty and Staff Benefits of the Association of American Colleges, plans for such a study were developed and support for it secured. In particular, William C. Greenough, President of Teachers Insurance and Annuity Association of America, Theodore A. Distler, Executive Director of the AAC and now its President, and J. Douglas Brown of Princeton, Chairman of the Commission, were active in this regard. Moreover, they have actively helped throughout the preparation of this report, as has Thomas C. Edwards, Executive Vice President of TIAA. Generous financial support was provided by the U.S. Steel Foundation. The Association of American Colleges and the American Association of University Professors also made contributions. The Teachers Insurance and Annuity Association of America donated free use of its facilities and the time of its staff. The University of Wisconsin cooperated in many ways.

By agreement with the Chairman, it was concluded that this report should be published without being submitted to the AAC Commission on faculty benefits, with the full understanding that the Commission may arrive at its own conclusions which, of course, might be at variance with those of the author. It was believed that the fullest consideration would be given to the subject if this book were published and reactions to its conclusions were available before consideration of its substance by the Commission. The budget of the study has funds set aside for conferences of the Commission and possibly of others on these matters.

The decision that this was to be a report *to* a committee rather than *of* a committee was welcome. So often I have written with an eye to the rewrite of a drafting subcommittee — which would mutilate the style, tone down the meaning, and write as if one had to be solemn to be serious — that this decision gave me a rather heady feeling.

It is partly because the report is not that of a committee that I have used the first-person singular throughout. This should remind the reader that the conclusions are the responsibility of a single person and are based on data, discussion, advice, experience, and perhaps prejudice. It should also help to distinguish between that which is reporting and that which is opinion.

But even if this is not a report of the committee, it also is not the product of a single person or of a small group of individuals. The data was furnished by many institutions in answer to a long questionnaire, and the judgments of experienced administrators were generously given. These judgments are not only quoted and paraphrased throughout this report, but they greatly affected the opinions and conclusions of the undersigned.

The author is grateful to the presidents and other administrative officers of colleges and universities who responded to the questionnaire (starting with St. Mary's College of Winona, Minnesota, whose reply was the first to be received), but especially to those of some thirty institutions who not only answered the questionnaire in its final form, but also in the summer and fall of 1962 cooperated in a trial run. He appreciates the courtesy of presidents of institutions, such as the one with only one full-time lay faculty member, who explained why the questionnaire was not being filled out.

In the formative stage the active help and the welcome advice of W. Robert Bokelman, of the U.S. Office of Education, and of Peggy Heim, of the American Association of University Professors, were of great assistance. Dr. Heim and William P. Fidler, General Secretary of the AAUP, also read the chapter on leaves and made useful suggestions. I wish to thank Kathleen McQuillan, Mary Tambini, Antonette Madden, Joanne Fricano, Giovanni Pilla, and Patrick Hanbury of the TIAA staff. I also thank the following members of the staff of the University of

Wisconsin: Mrs. Carol Grumann, who typed manifold drafts of the manuscript; Mrs. Nancy Miller, who organized the files of the questionnaires and correspondence, thereby bringing order out of chaos; and especially, Mrs. Helen Guzman, who helped throughout, assisting in organizing the questionnaire, turning my scrawls into a workable draft, and giving invaluable advice on both the content and phrasing of the final report.

Francis P. King, of the Educational Research Department of TIAA, collaborated throughout the study. He was the chief designer of the questionnaire. He directed the coding of the answers and the summarizing of these replies. It was a privilege to have such a colleague. The undersigned expected that King would be listed as one of the authors; it was his preference not to be. I can only express my gratitude to him. This arrangement makes it evident that the faults of this book are mine; I wish it could be made equally clear that many of its virtues are his.

MARK H. INGRAHAM

May, 1964

CONTENTS

*"The world is so full of a number of things
I am sure we should all be as happy as kings."*

LIST OF APPENDICES

THE OUTER FRINGE

Faculty Benefits Other Than Annuities and Insurance

CHAPTER 1

INTRODUCTION

THE most important compensation of a faculty member is the opportunity to do pleasant and useful work under conditions that make it effective and to live in a community of scholars without incurring undue economic hardship for either himself or his family. Therefore, we ensure first the conditions that make a scholar's work effective. These include library facilities, equipment, students, and a schedule of work that does not preclude performance of high quality. These also involve academic freedom, tenure, and administrative understanding. But, in addition to these, a degree of economic well-being and security is vital. Salary, retirement provisions, and various types of insurance are of major importance in this regard. However, other perquisites may be of great value and under certain circumstances prove of comparable importance with any benefits other than working conditions and salary.

The problem of the use of institutional resources to enhance the educational program, along with the related and interdependent problem of increasing those resources, is always complicated. How much should be spent on equipment, buildings, and supporting services, and how much on the salaries of the faculty? Unbalanced decisions in this regard may ruin an institution.

Even when the total faculty compensation budget is known, its distribution must be determined. How much goes to the young; how much to the old? Is the distribution made by a scale or largely by individual decisions? Note that this question can easily be asked so as to prejudice the answer. For example: "Shall we pay people by a rigid rule or on the basis of individual merit?" or "Shall we have an equitable, well-understood schedule of payments or leave it to arbitrary administrative decisions?" One of the privileges of being an ex-dean is not to worry about this problem.

Salary is a very good way to pay people. This is so obvious that any other mode needs justification. By means of salary the greatest degree of freedom is given the individual to use his compensation in the way he wishes. It maximizes liberty. By means of salary the clearest decisions as to merit or competitive status may be made; however, unless administrative decisions are wise, this may not be a blessing. Yet salary alone seldom provides the most effective compensation.

A retirement program is clearly a part of a wise compensation plan, but it immediately presents many questions: For instance, how much known present compensation should one sacrifice for future probable income? Who contributes to the retirement system? When *may* a man retire? When *must* he? Also insurance — life, medical, disability — all present problems and opportunities. Fortunately, the Teachers Insurance and Annuity Association of America has not only been run soundly from a financial point of view but has provided leadership in the analysis of these programs. Moreover, the sequence of books by Robbins, and then by Greenough, and most recently by Greenough and King, *Retirement and Insurance Plans in American Colleges,** both describe practices and provide counsel on these matters. The latest of these, although five years old, is still of major use, and most of the factual material is currently valid.

The purpose of the present book is to report and comment upon certain of the major faculty benefits other than salary, retirement provisions, and insurance that are being provided in the colleges and universities of the United States.

DIVERSITY OF CIRCUMSTANCES. One broad generalization may be made. The nature, value, and feasibility of the staff benefits described in this report vary more widely from institution to institution than do the nature of and need for salary, retirement provisions, and insurance programs. It is imperative in some places for the institution to help provide housing for the faculty. In others this is of minor importance. In between are institutions where housing is needed for new faculty only. Travel requirements are different in the Rocky Mountains where there are few national meetings from the requirements in Washington where there is a surfeit of them. Parking needs may differ not only with the size of the community but also with climate. From both Alaska and Texas we hear of the desirability of the car being close to the office because of temperature extremes.

Tax regulations, both state and local, enter into the planning of a

---

* William C. Greenough and Francis P. King, *Retirement and Insurance Plans in American Colleges* (New York: Columbia University Press, 1959).

benefit program, for example, in determining the amount of the contribution that the institution makes toward retirement annuities and insurance, or in planning a housing program. Changes in tax rules will affect the logic behind staff benefits, as in the case of recent changes in regard to moving expenses.

TYPES OF BENEFITS. Some staff benefits are largely means of compensating the faculty in ways that give them more than if the equivalent in cost were paid in salary. These may result in savings to the faculty because of the lesser cost of doing things on a group basis than on an individual one, or because of savings through use of the institution's favorable purchasing power. Examples are low rentals, low-interest mortgage loans, family education privileges, campus hospital and medical services, and purchases through the university. Others are facilities of minor pecuniary importance but affording conveniences or pleasant privileges, e.g., faculty club, athletic privileges, preferential treatment in regard to attendance at lectures, concerts, athletic events, and perhaps parking. Other items represent in part conditions of work and in part staff benefits, such as travel expenses and research leaves. Personal loans to meet family exigencies are hard to classify. Many benefits are not monochromatic but are represented by a number of lines in the spectrum: This makes the author's job interesting.

Among the benefits discussed are some which are included in this survey upon the insistence of many colleagues but which other colleagues consider merely conditions of effective work, e.g., secretarial help and adequate parking facilities.

In general this book consists of a sequence of chapters describing particular types of faculty benefits, giving in brief form the major facts about the present practices in regard to them while trying to analyze the purpose of each, the conditions which lead to emphasis on a particular item, the advantages and disadvantages of a benefit under varying circumstances, and the provisions which lead to the success of a given program. The author's judgments are frankly stated; his prejudices may be equally apparent.

Those benefits which, though often affecting his work, are chiefly for the financial or other personal advantage of the individual faculty member are discussed first. These are given in Chapter 2 through 6. Starting with Chapter 7 (on leaves) and going through Chapter 11, benefits largely ancillary to the work of the faculty member are dealt with.

Chapter 12 is devoted to the status of the retired faculty and widows of faculty members. Chapter 13 contains comments on certain miscellaneous topics and a large " 'They' Say" section. Chapter 14 gives my conclusions concerning staff benefits and suggestions for their review by individual institutions.

This report is based upon the answers to an elaborate questionnaire, upon visits to a number of different colleges and universities in order to understand more clearly the nature of the programs and the problems involved, and upon personal experience.

The questionnaire (see Appendix I) was mailed to the colleges and universities classified by the U.S. Office of Education as offering at least four years of work in the liberal arts leading to a degree. Institutions essentially a part of another institution were not counted separately. There were 999 institutions to which the questionnaire was properly sent (a very few on the mailing list turned out not to meet the above criteria). Of these, 745 returned usable questionnaires in time for IBM tabulation of the statistical results. An additional 12 responses were received in time to be included in the institution-by-institution listing of benefits in Appendix II. Since the larger institutions with few exceptions answered, we believe that about 90% of the faculty members of the institutions to whom questionnaires were sent are covered by the replies. (Only the lay faculty members of Catholic institutions were included in the study.)

We are really elated by the coverage.

Any educator who sends out such an almost unforgivably long questionnaire should pay for his sins. I have done so. First of all, there were many questions whose answers could not be tabulated on the IBM machine. I read the replies to all of these. Secondly, I have spent much time trying to decide what the replies meant. English is a common language in part only. Local usage differs greatly. What is a leave? There is no common answer. Worse yet, what is a sabbatical leave? If I ask you a question and describe your answers to a third party, there are three sources of error besides misinformation: your misunderstanding of what I ask, my misunderstanding of what you reply, and X's misunderstanding of what I say you mean. Thus do we secure the bases for intelligent action.

A feature which we hope will add to the value of this report and which we are sure will add to its interest is the inclusion, usually at the end of each chapter describing particular benefits, of a " 'They' Say" section quoting or paraphrasing answers in the replies to the questionnaire. Sometimes these add factual material but more often they represent the reactions to or evaluation of various programs by college administrators. A rather extensive "'They' Say" section is also included in Chapter 13.

Since many persons may desire to read only a single chapter on a topic uppermost in their minds, we have consciously repeated certain statements. This may annoy the rare person who reads the whole book; it should make it more useful for all others.

The main text is followed by four appendices. Appendix I is a copy of the questionnaire. Appendix II consists of a table in which certain items are tabulated individually for each responding institution. Appendix III contains a large number of summary tables based on the answers of 745 institutions. Finally, a chart of the advantages and disadvantages of the various benefits (admittedly in part subjective) forms Appendix IV.

It was difficult to determine how detailed the classifications of institutions should be in the summary tables. Clearly many facts are available that any broad classification disguises — such as those based on size, region, or financial resources. However, for most purposes we considered that a simple division into four categories — namely, private colleges, private universities, public colleges, and public universities — was the best available compromise. The author will be willing to furnish more detailed information to institutions which desire it during the period in which the data remain relevant.

CHAPTER 2

HOUSING

IT is fortunate that the discussion of particular benefits starts with programs for faculty housing since such programs present a large number of the aspects typical of other benefits. The need for housing varies greatly from institution to institution and among various groups within a faculty. A housing program often is expensive and hence many institutions cannot afford one. Local and state tax rules enter the situation. Public relations with banks, realtors, and house owners are affected by the program. The expansion plans for the academic campus and the desire to control the environment of the institution may be major considerations. There is no uniformly desirable goal to move toward as there is in the case of retirement plans or of salaries.

There are two distinct major divisions of housing programs, sometimes used together but frequently alone: the owning by the institution of accommodations for rent to the faculty, and the granting of mortgages on faculty-owned homes. Even these merge in the case of mortgages on faculty-owned homes built on land rented from the institution or on land with restrictions as to its sale. Since both housing programs are aimed at providing decent living accommodations for the faculty at reasonable rates, we shall treat them in the same chapter.

TYPES OF HOUSING PLANS

RENTAL. The rental programs tend to fall into the following overlapping types:

1. Extensive programs for a large portion of the faculty with long-time occupation permitted.
2. Plans for the housing of new members of the faculty for a few years.
3. Plans basically designed to protect or improve the environment of the institution, with preferential use of the land for housing of faculty members.

4. Plans incidental to campus expansions, the housing usually already on the acquired land and destined to be demolished at some later date.

In addition, incidental ownership of houses acquired by gift or purchase account for a fairly large number of faculty residences.

MORTGAGES. The mortgage programs also follow several general plans, more than one of which is often used by a single institution:

1. Low-rate first mortgages up to a higher proportion of the value of the house than is usually obtainable commercially.
2. Low-rate second mortgages.
3. Mortgages for homes on land furnished by the institution at low cost but with restrictions on the sale of the homes, frequently limited to sale to other faculty members.

In addition, many institutions with no plan for mortgages on faculty houses have made a number of mortgage loans to faculty members on an individual basis.

GENERAL. A few institutions have well-conceived and almost complete plans for faculty housing. These institutions are chiefly: (*a*) private, (*b*) well-to-do, (*c*) in not very large places. Such a plan for housing often has apartments for rent to junior staff, some rental housing for senior staff, land on which members of faculty may build houses but with restrictive clauses so that the continuation of the use of the homes by faculty members is assured, and mortgages at below commercial rates. In this connection, the plan at Princeton will be described later.

MAGNITUDE AND FREQUENCY. Approximately 60% of the institutions responding to the questionnaire had some housing which they rented to faculty members. There was no striking difference between public and private institutions nor between universities and colleges in this regard. However, the programs in private institutions cover a larger portion of the faculty. Of the faculties of public institutions, 5% are in housing owned by the institutions, whereas over 13% of the faculties of private institutions are so housed. In those institutions having such housing, 9% of the faculty in public institutions and 20% of the faculty in private institutions live in these accommodations. The total number of faculty reported in such housing by replying institutions exceeds 12,000.

The programs of mortgage loans for faculty, although important, affect about one-third as many faculty members as do rental programs, largely because the number of institutions making such loans is about one-third as many as those owning housing for faculty rental. To a high degree programs of mortgage loans are concentrated in private institutions. The total amount of mortgage loans on faculty houses held by institutions employing faculty members exceeds 46 million dollars. Of these 46 million dollars, over 32 millions are held by fifteen institutions each with not less than half-a-million dollars of mortgage loans on faculty homes.

RENTAL HOUSING

INSTITUTIONAL OWNERSHIP OF DWELLING HOUSES OR APARTMENTS TO BE RENTED TO FACULTY MEMBERS. As stated above, about 60% of the replying institutions own apartments or houses for faculty occupancy. Over a third of these house less than 10% of the faculty in such buildings. However, in the neighborhood of 15% to 20% of our institutions house a third or more of their faculties in this fashion. Many institutions combine this plan with providing mortgages at low interest rates for faculty homes.

PRIORITIES. Slightly more than half of the institutions which own dwellings for rental to members of their faculties have some established priority system for the assignment of housing. The most frequent priority classification is for new faculty members, and the next most frequent is "special need." Of course we find that, where there are only a few houses available, the decisions are apt to be on an individual basis; where there are a large number available, the order of applications may well be the only criterion necessary.

LIMITATIONS ON LENGTH OF OCCUPANCY. If a rather small number of houses are available chiefly for new members, then some limitation on the length of occupancy may be established. Frequently a specified number of years — such as one, three, or five — is used. However, most institutions do not specify the length of time houses or apartments may be occupied by a faculty member. One large university increases the rent after two years of occupation — a method, the effectiveness of which was not reported, to help preserve the limited amount of housing available for new faculty members.

At the other end of the employment period, other questions arise. May a faculty member occupy a house owned by the institution after retirement; and, if so, may his widow continue to occupy it? The evidence we have, although inadequate, would indicate that upon retirement the faculty member usually must relinquish the house. A few institutions have provided special rental space for retired (or near retired) faculty members, and this is clearly in the forefront of the administrators' consciousness at a number of other places.

RENTAL RATES. In rough figures, about 40% of the institutions that rent living quarters to the faculty estimate that the rental rates are about the same or slightly below the commercial rates for accommodations of approximately the same quality; about 40% at between 10% and 25% below commercial rents; and about 20% at a still lower figure. The centering on a figure from 10% to 25% below commercial rates is even more pronounced if we consider institutions with large housing programs.

The estimated cost of a rental program to the institution will be discussed later.

Housing furnished as part of compensation is of minor significance. Most institutions do not do this and those that use such a plan generally do so in only one or two instances.

The answers to the free-wheeling questions concerning special provisions, special problems, and special inherent values of the program were particularly interesting. Some of these will be described below; most of them have entered indirectly into the writing of this chapter. Others are quoted at the end of the chapter under " 'They' Say."

HOUSING FOR CERTAIN GROUPS. A number of institutions use the housing they own to rent to individuals belonging to specified groups who might otherwise have unusual difficulty in finding houses at suitable rates or whom, for one reason or another, the institution wishes to favor. As illustrations of these groups:

1. Visiting faculty members or other temporary appointees. This is particularly worthwhile if the houses or apartments are furnished.
2. Young instructors at the college who are doing graduate work at neighboring institutions.
3. Ministers belonging to the faculty. (In this connection one institution listed: "To provide housing or 'manses' for ministers who are entering education and have come to expect that housing be provided.")

Such accommodations have also been used to provide housing without regard to race, with special attention to groups which in the particular community would find it hard to obtain suitable dwellings near the campus. Some institutions also refuse to list housing which is subject to racial discriminations.

HOUSING CORPORATIONS. Some institutions have found it desirable to create housing corporations, legally distinct from the institution but in essence formed to serve it, which build and rent houses to faculty members in preference to others. This not only may remove from the college the strain inherent in the landlord-tenant relationship, but also may avoid difficulties that otherwise might arise between the institution and outside financial interests — especially where these interests, such as local banks, participate in forming the corporation. Further descriptions of some of these plans are given in the " 'They' Say" section.

SPECIAL PROBLEMS. Perhaps the most amusing reading among the replies to the questionnaire came under the heading of "Significant Problems" and, with the exception of the problems connected with parking, the frustration in the answers to this section "led all the rest." The customary human foibles show in the faculty as described and in the administrator in describing; but these do not keep the problems from being significant.

Many of the problems can be put into one of three groups: (1) those involving expenses; (2) those involving public relations; and (3) those involving landlord-tenant relationships. The discussion of the first two of these will be postponed until after the description of mortgage plans. The third we shall now discuss.

LANDLORD-TENANT RELATIONSHIPS. This is a generally recognized problem but is more in the front of the mind of the president in a small college whose office may be directly involved than of a president of an institution which has an adequate housing office. It is also increased in a faculty colony where a college feud may become a neighborhood feud or vice versa.

Some of the troubles reported are "unreasonable" demands for redecorating, repairs, etc. These are accentuated where turnover is great and the new tenant abominates the taste of the last. It was probably some such worry that led one administrator, a man, to put under the category "Significant Problems" "wives" (which is different from the answer of another, "pets").

A vice-president of a public university, with a substantial program for new faculty members in their first two years with the institution and with rents estimated to be between 10% and 25% below commercial rates, made the following thoughtful analysis:

(*a*) General Purposes of Housing Program:
 1. To enable new faculty people to more easily get moved into and established in a new community without incurring the cost and risk of an investment in housing.
 2. To help recruit young faculty people who are purchasing durable goods and incurring moving costs and who, therefore, need subsidized housing.
 3. To give young faculty people two years to decide whether they want to remain at the University and to make a decision about where they wish to live in the . . . community.

(*b*) Significant Problems:
 1. Some faculty people are reluctant to make the transition to privately-owned housing and sometimes look for University-furnished housing at another institution.
 2. A question exists as to whether it is good for morale of new faculty people to be housed in a single area rather than to be integrated into the general University community or the City residential area.

(*c*) Important Special Features:
 1. Major effort to provide good service on repairs, vehicles, maintenance, etc.
 2. Use of individual ground-level duplexes or apartments.

MORTGAGE PROGRAMS

Nearly 15% of the institutions replying make first-mortgage loans to their faculties for homes; an additional 6% make second-mortgage loans; and about 2.5% both. These programs are predominantly in private institutions.

SIZE OF LOANS. About half of the institutions limit first-mortgage loans to 80% or under of property value, and half go above this figure, 10% loaning up to full value.

Most institutions which make second-mortgage loans will go as high as 90% of property value and one-sixth of these institutions will lend up to full cost. Although a substantial number of institutions relate the size of the mortgage loan to the size of the faculty member's salary, the majority have no such rule. Again, although most institutions have no fixed-dollar limit on the size of the mortgage, over one-third of those making such loans do have.

INTEREST RATES. The interest rates on mortgages are clearly below current commercial rates, centering on figures between 4% and 5% inclusive, and some institutions even grant short-term, second-mortgage loans without interest. Often colleges require an increase in the interest payments when faculty members leave their employ.

PLANS WITH RESTRICTIVE CLAUSES AS TO SALE. Some 10% of the institutions have plans to aid faculty members secure land on which to build houses. Many of the more substantial plans are aimed at creating and maintaining a pleasant faculty residential community, usually close to the campus. Frequently the land is furnished at below market value by the college, sometimes at a nominal cost. The homes built on this land must meet appropriate standards. The institution has an interest in who may later occupy the house and frequently places some definite restrictions on the sale and rental of the property.

Typical restrictions are: (1) Houses may be rented (or subrented) only to faculty members or others who are approved by the administration. (2) Houses may be sold only to faculty members or others who are approved by the administration. (3) The house, before sale, must be offered first to the college at fair market value. (4) The college agrees to buy the house and the staff member to sell it to the college at some stipulated value determined in advance by the investment in the house or, in other cases, the fair market value. Modifications and combinations of these restrictions may be used.

SPECIAL FEATURES. Some of the special arrangements mentioned are worth recording. Institutions may limit the privilege of securing a mortgage from them to members of the faculty with tenure. Some institutions require that homes on which they hold mortgages be in the environs of the campus, "environs" having various definitions: "same town," "10 miles," or — as in the case of one women's college where the students may not drive cars — "within bicycling distance."

Just as in the case of rentals, certain institutions are served by a special corporation which makes mortgage loans to the faculty. Several institutions which do not make loans have special arrangements with banks to make mortgage loans upon recommendation, or even on the guarantee, of the institution.

OVERALL PLAN AT PRINCETON

As an example of an overall plan, a description of that at Princeton is given with admiration and also with misgivings. It is well thought-out and is chosen not only for that reason but because fuller details concerning it were furnished than in any other case. In addition, I made a personal visit to see the plan in operation. The misgivings are due to the fact that few institutions, even if they wished to, are in a position financially or administratively to operate such a plan, and hence a description may be of little value. However, the image of heaven has been of use on earth.

About 60% of the faculty either rent their homes from Princeton University or live in homes upon which the university holds the mortgages. In addition to the faculty, equivalent members of the administrative staff are eligible for all aspects of Princeton's housing program. Hence, when faculty is referred to in this section, the same applies to qualifying members of the administration.

The ingredients of the Princeton program involve:

1. Apartments for younger faculty members.
2. Rental housing for established faculty members but with an upper age limit.
3. Rental housing for members near and past retirement.
4. Tracts of land on which faculty may build (with loans from the university) restricted by a repurchase agreement.
5. Mortgages on faculty homes not under such restrictions.
6. A real estate office to service all of the above.

More details on each of these aspects follow:

1. APARTMENTS FOR YOUNGER FACULTY MEMBERS. Approximately 390 apartment units are available for younger faculty members. The rent is considerably below commercial rates, although no real standard of comparison is available. Moreover, the commercial rates might be higher if these apartments did not exist.

One feature of a large eight-story apartment building, beautifully located by Lake Carnegie, is the fact that each apartment unit is two stories high. It is reported that this is a very popular arrangement. "We like to put the children to bed upstairs." Although it would probably be an exaggeration to call these apartments "de luxe," they certainly are at least adequately comfortable.

2. RENTAL HOUSING FOR ESTABLISHED FACULTY MEMBERS. This aspect of the program involves apartments, housing developments, and an assortment of individual houses acquired for various reasons and by various means — as, for instance, in an expansion area of the campus or by gift.

Many of these, especially the larger ones, are rented with a stipulation that occupation must terminate at the age of sixty unless dependent children are living at home. They are not occupied by retired faculty members. Again, the rental rates are substantially below the otherwise high rates in the town.

3. HOUSING FOR RETIRED FACULTY MEMBERS. This aspect is perhaps the weakest portion of this program. However, Princeton, does own, as an investment, some attractive small housing units. These are rented at commercial rates and retired faculty members, or sixty-year-old oustees, have first chance for vacant units.

Princeton pays real estate taxes on all housing owned for rental purposes.

4. LAND-LOAN PROGRAMS. Princeton has several tracts of land which it makes available for faculty houses. The President's (1957) description of this arrangement, omitting that of location, follows. (I like the last sentence.) The upper limits specified have now been raised somewhat.

> The University will make building lots, improved with utilities, available for one dollar each, for construction of a home by the individual for his occupancy and that of surviving spouse. The condition of each transaction is that the University will repurchase the property on a no-loss no-gain basis in the following events:
> 1. Termination of association with the University;
> 2. At any time after retirement, as the individual elects;
> 3. On death of the individual, if the widow elects;
> 4. On death of the widow, if the widow has elected life occupancy;
> 5. Upon the decision of the widow.
>
> .   .   .   .
>
> *Financing*: The University will provide first mortgage assistance to cover the total cost of architect's fees, construction, driveways, utility connections, and landscaping in an amount not to exceed $30,000. Equity investment by the individual to be as follows:
> 10% of the first $20,000 of improvement cost.
> 20% of the next $15,000 of improvement cost.
> Any expenditures in excess of $35,000 are not subject to reimbursement by the University at the time of repurchase. Mortgages will bear interest at a flat 5% per annum with no amortization. An individual may increase his equity by lump sum payments if he desires.
> The above outline is purposely brief but is deemed sufficient to prompt preliminary interest and many questions.

5. MORTGAGE LOANS. Princeton also makes mortgage loans of the conventional type upon the homes of faculty members with rates and limits

which are very advantageous to the borrower. The loan may be made from up to 90% of the value of a small home to about 80% of a $30,000 home. The interest rate is 4% and amortization may be as low as 2% a year. If the faculty member leaves Princeton, the mortgage may be called or, if continued to a non-faculty member, will be at commercial rates.

6. REAL ESTATE DEPARTMENT. The great success of Princeton's housing program, and it is a great success, is due in part to a complete and well-run real estate department. This department manages the apartments and houses owned by the university and rented to the faculty; it also is the agent of the university for making land-loan arrangements or conventional mortgage loans. The multiplicity of the services performed and problems faced are staggering. Just a sample: appraising land, approving architects' plans, arranging financial provisions, fixing radiators, establishing priorities in laundries, persuading people who reach sixty to really move, dealing with the well-known faculty temperament (not at its mildest in the Ivy League), and being cordially courteous to those who want to study Princeton's welfare program. My gratitude is matched by my admiration.

The program at Princeton University is well adapted to its needs and is one from which others may learn much. (It will be noted that I warmed to the Princeton plan as I wrote about it.)

GENERAL REMARKS AND EVALUATIONS

Since I conclude that under certain circumstances housing programs are highly desirable, I shall now describe some of the problems connected with such plans — some inherent, some partly avoidable. I shall especially discuss three: expense, difficulty of relations with the faculty, and public relations.

EXPENSES. As previously stated, most institutions that have housing to rent to the faculty report that the rates are either about the same as commercial rates or are in the range from 75% to 90% of commercial rates. In each case the large majority of these institutions report that "rents approximately cover costs"; a few of those in both categories report a substantial gain from the operation; about a third of the institutions, where the rentals are at 50% to 75% of commercial rates, report that they break even. I doubt if these latter institutions use the same pencil in arriving at the conclusion that they use in computing "indirect costs."

The figures are affected not only by the local commercial rates but also by the standards of maintenance which are observed and by the decisions as to what are the correct charges against depreciation. State and local policies differ as to taxing housing owned by educational institutions. It would seem to me fair to state that housing for faculty will seldom bring in a financial return commensurate with the investment — in fact will, in general, pay no return on such an investment — but in many cases may not involve further financial loss. I believe, however, that the figures reported in the questionnaires are frequently overoptimistic.

At times when an institution has acquired, by gift or otherwise, old fine houses which are used for rental to the faculty, the maintenance costs are very high; these homes, built for large families with servants, are inappropriate for faculty dwellings.

The cost of mortgage loans are more readily assessed. Throughout the United States the commercial rates on first-mortgage loans on houses are at present not far from 6% with an upper limit on the loan of 60% of valuation. Second-mortgage loans are at higher rates, perhaps 7%, and the upper limits on the coverage of first- and second-mortgages combined go to about 80%. I am told that banks consider faculty mortgages to be first-class credit.

A second yardstick consists of the alternate investments for the institution's funds. Many institutions invest both in equities and in bonds, preferred stocks and mortgages. From 4.5% to 5% might be considered a fair return on such investments and is better than was expected a decade ago. The administrative cost of mortgage loans on houses is higher than that of handling bonds, although the paying of interest and principal through payroll deductions cuts down the collection expenses.

The institution that makes a first-mortgage loan up to 80% or 90% of the value of the property at 4.5% interest with repayment through payroll deductions has a good "piece of paper" and, even considering administrative expenses, probably is making within 1% of what can otherwise be made in non-equity investments. First-mortgage loans are therefore not as favorable investments as others being currently made, but probably are better than many still being held. When, as is often the case, mortgages are given at considerably lower rates, sometimes as low as 0%, the cost to the institution is obvious.

The distinction between second mortgages and first mortgages is somewhat blurred by the fact that many of the institutions will make first-mortgage loans up to, or above, 90% of the value of the property.

FACULTY RELATIONS. Unless an institution can provide all the housing that the faculty desires, and make mortgage loans to the extent demanded, it will have to provide a means of making choices.

Many institutions have found that without a priority system the administration may be charged with favoritism in the assignment of dwellings. Even with a priority system these charges are not always avoided, especially if the quality of the available housing varies greatly. Moreover, at times arbitrary decisions may be desirable when the obtaining or the retention of an outstanding faculty member is at stake.

Where there are large programs, rules covering the assignment of dwellings can usually be established. However, the owning of a few houses due to gifts, campus expansion, etc., leads to special decisions and hence to possible discrimination. The same is true when limited areas are set aside for the building of faculty homes on a land-lease basis or in cases where, without a system, a few mortgages are made. In spite of these dangers, I must report that complaints are less numerous concerning these decisions than might be expected. For instance, they have not led to the same complaints as variable retirement ages sometimes do. Perhaps this is because they do not so clearly involve judgments of current capability about which the elderly may be especially touchy.

THE PROBLEM OF PUBLIC RELATIONS. The problem of public relations involved in competing with local landlords or local financial institutions may at times be acute, but in its chronic form is usually mild. This problem, of course, also may arise when dormitories are built.

The usual argument of the local business community is that the relation of the town and gown should be that of symbiosis: that the town furnishes many facilities which the institution cannot and that, if the natural business relations between the faculty and the commercial interests of the town are warped by removing sources of reasonable profit, the services that can be rendered by the local community will necessarily deteriorate. In addition, if there is an aspect of using the tax advantages that the institution may possess (especially a public institution), this is said to introduce unfair competition in a way not intended by the law. The local citizen is happy to see salaries rise since this brings money into the community, but benefits that lessen the likelihood of these salaries being spent locally are suspect.

The clamor in this respect is, of course, loudest when a plan is being inaugurated. However, resentment may smoulder for a long period. The language can become rather violent at times: "faculty communists" and, in reply, "local vultures" are representative samples. The size of a housing or mortgage program relative to the size of the community has much to do with the intensity of feeling. New York City scarcely would become excited by any housing program of a local university. The economy of a small town may be vitally affected by the decisions of even a small college.

The plan of some colleges of granting second mortgages at very low rates, after first-mortgage loans have been made by the banks at commercial rates, is reported to be welcomed by the banks.

Even when it is felt that the attitude of the local community is too possessive and unreasonable, it is of importance and must be weighed in the formulation of any plans. A cordial relationship with the neighboring citizens and their loyal support are great assets to any college. However, it must be remembered that the student, the parent, the donor, and the taxpayer all have an interest, perhaps in conflict with those of the local businessmen, in having the college use its funds in the most effective manner.

ADVANTAGES OF HOUSING PLANS. There are numerous advantages to housing programs that in many particular situations may more than offset the disadvantages described above. Some of the major ones are: (1) financial saving to the faculty member; (2) assurance that new and temporary faculty members can secure satisfactory housing; (3) rehabilitation or protection of the environment of an institution; (4) making it easier through propinquity for faculty members to participate in the affairs of the institution and have contacts with the students; (5) development of the sense that "the institution cares"; and, of course, many incidental advantages in particular situations.

Financial advantages to the faculty. The advantages of low rents and low mortgage rates are clear; other financial advantages are not as obvious. Sometimes the effect on local rental rates of competing institutionally-owned housing is salutary (or depressing, depending on your point of view). There are certain localities where property owned by the institution is not taxed. This saving may either be passed on to the faculty through low rentals or used for other educational purposes. In certain states, however, real estate used for other than educational purposes by an educational institution (in some cases even public ones) is subject to taxes.

Control of environment. Frequently, especially in the case of urban institutions, the environs of an institution will deteriorate unless the institution itself takes an active part in preventing it. The acquisition of land and the building thereon of apartments and houses for rent to faculty, or providing mortgages on homes meeting certain standards built in such an area, are methods of maintaining a good environment. Use of these facilities may be limited to faculty members. When in a city, such as New York or Chicago, this limitation may not be feasible, the faculty may receive preferential treatment. Such plans may produce great improvements in the surroundings of a university or college and in certain places have produced an area of attractive houses with more space around them than is normal for the locality.

Propinquity and a faculty man's duties. In a great many places one of the chief reasons for a housing program is the belief that if the faculty members live near the institution they will participate more actively in college affairs and have more contacts with the students. (It will even ease the parking problem.) This consideration plays a larger part in the thinking of colleges than of universities — in my opinion, to the credit of the colleges. Many institutions hope that not only will faculty members participate in campus activities of the students, but that students will visit in their homes. As cited earlier, one women's college where no students except seniors may drive cars makes very favorable mortgage loans (2%) provided the home is built within bicycling distance of the institution.

In spite of a few administrative cynics who believe that a faculty living close together is more apt to quarrel than one scattered over a large area, this is not the general opinion. However, others point out with a good deal of validity that wholesome faculty community relations are curtailed when faculty colonies are created.

Other advantages. One of the uses of a faculty housing plan mentioned by a number of institutions is to mitigate, at least locally, the problem of racial segregation. This in some cases is even the chief motivating force behind a housing plan. Though the emphasis on this aspect may be greatest in the South, it is by no means limited to southern institutions.

RECOMMENDATIONS

May I emphasize again that appropriate plans for faculty housing depend, even more than in cases of most other benefits, on individual institutional circumstances and local conditions. If the institution is located in a community where housing both for rental and purchase is adequate at reasonable costs, it may be well to forego all housing programs for the faculty. The same may be true if the institution still is struggling to increase faculty salaries to an appropriate level and to provide a suitable retirement plan.

On the other hand, in an institution located where rents and costs of real estate are high, where commercial areas or slums may be closing in on the campus, where the retirement plan is based on contributions of 15% or more of salary, and even where the institution may be in a favorable position as to real estate taxes, a complete program of rental housing, land-lease developments, and mortgages may be a very wise undertaking.

In spite of the great local differences just referred to, it would seem useful to give my beliefs as to what under most circumstances may be sensible.

Usually, it would seem desirable that the faculty live fairly near to the campus, that most of those on tenure own their own homes, that junior members use rented space, and that it be not too difficult for retired faculty and their widows to remain a part of the academic community.

SPACE FOR NEW FACULTY MEMBERS. I believe that more often than not rental space for new faculty members to live in, until they find a suitable home to buy or while they do not have tenure, is the first portion of the program to emphasize. The new faculty member usually is not in a position to buy a house. He does not know the town. If young, he frequently has no backlog to help him finance a home, and he usually does not have tenure. He is often faced with a scarcity of good places to rent and, if the town is at all underbuilt, the rents may be exorbitant. If the university can rent him an adequate apartment or home at a moderate rate, it is very attractive. Moreover, such an arrangement may quickly acquaint him with his new colleagues. There is much that tends to make junior staff believe they are treated as second-class citizens: no tenure, lower salaries, heavier teaching loads with emphasis on elementary work. Marked differences in quality and cost of living quarters will accentuate this belief.

If an institution has a 10% turnover a year, it is quite possible that a third of its faculty will have been in the institution for less than six years and hence, if junior members, may not have secured tenure. If we use as a hypothesis that a quarter of the faculty is without tenure and that a fifth of these are unmarried, we arrive at a figure of about 20% of the faculty who might be served by a program for faculty housing for new members. In many places it can be assumed that half of these would have major difficulty in finding apartments or housing for rent. A program which would provide housing for 10% of the faculty, with priority for new members who would not continue in such housing beyond the point when their tenure is determined, would solve this particular problem. Even if 5% of the faculty could be so housed, the program would be of great use. Some housing should be available, if there is such a program, for new members with tenure, and some on a furnished basis for visitors.

If such housing can be provided at, say, 80% of commercial rates without undue cost to the college (this feasibility is indicated by many responses), doing this is probably better both for the individual and for the institution than paying to the faculty the small extra amount in salaries that otherwise might be possible. In spite of the fact that such a plan helps keep other rents down, a few of the faculty members who rent houses from commercial sources may be irritated.

If housing is available, it should be used for some category of the faculty which can be nearly or completely covered; otherwise, jealousies and a sense of grievance may arise.

If I were to make an arbitrary rule to which many exceptions might well be made, I would say a plan of housing for new faculty members should provide for at least 50% of those who arrive in any year, wish to live in such housing, and are eligible to do so. Morale will be much better if this is nearer 90% to 100%. This goal might be reached by having ample housing, but other means can be used when housing is limited, for instance: (1) limiting the housing to new faculty members with certain rank, say, assistant professors and up; (2) limiting the length of occupancy to a given number of years; and (3) keeping the rent high enough so that there is some commercial competition. These rules avoid arbitrary decisions which leave the administration in a vulnerable position. They may be relaxed if housing becomes more nearly adequate. All such rules, however, adversely affect the scope and usefulness of the program. Ideally a young man should be permitted to live in his rented quarters at least until the question of his tenure is settled. This may take as long as six years.

MORTGAGE PLANS. It is probably even more desirable than in the case of rentals to have explicit rules to determine under what conditions mortgage loans will be made to faculty members. These rules may be in terms of: (1) rank of the borrower; (2) type of house being built or bought; (3) cost of house, or dollar limit on loan; (4) percentage of value covered; (5) distance from campus. The presumption should be great that, if the stipulated conditions are met, the loan will be made. Moreover, the rules should be uniform from person to person though they may vary with the size of the loan.

In general I believe that these loans should be made only to faculty members with tenure, that usually the house should be a single-unit dwelling with the cost not incommensurate with the value, and that in most communities the house should be within a reasonable distance of the campus. Often the feature that makes a mortgage program particularly desirable is the high percentage of the value of the property which may be covered. The most important portion of the coverage by a mortgage held by an institution may well be in the range from 60% to 85% of the value of the property, since it is usually possible to get a first-mortgage loan from a bank up to 60%, and there might well be a 15% down-payment.

An institution with limited funds for loans on faculty homes could start a second-mortgage program at rates not far from the rates on first-class bonds, say 4.5%, with a dollar limit in the neighborhood of $7,500. Up to 85% of the value of the home could be covered by a commercial first-mortgage loan and a second-mortgage loan from the institution with a payoff of the second mortgage in five to ten years. Banks often will postpone principal payments on first mortgages for such a period.

In more detail, on the matters of upper limit to loan and of per cent of value covered by the mortgage, I would suggest something of the following sort: That the dollar limit on the cost of the house be uniform rather than a multiple of salary, since the future salary may be more important than the present. This dollar limit, however, might well consider not only the cost of housing in the community but also the general salary-scale of the faculty. Judging from replies of those who place dollar limits on the housing, I would estimate that first mortgages up to 80%–100% of the value of houses costing about two to three times the average yearly salary of a full professor, and limits of $5,000 to $7,500 on second mortgages, with total of first and second mortgages covering 90%–100% of cost, are not unusual and work well.

I may add that faculty committees should not be used to determine who should get a mortgage loan, especially if this involves examining an individual's financial status. This should be in charge of one person either in the real estate office, if there is such, or in the business office.

Since there is no saving based on group coverage, no sharing of any risk, and no federal income-tax saving, a low interest rate has of itself little advantage over giving the same money in the form of salary. However, if the institution has an extensive rental program that provides marked savings to the faculty, it may be only equitable also to give a special benefit to those purchasing homes. In addition, it may ease the problem of getting a more rapid turnover of rental space, thus having more of it available for new faculty members. When a mortgage program is accompanying a rental program with subcommercial rental rates, the interest rates on the mortgages may well be as low as 4.5%. Rates below this figure will normally represent a loss of income to the institution.

It is usually advantageous to the individual both as to rates and as to convenience to have his home covered by a single mortgage. Hence, an institution with sufficient funds may wish to establish a plan of first mortgages covering up to about 85% of the value of the houses. However, a program of second mortgages only will entail fewer public relations problems than one involving first mortgages.

FACULTY COLONIES. If an institution has adequate funds or land in the neighborhood of the campus, land-loan plans such as those described earlier will not only provide very nice communities for faculty members but will protect the environment of the institution. The basic ingredients of such plans are: land sufficiently near the campus to provide a number of contiguous houses, low-cost lease or sale provisions for this land, standards for construction, and restrictions on the sale of the property that ensures its continued use by the faculty or other persons approved by the institution or the retention of the title by the institution.

It is strongly recommended that such a program be accompanied by attractive low-cost rentals for new faculty members. It is also wise to accompany any mortgage program for restricted faculty colonies by a mortgage-loan plan that allows greater freedom of choice of house under mortgage rates and coverage not dissimilar to those within the restricted program.

Rental colonies for senior faculty members may serve as a supplement to those based on mortgages.

The house that comes as a gift or is on land being held for future campus development presents a special problem. Maintenance is often high and administrative worries great. Such a house rarely fits into any real planning and it is illegal to burn it for insurance. This is a local problem and must be solved as such. However, we should remember that an obligation often enters disguised as an opportunity.

HOUSING FOR RETIRED FACULTY AND WIDOWS. Housing provisions for retired faculty members and widows should be such as to indicate a continued concern for their welfare on the part of the institution. It would seem to me that an institution which allows faculty members to reside in institutionally-owned homes until retirement or near retirement should continue to provide for them, either through allowing the member or widow to stay in the same house or in other houses rented to them by the institutions. This, of course, does not apply to official homes such as that of the president or of the custodian-of-the-grounds. This problem naturally does not arise in connection with housing reserved for recent appointees.

I believe that providing housing for retired faculty members and faculty widows is one of the major benefits in which progress is needed.

HOUSING AND REAL ESTATE OFFICES. An institution with an ambitious housing program should see that it is adequately administered by a special office. This is no task to be taken on by the president, the deans, or their aides. Such an office should contain a person who knows both land values and housing costs, the real estate law, the local banks and real estate companies, and who has the skills of a landlord. Even if he is a paragon, it will still be one of his important functions to be blamed unreasonably.

(It is better that a dean be considered a blackguard than that a man consider his departmental colleagues to be such. It is better for the head of the housing program to be thought a scoundrel than that the dean be thought such. The distribution of the objects of wrath in an institution is of importance and the optimal distribution is not always just.)

In summary, the following packages seem to me to make sense:

1. Rental housing for new faculty members and visitors.
2. Investment-rate mortgages with high coverage.
3. A combination of 1 and 2 with lower mortgage rates if rentals are subcommercial.
4. The "full treatment": faculty colonies, mortgage programs, and rent-

als at least for new faculty members, with as far as possible equally favorable rates for all components.

Any one of these should be governed by rules sufficiently restrictive so that not many eligible will be excluded for lack of facilities.

"THEY" SAY

The following quotations or paraphrases from replies to the questionnaire are arranged in two main sections: first, material that is chiefly factual; and, second, that which is evaluative and expresses opinion. Insofar as practical, each section is arranged to cover rental program, mortgage program, or aspects that involve both or are general.

Since it was promised that the institutions from which evaluative statements arose would not be identified, names are omitted. The broad classifications of institutions are given.

FACTUAL REPORTS

Rental. The many descriptions of types of dwellings are omitted, for without rental rates and identifications they mean little.

The following quotations concern rates. The first three indicate attempts to use rental cost to encourage turnover where housing is intended largely for new members:

20% rent reduction for Instructors for first three years when occupying College owned housing. — *Private college*

Some faculty members tend to make this a permanent arrangement. Reduce rent for first three years or so, and then raise it in accord with prevailing rates. — *Private college*

We do not "evict" faculty members when the emergency period of occupancy is past, but we price them out. — *Public university*

The next two indicate plans of relating cost to salary:

Each faculty member receives a rent allowance of $125 per month less 10% of salary. — *Private college*

The College subsidizes the faculty members for rent which is in excess of 10% of their salary. — *Private college*

The above were typical but the following cannot be so described:

No faculty member pays more than $33.33 per month for house rent. This is a tradition extending back across 90 years. With the completion of new faculty houses, now under construction . . . a charge of $65.00 per month will be made — but for these new houses only. (The tradition referred to above for older houses and apartments will be continued without change.) — *Private college [paraphrased]*

Rental on "free will" offering basis. — *Private college [paraphrased]*

The next is a special arrangement which is reported to be of marked value:

The retired faculty housing facility, built with private funds, allows nine family groups (usually two per family) to live on the campus. — *Public university*

Mortgages. Some indication of features of mortgage plans follows:

Interest rate set at 1% less than the local bank rate. — *Public university [makes first-mortgage loans]*

The rate of interest on our second mortgage loans is the same as the first mortgage and runs for the same period of time. Our second mortgage loans require no repayment of principal until the beginning of the fourth loan year. It is intended that by the fourth year a person's salary will have risen sufficiently to overcome principal payments. — *Private college*

No penalty assessed against Faculty member for prepayment. — *Private college*

We help buy, build at reduced (wholesale) prices, and fund the debt over a period of years. — *Private college*

(1) The automatic reduction in interest rate when owner's equity exceeds 40% of value encourages rapid repayments. (2) All loans are on monthly payment basis — principal amortized over not more than 20 years. (3) When a faculty member finds it necessary to buy a larger house the University tides him over the difficult period of double ownership by waiving principal payments on the mortgage against the house to be sold; thus, in some cases avoiding necessity of quick sale. — *Private university [makes first-mortgage loans]*

Aimed toward assisting new faculty members purchase homes with a small down payment, and prior to their establishment of a proven credit rating in our city. [Significant Problems] Few: major problem is difficulty of disposing of a house if the Faculty member decides to move to another institution. This is particularly true if the real estate market is "slow" with new homes available at or near the same price as older homes. — *Private university [makes first-mortgage loans]*

Cooperation with outside financial groups is indicated in the next five:

By arrangement with the . . . , faculty and staff mortgages on housing may be arranged at a preferential rate of 5.5% (as compared to the local 6.5%). — *Private college [partly paraphrased]*

About fifteen years ago we sold land adjacent to our campus to a group of savings banks. These banks formed a corporation to construct and operate an apartment project of 180 units. University personnel have preference in available apartments and until now we have been able to maintain full occupancy from among University families. — *Private university*

Main advantage of an F.H.A. administered plan: (1) No direct college approval or rejection involved. (2) College will take up F.H.A. if desired regardless of length of time requested — where commercial sources like to get 10–12 years for completion . . . . Long-range housing easy this way. (3) College and collection problems separated thru F.H.A. program. (4) Faculty move, sell, etc. separated from employment. — *Private college [makes only F.H.A.-approved loans]*

The [university], in conjunction with [a lending corporation], has established the Home Purchase Plan to assist faculty members and administrative officers in buying their homes.

This program makes it possible to borrow up to 90% of the purchase price of a home. This is accomplished by a first mortgage loan made by [a lending corporation] and a second mortgage loan made by [the university]. Applications for both loans will be made at the same time, and all details handled at one closing, resulting in considerable savings to the home buyer. — *Private university*

Our policy is to provide financing only in cases where a member is unable to secure commercial financing. — *Private college [This presumably means that the college takes the poorer risks.]*

Types of faculty community projects are referred to below:

If the property adjoins other college property, the mortgage deed gives the college an option to purchase when the borrower leaves or dies. — *Private college*

Lots in college owned sub-division available for sale to faculty members at prices below prevailing costs in area. — *Private college*

University provides tax-free land on which faculty members can construct tax-exempt houses within minimum and maximum cost limits, with plans approved by University (20 have been built). — *Private university [ownership remains with institution]*

By charter and will . . . is forbidden to alienate any of its land. Accordingly, the Board of . . . adopted a program of permitting faculty members to build homes on . . . property under a repurchase agreement. In general, the College agrees to purchase the home of a particular faculty member at cost of construction or market value, whichever is lower, not to exceed $25,000. We presently have fourteen homes under an arrangement of this kind. To date, three houses have come up for purchase by the College; however, one of these was willed to the College. Since the original . . . tract cannot be sold, the land is leased for $1.00 a year. — *Private college*

EVALUATIVE REMARKS

Rental. I fear that the following quotations will seem less enthusiastic concerning rental housing than were the responses to the questionnaire.

The general tenor of the replies was distinctly favorable, but the special remarks were largely made relative to the problems that have arisen. I believe that in most cases they represent problems to be solved rather than avoided by not having a rental program.

 The first group of remarks indicate purpose to a greater degree than problems:

To furnish faculty housing at low cost to teachers. To keep faculty on campus and near work location. To increase faculty contact and influence on students. — *Private college*

To aid in recruiting faculty; removes anxiety about moving. Keeps rentals in community more realistic; aids standards. Becomes a way-station for 3–8 years frequently for young faculty until their incomes improve for excellent private home-building. Assists single faculty members into a tenable, attractive social system. — *Public college*

To assist new faculty to locate suitable housing until they have time to find something in the community they would like to buy. Some faculty are content to continue renting. — *Private college*

To provide adequate housing for new appointments allowing them up to three years to buy or rent non-college housing. A three-year limit is sometimes too short. — *Private college*

To aid young faculty member to become established, whose income does not immediately permit purchase of a home. It is hoped this will enable them to save enough after a few years to make a downpayment on purchase of a home.

Not enough such houses are available for all who desire them and a certain amount of dissatisfaction arises. Since there is no time limit set on occupancy, some faculty members have stayed for over 25 years — *Private college*

To assist our faculty members in getting settled on our faculty to give them a fringe benefit that will indicate the true interest of the institution. — *Private college*

Our situation in a small town makes it imperative that we own faculty housing units. Otherwise we could not attract and hold a good faculty. Our chief problem is in having the right size unit for new faculty members' families. — *Private college*

The University is located in a village, and it is difficult for a new faculty member to locate housing to suit his needs. The general purpose of the University is to provide "threshold" housing for new faculty members to allow them time to locate a home that will meet their needs. — *Public university*

Length of service, whether new or old, is the sole determining factor. To provide an increment to help off balance a below average salary scale. — *Private college*

Although assignment should work out in the order of rank, tenure, and need, in practice it works out in the order of need, rank and tenure. — *Private college*

Foreign exchange professors have lived in student dormitory's units; benefit of living on an American campus. — *Private college*

Apartments close to center of campus are invaluable to those members of the faculty with heart conditions. — *Private university*

Build "buffer" between College and non-college resident area. — *Private college*

It is expected that those faculty residing in college-owned apartments will participate somewhat more actively in the extra-curricular activities of the student body (80% of which resides on the campus) than other faculty living in the suburbs. Those faculty living in college property do not, except in a few instances, participate very actively in the general college activities. — *Private college*

The following represents a special need mentioned by a number of institutions:

We have an integrated faculty in a highly segregated environment. We live interracially in our college housing. Faculty people find it difficult to add value of housing when considering compensation. — *Private college*

The two sets of problems most often mentioned deal with the landlord-tenant relationship and with financial problems. I list these next:

Landlord-tenant relationship with a College's own faculty is apt to be difficult. — *Private college*

The obvious dangers are best described as those of the company town with the College serving both as employer and landlord. — *Private college*

Eviction of the retired after long residence. Noisy, ill-mannered youngsters — with insensitive parents — as nuisances. Restriction of pets. Some envy of privately housed faculty over our "pampering" of tenants (free services, etc.) and the moderate, under-market rents. Pressures for refurnishings, redecoration, etc. — *Public college*

Maintenance requests are more numerous with faculty residents than non-faculty residents. — *Private college*

Difficulty of satisfying whims of persons. — *Private college*

Keeping paint, color schemes, etc., satisfactory for occupants. Small families becoming large families in small apartments. — *Public college*

Bachelors apply for vacant apartments; then become virtually permanent residents. — *Private college*

Widows occupying choice college houses (sometimes for part of the year only) while junior faculty is unhappy in the choice available to themselves. — *Private college*

The employer-landlord relationship creates some difficulty. Lack of adequate space for large families. Conflicts arising from working together and living in such close contact. — *Private college*

Problem of personality conflicts due to close proximity, and close association. — *Private college*

Often tenants move during the year or in June. If the College limits rentals to faculty only, it means that houses may be vacant until the next school year when new faculty arrive. This creates a financial problem in running the housing program on a break-even basis. — *Private college*

Non-payment at the time of separation from the University of. . . . — *Private college*

The houses available for faculty use are owned by restricted funds of the College and must rent for enough to cover maintenance and depreciation plus a fair interest return to the fund. Our experience has not been favorable: (*a*) faculty usually can find more desirable housing; (*b*) they are apt to feel we are charging exorbitant rental; (*c*) they try for rent reduction where salary increases are not available. — *Private college*

Being in a purely college community, there were originally no private houses for rent. Consequently, the college had to build them. While salaries were low, rents were low. Rents have not gone up at the rate that salaries have, and are now approximately 60% of what normal rentals would be. — *Private college*

Situation today is different from 10 years ago. Only 7 out of a total of 14 college housing units are occupied by faculty. Abundance of retail housing units in community and reduced turnover of faculty have contributed to this change. — *Private college*

Cannot operate profitably because of special concessions, etc., to faculty — *Private college*

Maintenance of old spacious buildings, and gracious living at below cost for anything comparable. — *Private college*

Connected with the growth of families is the school problem:

Elementary and secondary public schools not of a suitable quality for faculty children. — *Private university*

Deterioration and blight of urban neighborhood surrounding College and dissatisfaction with schools and environment detract considerably from value of housing. — *Private college*

Only the common problem of the occupant regarding the University as the required provider of any item requested regardless of cost. We have a neighborhood problem of relatively poor public schools so our staff is not anxious to live on the campus beyond the first grade year of their children. — *Private university*

More definitely negative are the following:

Tends to lend to a transient faculty. — *Public college*

Opposition from local people to college owning tax-free housing — *Private college*

A question exists as to whether it is good for morale of new faculty people to be housed in a single area rather than to be integrated into the general University community or the City residential area. — *Public university*

We believe adequate salary for all is better than fringe benefits for the few who could occupy faculty housing. — *Private college*

We are definitely opposed to providing faculty housing or having the faculty live in close proximity on College land. We feel they should be dispersed among the neighboring communities and apart from each other. — *Private college*

Mortgages. The first group of quotations represents remarks concerning the purpose of a mortgage:

By aiding faculty members to build or buy homes we have a more contented and stabilized faculty. — *Private college*

Once they own a home they are not so interested in leaving for a slight increase in salary — *Private college*

Pride of ownership. Encourages longer tenure and more satisfaction. — *Private college*

Our program has achieved its purpose of moving faculty out of the college-owned units and into their own houses, thereby making room for new incoming faculty in the college-owned houses — *Private college*

Made to those we hope will stay — *Private college*

We will loan to any faculty member whom the Dean indicates he wants to keep — *Private college*

In the case of programs with a repurchase agreement, the difficulty of evaluating improvements is brought up:

In the case of faculty-owned homes on land leased from the college, the problem of evaluating improvements made without prior consultation with the college or filing of costs is a problem that comes up with some frequency. We are becoming more and more reluctant to add the cost of minor improvements to the cost on record.

In the case of faculty-owned homes on college land the college guarantees a purchaser if the owner does not find a ready buyer. In more than twenty years we have had to buy but one house and that one was sold later the same day the college bought it back. — *Private college*

The relation of the mortgage to the faculty member's financial situation is mentioned very often. The following are illustrative examples:

Few have accumulated even a token down payment. We feel a person should be able to furnish at least $3,000 of their own money to purchase a home — *Private college*

Younger faculty members sometimes are unable to pay as much as 20% of purchase price. This necessitates increasing mortgage loan above 80% of market value in selected instances. — *Private university*

Limited fund requires short amortization period. Therefore, limited to members who can "afford" second mortgages. Primary help then, has been in the

Science areas where "Summer Salaries" from grants is major source of quick repayment. — *Private university*

There is a tendency for faculty to want to buy more housing than they can afford. The University will not make secondary mortgage unless it is satisfied that the borrower can afford the total shelter cost. To date, there have been no defaulted loans. The second mortgage program is perhaps the single most important factor in increasing the percentage of faculty residence in the campus community to the present 70% level. — *Private university*

Problems sometimes arise when a faculty member wishes to purchase a house which is overpriced, or which is somewhat beyond his capacity financially. There is the further problem that this policy and its benefits is available only to faculty members who have money enough to make a down payment. Not all faculty members whom we might wish to retain on the faculty will have the down payment at the time they would like to consider permanent housing.— *Private college [institution makes 90% first mortgage loans]*

Remarks of general approval are frequent:

The second mortgage loan program has been invaluable in assisting faculty in acquiring own homes. — *Private university*

[Significant problems:] None. — *Private university*

GENERAL. A few quotations about the housing program in general follow:

College is in the country, near a village and a small town. Adequate rental housing units are not numerous and are often relatively expensive. Proximity to the campus is desirable to most faculty members and many prefer to take advantage of being in the country rather than in town — *Private college*

Small town, imperative to own many rental units. Has to be subsidized to an extent; difficult to administer. Occasionaly causes hard feelings.

To encourage home owning for faculty expected to be permanent. In a small community like . . . , there was a tendency for the faculty to remain renters until this program began. Although not necessarily significant, this program creates a great deal of additional work for the Business Office — *Private college*

We must honestly say that our faculty housing program came into being largely through acquisition of land for campus expansion and we have not given much thought to its purposes or its goals.— *Private college*

To provide temporary housing for new faculty so that they are assured a place to live upon arrival, and to enable them to become acquainted with the local real estate market before making a personal choice of neighborhood and a large financial investment.

[Priority Point System] 1 point wife, 2 points per child; 3 points first year; 2 points each additional year.

Housing is our greatest faculty problem. It involves the entire faculty family in greater status comparisons than rank or pay. The current point system for the assignment of houses and the economic advantage of occupying housing is directly in opposition to the avowed purpose of providing temporary housing for new faculty. At the present time housing is a special problem within the entire community. Rents and building costs are well above the national average. — *Public university* [*partly paraphrased*]

Too many faculty residences clustered together tend to isolate faculty members and families from the community. Faculty families are too sheltered. — *Private college*

Staff members on tenure should own their own homes, either on campus or off, or secure their own rental facility. — *Private college*

REFERENCES TO APPENDICES

Appendix I: Questionnaire, Sections 1 and 2.

Appendix II: Institutional Listings
  Ratio of faculty in college housing to full-time faculty
  First-mortgage home loans
  Second-mortgage home loans
  Ratio of faculty with college mortgage to full-time faculty

Appendix III: Summary Tables
  Rentals: Tables 2–10
  Mortgage Loans: Tables 11–20

Appendix IV: Evaluation Chart
  Rental: item 11
  Mortgage Loans: items 12, 13

CHAPTER 3

EDUCATIONAL PRIVILEGES
FOR FACULTY MEMBERS
AND THEIR FAMILIES

CHILDREN'S COLLEGE EDUCATION

IN spite of occasional provisions for the pre-college and the post-graduate education of the children of faculty members, the principal privileges dealing with the education of the family of a faculty member are aimed at helping to pay for the undergraduate college education of his children.

In few other major areas of benefits are the practices of private and public institutions as different as in this one. Whereas 93% of the private institutions waive some or all (in most cases, all) of the tuition for faculty members' children attending the institution, this is true in only 13% of the public institutions and even this figure is deceptively large.

Perhaps to a greater degree than in any other major benefit, educational aid to faculty members' children is based on an aspect of individual need. It is, however, an easily measurable aspect.

WAIVER OF COLLEGE TUITION FOR FACULTY CHILDREN. As stated above, 93% of the private institutions waive some or all of the tuition for children of their faculty members. This figure is almost the same for universities and colleges. Moreover, in each case about three-fourths of these institutions waive the full tuition.

In the case of public institutions, slightly above 20% of the universities and about 8% of the colleges have some form of tuition waiver. It should be remembered, however, that for public institutions "in-state" tuition may be quite low and the waiver of tuition in some cases merely consists of immediately treating a new faculty arrival as a resident. Moreover, a semantic difficulty may arise in a case where there is an in-state "incidental fee" and tuition only for out-of-state students; if the new faculty member's child is treated as the child of a resident, then tuition is said to be waived 100%. In most cases for public institutions it can be fairly said that the tuition charges for faculty children are not great, but no special preference is given to them as compared to the children of other residents of the state or city.

The costs of waiver programs to the institutions are hard to determine. For those institutions where there are many more qualified applicants for admission than there are students accepted, the costs may fairly be considered equal to the tuitions. There are, however, many institutions willing to accept a greater number of qualified students than now apply and where, even if the tuitions do not cover the average costs, the costs of educating a few more students may be slight. The marginal cost may be very different from the average cost. For instance, the average educational cost of a candidate for the master's degree in a given institution may be in the neighborhood of eight times the cost of educating a freshman, while the extra cost for an additional master's candidate may be actually less than that for an additional freshman (40 new freshmen = 2 new sections English + 1 new section mathematics + 1 new section chemistry + ..., whereas the 40 first-year graduate students may be distributed into many partially filled classes). In a number of instances administrative officers have stated that through tuition waiver a substantial benefit can be given to the faculty with little, if any, cost to the institution.

Variations in the basic waiver plan are numerous. Some institutions have a fixed-dollar amount of waiver, sometimes lower than the present tuition but equal to that in use when the limit was established. Some institutions require a certain length of service by the faculty member, or tenure, before the children are eligible for a waiver of tuition. However, this limits the recruiting attractiveness of the plan. Some institutions extend the privilege to the children of deceased or retired faculty members. One institution reports that it waives tuitions not only for faculty sons but also for grandsons. (This is the same institution that has free skiing privileges for its emeriti.) Of course non-coeducational institutions have their appropriate restrictions. So many institutions report (although the question was not asked) that the same privileges are extended to children of the non-academic staff as to the children of the faculty, that I believe this is the common practice.

AID TO FACULTY CHILDREN GOING TO OTHER INSTITUTIONS. The waiving of tuition for children of faculty members immediately raises the question of whether financial aid should be given to faculty children going to college elsewhere. This is a special problem in non-coeducational colleges.

Even if the child of a faculty member can secure a first-rate education at home, it is probably unwise to artificially increase the financial pressures for him to do so. In addition, the standards of certain institutions are such that many faculty children would not normally be selected to enter. It is, of course, unfortunate to lower admissions requirements for faculty children, but to discriminate between faculty children on an academic basis while favoring financially the parents of those admitted is rubbing salt into the wounds.

Two plans are frequently used to take care of this situation: the so-called "faculty children's tuition exchange" plan and its ilk, and grants made toward tuition of faculty children going elsewhere.

FACULTY "TUITION EXCHANGE." The faculty plan, "Tuition Exchange, Inc.," is basically an agreement among institutions (mostly private) to receive, tuition free, as many faculty children from other institutions belonging to the group as they will receive from you on the same basis. There is no attempt at direct exchange but only at a total balance of "imports" or "exports" accounted for on a clearing-house basis. Other institutions have set up twin relations. This is especially true of pairs of non-coeducational Catholic institutions in the same city.

The Tuition Exchange plan does not seem to have worked well. A few institutions with fine academic reputations are sought by the children of the academic community in far greater numbers than there are children of the faculty members of these institutions who desire to go elsewhere. These institutions cannot afford to stay in the plan — at least not without frequent moratoria on "imports". Unless these institutions remain in the plan, the total scheme has little attraction to others. College presidents also point out that the child of a faculty member is limited in the choice of his college through the Tuition Exchange plan in a manner that is not true in the case of a grant system. A number of institutions have reported withdrawing from the plan; others are considering doing so. A much smaller number report that they may enter the group. In conversations with administrative officers, many more expressed dissatisfaction with it than satisfaction. It is my opinion that its usefulness has largely gone but that it may linger on for some while unless there is a beneficent act of euthanasia.

TUITION GRANTS. The other attempt to solve this problem is far more successful but also far more directly expensive, namely, the making of grants toward the tuition of the children of faculty members going to other institutions. These are usually made directly to the other institution. In general the amount of the grant is limited to some fixed figure and will also not exceed the tuition at the college to which the student is going. When tuition is waived at the home institution in part or in whole, this same amount is the usual limit set upon such grants. Provision is frequently made to reduce these grants by the amount (or part of the amount) that may be received from scholarships or G.I. benefits or certain other sources. (The whole educational enterprise is riddled by competition not to be the source of funds that should be supplied once, but only once — scholarships, fellowships, travel grants, summer research, overhead.)

In the case of an institution whose marginal cost per student is less than the tuition, a plan of grants can be more costly than the Tuition Exchange plan but also more satisfactory.

LOANS. In addition to grants, a number of colleges, some of them with excellent salary scales, make loans to faculty members for the education of their children. These are often at rather low rates and for periods up to eight years. Some of these loans are made by institutions in addition to tuition waivers or grants made for tuition. In a number of cases this is the only purpose for which the institution makes loans to the faculty. In comparison with federal loans under the NDEA, the period is more restricted and the rates of interest often somewhat higher; moreover there are no "forgiveness" clauses for teaching. This "forgiveness" clause would, of course, be more attractive to faculty children if it applied to teaching at the college level and in private institutions. In contrast to the NDEA loans, these institutional loans are made to the parent, not the student. The upper limit is generally not very high.

EVALUATION AND CONCLUSIONS. In my opinion, for an institution which can afford to do so, the proper choice lies between (1) making salaries as high as possible but not aiding the children of faculty to pay tuition at home or abroad and (2) a plan of tuition waiver at home and an equal grant elsewhere perhaps supplemented by loans.

I happen to prefer the former plan because of its non-discriminatory nature either as between the fertile and infertile or between the faculty and the citizen at large. I cannot feel happy when the students of tax-supported institutions, or even tax-free institutions, are afforded special privileges because of the status of their parents as faculty members or alumni. To my mind one of the social disadvantages to all plans to help children of the faculty avoid paying tuition is that they may tend to make the faculty callous to the raising of tuition rates. This would be particularly unfortunate in the case of public institutions. On the other hand, there is much pragmatic value in the plan for tuition waivers and grants. Clearly colleges believe so, as indicated by both their practices and by their statements as to its significance. Moreover, in this manner large benefits can be given to individuals without leading to a noticeable amount of envy or attacks on administrators' judgments.

In spite of the competitive advantage entailed, it would seem unwise for public institutions to enter upon such plans. It is not as necessary for them as for high-tuition private institutions. It is better to exploit the advantages natural to them than to seek those foreign to their nature. However, the granting of "in-state" tuition privileges to the children of faculty members who have not been in the state long enough to become citizens would seem reasonable and on occasion important.

The weight of experienced opinion in private institutions is against my point of view. Although it is true that some administrative officers recognize this as "an inequitable form of compensation," no institution reports that it expects to eliminate its waiver plan. The institutions with programs to aid in the education of faculty children consider this a very important benefit from the point of view of recruiting and retaining staff. When one considers the prime importance of scholarly opportunity, salary, and retirement provisions, to have 191 institutions reply that this benefit is a substantial help in holding faculty and 200 others rate it as a moderate help means that there is very real importance placed upon this.

A wise and able university administrator gave me the following cogent statement:

It is increasingly evident that college costs of children are heavily concentrated in the period around a median age in the early fifties. This is generally well before peak earnings are obtained from either the university or from outside sources. Therefore, as a kind of "cost of children" insurance, tuition grants or educational loans are peculiarly appropriate in an academic situation. It is also true that faculty members are more likely than others of equivalent income to insist on sending their children to college. Their children assume that going to college — and to a good college — is "normal."

Without "family-education insurance," there is pressure on men in the middle years to seek increased gainful employment outside the University to meet heavy costs, or to capitalize too soon on their potentials by seeking another job paying more money, but offering less chance for self-fulfillment as a teacher-scholar. It is to the interest of the University to avoid excessive pressures in these directions.

One president says that "a high danger to the faculty morale is to serve as teachers in a college to which they may not be able to send their children."

Moreover, clear as I have made my inclinations, it is obvious that no institution should withdraw benefits, such as free tuition, from faculty members already at the college. This would be a breach of good faith. Phasing out of such a plan would be protracted and without marked increase in the salary scale would be competively disadvantageous. Whatever the ultimate plan may be, I believe private institutions are wise to work toward a program that will grant as much to the student who goes away as to the one who stays at home, and to remain out of or withdraw from the Tuition Exchange.

OTHER EDUCATION BENEFITS

The other financial aids for the education of staff families can be reported on briefly.

NURSERY SCHOOLS. Some 7% of colleges and 14% of universities maintain nursery schools where faculty children get preferential financial treatment. Others state that they have nursery schools used largely by faculty, sometimes with preferential admission but where fees are uniform.

AID FOR PRE-COLLEGE EDUCATION OF FACULTY CHILDREN. A few, but very few, colleges make grants toward nursery school, secondary school, or high school education for the children of their faculty.

Some institutions have special privileges for children of faculty members in a school connected with the institution; for instance, one institution allows these children to attend no matter in which school district they live.

ATTENDANCE OF FACULTY AND SPOUSES. Most private institutions and many public institutions allow faculty members to audit classes without charge, and a substantial number permit them to register for credit in courses without paying fees. The same statement (but to a less generous degree) is true relative to faculty spouses. Some institutions have found that when they grant tuition-free education to faculty wives the proportion who wish to take private music lessons is excessive.

It would seem that making every possible use of the educational facilities of the college by the faculty (or other staff) will enhance the quality of the faculty's work and should be encouraged. This is probably also true to a lesser but yet important degree in the case of faculty wives.

"THEY" SAY

In this section the "'They' Say" are arranged in five chief groups: (1) tuition waiver; (2) tuition exchange, under both "Tuition Exchange, Inc." and other agreements, bilateral or sometimes multilateral; (3) grants for college education of faculty children; (4) other specific benefits in connection with faculty family education; and (5) more general comments, some ranging over several of the above. Within each group the more factual statements come first and shade off towards those that are more purely opinions.

TUITION WAIVER

Available after death if he [the faculty member] dies in service. — *Private college*

Children of deceased faculty when the faculty member died in "harness." Children of faculty eligible to attend other [same denomination] colleges on an exchange arrangement. — *Private college*

Tuition exchange may be dropped and cash grant increased. Tuition credit does not extend to private lessons in art or music. — *Private college*

Faculty family children are immediately "resident." — *Public university [paraphrased]*

Full tuition waived in spite of being public institution. — *Public university [paraphrased]*

Also loans up to $1000 a year per child. — *Private college [paraphrased; this college belongs to "Tuition Exchange, Inc."]*

Based on length of service at 10% for 1 year to 100% for 10 years. Also provides waivers of tuition for brothers and sisters. — *Private college [paraphrased]*

Tuition remission is for 4 undergraduate years and one graduate year. — *Private university*

It is designed to encourage faculty children to attend college yet forcing them to assume some responsibility for paying a portion of costs. — *Private college [at this college there is partial waiver of tuition]*

Provides a maximum benefit to faculty at a minimum of cash expense to the institution. — *Private college*

This is provided frankly as a benefit of considerable financial advantage to faculty people but relatively inexpensive to the College. It is highly appreciated. Creates some difficulties with faculty offspring not capable of college work, or poorly motivated. — *Private college*

Financial help to compensate for inadequate salaries. — *Private college* [*paraphrased*]

It is an inequitable plan of compensation. — *Private college*

Some inequity is recognized in that only faculty with children are benefited, but this is not a critical issue — *Private college*

May eliminate and faculty children will have to be competitive for student aid. — *Private college*

Faculty Welfare Committee — composed of all lay people except one suggested that 50% tuition be charged — were opposed to total remittance — *Private college*

To enable faculty to purchase their own product. — *Private university*

Recognition of the great importance attached to quality of education by faculty members in all their thinking. — *Private college*

To follow through an ancient custom which is considered a right. — *Private college*

"TUITION EXCHANGE" AND RECIPROCAL ARRANGEMENTS. Two states report as follows:

Free tuition at U. of . . . for staff of state colleges — *Public college* [*paraphrased*]

Reciprocal arrangements are frequently reported:

Furnish tuition for children of members with tenure. Reciprocal arrangement for daughters at . . . — *Private college* [*paraphrased*]

Tuition benefits for children probably will receive attention. Possibility of exchange plan with other [same denomination] institutions to be considered this summer. — *Private college*

Dissatisfaction with Tuition Exchange is expressed in the following; however, one college and one university that I visited expressed satisfaction with the plan:

Consideration will be given to withdrawal from tuition exchange plan and substitution of a cash grant policy. — *Private university*

So far as Tuition Exchange is concerned, we find that as a small school there is no attendance at our school from outsiders to provide any basis for an exchange. — *Private college*

Difficulty under Tuition Exchange in finding desired school able to accept application. — *Private university*

Tuition Exchange has been a problem. We have few exports and many requests for imports. — *Private college*

Tuition exchange plan weakening, and many faculty prefer to have children attend another institution. Cash grant program needed. — *Private college*

Tuitions Exchange plan does not work well. Too many withdrawals of institutions once members. — *Private college.*

[Does your institution belong to Tuition Exchange, Inc.?] Yes, we did. We are fulfilling our obligation and withdrawing. — *Private college*

From Tuition Exchange plan to cash grants. — *Private college*

Would like to become involved in tuition exchange of some sort. — *Private college*

Considering joining Tuition Exchange. — *Private college [paraphrased]*

GRANTS FOR COLLEGE EDUCATION OF FACULTY CHILDREN

. . . the grant includes general fees as well as tuition. — *Private university*

Tuition grants for children going to other colleges in . . . . — *Private college [paraphrased; a grant arrangement but on a limited basis]*

[Changes contemplated:] Drop out of tuition exchange plan and give aid to faculty children in equivalent amount to tuition charge here. Limit of $10,000.00 annually set if more than 10 children qualify.

A fringe benefit which aids our faculty. We have always accepted Tuition Exchange students here but have been refused a like courtesy elsewhere on basis of "being full." Hence our proposed switch to new plan. — *Private college*

Some faculty now want cash grants which faculty as a whole does not approve nor does administration. — *Private college*

Not a uniform benefit (bachelors, childless couples) in institutions with tuition waivers and grant system. — *Private college*

May consider providing cash grants equal to our tuition charge. — *Private college*

[Hope to have cash grants for daughters equal to tuition grants for sons.] To prevent the irony of college faculty unable to provide college education for their children. — *Private university [partly paraphrased]*

A SAMPLE OF OTHER FAMILY EDUCATION BENEFITS

One-half of available capacity of nursery school is reserved for children of faculty. The nominal fee charged is the same for faculty and other residents of the community. — *Public university*

The University makes monthly contributions toward support of a nursery school and kindergarten, operated by a faculty wife, and conducted in a part of the campus dwelling occupied by the faculty member and his wife. — *Private college*

Sons granted ½ tuition at Prep School connected with U. — *Private college [paraphrased]*

Includes ½ tuition in prep school of . . . U. — Full tuition grant if 20 years service. — *Private university*

Affiliated school on premises with free tuition to faculty children. *—Private college*

Too many faculty children in campus school provides for an atypical situation. *— Public college*

Educational aid program providing actual cost of tuition, fees, books, travel and basic living expenses for those working on advanced degrees. ($1000 max. per yr.) *— Private college [this applies to faculty members themselves]*

GENERAL

Faculty children are eligible for free tuition in the Campus Elementary School. Faculty children are admitted free of tuition charge in the campus Secondary School. Fringe benefits have been helpful in retaining faculty members and in one instance provision for the education of children was influential in recruiting a faculty member. *— Private college*

We deplore the low salaries that require institutions to provide indirect subsidies and reciprocal agreements for the education of faculty children. Faculty youngsters should compete for entry and assume obligations to the same extent all other school people do, we believe. *— Public college*

The benefit with which we must deal next is providing assistance to faculty children in securing a college education. Reduction in tuition is now available only at . . . College. Faculty children who attend elsewhere derive no additional benefits and there is no tuition exchange arrangement with any other institution. This is a major concern and we must give it early attention. *— Private college [cash grant plan being considered]*

REFERENCES TO APPENDICES

Appendix I: Questionnaire, Section 7.

Appendix II: Institutional Listings
  Per cent of faculty children tuition waivers
  Member Tuition Exchange, Inc.
  Cash grants for faculty children's tuitions

Appendix III: Summary Tables 99 to 106.

Appendix IV: Evaluation Chart, items 14–17.

CHAPTER 4

HEALTH PROVISIONS

AFTER salary and retirement, health provisions are often considered by faculty members to be the most important staff benefit. Health services could be discussed, and must be mentioned, in many portions of this report: e.g., in connection with leaves, family emergency, improvement of conditions of work, and treatment of retired faculty members. It seems best, however, to make a somewhat detailed statement on this matter in a single place.

Unless a highly organized local system of "Medicare" is developed, the chief contribution of an institution toward the medical care of its faculty will be through insurance — of which the most important, though not most frequent, is major (sometimes called catastrophic) medical, surgical, and hospital insurance. The administration of any insurance plan involves expense, and it is cheaper for the individual to care for the minor misfortunes of life than to pay for insurance to do so. We do not insure our neckties against spots, nor should we afford overhead to pay for an occasional call by a doctor. There comes a point, however, where a health problem may wreck the finances of a family. Such events have a low probability of occurring but disastrous effects when they do. The costs of these should be shared through insurance and thus, through a small expense to each, protect the solvency of all. The plans for such insurance are discussed in Greenough and King, *Retirement and Insurance Plans in American Colleges.*

This chapter describes health services provided by colleges and universities to members of the faculty and their families, the policies of the institutions regarding continuation of pay during disabilty, and the relation of these policies to disability insurance.

HEALTH SERVICE

In broad terms the facts concerning various programs of health service are about as follows:

Three-quarters of the responding institutions (more than this proportion in universities) have facilities for emergency medical treatment, usually open to the faculty free of charge. In about 25% of the cases, these facilities are also open to the family of a faculty member, usually with a charge.

In about two-thirds of the institutions there is provision for consultation (other than an emergency) with a doctor; in about two-fifths of these the privilege is open to faculty members, and is free to about one-half of this latter group: $2/3 \times 2/5 \times 1/2 = 2/15$. The privilege is extended by about 10% of the institutions to the family of the faculty member, generally with a charge.

About 10% of the institutions extend regular medical treatment to the faculty and about 5% to the family, usually with a charge in both cases.

The figures for an annual physical examination are slightly lower than for regular medical treatment, as is also the case for the use of a hospital bed.

About 30% to 40% of the institutions with a particular health service available to the faculty extend it to retired members, usually at the same charge as for the active members. The proportion that extend such a privilege to the family of the faculty member is slightly higher.

Two of the medical programs have specially cogent reasons for adoption: emergency service and periodic health examinations. The former is frequently supplied; the latter not.

EMERGENCY SERVICE. The chief reason for emergency service is propinquity. When emergency help is needed, the nearest may well be the best. It would seem clear that, if there has been an explosion in the chemistry laboratory, help that is available to the student should also be available to the professor. If, moreover, many of the faculty live on or very close to the campus, this service can well be extended to the nearby families of the faculty members and to retired faculty members in the immediate vicinity. Whether this should be free is not as important as its availability.

PERIODIC HEALTH EXAMINATIONS. The question of the desirability of periodic health examinations for the faculty is a more complicated one. If compulsory, some faculty members will resent these examinations on the ground that they might jeopardize their tenure or their promotion. A very good case for such examinations can be made, but only in the context of an employment policy that is not only enlightened but generous. In the case of certain communicable diseases, notably tuberculosis, both the public and the individual are protected by early diagnosis. The administration that knows the health difficulties of an individual can plan better how to minimize his handicap and prolong his usefulness. A man under nervous tension may temporarily have a lightened teaching load or a different office mate; the office and the teaching of a heart case may be on the ground floor and his parking close to his office. It is not paternalism to show decent human considerations. Moreover, the faculty member himself usually postpones requesting "favors" beyond the time when the question first should have been raised.

To get the most out of periodic examinations, it must be understood that the doctor is a "company doctor" and may disclose information which would be considered privileged in the usual patient-doctor relationship. Moreover, any dean knows or surmises a great deal about the health of faculty members. Obvious vigor or lack of vigor, reports of departmental chairmen, students' observations contribute to this information. The degree that surmise is replaced by knowledge will be not only in the interest of the college but usually of the individual as well. To grant that there should be constant vigil against the abuse of administrative power is not to deny that most administrative officers are kindhearted, decent, and often harassed individuals. The president or the dean should have the knowledge to help him do his job well even if that knowledge could be misused. However, the faculty member must know what the rules are.

Even if it is decided, unwisely I believe, that all medical information is privileged, much value can be gained from periodic examinations not only for the individual but for the institution, since usually the administrative officer will be informed of any serious health problem either by the individual or with his consent. The doctor certainly should be allowed to take steps necessary for the safety of the students.

It is best to have this service free especially if it is required.

I believe that for the present it would be well to make routine X-ray chest examinations compulsory (in many communities these can be provided by free public health services, Red Cross, etc., and the results reported through the individuals to the institution). I would not go beyond this unless the faculty decided that they wished it. However, I do believe that a faculty recommending the initiation of such a program would be acting in the best interests of both the institution and of themselves as individuals.

Some institutions provide free immunization "shots." This is an enlightened health measure, of service to the institution itself.

As to the other health benefits, such as general doctors' consultations, regular medical treatment, and infirmary or hospital bed, no general conclusions would seem valid. Medical services are expensive; if a college does not have a good infirmary or a medical-school hospital, providing them will be more costly than using local facilities when these are adequate. The relation with the local medical profession may be complicated if the institution provides medical facilities for its faculty. If the institution has good plans for health insurance for its faculty and their families, it may well be that the same amount of money paid to the faculty as salary would be as well spent as in providing medical services. However, a community with inadequate hospital facilities, few doctors, and no specialists may be the seat of a college with an elaborate student-health clinic or even of a university with a medical school and, unless the institution provides the services, they will not be available to the faculty. The usual role even may be reversed, with the institution furnishing the hospital facilities for the community or cooperating in doing so. Thus, under certain local conditions, plans for consultation, regular medical treatment, and hospitalization are almost a necessity, under most circumstances marginal, and in some communities a liability. These are facts; not weasel words.

RETIRED FACULTY MEMBERS. Considerations of gratitude, of compassion, and of self interest would indicate that campus facilities, including health services which are open to the faculty, should be extended to retired faculty members. Current faculty members, administrators, and alumni are properly disturbed when a person who has served a college until old age is not treated with a modicum of generosity.

CONTINUATION OF INCOME DURING SICKNESS

SALARY. The problem of what should be done concerning continuation of salary during temporary disability due to sickness or accident is real in all institutions, even those with regulations covering the question.

About 60% of the institutions have no formal rule in this regard. However, the practices are quite different in public than in private institutions since nearly 60% of the public institutions have formal plans often prescribed by law, and less than 33% of the private institutions have such plans. It is also interesting, perhaps even surprising, to note that universities are less likely to have fixed plans than are colleges. Even institutions with formal rules often have escape clauses.

The institutions with fixed plans have widely varying rules as are seen from Table 152, Appendix III. Some of these limit sick leave to under four weeks, others have cumulative formulas that go beyond a year. In other plans the timing of illness seems crucial, since leaves terminate at the end of the semester or the end of the academic year. But even with all the possible types provided for in the questionnaire, about one-third of those with formal plans checked the description as "other."

The rules are in some instances quite heartless. The practice may be very different. The rules that are forced upon public institutions are often extremely restrictive and are broken by the administrations at their peril; yet most legislators would feel outraged if in practice the regulations were used cruelly.

In addition to leaves with salary, sick leaves without salary are often granted. This at least protects a man's position.

The first question that arises in regard to sick leaves for relatively short times is whether an institution should have a formal or an informal policy. The argument for the latter is that few administrators can persuade trustees (or legislatures) to formulate as generous a plan as they will actually observe. Even where there are formal plans, various exceptions are made either by regular action or by subterfuge. On the other hand, the faculty member has a certain sense of insecurity when he has no advance assurance of what will happen in case of illness, and individual decisions may be discriminatory or at least thought to be so.

In general the American faculty member is not treated poorly in this regard if he has secured tenure. The young man who has a prolonged illness is probably in financial difficulty.

Any policy regarding sick leave is in practice apt to be modified by administrators' actions or by a series of leaves that may be used, such as research or writing assignments while hospitalized; by use of the "president's fund"; by no official cognizance of illness, if not too long, provided colleagues shoulder work; by no special record-keeping or perhaps even bad record-keeping.

If there is no strong faculty sentiment to consider the matter and if the administration is allowed to be generous, I would not recommend trying to move from an informal to a formal basis.

If, however, there is a formal policy, it would be well to be sure it is generous enough and permits exceptions. A generous policy is usually not very costly because protracted illnesses are not frequent and because it is usually so difficult to get a substitute that colleagues shoulder at least the minimum extra work necessary to keep things going rather than try to make other adjustments. In general this mixture of self insurance and kindness is willingly exhibited by faculty members. The ease with which this is done, of course, depends in part on the size of the department involved. It should be remembered that, although a large university has more large departments than a small college, frequently it also has more small ones. The administration should strive to pay for substitutes and assistants when available in order to minimize the load on other faculty members.

In many areas colleges and universities tend to follow advertising methods and overpromise. In the matter of sick leave they often underpromise.

DISABILITY INSURANCE. It is desirable for an institution to provide (with or without individual contributions) long-term group disability insurance for its faculty. The relation of such insurance to the period of salary continuation needs careful study. It would probably be unwise, perhaps impossible, by insurance to fully cover salary during permanent disability. However, an institution may well wish to continue the salary of a man who may be expected to recover from a prolonged illness. If this is done, say, for a period of two years, while cases of permanent disability after six months are paid only an annuity from the disability insurance, inequities arise. I strongly believe in disability insurance and recognize that a policy based on a six-month waiting period is good, yet urge that, if an institution can afford it, the period of continuation of salary should be measured in years rather than in months. The relative number of these extended disability cases is not great and, since on the average you get about what you pay for in insurance, the extra cost of longer continuation of salary is approximately the same as the extra benefit the individual receives. For a reasonably long period salary payment may well be within the resources of most institutions. It is important that there be no lapse of time between coverage by salary and coverage by insurance.

I would recommend that institutions study their health programs in detail, since many of them seem to be made up of rather disjointed provisions. It must again be emphasized that the provisions best suited to local conditions will vary greatly. I believe that almost all programs should include major medical insurance, emergency services, routine X-ray examinations, a very generous sick-leave policy (perhaps unformulated), and insurance to cover long-term disability beyond the period covered by salary.

Health programs are frequently reported to be important both in retaining faculty members and in ensuring their effectiveness. It is well to report that discussions of benefits with representative faculty groups across the country indicated that health services form an area which they would like to see extended, not necessarily free but at "reasonable" rates. It should also be mentioned that often in universities the amount of expert medical aid provided at very low cost to the faculty by members of medical schools is extensive.

"THEY" SAY

HEALTH SERVICES

The faculty would greatly appreciate having their families taken care of through the University Health Service. This cannot be done at present. — *Public university*

University owns and operates hospital and charges are about ½ standard charges. — *Private college [paraphrased]*

Health Services supported 100 per cent by student fees. Faculty not permitted to use facilities or services. — *Public college*

Group Blood Bank Account. — *Public university [paraphrased]*

Free clinical medical service for administration and faculty and their families offered by two local physicians used extensively with effective results. — *Private college*

CONTINUATION OF SALARY DURING SICKNESS

Twenty days a year cumulative to 160. — *Public university [paraphrased; a typical formal plan]*

After 90 days of leave, the faculty member may borrow an additional 15. Only working days are counted. — *Private college*

[Sick leave] 1 month then salary of substitute taken from faculty member's salary — *Private college [paraphrased; I bet they fudge on this]*

A substitute is hired. Any amount of salary not used for this purpose is paid to the faculty member. — *Private college*

It is very expensive to make full salary payments to a teacher who is sick or disabled for a long period of time. Last year, a full Professor was out for the whole year and his salary was continued in its entirety. An Associate Professor became very seriously sick during the second semester and he too was paid in full. Because of his disabling illness, this latter individual has been teaching a greatly reduced schedule all this year. — *Private college*

Any absences in excess of the cumulative sick leave accrued to an absentee shall be taken without pay, except that the Board may, in cases of protracted illness or unusual hardship hear recommendations from the president that the bylaws be waived in exceptional instances without thereby establishing a precedent. — *Public university*

As a state institution we must have a formal policy, as indicated on this questionnaire; but the College acts in a manner more in keeping with the phrase "according to each case." Our ability to do so depends on the cooperation of the faculty. — *Public college*

Our informal arbitrary treatment of disability problems on a rather generous basis over the past 32 years, worked quite satisfactorily. — *Public university*

We have, on occasion, paid two or three years salary prior to retirement date. — *Private college*

We have been able to continue all instructional staff on payroll, even for extended illnesses, sometimes totaling as much as two years in a five-year period but averaging less than a month. In short illnesses other staff members carry extra load, but in longer illnesses temporary lecturers are employed. — *Public university*

We have supported a faculty member at full salary for over two years until his death. — *Private college*

We have not clarified the limits of our obligation. — *Private college*

Should formalize program to assure equity and knowledge of rules. — *Public university [paraphrased]*

There is some faculty pressure for a more definite sick leave policy, although in actual practice it could hardly be more generous than the informal one now followed. — *Public university*

REFERENCES TO APPENDICES

Appendix I: Questionnaire, Section 9, Subsection C, and Section 11, Subsection C.

Appendix II: Institutional Listings
  Emergency medical treatment
  Annual physical examination

Appendix III: Summary Tables 127–137, 151–155.

Appendix IV: Evaluation Chart, items 6–10.

CHAPTER 5

LOANS,
EMERGENCY FUNDS

*Question: Was Polonius a sage
or an old man in his dotage?*

PROGRAMS of personal loans to faculty members are
fairly extensive. About one-third of the private and about 8% of the
public institutions make such loans. A somewhat greater proportion
of the universities than of the colleges do so. This is perhaps somewhat
surprising in light of the fact that universities to a greater extent than
colleges are served by special credit unions often aided by the
institutions.

During 1962 the colleges and universities replying made over 6,000
personal loans to faculty members amounting to over $4,000,000. (How-
ever, a third of the loans [and half the amount] were made by a single
university.) These range from loans of significant size for an extended
period down to short-time advances on salary sometimes of less than
one month in duration.

Such programs usually are considered to be of negligible value from
the point of view of recruiting or retaining a faculty but not necessarily
from the point of view of morale.

In about half the cases, when loans are made at all, the number in
any year is at least 10% of the number of full-time faculty members.
This does not necessarily mean that in these cases 10% of the faculty
receive loans, since more than one loan is frequently made in a given
year to a single individual. This is attested by the fact that in a few
instances more loans are made in a year to faculty members than there
are members of the faculty.

SIZE, LENGTH, INTEREST RATES, REPAYMENT PROVISIONS, ELIGIBILITY.
Policy differs greatly as to size of loans. Either by rule or practice well
over half of the institutions making personal loans to faculty members
will, in any given year, make no loan of over $1,000. However, this
amount is exceeded substantially in a number of cases. Some loans are
for amounts even in excess of $10,000. Most institutions make no loans
for a period of more than one year and may require that the loan be
repaid within the current academic year. However, loans for two or
more years are not infrequent especially when covering the education
of the faculty member or of his children.

The rates of interest on these loans are clearly below the rates obtainable commercially. Over 40% of the institutions making personal
loans to faculty members charge no interest at all and none charges
above 6% per annum on unpaid balances. This is in marked contrast
with commercial plans sometimes charging 1% per month on unpaid
balances.

In three-fourths of the institutions making personal loans to faculty
members, repayment may be by payroll deductions. In many cases this
is mandatory. Payroll deductions for this purpose are significantly more
prevalent in private than in public institutions.

In general, there is no limitation by rank as to those eligible to receive
loans.

REASONS FOR LOANS. The most frequently given reason for personal
loans is listed under "family emergency" and the second under "study
for degrees." These two answers tie in with two other topics, namely,
what is sometimes called the "President's emergency fund," and the
general policy on leaves of absence especially for the education of
faculty members. These subjects are discussed later, the first in this
chapter under "Emergency funds," and the second in Chapter 7. A
number of institutions make loans to faculty members for the education of their children. This has been discussed in Chapter 3. Among
the purposes, under the heading of "other," several institutions listed
"consolidation of debts." Some institutions note loans for travel and for
such items as cars and outboard motors. Others, although limiting the
size of loans, have a definite policy of not inquiring into the purposes.
As mentioned above, some loans are scarcely more than advances on
current payrolls, often not more than payment before the normal date
of salary already earned. It is believed that in some cases these have
not been reported as loans.

CREDIT UNIONS. Instead of a loan policy, or sometimes supplemental to one, are credit unions specially serving either the staff of an institution or the staffs of more inclusive groups. These two types shade into each other as in the case of credit unions for all teachers in a state, or for all staff members of a group of institutions under a common governing board. Some sort of aid to these credit unions is often provided by the institutions in various forms, especially through the furnishing of office space, and through the privilege of repayments through payroll deductions.

It is believed that the amount of loans made to faculty members through such credit unions is far in excess of loans made to them directly by the institutions; this conclusion is based on only a very small sample and on the fact that these credit unions tend to exist chiefly in the larger institutions. It is a guess but I believe a good one.

One public retirement system covering several institutions reports that it is possible to borrow against the member's equity in the system. Any such plan tends to defeat the purpose of a retirement system and I believe should be avoided.

"EMERGENCY FUNDS." A number of institutions mention the existence of "president's emergency funds," sometimes established by gift. Through conversations it was learned that many institutions not listing these on the questionnaire have such funds. The uses of these funds vary with their size and with the natures of the presidents (or of the committees that in some instances act for them), but in almost all cases these uses include aid to faculty members in the event of personal or family emergencies. In the absence of major medical insurance, expensive illness or accident is frequently the cause of such an emergency. These funds have also been used to help in the education of faculty members seeking higher degrees. It is clear that, where wisely and tactfully used, emergency funds have been of substantial benefit to many faculty members and make a contribution to good faculty morale.

It would appear that these discretionary funds are dear to the hearts of many presidents. Through such a fund hardship may be mitigated, the institution benefited, and the paternalism of the president proven benevolent. Most presidents are warm, kindhearted men who day after day have to make hard-boiled decisions. A chance to be guided by the heart as well as by the brain has a right to be cherished.

These funds are described in this chapter because they not only often serve the same purpose that a loan might but also because in some cases they are intimately tied in with a loan policy. A loan may be made promptly; and if the financial strait becomes greater with time, some of the expenses may be transferred to a grant from the emergency fund rather than continued as a loan which had reached the point of being a real encumbrance to a man's future.

In a large institution it may be impractical for the president to administer the emergency fund personally, but it is unwise to have a committee do so. Matters of private distress should be discussed by a minimum number of persons. If the president does not administer the fund himself, he should delegate the work either to a single individual or to certain individuals, such as the deans of the various colleges, perhaps consulting among themselves as to policy but acting singly on individual cases.

Such funds can be used unwisely. It is also obvious that it takes great tact to use them without offense. I believe their total effect is good.

ADMINISTRATIVE OPINION RELATIVE TO FACULTY LOANS. It would be fun to preside at a meeting of college presidents discussing the wisdom of making personal loans to faculty. Even reading the answers to the questions concerning the evaluation of these programs is interesting. Lending money to the faculty is abhorrent to many. Others who "go along" still feel they have made easier the primrose path. Some feel such loans encourage faculty members to live beyond their means. The head of one institution whose salaries are at the bottom level in the AAUP scale says "loans not needed on our salary scale." But the above is not the whole gamut of opinions. Few of the institutions plan to contract their loan programs, some plan to increase them as the size of the faculties increases, and a few are striving to make them more adequate.

Some state clearly their opinions of the need for faculty loans:

To assist in the rare emergency when available cash is of critical concern.

A faculty member's economic situation is obviously related closely to the college (in most cases). If there is *ad hoc* need, not arising from irresponsible action, we think the college should be first to assist faculty member to meet this emergency.

EVALUATION AND RECOMMENDATIONS. It appears to me that one's attitude toward programs of institutional loans to individuals depends a great deal on one's social philosophy. (Obviously from answers received, this is true of college presidents and other administrative officers.) I find myself with two conflicting and deep-seated prejudices: First, I do not like to encourage people to live beyond, or even up to, their current incomes. Savings should be made. And, second, I do not wish young people to delay their education or unnaturally to postpone marriage and the rearing of a family in reasonable comfort.

Society is demanding longer and longer education of people, especially of those who become educators, and even more especially of people who become members of college faculties. This is almost inevitable, but it is tragic to have the traditional period of maximum employability and income moved later and later. Many students are helped by scholarships and fellowships, but it is still true that in academic circles the individual's periods of developing needs and of increasing income and capital resources are badly, increasingly badly, out of phase. In spite of the need of adequate security for the aged, I believe in a larger proportion of society's income being distributed to the young.

The natural reaction to the foregoing is to borrow. Borrowing is by no means always unwise. The use of a mortgage to procure a house is to a large extent planned saving. Borrowing to secure an education often is sensible, although this is balancing one handicap against another and is sometimes overencouraged by colleges and their faculties eager for funds derived from larger tuitions. From these prime purposes we have a descending scale of borrowing for items that approach more nearly luxuries and are of shorter term use — from near necessities such as cars, through automatic dishwashers and outboard motors, to more handsome clothes, more expensive drinks, and more cigarettes.

Of those few who enrich their lives by borrowing in their twenties and steadily increase their solvency in their thirties and forties by reducing their debts and ultimately building up reserves, there can be no criticism. But debt can become a mode of life, careless of the future, disregardful of the creditor, and irresponsible towards one's children.

How does this bear on the responsibilities of the college administration in relation to loans to faculty and the furnishing of facilities to credit unions? Here we must consider not only our attitude toward the "enjoy now — pay later" form of life but also the relation of faculty and administration. In general when a group such as a faculty wishes to form an organization such as a credit union, I believe an administration is wise to aid and abet the enterprise even if it believes the credit union may be used unwisely; hence the use of payroll deductions to repay debts should be arranged (for administrative reasons and to prevent a multiplicity of credit unions) and office space might be furnished. These organizations should cover the whole staff rather than the faculty alone.

However, it is quite another thing for the institution to become the source of loans to the faculty for general purposes. Here it might be desirable to have a fund which can meet general and overwhelming emergencies by loans and occasionally by grants. Loans to members of the faculty seeking advanced education could be another type of loan granted by a college. (This will be discussed further in connection with leaves of absence.) Beyond this I would not go. I believe that any advances on salaries and loans made casually, as is sometimes the case — for items such as cars, quasi-necessities, conveniences, and even luxuries — are not the proper business of an institution of learning.

"THEY" SAY

REASONS FOR LOANS. The first five quotations deal with loans for the faculty member's education:

Our loan program is specifically designed to promote advancement in professional training. We encourage new faculty members to teach a year or more and then go on to further their training for advanced degrees. — *Private college*

Loans are only made during leaves for professional improvement without salary. — *Public university*

Academic loans for advanced study generally made for the period of one year. Limited in number — repayment over a 5 year period at most. If 5 years, 1/5 of principal and interest cancelled at close of each year of teaching after return to . . . . If faculty member leaves, balance is due in cash, including interest. — *Private university*

Doctoral Completion Loan Program — Under this program, if a faculty member is in a position to complete all requirements for a doctoral degree within one year's time, . . . will lend him up to $2,500, and grant him a year's leave without pay, for the purpose of completing such requirements. There is no interest charge during his year of leave, and if he returns to his position at . . . , there is no interest charge so long as he is teaching at . . . . If he returns to . . . , 25% of the face of the note will be forgiven for each year he teaches at . . . upon his return. Should he not return to . . . or should he depart . . . before completing four years teaching service after he returns, outstanding balance of loan repayable in 3 years, at 5% interest. — *Private college*

Hard for faculty to pay back. Forgive up to $2,000 per faculty member if they return for at least four semesters of teaching. — *Private university*

Other reasons are indicated in the following:

Loans seldom and on emergency confidential basis. — *Private college [paraphrased]*

To relieve faculty of financing charges concerned with needs caused by incidents beyond their control. Misunderstanding and/or judgments relative to purpose. — *Private university*

To assist faculty members with personal financial problems, to prevent embarrassment or worry for them. — *Private college*

Loans chiefly to help new faculty get established. — *Private college [paraphrased]*

Loans chiefly for children's education. — *Private university [paraphrased]*

We encourage avoidance of long term or high interest loans by offering short term loans at low interest rate. — *Private university*

There is a faculty "kitty" for small advances (up to $25 or $50) from one payroll till the next no interest charged. — *Private college*

As long as funds are available loans are made for any reasonable purpose. — *Private college [lack of funds reported as a problem]*

No questions are asked *re* loans of moderate amount if a satisfactory repayment plan is accepted. — *Private college*

Reasons not asked for. — *Public university*

. . . no questions asked and no interest charged. — *Private college*

PROBLEMS. Among the problems mentioned and comments made are:

. . . repeaters — *Private university*

The only problem of which I have knowledge is that one professor failed to come to the college for help and borrowed money from a loan shark at a very high rate of interest. We were able to remedy this and are seeking to prevent it in the future. — *Private college*

. . . unplanned indebtedness. — *Private university*

We think that many persons due to facilities of credit are not living within their means. — *Public university*

Occasionally a faculty member adopts a bitter attitude when repayment is requested. — *Private college*

We feel that loaning of money is a banking function, and hence advise our faculty to go to the local bank. However, under certain conditions, we will advance salary up to one month before the normal payment date. — *Private college*

Local banks are most considerate. — *Private college*

"EMERGENCY FUND." Sometimes the "president's fund" is primarily to meet emergencies and at other times is a source for grants-in-aid:

President's Fund to administer as he sees fit. — *Public university [evidently sometimes used for loans]*

President's Discretionary Fund — to help tide faculty members over severe financial difficulties of a personal and temporary nature. — *Private college*

Without appearing too paternalistic, the College has and encourages special funds to be used in emergencies to help relieve the burden of extraordinary expenses and debts. — *Private college*

REFERENCES TO APPENDICES

Appendix I: Questionnaire, Section 3.

Appendix II: Institutional Listings
 Personal loans

Appendix III: Summary Tables 21–30.

Appendix IV: Evaluation Chart, items 20, 21.

CHAPTER 6

OTHER PROVISIONS
CHIEFLY OF PERSONAL
BENEFIT

MOVING EXPENSES

THE purpose of paying moving expenses is obvious. About three-quarters of private universities and over one-half of private colleges contribute toward the moving expenses of persons coming into tenure ranks. Only about 21% of the public universities and a mere handful of public colleges do so. The figures are slightly less for faculty entering the junior ranks.

Only a few institutions pay full moving expenses, limitations of 50% being frequent and fixed monetary limits being used even more often. Some pay only when "stealing" faculty, not when recruiting new Ph.D.'s from graduate schools. Some institutions have a normal scale of reimbursement, ranging in one instance from $400 for a move of 200 miles to $1,000 if the move is over 800 miles. One institution provides free use of a moving van. Many institutions that do not make a practice of paying moving expenses may make exceptions. If the fruit dangling from the tree of knowledge is luscious enough, Eve may be tempted. (If the apple was labeled "prestige," prima mater and alma mater have much in common.)

Since moving expenses were not deductible from federal income taxes before 1964, the benefits to the individual from such payments were reduced. A large reimbursement might place the individual in a higher tax bracket. Hence some institutions avoid paying moving expenses in favor of paying the equivalent amount as salary over an initial period of several years. Under most circumstances moving expenses may now be deducted from income for federal tax purposes.

Institutions may therefore wish to re-examine their policies in regard to reimbursing faculty members for moving expenses.

On the whole the payment of moving expenses seems a good benefit, if it can be afforded, and one that helps a person to decide, without bias because of the immediate expense of moving, whether he prefers to stay where he is or accept the offer from elsewhere.

DISCOUNT PURCHASES

A slight majority of private institutions, but under 20% of the public ones, report that they extend the discount privileges of the institution to the faculty. This is done by purchasing items for faculty and other staff members through the business office. Of course, most institutions which maintain "bookstores" give discounts to the faculties, and in many cases these stores rival the contemporary drugstore in the variety of items sold. A few institutions may have reported this as extending discount privileges to the faculty. I believe the number doing so was small.

The kinds of arrangements made to provide discounts are numerous. Some place practically no limit upon such a plan. Others will not secure discounts for faculty members except for certain classes of items or items above a certain value, say $50. Others make a charge to cover administrative costs. Some give discount privileges primarily in connection with furnishing new homes being built by the faculty members. In a few cases local merchants extend discounts to individuals upon request of the college.

Local circumstances make a deal of difference. An institution with an extensive dormitory system, located in a small town which provides limited foodstores, allows the faculty to buy from the college commissary, thus not only saving money for the faculty members but increasing the variety and quality of the food available. On the other hand, in a city with ample "discount stores" the advantage of buying through the college may be slight.

Almost but not all of the administrative officers with whom I have discussed the subject and whose institutions extend discount privileges to the faculty say that it is a "headache" but they do not know how to get rid of it.

The disadvantages are threefold: First, and least important, is the administrative cost, rarely completely recovered, if at all. Second, especially in smaller communities, buying through the college is greatly resented by local businessmen. This may be of considerable importance to the college and it may lead to decreased service of these business-men to the faculty. Third, the relation of the college to the buyer may be an unfortunate one. The car, the washer, the furnace must be serviced and the institution is not equipped to do this. The local merchants resent doing it or may charge extraordinarily high prices because they did not furnish the item originally.

No administrative officer with whom I discussed discounting would recommend that a college which has not had a discount plan start one now. However, it must be admitted that few expected to abolish the program. The opposition to doing so comes as much from the non-faculty staff (to whom the same privileges are extended) as from the faculty. In fact, the one provost who reported that a conscious effort had been made to do away with the plan said it was thwarted largely by the staff in the treasurer's office, where it was especially convenient to make use of the privilege. A report I received frequently in conversations, and a few times in writing, is that the difficulties connected with discounts are minimized by not publicizing the plan. In particular, the new faculty member may be ignorant of the practice. In such a connection the "what-you-don't-know-doesn't-hurt-me" philosophy, though natural, seems to me hard to justify.

My judgment is that an institution is unwise to enter into a discount plan except for such items as cannot be conveniently procured without institutional help. Incidentally, arranging a discount for items, such as typewriters and microscopes, needed by a faculty member for his professional work is a poor way to salve the institutional conscience for not providing them.

"THEY" SAY

Generally, the Purchasing Office directs faculty members to suppliers who will give them the university discount. In some cases, the Purchasing Office makes the purchase and sends the bill to the faculty member who pays the supplier by personal check. In a limited number of cases, where the supplier will not accept a personal check, the University pays for the item and then bills the faculty members. — *Private university*

Discount — Institutional rate *plus tax.* — *Private college [paraphrased]*

Business office orders item, deducts from salary. — *Private college*

The arrangement is informal. Business Office assists faculty members in buying furniture, appliances, etc., at a reduced rate. — *Private college*

On institutional physician's prescriptions. — *Private college*

Only for standard pharmaceuticals available without prescription. — *Private college*

Meat, etc., purchase through commissary at Institution plus a 10% handling charge. — *Private college*

[Discount, no] not that I know of . . . . They occasionally get articles which the college is purchasing in quantity. — *Private college [partly paraphrased]*

Discount rare, some special "buys" available. — *Private college [paraphrased]*

Because of local retail business attitudes, this service is not advertised. However, any faculty member who requests it may obtain discount rates through bookstore or business office wherever feasible.— *Private college*

Informal, not advertised to faculty, and infrequently used. — *Private college*

RECREATIONAL ATHLETIC FACILITIES AND SPECIAL EVENTS

Where athletic and recreational facilities exist they are almost always open to the faculty member and very generally to his wife and children. This statement is limited by the non-coeducational character of some of these facilities. The use of swimming pool, gymnasium, tennis and handball courts are usually free; of golfing, billiard, and bowling facilities, with charge.

The athletic events are, of course, usually open to the faculty, their spouses and children — in private colleges usually free, in public colleges and in universities at reduced charges. Probably in most cases the faculty and the students are treated alike; sometimes, however, the students may pay a general activity fee after which admission is free, and the faculty receive free admission without the payment of such a fee. A similar situation exists in respect to student dramatic events. Student concerts are usually free. Professional drama and professional concerts are usually free for faculty members in private colleges but not elsewhere. Most special lectures are free to faculty members in all types of institutions — I presume as a type of professional courtesy.

"THEY" SAY

It is a very complex problem with many varied solutions. As a rural University we try to provide community centered life for both student and faculty on campus. — *Public university*

Local community would like privileges while faculty would like free or at least preferential seating. — *Public university*

Oddly enough the absence of any charge for all such events seems to depreciate the interest which faculty express in such events. — *Private college*

MISCELLANEOUS BENEFITS
(some amusing but none ludicrous)

Perhaps the way that certain benefits arise can best be indicated by a true story. Many years ago a certain church-related institution had a Chinese student sent by a missionary society. He died while attending the college. In order to bury him, a lot in a cemetery was bought. It had spare space. For a while faculty members who had given long and distinguished service to the institution received free interment therein. But this, like granting honorary degrees within a faculty, led to envy and jealousy. The space is now reserved for presidents.

Many of the benefits described below, as that above, seem odd when described out of context. Almost all have a natural origin and a definite, albeit a limited, use.

In the spirit of the above story, we find the institution which hopes to provide "free cemetery lots and monument markers for selected individuals" but did not inform us whether a faculty committee or the administration selects the individuals.

The two special benefits not included in the questionnaire which were reported most frequently were various types of cash bonuses and either free meals or meals at reduced rates (and the associated special provisions for coffee).

BONUSES. The most frequent type of financial bonus is an annual allowance for minor children. This is apt to range from $100 to $200 per year per child. Sometimes a special gift is made upon the birth of a child.

One college reports:

The College makes a grant of $150 per year to the Faculty Member for each child under 18 years of age.

This family allowance plan is probably the most prized and greatly appreciated fringe benefit that the College offers. Over two-thirds of the Faculty qualify for the benefit and the plan costs the College annually over $20,000. This has been in effect since 1956.

The plan is an attempt to bring extra help to those with greater need, i.e., younger faculty members who have a number of small children and who are not yet in the upper academic ranks. The plan has been hailed by those who share in its benefits as well as by others who recognize how logical it is and how well calculated it is to achieve its objective without exposing the College to the charge of favoritism.

Prospective faculty members never fail to comment upon this plan and we feel that it has made a very substantial contribution to our program of recruiting and retaining faculty. — *Private college* and another

According to this plan a ranked faculty member receives an annual allowance of $200 for each dependent child. A dependent child is understood to be one living at home who will not reach his nineteenth birthday on or before May 31 of the year a contract is negotiated, and who is not receiving the benefits of the college's free tuition privilege for faculty children.

The amount of the family allowance is determined each year on February 1, when new faculty contracts are issued. In the event of the birth of a child entitling a faculty member to an increase in the amount of the allowance between February 1 and the last day of the fiscal year, May 31, inclusive, the amount of the family allowance will be increased accordingly. It is the responsibility of the individual faculty member to keep up-to-date at all times, in his personal file maintained in the Dean's office, the data concerning the number of his dependent children.

The full amount of the family allowance will be paid for a child born before the day on which classes start for the fall term.

A $100 allowance will be paid in the case of a child born between the first day of the fall term and the end of the calendar year — *Private college*

One institution has in the past made a Christmas present to the faculty but plans to stop the practice. Another pays bonuses from the interest on a "Ford Grant."

Perhaps this is the place to mention the very pleasant custom reported by one college of giving a wristwatch as a present when one is inducted into the "Quarter Century Club."

A few places buy professional journals for individual faculty members.

FREE MEALS AND FREE COFFEE. A number of institutions have provisions for free meals or meals at reduced rates. In Catholic institutions refectory privileges may be extended to the lay faculty, especially if their number is small. Most of the plans are limited to free lunch on work days; others, however, exhibit a variety of purposes and provisions.

Free lunches in college dining hall. Used by about 80% of faculty. Great convenience to faculty — makes for esprit de corps. — *Private college*
1. Meal Tickets — provides 12 lunches a term per faculty member.
2. Used almost 100 per cent.
3. No cost to faculty member.
4. Objectives are to encourage faculty-student contact and to increase faculty participation in committee and department meetings. — *Private college*
Have several banquets each year served to faculty members and their wives free of charge. A tremendous amount of good will is developed. — *Private college*

Special rate in college dining room for 1, 2, or 3 meals a day. — *Private college [paraphrased]*

No club but weekly free luncheons — other meals at student rates — *Private college [paraphrased]*

Free noon day meals every day and free meals any time they are on campus at meal time. — *Private college*

Free cafeteria lunches. — *Private college [paraphrased]*

Free coffee is often provided, especially in small colleges where one room for the purpose may be sufficient. An absolute statement was:

Coffee is available free of charge all day. — *Private college*

Some of the benefits listed by a number of institutions follow:

BABY-SITTING. Various free baby-sitting arrangements occur. One of the most clear-cut descriptions of the relation between faculty responsibility and baby-sitting is given in the faculty handbook of . . . College:

Faculty members in a small college like . . . are expected to interest themselves in student activities, at least to the extent of being willing occasionally to chaperon social events. . . . The organization holding the activity will provide baby-sitting service for faculty members acting as chaperons. — *Private college*

Another college reports:

Free baby sitting — 200 hours per year. Basic purpose is to enable faculty with children to attend college events, but its use is not restricted to this purpose. — *Private college*

CABINS AND RETREATS

Faculty cabin used by individuals and groups. — *Private college [paraphrased]*

A Faculty Retreat is held annually in February at . . . State Park for the purpose of discussing in a social atmosphere free from academic duties matters which are of particular concern to the total faculty and the administrative staff. The Retreat is planned by the Faculty Retreat Committee. All academic functions on the campus are suspended during the Retreat. — *Private college*

Another institution reimburses the faculty members for expenses of a religious retreat.

Several institutions reported fine recreational areas available to the faculty.

AGENCY FEES. Several institutions who recruit through teachers' agencies pay the fees for the newly acquired faculty member.

SPECIAL RECREATION OR CULTURAL TRAVEL FUNDS

An endowed fund provides $6,000 to $7,000 annually to be used by members of the faculty for "recreation in the best sense of the word." Administered by a committee of the faculty (Chairman, Dean of the College) used largely for travel in United States or abroad. Seniority at . . . most important factor in determining eligibility. — *Private college*

We have a Faculty European Travel Plan whereby approximately 1/4 of our faculty are eligible to travel in Europe for 6–7 weeks each summer. College pays $1,000 and faculty member pays $500. This has been a tremendous stimulation to our faculty. — *Private college*

INVESTMENT FACILITIES

Faculty Investment Club. Voluntary membership limited to 25 members. — *Private college [paraphrased]*

Investment by payroll deduction. — *Public college*

or even with matching funds:

Opportunity to invest in stock, such as MIT Cumulative Trust, or Texas Fund. Three per cent deducted and matched. Faculty likes plan. — *Private college [paraphrased; this institution, however, had no retirement plan as of 1959]*

TAX PRIVILEGES. Under the amended charter of one private . . . university, as interpreted by the courts, the homes of full professors and the president are exempted from local taxes up to a maximum of $10,000 property valuation.

The following have been mentioned by a single institution but the benefit may be available in several places that did not mention it; certainly this is true of the first of these:

Extensive employment of faculty wives. — *Public college[paraphrased]*

Reimbursement to faculty member for entertainment of students. — *Private college [paraphrased]*

College operates its own laundry and the rates are set up at 50% of commercial for faculty. — *Private college*

A person with tenure and 10 years of continuous service may elect with proper approval (during final 2 years) (1) Increase of 1/4 of salary or (2) reduction of 3 hours teaching per semester. — *Private college [paraphrased]*

Aid in getting exemptions from jury duty. — *Public university [paraphrased]*

The next would not be considered a benefit by many:

Special — Smoking in classroom if ashtray and no member of class objects. — *Private college [paraphrased]*

The environment is often mentioned as a benefit, including the cultural opportunities of New York City, the chance to live in the country, the beauties of the New England mountains, and the semi-tropical climate of New Orleans. A college in Vermont mentions skiing and one in Virginia horseback riding. (Soon after I was made dean at the University of Wisconsin, an irate faculty member said to me: "Dean Birge used to say Lake Mendota was worth five hundred dollars on everyone's salary; Dean Sellery, a thousand. Just what are you trying to get by with?")

I must add to the list of benefits (though not mentioned as such in the questionnaire) the fact that a number of institutions have no academic rank. What a relief this must be to at least one type of administrative headache!

I think this list covers all of those benefits mentioned in the report of Committee Z of the AAUP in 1963 except "uniform allowance" (which was also reported to us), the "hanging of screens and storm windows," and "choice dahlia bulbs."

Certainly the college administrator who, after reading our questionnaire, with kindly irony said, "You must have thought of everything," was in error.

REFERENCES TO APPENDICES

Appendix I: Questionnaire
  Moving Expenses: Section 4, Question 8
  Discounts: Section 9, Question 2
  Recreational Athletic Facilities: Section 9, Subsection A
  Special Events: Section 9, Subsection B
  Miscellaneous Benefits: Section 11, Subsection D

Appendix III: Summary Tables
  Moving Expenses: Tables 37–40
  Recreational Athletic Facilities: Tables 114–120
  Special Events: Tables 121–126

Appendix IV: Evaluation Chart
  Moving Expenses: item 22
  Discounts: item 23
  Athletic Facilities: item 27
  Special Events: item 28

CHAPTER 7

LEAVES

"American faculty members are telephiles."

THERE was not much need to consider the varying purposes of the institutions in connection with the benefits already discussed. In developing programs of leaves, the institutions which place a major emphasis on research must meet different problems from those which consider research only a minor function of the faculty. The college whose faculty consists almost wholly of persons with the doctorate has other problems than the one with a substantial portion of its faculty still desiring, or at least expecting, to do more graduate work.

Even the meaning of "leave of absence" and particularly of "sabbatical leave" will differ from place to place depending on how closely related to the purpose of the institution is the purpose of the individual in taking a leave. One administrator will say that a man is on "leave" when he is paid by the institution and is in his office, his laboratory, or the college library doing research, since he is not teaching and teaching is the predominate assignment of the faculty. At another institution a man may be in Turkey digging dirt from precious records of the past, or in the British Museum removing dust from less ancient but even more precious records and not be considered on leave since he is fulfilling one of the major functions of the university. It is doubtful if any questionnaire could have gotten consistent answers from American colleges and universities on this topic; certainly ours did not. Although the distinction between leave without pay and leave with pay, and the distinction between leaves on contract or grant funds and leaves on the regular funds of the institution are clear, the boundary between sabbatical leaves and other leaves on pay is not agreed upon. Even a definition given in the questionnaire appears to have had little effect on the use of the phrase "sabbatical leave," which seems on each campus to be well established but without uniformity among institutions. However, there is much meat in the replies and they lead to a good deal that is worth saying.

PURPOSES FOR WHICH LEAVES ARE GRANTED. There is no other portion of the questionnaire that should be so sharpened if it were to be used again as that dealing with the purposes of leaves of absence. Most institutions which report that they grant leaves of absence state that any of the following are valid purposes: research, writing, studying, or teaching improvement. This does not indicate the fact that many institutions grant the large majority of their leaves for the first two of these and other institutions for the last two. Moreover, it must be noted that the questionnaire, although supplying a place to describe other purposes, indicated what were expected to be the most frequent. This somewhat handicapped the flexibility of responses, but without such limitations the summarizing of the answers would have been a hopeless task. Moreover, the infrequency of "others" and the diversity of the descriptions lead us to believe that the major categories were listed. However, if it were to be done over again, it would be wise to separate study for a higher degree from study as a means of updating or refreshing one's knowledge after the more formal aspects of education have been completed and to ask for an estimate of the relative numbers coming under each category.

The fact is clear that the chief purpose for leaves in the university is for research, writing, and study at the level of a trained active scholar furbishing, or sometimes refurbishing, the tools of his craft. In contrast to this, the most frequent reason for leaves from most colleges is advanced graduate work often aimed at the attainment of the doctorate.

Among "other purposes" is listed creative activity, such as painting, and rest and recuperation are frequently given. Some institutions not only weigh carefully the reasons advanced for a leave, but upon return require a report concerning what has been done. Others do not require any formal justification for leaves, at least sabbatical leaves, treating them essentially as benefits to which the faculty members become entitled through service. Between these extremes are those institutions which, recognizing that leaves are for the benefit of education rather than the individual, nevertheless take a relaxed attitude toward the question of purpose, granting "any reasonable request." An enlightened statement of the middle ground, from a private college says:

We hope that our leave program will make better teachers of our faculty, either through additional education and experience, through travel or research, or through a rest and "change of pace." It is our thought that persons with a rested mind and a relaxed nervous system can get a better grip on reality with the result that they become better equipped to meet the challenges of higher education.

INSTITUTIONAL USE OF TYPES OF LEAVE

SABBATICAL LEAVES. Of the institutions replying, 57% (with a small range either side of this figure for the various categories of institutions) report that they grant sabbatical leaves.

LEAVES OF ABSENCE OTHER THAN SABBATICAL

On institutional funds. Just under 60% of the universities, but less than 40% of the colleges, grant leaves other than sabbatical on pay from institutional funds to faculty members. Some of the institutions that do this have no regular sabbatical leave plan.

On funds from special grants and contracts. The large majority of universities grant leaves of absence financed by funds from special grants and contracts. Probably the universities that report not doing so differ more in accounting procedure than in practice.

Unfortunately, the question asked concerning these leaves was so phrased that some institutions reported what the actual experience was and others what their policy would be if they had a chance to decide. Hence some institutions answered that they did not give leaves on funds from outside grants but that they would be glad to do so. The figures state that about 40% of the colleges grant leaves on pay where funds are provided by outside grants. It is my belief that somewhat less than this number actually are doing so currently but that the large majority would be willing to do so.

Leaves of absence without pay. The great majority of institutions are willing to grant leaves of absence without pay and many for an extremely wide variety of purposes. These are often limited to a year in duration.

Summer leaves. The answers to the question concerning summer leaves ran into insuperable semantic roadblocks. Many places which are closed in the summer said all were on leave; and if these institutions happen to pay on a twelve-months basis, then they were on leave with pay. Others said they had no summer leaves on pay, but sometimes made appointments for research.

It is clear that many universities and relatively fewer colleges will make special grants for projects carried out in the summer. It is interesting that some 14 universities and 46 colleges make grants for summer travel.

THE NUMBER ON LEAVE. The 745 institutions answering the questionnaire reported 7,785 faculty members as taking leaves in 1962–63 as compared with 146,443 full-time members in their faculties. This factual statement can be misinterpreted in two ways: In the first place, some of the leaves were probably granted to part-time faculty members; in the second place, many of them were for less than a year. This might be as large a portion as a third. Hence, to conclude that at any one time about one person in twenty on the full-time faculty is on leave of absence is clearly an overestimate.

It would be even less justified to conclude that the number of full-time faculty members away from the campus for at least a term in a given year is about 5%. I would hazard a guess that this would be an overestimate in the case of most small colleges since a relief from teaching for special work on the campus may be reported as a leave. For reasons explained earlier, I believe this is an underestimate in the case of universities where many research appointments, whether at home or away, are not reported as leaves.

TABLE I
Ratio of the number taking leaves in 1962–63 as a per cent of full-time faculty in all institutions answering questionnaire

	Sabbatical	Other on inst. funds	Other on grants	Without pay	Total
All institutions					
Total	2.1	.8	.5	2.0	5.3
Universities	2.1	.7	.4	2.0	5.3
Colleges	2.0	.9	.6	1.8	5.3
Public institutions					
Total	2.0	.5	.4	2.1	5.1
Universities	2.1	.6	.4	2.2	5.4
Colleges	1.7	.3	.4	1.7	4.1
Private institutions					
Total	2.2	1.1	.7	1.7	5.7
Universities	2.2	.9	.5	1.6	5.2
Colleges	2.2	1.3	.8	1.9	6.3

In spite of the above qualifications, Table I is of interest. The most striking feature of this table is the constancy rather than the variation of the figures. However, among the variations we should note the markedly lesser use of leaves by the public colleges. This may in part be due to the fact that they are rapidly expanding and thus have a high percentage of their staff who are relatively new and presumably not eligible for leaves. It also reflects the unfortunate extent to which these institutions are limited by outdated state or municipal regulations. The public universities also suffer from this disadvantage but to a much smaller extent. The relatively large proportion of the faculty of private colleges reported as on leave supported by gifts, grants, etc., is heartening and to some may be surprising. This fact must not be overemphasized since, as mentioned above, it may in part be derived from reporting as leaves what in some universities would have been classified as research assignments.

POLICIES AND REGULATIONS
REGARDING SABBATICAL LEAVES

A number of conditions must be met before a person receives a sabbatical leave: In addition to willingness, a person must be eligible, must usually have a suitable purpose, must be selected in case more persons desire leave than the funds or the educational program of the college will allow, and frequently must agree to return to the institution after the leave is completed.

ELIGIBILITY. The eligibility to be considered for a sabbatical leave usually depends on length of service before the initial leave or since the last leave, and often on the rank and tenure status of the individual. The majority of the institutions require six years of service in the institution before a sabbatical leave is granted.

A number of institutions, which as a general rule observe the six-year provision, have special exceptions by which such leaves may be anticipated, especially by persons working for their doctorate. For instance, at one state college a junior staff member after three years may have a leave at 24% of salary. This percentage increases until, after six years, he may take a leave at 50% of salary.

Almost without exception, professors and associate professors are eligible as to rank and only about 15% of the institutions with sabbatical leaves exclude assistant professors — although rules in regard to tenure and length of service might do so in many cases. About one-third of the institutions will grant leaves to instructors who are otherwise eligible.

One institution grants leaves only to instructors and assistant professors with the single purpose of working for an advanced degree. A few institutions are not blessed (?) with ranks. Somewhat over half the institutions granting sabbatical leaves require that a faculty member have tenure before he is eligible for leave; and in the case of many of those which do not so report, it is actually required because, before a man has served long enough to have a sabbatical leave, his tenure status will have been determined.

LOCATION. Slightly over 15% of institutions with sabbatical leaves require that the recipient be absent from the campus.

OCCUPATION WHILE ON LEAVE. The large majority of institutions do not permit full-time teaching during sabbatical leaves; a lesser majority do not permit part-time teaching. About half the institutions permit some other type of employment, often requiring prior approval. And 80% permit study for an advanced degree — indeed, in many institutions this is the major purpose of sabbatical leaves.

REQUIREMENTS TO RETURN AFTER LEAVE. In 80% of the institutions (more than 90% of the public ones) there is a requirement that persons return from sabbatical leaves, usually for one year but, deplorably, often for a longer period. In some cases this is described as a "moral obligation" or the rather strange "only a moral obligation." Others require written agreements or go so far as to give the salary while on leave in the form of a loan "forgiven" after the required period of service subsequent to the leave. In certain states regulations governing service after leave are set up by state law. Some institutions admit that they do not know whether their regulations in this regard are legally binding and probably would not try to enforce them. Later this topic will be considered at some length.

LENGTH OF LEAVES AND FINANCIAL ARRANGEMENTS. Financially the typical plan is a half year on full pay or a full year on half pay. Variations for institutions on the quarter system and for special summer situations are numerous.

Other variations are more vital. In some cases there is no full-pay option; in others, it is rare to allow any period on part pay. A number of institutions have ways to supplement sabbatical leave pay — in case of travel, etc.; others use a fraction of pay greater than 50% for these year-length leaves.

One type of plan involves loans, of a forgivable nature, but appears to be used with a variety of motives. In one instance, as mentioned above, the man who is eligible by length of service and rank for a sabbatical leave is required to sign a note for his salary, but 25% of the loan is "forgiven" for each year after his return. A sort of indentured servant clause! Another with almost the same form is given to young men within a year of their doctorate as a leave without pay but with a similarly forgivable loan. The intent of this, although also possessive, is clearly generous.

Another variation on pay seems to be the greater of 50% of pay or salary up to $5,000.

Some institutions, forgetting the clause in the Lord's Prayer: "Lead us not into temptation," pay the individual on leave the difference between his salary and that of the substitute.

Other arrangements depend on reasons for leave; for instance, those on sabbatical leaves for health may be paid less than for research, or research leaves are at less than regular salary.

Usually the contribution to the retirement plan follows the choice of type of leave, being full when leave is on full pay and partial otherwise. In general, coverage by the group insurance plans of the institutions is continued.

About half the persons taking leaves take them on half pay for the longer period and about half on full pay for the shorter time.

A good majority take leaves when they can, but the number who do not is sizable. In some institutions over 75% do not take leaves when they are eligible. In some of these latter institutions the one-half salary provision is the only one available and the faculty members do not feel they can afford leaves under this provision. In others the purposes of leaves may be restrictive. In still others it is possible that the obligation to return for a prolonged period may make some hesitant to accept a leave.

In some institutions the possibility of taking leaves is restricted not only by eligibility rules and possible interference with the educational program, but also by limitations of funds. However, about 80% of the institutions reported that the funds were usually sufficient. Often this is made possible by the fact that many faculty members do not desire (at least under the financial and other conditions imposed) to take leaves although they may be eligible for them.

The plans for sabbatical leaves are so inextricably connected with policies concerning other leaves that a discussion of many of the questions that occur with regard to them will be postponed until the facts regarding other leaves with pay and leaves without pay are presented.

In particular, the evidence of the institutional and faculty opinions concerning these leaves will come later.

LEAVES OTHER THAN SABBATICAL

FROM INSTITUTIONAL FUNDS. When leaves from institutional funds are granted, they are usually for the same purposes as sabbatical leaves. However, some institutions with extensive research functions find a program of such leaves more adaptable than a periodic plan. Other institutions, which cannot afford a fully developed sabbatical plan, can and do occasionally grant leaves on pay for various reasons from health to a particularly interesting research project or curriculum study. Some institutions supplement the regular sabbatical leaves by other leaves, sometimes on a fellowship basis and sometimes as special awards.

The financial arrangements are more flexible than in the case of a sabbatical leave, sometimes full pay for a full year, sometimes a special summer appointment. Leaves on part pay, besides sabbatical, are also given.

Most institutions that grant these leaves insist that the faculty member return, although the practice is not as widespread as in the case of sabbatical leaves. On occasion the institution insists that a man not return.

About half our institutions will sometimes supplement a grant or fellowship received by a faculty member in order to make it financially possible for him to take advantage of it. This is the way the Guggenheim Foundation selects the persons who will receive grants from the universities.

Fellowships from foundations, even those related to an institution, may have tax advantages for the individual not present in the case of continuation of salary.

LEAVES WITHOUT PAY. Most institutions are willing to grant leaves without pay to all ranks without any special prior minimum period of service. Limitations on frequency of such leaves is usually on an individual basis. Even with leaves without pay, 20% of the institutions require that the faculty member return.

The employers' contributions to various retirement and insurance benefits are usually stopped while a man is on leave without pay, but this is by no means universal, especially in respect to the group insurance plans.

GENERAL

LIMITATION ON THE NUMBER ON LEAVE AT A GIVEN TIME. Although institutions must control the number of persons who are on leave at any one time in order to protect the functioning of the institution — and sometimes also the budget — only about 50% of the institutions have a fixed institution-wide rule in this regard. Some have rules relating to the number on leave from a department and many handle the matter by ad hoc decisions.

Budgetary considerations chiefly affect the total number of persons on leave on pay from institutional funds, either sabbatical or otherwise. However, this is not always the case since special endowments sometimes exist, limited in use to a certain department or some other faculty group.

Educational considerations take into account the particular program for which a man may be responsible and the ease of securing a substitute or temporarily foregoing some activities by omitting courses, etc. Decisions must often be made within departmental context and, since the size of departments and the substitutability of individuals are involved, are not subject to rule as much as to individual considerations. It may not be relevant whether a leave is sabbatical, nor from what funds it is paid, nor even whether it is a leave without pay. Moreover, the staffing problem is affected by persons who may not be on leave but may have special assignments that remove them in whole or part from their regular duties. In a college without graduate work the manning of essential courses may be the central problem. In a large university this may be relatively easy, but the plight of thesis students can be made distressing by the absence of major professors.

The fact is that hard choices must be made. The institution can afford five sabbaticals but seven eligible persons wish them. How do you choose? Or, one man in a department is eligible for a sabbatical, a second has the possibility of a research grant, a third a Guggenheim. The department cannot readily spare more than two. Which should stay home? Or perhaps let the students suffer?

How are these decisions made? Within the sabbatical leave plan certain practices are by regulation or custom often observed. The length of time since the last leave may be a major factor. The seniority of the staff member and sometimes a judgment as to the project enter in. A rather subjective one is reported as "the member's value to the University." The more complicated decisions involve various types of leaves. One college determines two years in advance who will be on leave with pay. (Of course exceptions are possible.) This provision should help both the college and the individual to make plans.

One question was asked to elicit information as to "who reviews and decides upon requests for sabbatical and other leaves of absence?" The answers, though technically correct, gave little insight into the real processes. An answer such as "the trustees" is probably purely formal. Perhaps the most important information gained is that, in general, the decision is not made by a faculty committee (yet this method is not rare); that, depending on size of the institution, the person whose "yes" or "no" sticks is either the president or the dean; that, where the problem is not chiefly budgetary but one of providing for the work of the absentee, the department, speaking through its chairman, is the essential adviser in the matter.

HOW IS THE WORK OF THE ABSENTEE CARED FOR? The answer is just as you would expect. Almost all of the institutions replying try at times to get substitutes. Most institutions do some dividing up of the work as extra loads of individuals. This process merges into that of the institutions that definitely staff their departments to have some on leave. (When I was dean I once complained to a department that had an excessive number of persons on leave, mostly without pay. The chairman replied: "Mark, someday we will all stay home – then you will scream!") Finally, a quarter of the institutions admit to reducing programs.

LEAVES OF ABSENCE AND TENURE. Of those institutions which have a fixed period within which tenure must be determined, somewhat over half do not count the time while a man is on leave as being within that period. This tendency is greater in public than in private institutions. However, even in the case of leave without pay, promotion and salary are not usually delayed by taking leave. A leave, well spent, may even speed up promotion.

PROBLEMS AS REPORTED BY PRESIDENTS. The commonest leave problems reported by administrative officers are:

(1) Lack of funds.
(2) Difficulty of finding substitutes.

(3) Unwillingness of those who need them most to take leaves.

(4) Failure of faculty members to return.

The first needs no elaboration and it affects both (2) and (3).

Substitutes. The securing of adequate substitutes for absent faculty members is at present extremely difficult. It costs more to live away from home than at home; hence an institution must either plan to get a lower-salaried individual or pay more for the substitute than for the man leaving. Thus the additional cost of the leave may actually be greater than the salary paid to the absent member. There is also a chain reaction by which a single man, a, on leave with pay at college A may cause individuals at X, Y, and Z to go on leave without pay; that is to say, a and x have pay from A, y from X, and z from Y, and Z does without. Z has been hurt as well as bothered. Moreover, each successive arrangement in the chain is made at a later and hence, usually, a more inconvenient time.

A goodly number of presidents reported that this difficulty of finding substitutes is accentuated by the late date at which foundations and government agencies make their awards or offer contracts.

Short leaves make for special difficulties in securing substitutes. One institution noted the convenience, if two men in a given department are each to have a half-year leave, of their taking them in different semesters so that a single substitute employed for the year can be used. Large departments may staff for a given number regularly to be away but, as indicated earlier, this system also at times breaks down. For a given institution more money would help secure substitutes. For higher education as a whole the problem would still be with us.

The possible use of the "Retired Professors Registry" (which is under the management of the AAUP, assisted by financial contributions from the AAC and TIAA) might often help in securing substitutes.

Where leaves are concerned we live with compromise — sometimes at the expense of the faculty member, sometimes of his colleagues, and often of the students. To have everyone stay at home would be even harder on all. In a few places the number on leave may be so great that, even if the departments can carry on their work, the proportion of senior staff present in the college becomes undesirably low.

Those who will not take leave. Inertia, lack of funds, family problems including education of children, and at times just the love of teaching keep people from taking leaves for which they are eligible. To the extent that a break for research, study, or plain rest is necessary to the continued effectiveness of the scholar-teacher, such failure to take leave is a detriment to the college. From the point of view of the college, the lethargic need leaves more than the avid. This particular complaint comes more from the colleges than from the universities and of course is connected with the generosity of the plan for leaves. The figures reporting the number of eligibles who do not take leave (See Appendix III, Table 57) show that this complaint is by no means fictitious.

Failure to return. More than one place reports that sabbatical leaves lead to loss of faculty particularly when the leave results in the individual's receiving a higher degree. This is especially true for institutions with less adequate financial resources and a limited number of faculty members holding the doctorate.

Another fear is sometimes mentioned, namely, that sabbatical leaves may "degenerate into paid vacations."

THE VALUE WHICH INSTITUTIONS PLACE UPON LEAVES. An adequate program of leaves is considered among the most important benefits that an institution provides. The evidence for this is based both on the statistical data that can be tabulated and on the personal testimony of the profession, administrators, and others.

Of the institutions with sabbatical leaves, over one-third state that they are of substantial use in retaining the faculty and about 85% rate them as at least of moderate value. Other leaves with pay make a substantial contribution toward retaining staff in nearly 20% of the institutions and at least a moderate contribution in 55%, while even leaves without pay make a substantial contribution in over 10% of the cases and at least a moderate contribution in 55%. The testimony relative to the power of these leaves in recruiting staff is only slightly less impressive. The exact figures differ between private and public institutions and between colleges and universities but tell essentially the same story.

Another piece of evidence in the same direction is that, in spite of the fact that in at least half the cases faculty members taking sabbatical leaves do so at a financial sacrifice, still over half of those eligible to receive sabbatical leaves accept them; and non-acceptance is often only postponement.

The greatest evidence of value, however, comes from the constant testimony given by college administrators. This frequently involves statements as to the high relative importance of leaves, statements as to plans to expand the program when funds become available, statements as to the relatively high importance that faculty members place upon the privilege of leaves — especially on pay — and, perhaps most significant of all, the witness borne to the fact that those leaves actually contribute to the value of the faculty members as scholars and teachers.

However, one president believes the chief use of leaves is to "satisfy desire of faculty members."

The value of leaves as compared to research assignments is touched on by the university which reports: "Popularity of 'leaves' has diminished in recent years, under impact of competitiveness on all levels of teaching. Professors prefer to stay 'close to the home grounds' and develop from that base of operation."

RECOMMENDATIONS WITH REASONS THEREFOR

The reasons for leaves are both the intrinsic value of what is accomplished while a man is on leave and the effect of the leave on the individual faculty member. When research is a major function of an institution, the emphasis well may be split rather evenly between these two objectives. For most colleges and some universities the concern will center on the enhancement of the effectiveness of the individual.

PHILOSOPHIES OF LEAVES. There are two contrasting philosophies as to the reasons for having a system of leaves, especially sabbatical leaves. I presume in their pure form these are held by few persons; but as they are approached, very different policies emerge. First, leaves, especially leaves with pay, are given to increase the usefulness of the faculty member to the institution he is now serving. Second, leaves with pay, especially sabbatical leaves, are a form of deferred compensation.

If you hold the first view, you tend to insist on persons returning from leave, on not giving leaves to men near retirement, and on an educational purpose for the leave.

If you hold the second view, there is little insistence on or even belief in the obligation of the faculty member to return; leave is granted right up to retirement — often including the terminal year; rest and recreation are ample purposes for a sabbatical leave; and you wish some system were devised to fund leaves so that a person would be assured of a leave on schedule even if he changes the institution which he serves.

Another view, which some will not accept but which I believe is compatible with the best practices actually used, is that the institutions' policies should be such as to develop the scholar's and teacher's (or, perhaps even better, scholar-teacher's) total effectiveness for the good of the profession with full recognition of the value of his personal development both to society and to himself. This point of view should not be held too rigidly, but it seems to me to be more in the public interest and to rationalize a better policy than the first two.

Thus one does not consider a leave as deferred compensation but, on the other hand, does not try to use a leave to immobilize the recipient. Moreover, one would recognize the need for leaves at nearly regular intervals even if a man is shifting from one institution to another. It would also recognize that rest is no reason for a leave unless rest is clearly needed; also that a man's cultural life and social usefulness do not end by decree at age 68 or 70. An institution which turns out educated bachelors but fossilized emeriti has failed in one of its educational functions. Moreover, it is probable that the second would preclude the first.

Perhaps the chief practical difficulty of this "good-for-the-profession" policy is that to some degree the colleges would be divided between the exploiting and exploited. Moreover, it would be the financially less privileged colleges that would be exploited. The college which wishes to increase the number of its faculty holding the doctorate and helps them to acquire it by granting educational leaves may lose these very members to the college that can afford to do most of its initial recruiting at the post–Ph.D. level. I shall harp on this again.

PLAN FOR UNIVERSITIES AND COLLEGES WITH EMPHASIS ON RESEARCH. I believe that almost all universities and many colleges that emphasize research should have a plan something like the following:

The faculty should have opportunities for full-time research duties at frequent intervals but not necessarily strictly periodic. (It would be interesting at times to give research men an opportunity for full-time teaching.) The terms, length, and locale of these assignments may depend in large part on the research programs of the individuals. However, the stage of development of the candidate for leave, the needs of his discipline as to library, laboratory, or field work, and the balance of both the individual's and his department's emphasis on teaching and on research must enter the picture. Funds from outside sources and internal funds should be distributed to produce as balanced a program as feasible. These should be considered as assignments, not leaves, whether the man is in his own laboratory or in Zanzibar — indeed, Zanzibar may be his laboratory. In general there should be no regulations against a man's remaining on the campus during such assignments. Although for general social reasons the young men should be favored, no cutoff point short of retirement should be fixed. The institution inviting a man to come from another institution should consider the length of time since his last research assignment in determining how soon he may have another. If he is assured on this subject when he moves, it is not only helpful to him but good bait.

In addition to these assignments, occasional leaves on pay for reasons of health or cultural travel may well be granted, but these need not be as frequent as every seventh year.

The research assignments should be granted more frequently than once in seven years to active scholars. However, scholars continuing their work, even if less active and distinguished than the leaders of the profession, should still get these assignments as frequently as they now get so-called leaves.

Naturally on such assignments all the usual employment benefits, such as contributions toward retirement and insurance, should be continued.

At times, also, special assignments may stress research without completely excluding teaching; thus a person might not be assigned to classroom teaching for a year but would still guide his thesis students.

The granting of these research opportunities when not done by rule may occasionally lead to unfortunate discrimination and even more often to the charge that it exists. This may be lessened by placing a large part of the money budgeted for these assignments in charge of a research committee. This is probably wise but has two disadvantages: (1) a great deal of time of first-class men is used (not without some educational benefit to them); and (2) a committee which operates will always generate a plethora of rules to protect itself from being charged with discriminatory actions. In my opinion, the deans of the colleges should have some research funds to arbitrarily spend on exceptions. The usefulness of the dean who hasn't the power to make mistakes is nil. Put him in the clean-up position, but watch his batting average!

LEAVES IN COLLEGES WHERE THE RESEARCH FUNCTION IS MINOR. The problem of leaves for the college without research emphasis is truly different and perhaps more difficult than for institutions with emphasis

on research. The teacher who does not have of necessity the stimulus
of research, which clearly has an enlivening influence (but also com-
petes with teaching for time and attention and may be narrowing),
must, to remain effective, have scholarly interests that at times should
be given full play. Some system of leaves is almost a necessity. Since
these leaves are usually a break in his duties rather than a temporary
shift in emphasis, it is harder to determine their nature and frequency
on the basis of the individual program. They may well, therefore, tend
to be more nearly periodic, more truly sabbatical, than in the case of
research assignments. The purpose should still be defined, and be rest
only when rest is needed. However, this is needed more often than is
admitted. (What faculty member desirous of salary increases wishes
to plead exhaustion, either physical or mental?) Travel, when seriously
pursued for its cultural benefits, should be a justification. In fact, I
am depressed by the terrible purposefulness of leaves. A student appreciates a teacher who is relaxed rather than taut. The same quality
would be appreciated in an administrator or, for that matter, in a
faculty policy declaration.

The "half-on-full or full-on-half" may well be an appropriate formula.

I still believe that the older men should not be excluded, but emphasis on the younger should be strong. The length of time since a
man's last leave should be considered even when he moves.

In spite of the danger of gratuitously preaching a sermon that is only
partially relevant to the subject, I want to strongly urge that consideration be given to the best way of using in institutions that are not strongly
oriented toward research the leaves of persons without Ph.D.'s. If a
man is reasonably near his doctorate, is making progress on his thesis
while teaching, and can finish or nearly finish his work with a year's
leave, the opportunity should be used for this purpose. But a prolonged period with only occasional intervals of intensive work toward
the doctorate — even if the work culminates in a degree — does not do
the most to develop the individual as a teacher and an academic citizen,
and rarely does it produce an investigator. Far better, for a man with
the master's degree, to periodically take work which will bring him
up to date in his field, allow him to observe first-class exposition of
his subject, and to pay attention to the development of the curriculum
changes and new teaching programs of interest to him!

This dream will not happen unless: (1) accrediting associations decrease the pressure for their formal requirements relative to number of Ph.D.'s on the faculty; (2) universities plan courses which will be of maximum use to such teachers; (3) colleges reward excellence in teaching; and (4), if possible, some plan be developed to make the good teacher visible beyond his campus. Competition for excellent teachers, rather than meanly hiding one's treasure (even if appreciated), would be wholesome.

REQUIREMENTS TO RETURN FROM LEAVE. As indicated above, I believe American education is served best if there is no requirement for a person to return from leave. This seems clear to me in the case of leaves without pay, although of course there is the same obligation to give adequate notice as there is for a man in residence. However, some institutions believe it is best to require that a man return from a leave without pay.

In the case of leave with pay for research, the argument for mobility and freedom is, in my opinion, nearly as persuasive. In spite of the greater justification for a hard-boiled policy relative to return to an institution which is investing in a man's education by granting him a leave, I believe such a policy is undesirable. It is fair to ask a man his intent when he applies for his leave and take this into consideration in determining whether to grant leave or not. The individuals who will not take fair play into account are probably few and not desirable. Moreover, the individual's value to an institution is greatly diminished if he is forced to remain when he wishes to go elsewhere.

I am not pleading for looser practices on the part of individuals in relation to their institutions but that institutions rely, as they do in so much else, on the individual's sense of fair play instead of on contractual relations. Even if this does not work perfectly, it works better in other relations than rigidity. I believe it would here. Often we may expect what it is unwise to demand.

Moreover, the scare technique is unacceptable. Administrators have told me, both in private and on the questionnaire, that (a) they were not sure that their rules would be sustained in a court, and (b) they would not try to enforce them if there were a showdown. This technique is as reprehensible as a faculty member's trying to get as much mileage as possible out of an offer he does not intend to accept.

Some institutions, inviting a man who is on sabbatical leave to join their staff, have indicated their willingness to pay part or all of his salary for the period of his leave if he agrees to join their staff at the termination of his leave. It might be well for this to become the accepted practice.

WHO SHOULD DECIDE ON WHO ARE GRANTED LEAVES? This problem has been described earlier. I have already stated that, in the case of special research assignments or leaves based on projects, the expert advice of a research committee is valuable.

Frequently, however, the project is not the most essential consideration, especially in the case of sabbatical leaves; and yet there may be more applicants than leaves available. I am one who believes that the faculty should have a very large role in academic government and that to a large degree it should determine what that role should be. Yet I believe the faculty is wise if it participates very actively in the determination of policy and, on the other hand, shows real reluctance to assume the administration of that policy. Hence it would seem to me appropriate to have the leave policy developed initially and reviewed from time to time with full faculty participation. If there is a faculty committee that now deals with questions such as individual salaries and promotions, it might also advise on the choice of persons to receive leaves; if there is no such committee, it would seem better not to create one merely to handle questions of leaves.

LEAVES, TENURE, AND PROMOTION. It would appear that in the case of most leaves — and certainly of research assignments — the process of securing tenure, being promoted, and receiving salary increases should not be slowed down by a leave of a year or less. However, leaves of unusual length and leaves for non-academic purposes (such as industrial employment or military service) raise questions that must be decided on an individual basis. In some instances, the postponement of a decision is a kindness to the individual.

INSURANCE AND RETIREMENT CONTRIBUTIONS. It is important to be certain that a man's program of insurance is not affected adversely by leaves. It is not so important whether the institution or the individual pays for these provisions as that they be continued. It is not costly for an institution to continue its contributions and to ensure no accidental lapsing of the insurance coverage.

Retirement contributions are another matter. It would seem fair to continue them to the same extent that the salary is continued: full if on full pay, half on half, and zero on leaves without pay. However, even if fair, this practice may not be wise. Any lessening of contributions toward a retirement annuity will in general mean a less adequate provision for retirement. This is unfortunate for both the individual and the institution. A large number of institutions continue their contributions during leaves without pay; what proportion of these are on a matching basis is not known. I strongly recommend some plan be worked out in each case so that the total contribution toward retirement not be decreased. The details may depend in part on the relations of the individual to the employer whom he has during his leave.

Often it is possible to get a foundation or government agency, which is paying for an individual's salary, also to provide for the institution's normal contributions to his retirement annuity and insurance benefits.

"THEY" SAY

PURPOSE OF LEAVE, BOTH INSTITUTIONAL AND INDIVIDUAL

To encourage faculty to be scholarly and professionally alert by attending professional meetings. To encourage faculty to write and publish. To keep the faculty and the college aware of trends, especially in the field of teacher education. To meet accreditation criteria. To help create a national or regional image for the college. — *Private college*

To encourage faculty to participate in scholarly and professional meetings. To enable faculty to know what their colleagues at other institutions are doing — teaching methods, research, etc. To encourage and promote academic and professional development of the faculty. To perform the research and service functions of the University. — *Public university*

We do not require a statement of intent. We do require that the sabbatical be used for increasing the effectiveness of a teacher in the academic area concerned.

We hope that our leave program will make better teachers of our faculty, either through additional education and experience, through travel or research, or through a rest and "change of pace." It is our thought that persons with a rested mind and a relaxed nervous system can get a better grip on reality with the result that they become better equipped to meet the challenges of higher education. — *Private college*

Ninety per cent of those who are eligible timewise do not take leave because they do not have an eligible program. — *Private college [paraphrased]*

Report of accomplishment shall be made at conclusion. — *Private college*

GRADUATE WORK

Most distinctive feature is a $25,000 grant which the College matched to assist present faculty to work on advanced degrees. — *Private college*

To help younger faculty members complete their doctoral program. College allows $500.00 credit for each year of service. Will advance money if credit earned is not sufficient. — *Private college*

For graduate study we have a plan for those above M.A. to work toward Doctorate and school can grant a maximum of $3200 plus tuition for ten months. — *Public college*

I fear that the possible distinction assumed in the following is valid:

So that faculty may advance their minds and their degrees. — *Private college*

FINANCIAL ARRANGEMENTS BETTER THAN AVERAGE

Effective 1963–64, sabbatical leave stipends for two semesters will equal half salary if the individual receives outside support; otherwise, 3/4 salary up to a maximum of $9,000. — *Private college [context would indicate $9,000 as possible maximum payment rather than maximum salary to which rule applies]*

One year's leave at 3/4 salary. — *Private college [paraphrased]*

Faculty Fellowship Program: Fellows receive full compensation and grant not to exceed $2,500 in support of travel or other expenses related to full year of study, observation, or creative activity; complements sabbatical and other award programs. Recognizes the need of the teacher-scholar for uninterrupted time to pursue his professional development. Prof. or Ass't. Prof. eligible with emphasis on latter. Currently 3–4 awards per year. — *Private college*

Fulbright grantees get 1/6 of their salaries and regular fringe benefits to supplement their Fulbright grants. Others may get special travel allowances when it is to the advantage of the University program. — *Private university*

TIMING OF LEAVES

Younger men may apply earlier than older (after 5 years if under 40, after 7 otherwise). — *Private college [paraphrased]*

Sabbatical leaves available at 1/2 pay for semester after 6 semesters. — *Public university [paraphrased]*

Junior sabbatical after 3 or more consecutive years of service. — *Public university*

Borrowed leave, whereby faculty members after 7 quarters, may take 2 quarters leave, of which one is earned and one is borrowed against 7 quarters of service after return to campus. — *Public college*

Our only problem is that each person gets about *one* leave during his lifetime. We can't finance a leave for everybody every 7th year.

[Important Special Features:] The fact that some of our leaves are automatic by virtue of seniority; the fact that at age 57 every professor becomes eligible for a leave with pay regardless of seniority; the fact that several leaves are available to the faculty at large regardless of rank. — *Public university*

No leave within 5 years of retirement (at age 65). — *Private college [paraphrased]*

Leave without pay counts as breaking continuity of six years of service required for sabbatical. — *Private college*

OUTSIDE JOBS

His total remuneration from job and sabbatical allowance may not exceed his regular salary. — *Public university*

RETURN OF FACULTY. This is a frequently mentioned problem. Many of the following quotes would be found very often. Note in the first four quotes the distribution of types of institution.

Often the person does not return — a better opportunity has come along. — *Private university*

Attracting them back after their enhanced visibility elsewhere in the Nation. — *Public university*

Tendency for faculty on leave to become interested in narrow aspects of their respective fields and thus decide to go to positions in large universities where they can specialize. — *Private college*

Loss through resignations — particularly last-minute resignations. — *Public college*

Avoiding the role of simply providing "job insurance" to a person who wants to try out something but does not choose to risk being out of a job. — *Public university*

Some faculty members do not return. — *Private college [This institution expects people to return for three years.]*

Occasionally person granted leave without pay fails to return. Then department involved suffers, having managed with a temporary replacement for a year. — *Private college*

In the past the faculty members have left our employ after a year back on our campus. — *Private college*

No, but a moral commitment is recognized. — *Private college [paraphrased]*

Obligated — yes; compelled or required — no. — *Private college [paraphrased]*

But he would not be held to this obligation. — *Private college*

For leave without pay return for equal time. — *Private college*

Policy has been changed to require 4 years of service after a sabbatical leave. — *Private college*

Reconsideration of policy of obligation to return to position after taking leave. — *Private college*

SUBSTITUTES AND HARDSHIP ON STUDENTS

Our greatest single problem in faculty recruitment is, and will continue to be, finding faculty members for short-term appointments for regular faculty members who are on leaves of absence. The recent liberalization of our policy governing leaves of absence notably increases this difficulty. So many positions offering the possibility of permanency are available elsewhere that good candidates are understandably reluctant to accept what is only a temporary appointment as replacement for someone else. — *Private college*

We have experienced no particular problems outside of the difficulties of securing adequate replacements on a temporary basis. Also students object to losing out on dynamic teachers. — *Private college*

Adjusting departmental teaching programs, particularly to prevent graduate students from very great changes of schedule due to unavailability of essential courses for a full year. — *Private university*

1. Replacement is not always competent.

2. Students dislike absence of professor under whom they have been working.

3. Financial hardship of two salaries for the work of one person. — *Private college*

TRAVEL, I.E. WORK VS. VACATION

Our program is one of travel *and* research. My main criticism of the program which is wholly managed by a faculty committee is that there is a lot of travel and not enough research paid for out of the appropriation. — *Private college*

Seemingly each person granted a sabbatical feels that he must go abroad. Whether a sabbatical leave degenerates into a paid vacation is still to be determined. — *Private college*

Automatic leaves tend to encourage dilettantism. Faculty committees do not like to turn down those long in service, no matter how flimsy the rationale. — *Private college*

FACULTY FINANCES

Half-pay sabbaticals are not financially feasible to many faculty.

Young faculty with incomplete doctorates need financial help to afford leaves. — *Private college*

Half salary makes it difficult for young faculty members with families to take such leave. We try to secure additional help from foundations etc., to give additional aid. Have succeeded in most instances. — *Private college*

INSTITUTIONAL FINANCES

Funds for needed staff must be diverted for this purpose. — *Private college*

Budget never permits leave time schedule to be carried up to date. — *Public college*

Very expensive program for a college of modest means.

Education Department given priority on funds. — *Private college*

STATE LAWS

Prohibited by state law. — *Public college*

Lack of a state policy which permits sabbatical leaves. — *Public college*

LATE REQUESTS

Most of the problems occur in the Fulbright Program and government service. The award or appointment is made definite too late in the year to find suitable replacement. Moreover, too near the end of the period of leave there is often a request for an extension. — *Private university*

HOW ARE SELECTIONS MADE?

One illustration of faculty participation in the selection of candidates for leaves is:

The President and the elected chairman of the department for sabbatical leaves (which are never questioned unless a staffing problem exists) and for leaves without pay; for early leave with pay for faculty not yet eligible for sabbatical leave, the President and the elected Faculty Appointments Committee. — *Private college*

REFERENCES TO APPENDICES

Appendix I: Questionnaire, Section 5.

Appendix II: Institutional Listings
Sabbatical leaves
Maximum time sabbatical leave on full salary
Maximum time sabbatical leave on half salary
Leaves with pay other than sabbatical from institution funds
Ratio of faculty with leaves during year to full-time faculty

Appendix III: Summary Tables 41–88.

Appendix IV: Evaluation Chart, items 18, 19.

CHAPTER 8

FACULTY
TRAVEL EXPENSES

A FEW facts are clear about reimbursement for travel, but the questionnaire was not adequate to reveal many details. What a horrendous questionnaire it would have been if it had been adequate!

RELATION OF PURPOSES OF TRAVEL TO REIMBURSEMENT. Most institutions pay without question the full expenses of administrative officers or other faculty members traveling on official business.

The following pattern of reimbursement for attending meetings occurs frequently, ranging from least to most generous: (1) no reimbursement or infrequently on ad hoc basis; (2) no reimbursement unless person is giving a paper or has some other special connection with the program (such as being a society officer) and then only for transportation; (3) to all attendants transportation only (often with limitations on frequency and distance); (4) to those not giving papers transportation only, but full expenses to those giving papers or to officers, etc.; (5) full expenses to all (often with limitations as to frequency and distance).

Reimbursement for those attending special conferences is usually on an individual basis but conforms as nearly as possible to the general policy for those attending meetings.

About 40% of the universities (50% of private universities) will pay toward travel expenses of persons on research leave. This is true in less than a quarter of the colleges.

Usually institutions will allow reasonable expenses, both transportation and other, on grants from outside sources.

BASIS FOR REIMBURSEMENT. The basis for transportation expenses is often stated, examples being: "tourist air," first-class rail + pullman," "rail coach," "actual." Some limitations are also placed on other expenses even when reimbursements for these are permitted. In public institutions reimbursements frequently are controlled by regulations covering all state or municipal employees.

In general a person using his own car gets an allowance, in most cases either seven or eight cents per mile, sometimes with higher limits if more than one faculty member go in the same car. But one institution reports occasional difficulty in getting members to travel in the same car.

Since one must eat even at home, meals are sometimes explicitly ruled non-reimbursable.

Some large institutions run travel bureaus (in fact, if not in name) and provide traveler's checks without the usual service charge.

A large number of institutions, within some framework of what items may be paid for, allot travel funds to the departments and allow them to make the decisions as to who should go and how the "kitty" is to be divided.

Administrators of the institutions with generous plans believe reimbursement for travel has at least a moderate effect on recruitment and retention of staff. Moreover, many complain of lack of funds for travel.

VALUE OF THE PROGRAM. The faculty member who never travels is crippled, and the one who travels too much is constantly out of breath — and frequently out of place. It is in the best interests of the profession and of the institution for faculty members to meet with colleagues, to keep aware of what others are doing even before publication and of what is thought about the importance of varying scholarly activities, to know the men in the field and to assess their scholarly achievements, their personalities, and their probable teaching skills. Visitors to the campus and travel away from the campus are both ways to make the community of scholars that form a faculty a part of a still larger community. However, national groups sometimes unduly tend to isolate themselves along professional lines. Many institutions frankly admit that the value to their public relations of having members participate in meetings, or even just attend, is significant.

A reasonable travel budget seems justified. Moreover, as will appear later, this may be the only way to equalize the opportunities of faculty members in various branches of learning.

The institutions of higher education, especially universities, face the problem of keeping the staff at home. Frequent leaves can create major difficulties (especially for the graduate students) but provisions to solve them often can be systematized. Constant traveling to meetings, conferences, and committee sessions is disruptive of classes, of the university's own committees, and even of its social life. (Dining clubs to which I belong used to expect full attendance but now often find that nearly half the members are away at any given time.) We have the witness of one president that "attending meetings becomes a disease which infects a fair number of the faculty." It is not too soon to struggle with the problem of too many meetings. There must be some middle ground between the rusty and the worn.

Of the policy problems worthy of discussion, I shall consider four: (1) the problem arising from more generous treatment of expenses paid by grants; (2) the questions of what are reasonable expenses and the value of a per diem policy; (3) state or other elaborate regulations; (4) the policy of paying more to persons participating in the meeting than to those merely attending.

INEQUITIES CAUSED BY GRANTS. Until recently it was reasonable, perhaps even enlightened, to try to keep salaries as high as possible, to reward the active, but to expect the scholar to pay his own way to meetings. When, however, it became less difficult in certain areas to get money on research grants for travel, to obtain grants for conferences including expenses or at least transportation for a large invited list, to set up committees with a travel budget supported by a foundation, when these meetings often were contiguous or overlapping in time and place with society meetings, and when it became clear that the ease of getting such funds was much greater in some areas than others (for instance, physics had more funds than French; for that matter, Telugu or Swahili also might be relatively better off than French), the universities and colleges were forced to try to use their own funds to equalize the opportunities of the members of their faculties. The inequities often are within departments as well as between departments.

Hence a system to provide for the expenses of faculty members who have no outside support for travel is important. This support should not be so generous as to assure that all members of the faculty, instead of just some, are away from the institution more than is desirable or perhaps even desired.

REASONABLE EXPENSES. The question of reasonable expenses is, of course, a difficult one. The transportation by coach for relatively short

trips and pullman or air coach for longer, with equitable provision
for travel by private car, are not points of major dispute. An institution
may, for financial reasons, or because some of the living expenses would
be incurred at home and much of the benefit is personal, decide that
transportation expenses are all that will be paid except for travel on
institutional business. However, if this is not the case, some limitations
will probably be desirable. Various groups use certain per diem allowances to solve this problem. But reasonable reimbursement for living
expenses in Washington, where all expenses are unreasonable, is different from reasonable reimbursement for living expenses in Eugene
(better scenery at less cost). Consultants for the National Science
Foundation get $16 per day for expenses. The Internal Revenue Service
allows commercial concerns to give per diem of $25 without special
questioning. One of the more generous college provisions is 10¢ a mile
by car plus $20 per diem. One of the less generous pays only for gas
and oil. The N.S.F. allowance is not bad except when a person is a
captive. Conventions in large high-priced hotels often are more useful
for those who stay in these hotels than for those who do not. Banquets
are habitually higher priced, poorer served, with food of lower quality
than in other dining facilities in the same hotel, and yet for many are
almost obligatory.

I believe an institution would be reasonable if, in addition, to transportation, it gave an individual a per diem of $15. One meeting a year
per person on this basis would seem ample. A choice should be available
between a per diem and actual costs, but a man should not be allowed
to change his choice too readily.

In spite of the expense, distance should not be tightly controlled.
However, I liked the regulation of a small college in New York City
which paid no travel expenses to go out of New York to persons who
did not attend the meetings within the metropolitan area.

Others have a minimum distance for which they will make reimbursement. This is an important protection in the neighborhoods of
popular centers for meetings such as New York and Washington.

Some institutions on the West Coast early developed generous travel
policies so that their faculty members would go to Chicago and East at
frequent intervals. Some of the eastern rules, however, still reflect the
well-known reply of the Boston lady: "No, I've never ridden in a Pullman; I was born here." There are many in America who will not worry

too much about the problem of one institution which complains of the "increasing tendency to have meetings in places more than 1,000 miles from New England."

Other institutions, without placing distance limits, do place dollar limits on travel which have similar effects but give the individual more freedom and provide substantial, if not total, aid for long trips.

It would seem that persons who have grant or contract travel funds should also be controlled as to reasonableness of charges for which they are reimbursed.

STATE AND OTHER REGULATIONS. The state or other public regulations regarding travel may present problems. Often these difficulties are real, but frequently are chiefly psychological. Where these regulations take permission to travel out of the jurisdiction of the college or university, they create a nuisance and sometimes bad decisions. Beyond certain basic principles the solution for administrative abuses is not more regulations (sometimes it is better administrators) but very frequently decisions at levels intimate with the problem. In the absence of evidence to the contrary we should assume, even if wisdom goes with authority, that the president of a university can make a better decision about the travel of an individual faculty member than the governor (or his assistant), the dean than the president, the department chairman than the dean, and the individual than the chairman. Of course there are instances where evidence to the contrary is not absent.

Most of the regulations as to what are inadmissible expenditures are sensible: no liquor, no entertainment, etc. However, the frequent regulation against tips is unrealistic. The regulations covering receipts for expenses often are an unnecessary nuisance but, if some flat charge is allowed in lieu of receipts, form no major hardship. Moreover, the increasing use of credit cards is lessening difficulties from this source.

THE POLICY OF MAKING GREATER REIMBURSEMENT FOR THOSE GIVING PAPERS. Many institutions pay more toward travel for persons giving papers than for those who just attend. Presidents of real wisdom and great experience argue that this is a stimulus to the scholarly and professional activities of the faculty. To the argument that professional advancement can be recognized through salary and promotion, the reply is made that salary and promotion should not be based on an individual act but only on the growth in usefulness therefrom; yet some direct stimulus to a presumably worthwhile activity is desirable. Moreover, recognition in salary and rank for papers might just increase the "publish-or-perish" league which already is big enough.

On the other hand, there are temptations which are too frequently yielded to in the "pay-if-you-give-a-paper" system. Among these are the temptation to give a paper before it is completed and polished, the temptation to fractionate a paper, and the temptation to give papers far away. (However, the mathematician who spent ten minutes telling how important his new theorem was and at the next meeting another ten minutes telling how much ingenuity it took to find the error in the previous paper lived near the meeting place.) My own experience has shown me what a bad effect upon a scientific meeting this system can have. I am sure in institutions where there are already many stimuli to research and publication this practice is pernicious; in others it is at least dubious.

It would be difficult, without a depression, to decrease the reimbursement for those giving papers; but whenever more funds become available for travel, the discrimination against the intelligent listener should be lessened. Yet it may be well to discriminate in favor of those who are officers of professional societies or who upon invitation are participants in a major manner in the program.

Reimbursement for travel to meetings seems to me important if without it there would be inequities between departments. The degree of generosity to some extent will depend on the degree of inequity. The location of an institution may make help toward travel imperative. Although there may be cogent reasons for reimbursement of travel to meetings, most of these depend on the individual circumstances of the institution. In their absence I must say that the greater freedom granted the individual by using these funds for compensation (salary, retirement annuities, insurance, etc.,) rather than for specific reimbursement for travel appeals to me. Sometimes it is easier to get additional funds for travel than for salaries. In many institutions the balance between too little and too much travel has shifted drastically in the last two decades.

One last word of warning: If the policy of the institution concerning travel funds is "tight," then the travel of administration officers should also be scrutinized. It is scarcely more important to inspire a dean than a teacher and perhaps even more difficult.

TRAVEL EXPENSES OF "PROSPECTS." Besides provision for official travel of the staff and of faculty members going to meetings, panels, conferences, etc., it is important to have adequate funds to bring to the campus persons who are being considered for, or who are considering, offers to join the faculty. Some institutions deplore the lack of such funds.

"THEY" SAY

PURPOSE

The faculty is presumed to have interests in various professional and learned societies. The College looks with favor upon attendance as the individual is likely to be a better teacher from having made stimulating contacts and heard challenging papers and discussions, and it is excellent public relations for the College. The College has successively increased the allowances to aid faculty members desiring to attend these conferences. All of the faculty are considered rather than concentrating on a few. No rule of thumb as to the number of such trips is made, but it is assumed that discretion and courtesy will be used. Expenses are determined by the least expensive means of travel possible. — *Private college*

To take care of programs of the college that require faculty travel. To carry on essential college business. To provide opportunity for faculty to render services. To provide participation in professional organizations and learned societies. To aid faculty in keeping up with professional association activities. — *Public college*

Refresh faculty and make them happy, in comparison, that they are where they are: Enrich and expand points of view. — *Private college*

To meet accreditation criteria. — *Private college*

VARIOUS ARRANGEMENTS

For each full-time faculty member, for the attendance at one such meeting each year, the college will contribute the expense of: (1) registration, (2) travel: by first-class air coach or a 10¢ allowance per mile by car, and (3) up to $15.00 per day for living expense. — *Private college*

First-class transportation or member may save on transportation and apply balance toward other expenses. — *Private college [paraphrased]*

8¢ per mile — if college-owned transportation is not available. 3¢ per mile — if college-owned transportation is available but faculty prefers to use personal car. — *Public college*

$75 allowance may accumulate 2 years. — *Private college [paraphrased]*

A faculty member may apply for a travel allowance on a biennium basis, allowing $150.00 to be extended over a 2-year period. — *Private college*

Actual cost not including entertainment. — *Private college*

Have recently added a limited program for overseas travel. — *Public university*

Travel reimbursement for transportation only but up to $500 abroad.— *Private university [paraphrased]*

We try to provide enough money for each faculty member to attend (at full cost) the professional meeting of his choice. — *Public university*

A local transportation firm will deduct 10% if billed through the college. — *Private college [paraphrased]*

Reimbursement out of U. budget only for travel on official U. business. — *Private university [a university with a good salary scale]*

PROBLEMS

Only those problems resulting from strict adherence to State Code, Budgets and university policy. — *Public university*

Receipts for items over $2.00 required by state are a "nuisance". — *Public university*

Approved by Governor (out of state). — *Public university [paraphrased]*

Education Department is always wanting to go to multitudinous conferences: Our answer is frequently, "No!" — *Private college*

Having general faculty travel rather than a few members wanting excess amounts. — *Private college*

How to get those who need it most to attend. — *Private college*

Some persons are likely to neglect their campus responsibilities. — *Public university*

Staff members explore the labor market and obtain other offers. — *Public university*

Where travel to a departmental (example, Modern Language) conference is involved, it would appear that we might be financing a member of our faculty to go to a place where he can more easily find a position somewhere else. On this basis it would appear to be a poor investment. — *Private college*

Lack of funds and peculiar situation of West Coast schools in relation to great majority of meetings in the East or Mid-West. — *Private college*

Not west of Chicago without special permission. — *Private college*

. . . east of Mississippi River. — *Private college*

Naturally, the constantly increasing cost is still the main problem. Contributing to this is the fact that many research grants have generous sums for complete coverage of travel, and of course, we cannot yet afford to offer the same opportunity for all faculty members. — *Private university*

CRITERIA FOR GRANTING

In general, faculty members giving papers at meetings, and those who are productive in their respective research fields would be more likely to receive all or part of their expenses for travel reimbursed. — *Public university*

Active attendance all sessions. — *Private college*

Distribution of funds by "secret" faculty committee of which the Dean is chairman. — *Private college [paraphrased]*

REFERENCES TO APPENDICES

Appendix I: Questionnaire, Section 4.

Appendix III: Summary Tables 31–36.

Appendix IV: Evaluation Chart, items 24, 30.

CHAPTER 9

FACULTY CLUB

WHERE there is a well-developed faculty club it is generally believed to make a real contribution to the recruitment and retention of the faculty. Yet its use should not be judged chiefly on this basis. Social and intellectual contacts within the faculty help to unify the institution, give its faculty members broader intellectual viewpoints, emphasize the college as against a too great absorption in the department, and lead to those informal discussions of academic policy from which wisdom is derived to a much greater extent than from formal faculty meetings.

Physical facilities which encourage this are highly desirable. The importance becomes greater as the size and complexity of the institution increase. Neither the kind of facility nor the kind of organization is stereotyped. In its simplest form the facility consists of a small room, a coffee urn, a few cups, a dish for dimes, a few voluntary dishwashers and coffeemakers. At the other extreme, it is a formally organized club owning a building with living quarters, guest rooms, dining facilities including private rooms, bar service, and game rooms with adjacent tennis courts or, in one case, a swimming beach.

The more elaborate organizations naturally are chiefly at the large institutions, where individual departments may have a facility of the "coffee break" type. Our questionnaire was centered around the facility rather than the organization. We will first of all say a little about the latter.

ORGANIZATION. Of 341 institutions that have special social facilities for the faculty, 140 are used by a formally organized faculty club. However, 75 of these clubs are in the 100 universities which have such facilities, whereas in the colleges only slightly over one-quarter of the social facilities for the faculty are organized as a club. In the formal club the vast majority admit both men and women to membership, but only about one-quarter have membership from outside the faculty. Some places admit town members at dues above the rates for faculty. This helps financially, but at the price of coherence. Some clubs are organized as "faculty-alumni clubs" and serve as unifying influences among the alumni. These "outside" members make ambiguous any comparison between numbers of club members and full-time faculty members.

FACILITIES. Three-quarters of the faculty social facilities include a lounge and equipment for coffee breaks. Dining facilities, often of the cafeteria type, rate next; and conference and reading rooms are frequent. A perusal of Table 90, Appendix III, gives a far better idea of facts of this sort than any running text can.

In some places the club affords living quarters for single faculty members and in 52 institutions, guest rooms. A number of institutions have guest rooms independent of the faculty club.

Twenty clubs report a bar serving alcoholic beverages. In some cases a compromise between no liquor and bar service consists of lockers for one's private store. (The author, although a teetotaler, has sometimes kept his own maple syrup at the faculty club.)

A special feature of one club in a relatively small college is that new library books, within certain categories, are placed for a period in the club.

The growth of student unions has of course affected faculty social facilities. Sometimes the "faculty club" is in the union; and sometimes the union is so open to the faculty that a club has not seemed necessary. No institution should plan its program of social facilities for the faculty without studying its relation to an existing or planned union.

As a checklist of adequacy, most clubs seem to be well located and over half are of sufficient size. Where dining facilities are a part of the program, they are usually adequate, but the guest facilities inadequate.

FINANCES. A large majority of the institutions make a financial contribution to the club. This is seldom a direct monetary grant but usually is either a contribution toward or actually furnishing of building, rooms, or utilities. In somewhat less than half the cases the institution furnishes at least some of the operating personnel. In something over one-quarter of the cases the dues and operating receipts cover operating expenses, and in about the same number fall below half enough to do so. The clubs at universities seem to be somewhat more successful in this regard than at colleges. At least one club calls for a deposit from each member, in addition to dues. This seems to be designed to provide a sort of joint ownership and the interest thereon helps to finance the club.

ADMINISTRATIVE OPINION. Clearly the facility is in general considered by administrative officers as highly useful, though frequently not meeting its full potential. One administrator states that it enhances the prestige of the faculty.

Two less favorable responses came from an eastern university where it was declared that the faculty club is "primarily for the benefit of faculty wives," and from a state teachers college which reported under *Purpose*, "contributes to staff morale," but under Significant Problems, "too much wasted time."

EVALUATION AND SUMMARY. The problem of bringing the faculty together on a semi-social basis varies greatly with the size of the institution. A college with a single large building in which the faculty have their offices or perhaps two or three adjacent such buildings can be well served by a lounge with coffee-break facilities. No department in a small college is self-sufficient, even psychologically; and with at least the minimum facilities, gregariousness alone will lead to their use. If, in addition, the institution is in a small town where it is customary to eat lunch at home, such a minimum facility is all that is needed.

On the other hand, in a large university where many departments have a building to themselves or share it with closely related departments, where many of the faculty do not go home for lunch, the need of a facility that will bring the faculty together in a way that crosses departmental lines is great. However, this goal is difficult to attain. As a specialty becomes more intense, it becomes less responsible to society and develops a thicker and harder protective shell. Hence, one of the great problems of a faculty club in a large university is that its use may decrease as its need increases. The club is neglected by departments who live unto their specialty. The very people who most need to brush up against intellects in other fields and to participate in university policy determinations gather into a variety of homogeneous cells. A club, if used, can be a great corrective; but to be used, it must serve good food at reasonable cost, be in a cheerful, well-located building, and, in addition, have a group of devoted faculty advocates.

No club should be forced on a group by an administration but it is a good institutional investment to give a faculty club every possible aid.

To be personal, my life at Wisconsin has been a far happier, and I hope more useful, one because of the faculty club.

"THEY" SAY

It provides dining, meeting, and lounge facilities for faculty and administrative staff. It also makes it possible for the university to accommodate visiting lecturers, dignitaries, and similar persons right on the campus instead of housing them at some distance from the University.

The main problem in operating our Faculty Club is a financial one. Because there is essentially only one meal per day served at the facility, it operates at a substantial deficit that the University must meet out of general funds.

The interior decor of the Faculty Club is extremely handsome, and makes it a facility of which the entire University body (faculty and staff) are exceedingly proud. It is thus an ideal facility for receiving and entertaining distinguished visitors. — *Private university*

The faculty club shows a substantial fiscal loss due to the lack of participation on weekends and at evening meal periods. — *Private university*

Institution pays all expenses of operations including coffee. — *Private college [partly paraphrased]*

University pays 1/2 of first-year dues as incentive to membership. — *Private university*

Makes up any deficits in the operating accounts. — *Public university*

Club for faculty women. — *Private college [paraphrased; this institution is coeducational]*

Facility is primarily a retreat. — *Private college*

Considerable effort at present to secure more suitable facility. Serving of alcoholic beverages, relationship of club to University, etc., are questions which bear on success of program. — *Public university*

Wine and beer only. — *Private college*

Bottle club. — *Private college*

A rather small town where most individuals prefer home recreation. — *Public university*

Our excellent Faculty Club is mentioned by many as a significant recruiting aid. — *Public university*

REFERENCES TO APPENDICES

Appendix I: Questionnaire, Section 6.

Appendix III: Summary Tables, 89–98.

Appendix IV: Evaluation Chart, item 25.

CHAPTER 10

PARKING

THIS chapter is written reluctantly because I once said: "Every administrative officer has a right to be uninterested in one subject and I have chosen parking." Even now it is doubtful that this report on parking will be of much value, since more than in other portions of this inquiry the problems and their solutions, if any, depend on local circumstances. Moreover, I fear that replies in this field are somewhat less reliable than in others. The dual fact that the president usually has a reserved parking place next to his office (or even a driver) — and that in most cases he was brought up when being asked to walk was not considered an outrage — leaves him unsympathetic to the plaints of his faculty. (In general the president represents the faculty much better than it believes, but in this area the faculty might be surprised at the partly disparaging and partly spoofing remarks of the prex.)

The inadequacy of parking is limited to about a third of the institutions and, as is to be expected, the situation is worse in universities than in colleges.

The basic problem is one of getting enough space close to the places where faculty members work. The fact that 611 institutions answering the questions as to parking spaces existing and needed reported 164,000 available and 189,000 needed does not begin to depict the acuteness of the local situations, since two-thirds of these institutions reported adequate or more than adequate parking facilities. Moreover, many reported the number of places adequate but their locations poor.

Beyond this, however, there are problems that exacerbate the situation. One of those frequently mentioned is that of the persons who wish parking permits for more than one car. It is of course natural for a family with two cars to desire flexibility in their use; this flexibility is cut down if only one car can be used to park on the campus.

Of course many parking lots are on sites where new buildings will be erected. When this happens, not only is the supply decreased but the demand is enlarged. This is a frequently reported source of intensification of the problem.

The policing of parking areas is expensive but never quite adequate. Some universities are using a card-key system to control entrance to parking lots or individual stalls. Related to this is the often reported problem of assessing fines against faculty members. One institution is making a "hard try" at being sure that the dean's position is untenable by turning the assessing of fines over to him.

Climate comes in for its share of the blame. Summer walking in Texas is reported as most uncomfortable, and winter walking in Alaska as dangerous.

Various methods aimed at ameliorating the conditions are in use. Most institutions have special spaces reserved for the faculty, sometimes by individual stalls. The latter plan is pleasant for the installed but is a space-waster, since area allotment can allow 10% overage with little danger of becoming filled with those really having permits.

Control of student cars is often urged as a safety measure, but with more vehemence if there is inadequate parking for the faculty. One New England college uses a plan that I believe would lead to dire results in the Middle West: senior and junior men may drive but only senior women. In my opinion, rules controlling general use of cars by students, beyond those of public law, are essential abridgements of the rights of citizens and should never be invoked merely to make the lives of the faculty or the townsfolk pleasanter. However, control of on-campus traffic and of parking is fully justified, and frequently the problems are accentuated and the faculty embittered by students parking in faculty areas. The parking by faculty in "No Parking" zones is by no means unknown.

Frequently there is a charge for parking. This is sometimes inaugurated in the futile hope that it will cut down the competition for space. However, it frequently serves the very useful purpose of paying for the upkeep of parking lots and the development of new ones or the construction of enclosed parking.

Various priority systems are also established based on such factors as health, seniority, and propinquity both of office to lot and of home to institution. Clearly those with the types of health problems which make walking difficult, painful, or dangerous should be granted special privileges.

On some large or divided campuses bus services have been established. Forty-five institutions report these. The comments made concerning them have generally been favorable. They partially solve the problem of the person with multiple locations for work, and they make possible the use of large peripheral parking lots. They tend to decrease, perhaps unfortunately, the amount of walking done by faculty members.

Another problem is posed by the conflict of interests between the looks and the convenience of the campus. As far as I know, there is no such thing as a good-looking parking lot. Some are more successfully hidden than others. Fifty people, whose health would be improved by a short daily walk, should not be allowed to take priority over the thousand who daily would be deprived of the beauty of the campus by the intrusion of ubiquitous parking lots.

"THEY" SAY

SOME SPECIAL PROBLEMS

Snow removal. — *Private college*
Keeping students out of parking area. Snow removal. — *Public university* [*paraphrased*]
Assignments made by staff member. [This] leads faculty to feel it has less preferential treatment than staff. — *Public university*
The lines are so close wide women have trouble getting out of their cars. — *Private college [this college has a male president]*
Student objection due to vacant faculty spaces when student facilities are full. — *Private college*

REACTIONS TO PARKING FEES

There is much objection to charge set by state. — *Public college*
Faculty extremely unwilling to pay cost of multideck parking: expect the state to provide same free. — *Public university*
Mental attitude that parking is a right not a privilege. — *Private university*

ATTITUDE TOWARD WALKING

Most of them walk to work. — *Private college*
If a walk of less than ten minutes can be considered reasonable, . . . offers adequate parking. — *Public university*
. . . planners are moving towards lots of 100–200 near/on the perimeter of built-up areas. This plan will result for many faculty in an excessive walk from parking space to office. — *Public college*
We have plenty of parking spaces as the above shows. However, many of the spaces are several blocks away from classrooms and faculty offices;

hence, some of the faculty complain about the distances that they must walk! — *Private college*

Plenty space within 1/4 mile but this does not satisfy members. — *Public university [paraphrased]*

One half of our faculty could and should walk to the campus. It is less than three minutes walk for this group. — *Private college*

To convince students and faculty that walking 300 yards is not burdensome. — *Private college*

In general, faculty and staff resist use of fringe parking areas involving walking distances of as little as 200 yards. — *Public university*

Reluctant to walk any distance to their home building. — *Public college*

One can seemingly never reserve parking space close enough to the buildings. — *Private college*

The "adequate spaces" are not very distant from offices (3 minutes' walk) but everyone wants to park in area immediately adjacent to offices. — *Private college*

Can't park car next to office door. Might have to walk half a block. — *Public college*

Nobody wants to walk more than 50 feet. — *Private college*

No one wants to walk more than a few steps from the entrance to his building. — *Private college*

They all want to park alongside their desks. — *Private college*

GENERAL ATTITUDES

Although classrooms and faculty offices are located on less than 25 acres of the campus the faculty prefer small lots near their offices rather than use a large centrally-located area. Faculty members object to $1.00 annual parking fee. Faculty members feel they should not be fined for traffic or parking violations. Faculty members would like individually reserved spaces. Faculty members do not appreciate the need for parking students. — *Public university*

Too much space is being used for parking. — *Private college*

[Are parking facilities adequate?] Yes. My opinion — many faculty members would disagree. — *Private college*

No area of faculty personnel management seems as sensitive as this. Why the location of parking becomes even a major issue is not clear, but such is the case. With a growing enrollment dependent on non-public transportation to reach the University, this problem will become more aggravated. No satisfactory solution seems in sight. — *Public university*

The institution's location in an urban area seems to preclude availability of adequate parking for faculty, student, and business needs. — *Public college*

Such items as a parking space with a professor's name attached is mainly for prestige value. It really makes no difference in recruitment or retention. — *Public college*

Faculty parking is certainly low on any list for the type of person we would hope to recruit and retain at . . . . . — *Private college*

Lack of adequate parking areas give rise to the following problems that *must be met* in some manner:

A. It is a faculty morale factor of significance.

B. It is causing a contempt of all parking rules and regulations.

C. It appears as though lack of space is causing some degree of a recruiting problem. — *Public university*

The least of our problems. — *Private college*

REFERENCES TO APPENDICES

Appendix I: Questionnaire, Section 8.

Appendix III: Summary Tables 107–113.

Appendix IV: Evaluation Chart, item 26.

CHAPTER 11

SECRETARIAL HELP

WHEN we started to frame the questionnaire, we assumed that secretarial help, like teaching assistants, assistant professors, or, for that matter, blackboards and stationery should be taken for granted as part of the working structure of the college or university. The number of persons that said this was not the case led to the insertion of one question concerning purposes for which secretarial help is furnished. The variations in the answers showed that this query was needed.

Almost all institutions furnish secretarial help for official institutional business but what this is considered to be clearly varies greatly. Typing of research articles is regularly provided by a little over a third of the colleges and about half of the universities. However, nearly 80% of the colleges and nearly all universities do this either regularly or "sometimes."

The typing of scholarly books is done regularly by only about 20% of the institutions, but another 40% take care of it "sometimes." The large majority of universities take care of this regularly or occasionally.

The overwhelming majority of institutions provide for the typing of instructional material. The typing of textbooks is cared for about as frequently as the typing of scholarly books. (I presume there is some overlap in these categories.) Speeches and essays seem to be treated about the same as research articles.

Few institutions regularly provide typing for personal business but about 20% sometimes do. My guess is that a good deal of such help is given on an informal basis.

When one talks with faculty members across the country, the impression is gained that secretarial help is insufficient in quantity and spotty in quality. Many faculty members, including presidents and deans, need a good deal of guidance through the practicalities of life. In the work of the college this is furnished primarily by secretaries. The questionnaire itself would seem to assume that typing was the chief role of secretaries. The author has no such low valuation of their services. In a large department it is the secretary who keeps the class schedule straight, sees that books are ordered, makes appointments (or skillfully does not make them), is the most reliable source of information to students, controls expenditures, and persuades professors to do things nearly enough on time to keep things going. When the department loses an assistant professor there is disappointment, a slight sense of lost prestige, and a sour-grape attitude towards his scholarship. But lose a good secretary and the department goes into a tailspin.

At the level of president and dean the functions are different but just as varied and usually even more responsible. I believe that added secretarial help would often do more for the administration of our universities than does the creation of a plethora of administrative offices. One could add 50% to the secretaries' salaries and still be ahead financially.

Clearly economy, effectiveness of work, and morale would all be enhanced by more and sometimes better secretarial help. One gains the impression, however, that the really professional secretaries (in contrast to student help and new temporary typists) who serve our institutions are a dedicated, industrious, intelligent group who, in spite of coffee breaks, produce an enormous amount of first-class work.

"THEY" SAY

[In general rather generous but] if the sale of the book, etc., results in income to faculty member, secretarial assistance has to be reimbursed. — *Private college [partly paraphrased]*

[Purpose for which secretarial help is provided:] Dissertations. — *Private college*

Dissertations. — *Private college*

Lack of sufficient secretarial help is of increasing importance as student loads increase. — *Public college*

[Benefits you would consider developing or expanding for the future:] Retirement and secretarial help. — *Public university*

REFERENCES TO APPENDICES

Appendix I: Questionnaire, Section 11, Subsection A.

Appendix III: Summary Tables 144–150.

Appendix IV: Evaluation Chart, item 29.

CHAPTER 12

RETIRED
FACULTY MEMBERS
AND WIDOWS

RETIRED faculty members and faculty widows are beloved and welcome members of the academic community, but they are frequently neglected. People want them around; only rarely does anyone wish them to be in Florida. Clear expressions of respect and affection for them come from all parts of the United States and are in complete accord with my own observations and experiences over many years.

But more thought is needed in regard to their status. Thought and effort have gone into the retirement annuities and life insurance programs. For people now retired few institutions have succeeded in providing annuities which fully meet satisfactory standards. However, we may expect a system where the total of institutional and individual contributions is from 12% to 15% of salary, where there is no long waiting period before starting such contributions, where a variable annuity is elected, where retirement is at 68 to 70 years of age or older, and where the institution participates in OASI, to be reasonably satisfactory in the long run. Aside from annuities and insurance, the institutions' relations with retired faculty, faculty widows, or their faculty members as prospective emeriti have not been given full consideration.

Many questions on this general topic were inadequately answered. This may in part have been due to natural weariness as one approached the completion of a long questionnaire. I also believe in some cases it was because there was no general policy upon which to base the answers.

In spite of many aspects of the situations of retired faculty members, or the widows of faculty members, which differ, we treat the two together except that retirement working conditions seldom are relevant to widows.

WORKING CONDITIONS. If a scholar is vigorous when he retires, he will regret but not resent having his salary replaced by the smaller income from his retirement annuity, but he will greatly miss the facilities for work and for professional as well as social contacts.

Some institutions, even where space is at a premium, make strenuous efforts to help these individuals. Library and parking privileges are usually continued. Most of the universities and many colleges provide office and laboratory facilities for those who desire to work in them. It is not uncommon to provide research assistance and secretarial help.

Often men continue steady and valuable post-retirement work. It is rare to find one who stops for a prolonged period and then returns to such work. Hence, a real problem is presented by those who imagine they would like sometime to continue their work and try to retain space they do not currently use. The morale of the staff, especially of those near retirement, is greatly improved by the security of the rug on which they stand. But they will not resent knowing that work (if not results) is a condition of that security.

It would be logically nice if retirement age could be gauged by vigor and effectiveness. It would then range from 50 to 85 years of age, aside from the instances of those who never should have been appointed. But this would create such insecurity and tensions that much effectiveness would be lost. So some maximum age of retirement for men in reasonable health is usually required. If this is, say, 68 or 70 years, it is hard not to seriously hurt peoples' feelings if any considerable number of persons are continued beyond this age at full salary. (Even reduced salary appointments lead to some injured sensibilities, but are at times justified if voting, committee, and administrative status is relinquished.) This hurt has little to do with favoritism, real or alleged. In fact, the hurt may be deepest when the judgments are clearly disinterested.

I have not heard of anyone who personally resents giving every facility to a retired man who is still effective and wants to do scholarly work free of charge. An institution cannot, however, afford to allow a retired faculty member to determine that he teach. It must protect both the other faculty members and the students.

It should be recognized that the services of retired faculty members are sometimes used in emergencies; in the war years this was important.

HEALTH SERVICES. All group health plans of the faculty should be continuable by retired faculty members: Keeping the cost on a group basis is important; unconditional ability to continue on some basis is vital.

Unlike athletic facilities, social privileges, and admissions to special events, the availability of the medical services of the institutions in many places decreases strikingly upon retirement. The extent of this change can be gathered from Table II. This is an area requiring further

TABLE II
Health services available to various groups

	Faculty member		Spouse		Retired Faculty member		Widow	
	Avail-able	Free*	Avail-able	Free*	Avail-able	Free*	Avail-able	Free*
Doctor consultation	214	110	86	19	68	20	43	11
Regular medical treatment	89	30	49	8	37	6	26	3
Emergency treatment	471	324	148	72	134	60	91	37
Annual physical exam	69	33	26	5	29	5	15	1
Infirmary bed	83	24	39	4	34	3	21	2

* Figures for free services are included in the figures for available services immediately preceding them.

consideration. In particular, the privileges of widows should not be less than of retired faculty members if the morale of the faculty is to be bolstered by these privileges.

HOUSING. The problem of housing for emeritus professors is being given more attention. If an institution has no rental housing for its faculty or if the rental housing is basically for new members of the faculty, the question of continuing a retired faculty member in his rented home does not arise. If, however, the house may be rented throughout employment, the institution is faced with a policy question. We do not have clear statistics on how this is resolved. We do know instances where the house may be retained by the member or his widow; in other places this is not so. Princeton's plan in this regard has been described in the chapter on housing.

In general, where mortgages are given for homes in special land areas with resale restrictions, the individual may live in the home after retirement. His widow may do the same.

It is, of course, often true that with reduced need for space and frequently reduced income, the emeritus professor, or the widow, will voluntarily seek more modest accommodations; the number, especially in the North, who move away from the locality of the institution is considerable.

The athletic facilities, the faculty club, and special events are usually open to the emeritus members and to the widow or to the spouse on the same, or less expensive, basis as to the faculty members. Frequently club membership is free, sometimes depending on length of previous membership.

In some institutions the availability of a pre-retirement consulting service on a formal or informal basis has proved useful.

It is my belief that few developments would so increase the contentment of the faculty members past fifty years of age as improvement in the lot of the retired faculty members and faculty widows. The young man is worried about what will happen if he dies; the old man, about what will happen if he lives. Some expense is involved — but even more planning. Institutional self-interest and decent human behavior both call for more attention to this matter. One should consider:

Retirement provisions based on contributions equaling 12% to 15% of salary.

Continued health insurance.

Facilities for continuing work (usually without pay).

The same medical services for emeritus faculty members and widows as for active faculty members and their wives.

Adequate housing wherever there is a housing program that includes regular long-term faculty members.

The use of campus facilities and admission to special events.

"THEY" SAY

PURPOSE

We regard it a normal courtesy of academic life to treat the emeritus and widows like active faculty members and wives, so far as facilities permit. — *Private college*

The college feels the same responsibility to the retired faculty members as active faculty members. — *Private college*

The College is both appreciative and compassionate in its view toward retired faculty and widows and it values their contributions during active service and is restless in the knowledge that generally speaking retirement benefits in private education frequently falls far below those enjoyed by retirees from public education or private industry. While this questionnaire has not indicated any concrete plans for betterment in retirement benefits, ... is tremendously interested in improving both the substance and status of those in retirement years after spending the major portion of their working years in this institution. — *Private college*

It is respectfully owed them because of their former association and it rebounds to the present good of faculty because of their wisdom of the years. — *Private college*

Appreciation of years of service. Respect and courtesy. We will all be retired some day. — *Public university*

PROGRAMS

In general, a lack of facilities prevents us from providing any essential privileges. — *Public university*

Space requirements — short office area and acute budgetary problems — prohibit us from granting to emeritus faculty a number of privileges we think they should be accorded. Many do not remain in the community because of cold winters and are resident in California, Arizona, Florida, or other milder climates.

Retired faculty and spouses are always given special invitations to "prestige" events, are included in all faculty social hours, are honored in various programs, are asked occasionally to serve on college committees, are aided with some special problems. — *Public college*

Age is not merely a function of chronology and greater flexibility is needed when a person reaches 65. With expanding faculty it is difficult to provide the facilities and helps one would like for those in various stages of retirement. — *Private university*

We have not studied this in detail, but in general our paternalism ends with the last salary check except for business consultations when needed. We do start well in advance with retirement discussions with staff members. — *Private university*

They are part of the organization. — *Private college*

Emeritus can have office space. — *Public university [paraphrased]*

May retain insurance programs at regular faculty rates. — *Private university [paraphrased]*

One source of worry for me of our personnel is the lack of desirable policies for medical and hospital care after they attain the age of sixty-five. — *Public university*

REFERENCES TO APPENDICES

Appendix I: Questionnaire, Section 10.

Appendix III: Summary Tables 133–143.

Appendix IV: Evaluation Chart, items 31–34.

CHAPTER 13

REMARKS

IN any report of this nature it is convenient to have a place to list miscellaneous items, as in Chapter 6, and also a collection of comments that do not belong elsewhere. For a mathematician it would be profane to call this collection "Pensées," but this was a temptation.

This chapter includes a group of comments of my own and an extensive "'They' Say" section of a general nature. The latter draws heavily upon replies to Section 12 of the questionnaire (see Appendix I) which asked for general comments concerning faculty benefits, particularly in relation to their effect on securing and retaining staff, their contributions toward obtaining the objectives of the institution, and the future plans of the institution in regard to these benefits.

SOME REMARKS ON THE TYPE OF INSTITUTION IN RELATION TO THE PROBLEMS OF SECURING AND RETAINING FACULTY. One of the facts that became clear in reading the general comments is that for purposes of securing and retaining faculty our institutions fall into many groups which, except perhaps in making initial appointments for individuals who have completed their formal graduate work, do not compete extensively with each other. The smaller colleges, with lesser financial resources, often report the least trouble in retaining staff. The reason usually is not reported and, when it is, some institutional loyalty may creep into the reporting. Practically all the large universities that consider research as one of the major functions of the faculty report increasing difficulty in securing and retaining the staff they desire. The competition for research talent appears to be greater than for teaching talent. This may in part reflect institutional value judgments. I believe, however, that these judgments are not the only, perhaps not the chief, factors. Many university administrators and faculty members care deeply for good teaching. They also value research. Topnotch investigators are rare, but so are topnotch teachers. Research, with its concomitant publication, is visible on the national or even international scene; good teaching may be known only locally. A year or less after a competent piece of research is published the investigator is known throughout the country by the active men in his specialty. A brilliant teacher is recognized at once at home; away at about the time his students get in the National Academy. In order to improve higher education we need to widen the competition for good teachers.

Another reason that many institutions have little trouble in retaining faculty members is that the religious views of the faculty are in accord with the church affiliation of the institution, so that institutional loyalties are reinforced by religious loyalties.

A lesser, but not unimportant factor, in holding personnel is that the city lover and the country lover are unwilling to move from a congenial environment to the loneliness of the field or of the crowd.

A large university which made a study of the institutions from which it secured faculty or to which it lost faculty discovered that almost always these were also large universities.

CERTAIN CONTRASTS BETWEEN PUBLIC AND PRIVATE INSTITUTIONS. There are few better illustrations of a connection between a fence and green grass than the envy (sometimes, I fear, jealousy) in the attitudes of the administrative officers of private and of public institutions toward each other. This note is written to point out the nature of the difference between the two types of institutions as regards benefit programs and to state why I believe this difference is less than many think.

In general, public and private institutions serve the same purposes with perhaps a greater emphasis on liberal education in most private colleges than in the average public institution. The spectrum from poverty to wealth is about the same. The degrees of emphasis on research cover a similar scale. Size tends to be considerably greater in the public institutions. There are probably more private institutions with extremely high admission requirements than public ones, but the range is nearly the same.

There are, of course, real differences between private and public institutions, but these are of less importance than the differences between large universities and small colleges, between the wealthy and those of meager means, between the highly selective and those whose latchstrings are ever out. Granted: There is a tendency for public institutions to try to secure a budget commensurate with their size, and for private ones to limit their size by the budget. Moreover, there are marked differences between church-related institutions and others, but the others include many non-sectarian private as well as public institutions.

In regard to benefits the most marked difference occurs in connection with family education. But this difference is lessened by the fact that, although in most public institutions there is no waiver of tuition for faculty children, the "in-state" (or "in-city") tuition is usually lower than in comparable private institutions.

One major difference that affects benefits such as leaves, travel expenses, retirement and insurance plans is that frequently in public institutions many of the regulations which control the institution are the same as those that control the rest of the state's (or city's) public service, and at times are ill calculated to strengthen an educational institution. However, the freedom of some public institutions from this difficulty indicates that even this difference is not without exception.

HANDBOOKS. The faculty handbooks sent in with the questionnaire were of very great interest for the study and I am grateful for them. Some of these give information concerning benefits and must be of real help to the faculty. Retirement and insurance provisions are frequently described in detail. Many also define the freedom of the faculty and give the tenure regulations. The purpose of the institution is often stated, and the relations of this purpose to the teaching assignments, the committee work, and even the chaperoning duties of a faculty member may be described.

A few of the handbooks seemed to be a bit "suped up." Most are solid and informative, even if slightly dull. A few, such as that of Columbia University, are distinguished.

To provide one of these for a complex university is an arduous and expensive undertaking and even to produce a mimeographed one for a small college is not an easy task. The large majority of those sent in with the questionnaire are useful and worth the effort.

SOME BENEFITS OUTSIDE THE SCOPE OF THE STUDY. Mention should be made of three items not covered by the study or that of Greenough and King:

1. Unemployment Insurance: The academic community may wish sometime to seek legislation that will bring it under provisions for unemployment compensation as was done in regard to the old-age and survivors insurance of Social Security.

2. Some institutions are currently studying group insurance to cover the liability of teachers in regard to work-related accidents as, for instance, in a chemistry laboratory or on a field trip.

3. The systematic use of "tax-deferred" annuities, a topic concerning which information has been furnished by TIAA.

A REMARK ON THE PRESIDENT'S JOB. To paraphrase an old quip: "All presidents are equally busy but some are more so." In a small college the president fulfills many functions that are delegated in a large university. This makes it possible for a wise and able man to assume a type of leadership in a college that no person is likely to attain in a university. It also makes it possible for a foolish man to foul up a situation in a manner that would be extremely difficult where authority is diffused and the administrative momentum great.

The small college has a large opportunity, but that opportunity is lost if the responsibility of the individual faculty member or the department is too curtailed. In some colleges there appear to be more links in the chain between a faculty member and a decision than in the large university. An example is the state college where, probably because of state regulations, long-distance telephone calls must be approved by the president's office. Benefits exhibit many contrasting operating procedures: Who authorizes that pink paint in a rental house be covered by a geometric wallpaper? Who decides that a mortgage loan should be refused because the house would be too costly? Who determines which faculty member can go on leave or travel to our most southern or our most northern state at college expense?

In the matter of benefits much should be decided by policy in the forming of which the faculty has participated. But there will always be, even within a policy, individual decisions to be made; and the president — who must represent the institution to the public, interpret the trustees and the faculty to each other, and greatly influence fundamental academic decisions — should be handicapped as little as possible by the irritations he creates and the time he consumes through being enmeshed in trivia.

The president, of course, may have administrative hobbies. I have known one president of a large university who took personal interest in its horses and its cows, another of a private college who knew almost as acquaintances the persons whose portraits were hung in its buildings — including the institution's only alumnus who, in addition to his portrait, was himself hung. Such interests yield relief, not annoyances. The use of the president's time should be determined by a hierarchy of values and by personal inclinations. It is a risk to ignore either.

"THEY." Administrative officers often evince a sense of injury because of being referred to as "they." Sharing the blame does not compensate for loss of personality. However, administrators should realize that the "theyness" in faculties' attitudes toward them is often matched by their attitude of "theyness" toward the faculty (think of a dean's reaction when the faculty does not approve a curriculum change he believes necessary, or demands more convenient parking). It is an interesting phenomenon of our language that a pronoun which can stand for saints, sinners, or just ordinary citizens is also used to impute obduracy and low motives. One reason for including " 'They' Say" sections in many of the chapters and especially in this one is that most of the quotes should help to rid the word of some of the connotations that now besmirch it.

Some day I would like to write an essay entitled "Introductions" and start it with "You two should know each other, Professor Doe please meet President Roe."

"THEY" SAY

Most of the quotations given below are excerpts from replies to Section 12 of the Questionnaire.

A FEW COMMENTS ON RECRUITING AND RETAINING

Recruiting fully qualified and thoroughly competent faculty members has been a serious problem. Retention of faculty members has been a minor problem during the past five years, whereas during the preceding five years it was a much more serious problem. — *Public college*

It is always a problem to find specialists in one field who are also able to participate in our required Humanities program and who are interested in doing so. The teaching climate at . . . apparently appeals to faculty members, for it has not been too difficult to retain faculty members once they have accepted appointment. — *Private college*

Except through normal retirement procedures, the annual loss of full-time staff at the University of . . . is a negligible percentage of the total staff, perhaps one-fourth to one-half of one percent. Increasing difficulty is being experienced, in recruiting new staff in Mathematics and in Engineering. This difficulty seems to stem more from the salaries available in these disciplines over the country than from a consideration of staff benefits. — *Public university*

Each of the past five years, with increasing intensity, has been a period of difficulty in recruiting and retention of faculty — as is to be expected, with needs increasing and the supply of first-rate persons not keeping pace. — *Public university*

Can recruit at masters level; difficult at doctors. — *Public college [paraphrased]*

I was surprised at how infrequently replies similar to the two following occurred:

No difficulty in recruiting but some in retaining. — *Private college [paraphrased]*

Considerable difficulty — large institutions tend to raid our faculty for top personnel. — *Private college*

THE ROLE OF SALARY

We have always operated on the philosophy that the College should put as much as possible in the pay envelope and economize on fringe items. — *Private college*

We must increase salaries before investing more in collateral benefits. — *Private college*

The faculty generally appear to prefer an ever increasing salary scale so that they can make their own decisions in preference to a lower scale supplemented by institutional benefits. We live in an area rich in all sort of opportunities so that personal and family lives do not depend exclusively on university resources and activities. — *Public university*

We do not anticipate developing the benefits listed, since we feel that if we can develop basic faculty salary to where it ought to be, that will be sufficient to recruit and retain faculty. — *Public college*

We have considered group life insurance and health and hospitalization, but the faculty itself has voted to receive the money instead of the insurance. If the faculty should change its mind, we might move in those directions. — *Private college*

If we did not offer these benefits we might encounter greater difficulty. [We] would prefer to use additional institutional resources in regular salary increases. — *Private college*

Prospective faculty members primarily interested in size of salary, and then rank, and then hours per week of class-room teaching. — *Private college*

Salary and . . .

Our main difficulties in recruiting staff have been related to salary levels rather than fringe benefits.

Our first need is the development of a more adequate retirement system before we can give any great attention to these other benefits. — *Public university*

Two factors which contributed most to easy recruitment and retainment —

progress in faculty salary and proximity to New York City. — *Private college [paraphrased]*

TIAA and housing are important in recruiting and retention, but much less so than rising salary schedules and a dynamic academic program. Emphasis and insistence on quality have no substitutes. — *Private college*

If our faculty salary scale were up to what we think of as a normal and proper minimum we would then wish to add salary raises by means of group insurance and group retirement plans, rather than by straight salary raises. — *Private college*

The problem of expanding benefit plans is the more you expand the greater the inequities grow between single men and married men with families. I have real concern over this growing gulf. If I were starting anew I would be inclined to pay as large as cash salary as possible, not provide any benefits except perhaps pension and sabbatical leave, and let each one purchase whatever he wishes. Also, the more you pay in benefits, the less it is considered when salary is discussed. It is the actual take-home pay that is considered. — *Private college*

But College should weigh carefully the preferences of faculty members to avoid increasing fringe benefits which occur to some members only at expense of general salary increases. — *Private college*

but

The answer is that more money and advantages is not the sole answer to educators today — it is just the first step. Those in the profession must continue to grow in order that their talents will grow and they will be worth the higher salaries they hope to acquire. Just sitting back and complaining about the need for more money can never be the answer. It is already available for those who are capable and willing to work for it. — *Private college*

THE GENERAL NATURE OF THE INSTITUTION

Fringe benefits, while helpful, do not seem to be the determining factor in attracting younger faculty. More important are the quality of one's colleagues, the overall excellence of the institution and its prospects for the future, and the availability of the equipment and conditions necessary for the individual to pursue his special academic interest. — *Public university*

Good salary scales and generous fringe benefits are becoming routine and the situation is moving so fast that any competitive advantage is usually only temporary. In talking with prospective candidates for appointment I have found that while fringe benefits of various kinds are an important consideration, the most significant single factor is the assurance of institutional interest and financial support for research and other scholarly activities which make up the professional work of a faculty member outside his formal instructional duties. — *Private college*

. . . but much more important are (*a*) an educational idea, (*b*) the caliber of the students, (c) a chance to be both a generalist and a specialist in a field, (d) a tradition for freedom, and (e) salaries. — *Private college*

If salary, rank, and tenure are their first interests they nearly always inquire about them last. — *Private college*

I have found that the fringe benefits of scholarly association and atmosphere mean more to a dedicated teacher than monetary fringe benefits. We try to emphasize the former in our recruitment of new faculty members. — *Private college*

The ease of recruiting varies, in the main, with the quality of the department. — *Public university*

No doubt the faculty benefits listed are a "sine qua non" of employment. Faculty comments on persuasive reasons for employment here are location, climate, beautiful campus, good reputation. — *Private college*

Young people tend to shift to coasts and recreational areas. Benefits not up to competition and this hurts. — *Public college [paraphrased]*

There has been some hesitation on the part of a few individuals to consider joining the staff because of their evaluation of the attitudes and mores which they assume to exist at institutions in the South. —*Public university*

If possible we will do more to keep our housing economical and gracious for the junior faculty. One of the unmentioned fringe benefits that we can provide is a beautiful location and relaxed community. This we shall safeguard as best we can against the march of population and commercialization. — *Private college*

We have had some difficulty in recruiting during the past five years; but the principal reason for this, in my judgment, is the fact that we have had a heavy teaching load. . . . Apart from the benefits considered in this study, the most important step we must take is a further reduction in the teaching load. — *Public university*

First objective — reduced teaching load and higher salary. — *Public college [paraphrased]*

Very difficult to find physics Ph.D.'s willing to teach undergraduates. Likewise pharmacy.— *Public college [paraphrased]*

[Major Problem] Seemingly, they (regardless of training, experience or rank) want to eliminate instructing of students from the University load. This is in line with the current trend away from the classroom toward travel, research, and consultative work for foundations, work on government contracts. If instruction is necessary, applicants desire, as soon as possible, to be relieved of instruction, at least as fast as research contract can be secured. — *Public college*

. . . ever decreasing supply of adequately trained and experienced men and women who are willing through percept and instruction to constribute to the perpetuation of the objectives and philosophy of the Christian College. — *Private college*

Chief concern not salary or benefits but:

We find difficulty in finding faculty who are academically excellent and who still feel responsible as members of a community of Christian Scholars to contribute to the development of the whole person. — *Private college*

Recruitment affected by being "strong evangelical Christian college." — *Private college [partly paraphrased]*

It seems virtually impossible to find a candidate interested in a program that does not include research. Our good fortune is being able to retain qualified personnel after successful recruitment and this is due largely to a deep sense of dedication and commitment to the cause of Christian Education. — *Private college*

Staff members who share the religious conviction of the school are difficult to get, but once they come they have been relatively easy to retain. — *Private college*

It is probably true that the majority of the lay faculty members of this college prefer to be associated with a college of their religious affiliation. Hence, they look upon their work both as a profession and an apostolate; on the other hand, financial needs make it imperative that they be kept on an equitable level regarding salaries and fringe benefits. — *Private college*

ANNUITIES AND INSURANCE

It has been our experience that younger faculty members ask more questions concerning institutional life insurance and medical, health, and accident benefits, especially if newly married. Those with doctorate degrees and over 35 years of age usually subject our retirement and long range benefits to excessively close scrutiny. — *Public college*

The . . . College faculty members naturally appreciate those benefits listed in this questionnaire which we are able to make available in our own college. However, in my judgment the only one which has any material effect in our ability to secure and retain staff members is our retirement program under TIAA. The faculty travel expense is much appreciated, but its value is greatest in giving us a better informed and more alert faculty. Sabbatical leaves are second only to the retirement plan in helpfulness. — *Private college*

As benefits which have been helpful in recruiting faculty, none ranks so high as the 10% contribution which the employer makes to TIAA. Faculty members quite generally regard this as equivalent to a significant increase in salary. In the retention of staff members, probably contributions to TIAA, mortgage loans, leaves of absence, and allowances for faculty travel have been among the most important. — *Private college*

We hope to liberalize our TIAA program by lowering the age at which one begins participation and to improve our life insurance program. Part of the difficulty of doing so will be the reluctance of faculty to jointly participate in the cost. — *Public university*

We need to increase TIAA to 15% as soon as we can. Then to increase life insurance to perhaps $20,000. — *Private college*

The only benefit that would really help us would be a more liberal retirement system. We are under a State system that has late vesting rights and pays rather modest benefits. The retirement situation is the only one currently giving us significant concern. — *Public university*

TUITION WAIVER

Our fringe benefits, particularly remission of tuition for faculty dependents, has been of particular influence in the recruitment and retention of faculty. Of minor importance in attaining other institutional objectives. — *Private university*

NON-FACULTY STAFF BENEFITS

Extension of benefits to clerical and maintenance personnel have helped college program. — *Private college [paraphrased]*

A SPECIAL PROBLEM

It is somewhat surprising that advantage is not taken of all benefits by many staff members. Applications for the Off-Campus Duty Assignment privilege have been surprisingly limited. Twenty to twenty-five percent of the staff are not now availing themselves of the full University contribution to a retirement plan under TIAA and approximately thirty percent of the staff do not participate in the group hospital plan made available to them and to which the University makes a contribution.

Action is currently underway to encourage all staff members to participate fully in TIAA and in hospitalization and life insurance benefits. — *Public university*

PUBLIC AND PRIVATE INSTITUTIONS

Handicapped by state regulations and limitations. — *Public college [paraphrased]*

The independent college has at least one arm tied behind its back in this fight [recruitment] against the public institution. — *Private college*

HOW MUCH ARE BENEFITS APPRECIATED?

Not having them would be bad:

The fringe program has been helpful in both recruiting and retaining faculty members, but not a major factor. I consider the value of many of them lie in helping to achieve a sense of belonging to the college community. — *Private college*

The greatest drawback of present or future benefits is that staff members take them for granted and fail to recognize their total significance, both tangible and intangible. For this reason, our policy in the future will probably be to keep from expanding them but rather to concentrate on actual increases in salaries. — *Private college*

So-called "fringe benefits" are of great value in recruiting and retaining faculty. They contribute to higher faculty morale and therefore aid in attaining our institutional objectives. We note, however, that as salaries and benefits are increased, there is a corresponding increase in attitude of demanding more on part of a minority of faculty and staff and a heightening of unrest and unhappiness. — *Private college*

It is human to become accustomed to benefits, and consider them a "right" rather than a valued privilege. — *Private university*

I am not aware that the staff benefits have played an important part in recruiting staff. If the College did not have any benefits, then recruitment would be impossible, but the benefits we offer are the usual ones found in institutions of higher learning and are of such a minimum nature they offer no special inducements to a strong candidate one would like to attract. — *Public college*

Our experience has been the absence of a fringe benefit increases problems — the advantages of a fringe benefit are soon forgotten. — *Private university*

I think that fringe benefits, except for sabbatical leaves, have been of only moderate importance in retaining faculty members in comparison with the factors listed above. However, had we not had other fringe benefits we would have had to inaugurate them. Faculty members would have asked for them and absence of benefits would have been interpreted as lack of regard for teachers. — *Private college*

We find that it can hurt us in recruitment if we are not competitive in staff benefits but it does not appear that staff benefits alone can be especially effective in attracting new faculty. — *Private university*

Poor staff benefits lend to belief administration does not care for faculty welfare. — *Private college [paraphrased]*

Special faculty benefits are significant to the degree they reflect the concern an institution has for the welfare of its faculty members. The most significant factors of all are a healthy salary schedule and a creditable academic reputation. — *Public college*

HOW MUCH DO FRINGE BENEFITS COST?

It is my experience comparing the benefits of other institutions that we are more than generous in these fringe benefits. We tell prospective faculty members that the benefits, excluding tuition grants to family members, equal more than 11% of their base salary. — *Private college*

All benefits will increase from a total of 10% now to a total of 18% in 1970. — *Private college*

Another institution estimates that if base salary is $5,000, supplemental benefits are an additional 20%; if $7,000, 18%; and if $9,000, 17%. In many institutions the cost would be more than those indicated.

My opinion may not fit in to this pattern, but frankly this is what I observed: Faculty members like to get enough salary to be as independent as possible. They do not appreciate the monetary sacrifice the college makes to provide fringe benefits. It's easier on the administration if the faculty member gets his own housing and handles his affairs independently. It's bad enough to be work boss without being landlord, health officer, insurance agent, loan shark, etc. The greatest fringe benefit is a stimulating academic atmosphere, congenial people on administration and faculty, and a favorable climate for raising a family. — *Private college*

I find it difficult to respond to the second half of this question referring to the attainment of other institutional objectives. From one point of view, the rather rapid growth of fringe benefits is, in my judgment, antithetical to the attainment of the institution's objectives of preserving and enhancing the freedom and independence of the individual. On the other hand, in recognition of society's present values which seem to place an inordinate high priority on security and the denial of responsibility to the individual, these benefits may have something to do with the attainment of a better staff morale. — *Private university*

The effect of fringe benefits on recruiting and retaining faculty depends primarily on the comparative value of the benefits rather than on their absolute value. Sabbatic leave policies, for example, do not vary significantly among good institutions and therefore do not play an important role in attracting or retaining faculty members. Blue Cross and travel accident insurance are probably in the same category. On the other hand, our tuition payment plan for faculty children, which is unusually generous, has played an important part in a number of cases in bringing men to . . . or keeping them here. Major Medical Insurance is important to us now but will probably lose some of its comparative advantage as it is more generally adopted. Very few institutions, I believe, provide this coverage for retired faculty members as we do. — *Private university*

The most important factor, we have found, in recruiting faculty are salary and the reputation of the College. Fringe benefits have not appeared too important, partly because . . . is located in a fair-sized community which offers many natural advantages in cultured activities and civic benefits, such as an excellent city government and public school system. — *Private college*

As faculty salaries continue to soar and the market becomes more highly competitive, it may be assumed that fringe benefits, will become of less importance, particularly to younger faculty members. — *Private university*

The faculty benefits covered by this questionnaire have not been of major importance in our gaining or failure to gain, or in retention of, faculty members. We have found that a sound retirement annuity program and disability and other insurance benefits are significant considerations for prospects. Probably the most important of the benefits covered by this questionnaire in our situation is the provision of travel expense to professional meetings. I am sure that the absence of reasonable provisions here would be a discouragement both to members of our faculty and to prospects. Undoubtedly our mortgage loan program, which enables members of our faculty to secure their own housing on a basis which would otherwise not be feasible, has been a significant factor in retention in several instances. In the absence of a sabbatical leave program, we have undertaken to enlarge our provision for summer and research opportunities. This has been done, however, more out of our recognition of its value in enhancing the professional effectiveness of our members, than for its benefits as a recruiting or retention inducement. — *Private college*

Benefits for faculty members, in my experience, have had a much more important effect on retention than on recruiting. This seems natural; most of our new appointments are of men and women fresh from graduate study. Retirement seems a long way off to them, and, moreover, they seem to make the assumption that benefits in institutions of comparable quality are fairly similar, and in almost no case has a prospective new member at a junior rank asked very many questions about the benefit program. As we have been able to increase benefits, I feel sure that has had an important effect on retention. Even so, however, the benefits should not be considered as a substitute for salary increases. In this period, our salary levels have increased substantially, and it is therefore impossible to separate what effect this has had from the effect of increased benefits. — *Private college*

Recruitment of qualified college staff under current conditions of expanding enrollments is becoming increasingly difficult. Our salary scale is competitive but we find our qualified applicants concerned about many of the items covered in this questionnaire. Of particular interest to new faculty are financial and housing problems, travel expense, sabbatical leaves, and secretarial help for the preparation of professional materials. . . . [We] hope that provisions for sabbatical leaves and financial assistance for attendance at professional meetings will be improved. — *Public college*

In the current world of academic fluidity, we shall have to add as many benefits as possible to compete for sound teachers. — *Private college*

Greatly enlarged retirement benefits beginning age 65 along with a number of cooperative ventures in group insurance, group buying, and catastrophic benefits developed to take major worries off the faculty mind with the hope this may be done without pampering the faculty so they lose their fibre. We are not much impressed with the value of free golf, free bowling, etc., queries included in this questionnaire. — *Private college*

Almost all of the non-retirement and non-insurance benefits which are the subject of this survey are helpful in recruiting and retaining staff members, and hence in attaining overall institutional objectives. It is, however, primarily in cumulative fashion that these benefits help; many do not lend themselves to strict evaluation apart from the whole. — *Private university*

Without question the matter of benefits covered by this questionnaire has been helpful in recruiting and retaining staff members. — *Private college*

One of the most useful devices has been the TIAA–CREF program in recruiting and retaining staff members. Money spent on what is commonly referred to as fringe benefits which includes retirement has been more effective with us than outright increases in salaries. Apparently very great importance is attached by faculties particularly in the direction of retirement and hospitalization and medical care. — *Public university*

We believe that our institution has a well-balanced program of fringe benefits, even though there are some areas (e.g., tuition for faculty children, moving costs, mortgages) in which as a public institution we have felt we could not provide support. Our program has been invaluable to us in recruiting and retaining faculty members. In our judgment, in the near future an institution will not be able to compete unless it has a soundly conceived program. — *Public university*

FUTURE PLANS

The area in which we will probably expand benefits in the near future will be an increasing of the amount the college contributes to the retirement program. — *Private college*

In the future we are hoping to (*a*) increase TIAA percentage paid by the College from 7 1/2% to 10%; (*b*) improve life insurance, medical, and disability plans for professional and (we have much to do here) non-professional employees; (*c*) reach a universal policy on retirement age, with certain waivers; (*d*) increase benefits for children of professional employees (and in some cases non-professional) going elsewhere to College. — *Private college*

It is probable that we will expand and improve our annuity benefit program in the near future. — *Private university*

I think our program of benefits would be strengthened by making medical protection possible for faculty members after retirement. I think we must add total disabilities coverage. I would hope also that the College could increase its share of payment for other insurances. It is possible we should introduce leasing of college land for faculty-built houses and, perhaps, loans to faculty members to build. Too, we should improve the provisions for faculty travel expenses. — *Private college*

Larger tuition grants to children of Faculty, assuming larger share of TIAA premiums, larger grants for research, increasing value of medical and hospitalization benefits, limited expansion of sabbatical program. — *Private college*

From the Self Study project have come suggestions that we attempt to expand the policies related to encouraging professional growth (i.e., leave of absence of various kinds, funds for attending professional meetings, etc.), and that we seek to extend the retirement plan, particularly as it relates to persons of long service to the College. — *Private college*

The most immediate fringe benefits which we are contemplating will be an expansion of our summer fellowship program in which we make out-right grants for summer work or projects of individual faculty members, and also we hope within the near future to establish a program of cash grants to those faculty members whose children wish to attend some other educational institution. — *Private college*

(a) More secretarial service to faculty.
(b) Private offices for faculty.
(c) Sabbatical leave policy which has just been initiated.
(d) Increase of University contribution to retirement.
(e) Increase in Basic Research Fund. — *Private university*

We are considering for the future possible adoption: (a) Major Medical; (b) Disability Insurance; (c) sabbatical leave with pay; (d) expansion of stenographic service to faculty; (e) since each man has a private office the possible installation of a private telephone in each office is being studied. — *Private college*

INSTITUTIONAL REVIEWS OF BENEFIT PROGRAMS

Institutional reviews of benefit programs are discussed at the end of Chapter 14. Relevant quotations are included here.

The questionnaire by itself may be of some use. In fact, I suspect that in some cases policy was determined to make an answer possible:

Our institution is only 16 years old and our Faculty is not yet large enough for many of these questions to be relevant. I doubt the truth of the last six words in the sentence below over your signature. — *Private college* [*these words are at the end of the questionnaire*]

Our questionnaire will not contribute to your study since we do not have any of the usual fringe benefits described therein.

We have cooperated in this study because we realize that you should have replies of this kind and because we know that we must set up at least a limited program of fringe benefits. We hope to receive a summary of the results for use in our own study of the problem. — *Private college*

This questionnaire makes one conscious of the many fringe benefits that a faculty member may receive. — *Private college*

The questionnaire has been studied carefully. I am sure that it will prove to be beneficial. — *Public college*

Please don't give us a questionnaire as complicated as this very often! — *Private college*

All these matters come up for review regularly and will next be considered by a special committee in the Spring of 1964. — *Private college*

We have a University Committee constantly working on various approaches to improve our fringe benefits but the political problems of trying to separate the University personnel from other state employees as well as the economic realities has regularly led to a decision to go for higher salaries rather than extending significantly our fringe benefits. What the decisions in these areas will be in the immediate years ahead I cannot predict. — *Public university*

The development of policy regarding fringe benefits for faculty is done through a committee of faculty and administrative staff. The faculty members are appointed on a three-year rotation basis by the President, and an effort is made to keep the membership representative of the eight faculties within the University as well as the various age groups.

Proposals are studied and investigated by this committee and recommendations are made to the President. Presently under study is a Disability Insurance program which if adopted would have some bearing on Item C. — *Private university*

REFERENCES TO APPENDICES

Appendix I: Questionnaire, Section 12.

Appendix IV: Evaluation Chart.

CHAPTER 14

CONCLUSIONS AND
INSTITUTIONAL REVIEWS

THIS chapter deals with (1) conclusions and (2) suggestions as to methods by which an institution can study its faculty benefits. Quotations from replies to the questionnaire relevant to this chapter are included in the " 'They' Say" section of the preceding chapter.

CONCLUSIONS

The chief purpose of a benefit program is to enhance the educational service of a college or university. This is done by directly increasing the efficacy and morale of the faculty members, and by its effect upon recruiting and retaining a strong faculty. Thus, the choice of benefits depends on how directly and how greatly these benefits affect the work and spirit of the faculty and the attractiveness of the institution. The choice and the pattern of benefits also depend on their cost in institutional resources and the alternative uses of these resources. Hence considerations such as the advantages derived from group or institutional action and the tax advantages of one use of funds compared with another must be taken into account. So also must many lesser or less frequent considerations, whose sum often is major and whose importance varies from campus to campus. Moreover, some institutions have resources — such as land, houses, or special gifts — whose purpose is restricted. These may provide an opportunity to help the faculty but have few, if any, alternate uses.

Some of the factors that affect the quality of a man's services are: (a) education, (b) range of continuing intellectual contacts, (c) freedom, (d) the absence of interfering worries or obligations, (e) health and vigor, and, of course, (f) native ability and character. To point out the relevance of these factors to faculty benefits may be to belabor the obvious. But I run the risk.

(*a*) Many schools have as their primary purpose of leaves of absence the completion of graduate work. Others make special arrangements for attendance of faculty members at neighboring universities or at their own institution and arrange the teaching schedules to facilitate such attendance. Still others make loans to faculty members in order that graduate work may be possible.

(*b*) Reimbursement for travel to meetings as well as the program of leaves, research assignments, post-doctoral fellowships, and cultural events on the campus serve to foster the intellectual life of a faculty.

(*c*) Academic freedom is protected by tenure, and the liberty to develop one's own intellectual interests is generally accorded faculty members. The extensive and frequently institutionally inconvenient granting of leaves without pay provides an opportunity seldom found outside the academic world for a faculty member to choose his own activities.

(*d*) Salary, retirement provisions, insurance, aid for children's education, and other benefits that make a direct financial contribution to a man's well-being not only lead to his peace of mind but reduce the temptation to participate for pay in non-academic activities. Aids to his work — administrative, secretarial, and even mechanical — reduce the waste of time of highly trained scholars. We should remind ourselves, however, that no one lives his whole life at an intense pitch of creativity. It is by no means certain that, when a man is relieved from routine duties, all of the time saved will be used in more useful pursuits. Much of the gain from secretarial help is that the secretary does the job better.

(*e*) Programs of medical services and medical insurance for the faculty help in regard to health and vigor. Perhaps of greater importance are programs that make it feasible (by providing support to the aged and the disabled) for an institution not to be tempted to use the services of persons who may have lost their effectiveness on account of age or loss of health. Retirement annuities, disability insurance, and short-time sick-leaves all serve this purpose.

(*f*) A high-minded faculty of native ability is secured only through a combination of the competitive attractiveness of an institution and the insight and judgment in selection of individuals. In this regard it is important to note that competition is not only with other educational institutions but with industry and government. Those administrative officers who express frustration over the fact that in the academic circles they can only keep up with — not ahead of — the Joneses should remember that they share with the whole profession in any progress it may make in relation to non-educational competition. In this, benefits play a part. Even if educational institutions cannot offer stock bonuses or participate in the galaxy of privileges provided by private industry or use the franking privilege, they can help create through benefits appropriate to their nature a community where talent will thrive and feel at home.

We now pass to secondary but often determining considerations.

As compared with the individual the power of a group or institution to save money in making purchases is often the reason for providing certain benefits, sometimes with little or no expense to the institution. Thus group insurance and annuity plans diminish administrative costs and decrease or eliminate the commissions for agents. These plans can be adapted to the needs of the faculty and have the important advantage of making it possible to cover the individually uninsurable. Suitable housing may not exist unless the college provides it. It often is cheaper to aid a student by a waiver of tuition than to pay the same benefit in salary to his father. The use of the purchasing power of the institution to secure discounts for faculty members is also a means of saving money for the individual though, in my judgment, seldom a wise one.

The study of how to receive and disburse funds in an honorable fashion with the least taxes is both useful and fascinating. Some appear to believe that, like algebra, it involves a low form of cunning. But, like algebra, this is not its basic characteristic. It is true that tax laws, like other laws, are affected by pressure groups, even educational pressure groups, and legal subterfuge at times may twist their intent. But fundamentally tax laws embody well-considered public policies. Among these policies are aid to religious, charitable, and educational institutions, the encouragement of saving toward old age, the investment in the means of production, and the facilitating of state and municipal enterprises. It is not wrong, but rather demanded by public policy, that individuals and institutions utilize their tax privileges. An individual giving $1,000 to the Community Chest may thereby pay $300 less in income taxes, but save the public more than the $1,000 he gave by the prevention of situations that, if they arose, would cost it dearly. Some states have decided it is wise not to tax even the commercial property of educational institutions, in the knowledge that income from such property will be devoted to the public welfare. We may debate about tax policy; but when it is determined, an institution should by honest and straightforward means make use of any advantage given to it. This is not simply a privilege but a duty, the fulfillment in an effective manner of a public trust.

Let me try to note in an order, depending on the degree of importance and the frequency of this importance, some of the more valuable staff benefits other than salary. Within the categories, the more important tend to come first, but such order does not mean much. Local conditions could dictate different, sometimes drastically different, conclusions at various places. Moreover the variations of human judgment enter into any such listing.

    I. In the first category I would place:

        1. A reasonable retirement policy and provisions for post-retirement annuities including Social Security benefits.
        2. Time for continued scholarly activities. This involves leaves of absence for research or individual education, research assignments, or a combination of the two, and sometimes aid for scholarly work in the summer.
        3. Major medical insurance.
        4. Continued benefits and privileges for retired faculty members and widows. These include major medical insurance. Work facilities for retired members are of special importance.

(I consider secretarial help a condition of work, but if it were considered a benefit, it would go in this first category).

    II. In the second category I would place:

        1. Housing — especially for new members. (At some places this would belong high in category I.)
        2. Group life insurance.
        3. Children's education. An effective plan is a combination of tuition waiver and grants to go elsewhere. I strongly urge that, if a waiver is provided, grants should also be. (There is no question concerning the importance of this program, yet as I have stated in Chapter 3, on grounds of social philosophy, I do not like it.)
        4. Provisions for income during disability caused by sickness or accident. This may be approached during a short-term disability or in the initial period of a permanent or long-term disability by an informal or formal policy of salary continuation, and at a later by disability insurance.

    5. Health services and basic group medical insurance such as Blue Cross–Blue Shield. What health services should be rendered depend largely on local conditions.

III. In the third category I would place:

    1. Faculty club and social facilities.
    2. Travel expenses to meetings (especially to equalize departmental opportunities).
    3. Parking.
    4. Moving expenses.

IV. And at a fourth level:

    1. Credit unions.
    2. Athletic facilities.
    3. An emergency fund — "president's fund." (In some places, this has proved of more importance than this ranking would indicate.)
    4. Campus events.

and I would give negative ratings to

    –1. Discount privileges.
    –2. Institutional loans to faculty.

SUGGESTIONS CONCERNING INSTITUTIONAL REVIEWS OF BENEFIT PLANS

THE IRREVERSIBILITY OF BENEFIT PLANS. The history of benefits indicates that they are remarkably permanent. Few are abandoned unless they can be replaced by something more adequate or, even occasionally, more lush. The old office of the dean that was once adequate is now a "barn." The present one is "dignified." This is a symbol of fringe benefits that are struggling to become necessities. We may be amused, yet approve. There is no reason why intelligent, trained, devoted servants of the community should not share in the growing economic and social opportunities of our society. Many of the benefits provided by institutions help to make this possible in ways that could not be done through additions to salaries. However, I believe that scholars should have enough sense of history to realize how rapidly luxuries are subsumed under necessities, privileges under rights.

In light of the above, it is startling how often a benefit program comes into being with great casualness. A gift, a decision as to how to keep a professor, a distressing accident, may start one going. Many new lands have been discovered by drifting or being blown off course, but even a windfall or a landfall may be exploited systematically.

GENERAL REMARKS. It is surprising how few institutions, as far as I know, have made comprehensive studies of their benefit plans. This does not mean that many committees have not worked on retirement provisions, many others on insurance, others on leaves, and still others on housing. One pressing need has often been compared with another, especially where the "part of the first part" is salary. But I believe attempts at overall assessments are rare. They are not unknown since a few institutions have reported periodic reviews of staff benefits or standing committees on the subject.

Few institutions would claim to have a well-developed and perfectly balanced program of faculty benefits. The details of even such a program would tend toward obsolesence. Almost all institutions have some staff benefits other than salary. Hence I will assume that an institution's survey of staff benefits starts neither with a void nor a perfected program. There will be customs — some good, some inadequate, some perhaps harmful. There will be explicit or implied obligations. There will be lessons to be learned from other institutions. Many conclusions must come from a close study of local circumstances, including the sources of competition for staff. However, what follows is intended to help not only those that are studying an on-going situation, but also young institutions and church institutions which have had until recently few lay faculty members.

We should not start with detailed objectives. Let them grow simultaneously with the growth of means.

In seeking the best we must use instinctive judgment as well as analysis. Often we know that a thing is good before, if ever, we find out its purpose or the reason for its excellence. Witness: Shakespeare's plays, sunsets, apple pie, and certain theorems of number theory. However, we must start with some realization of the benefits of "benefits." As mentioned several times before, it is hoped that they will increase the welfare, morale, and effectiveness of the faculty and make the institution more attractive to scholars of the type it wishes to have on its staff. Even this rather vague statement has corollaries, an important one being that in a study of benefit programs the faculty must be represented and by people they trust.

THE COMMITTEE, ITS NATURE AND ITS APPOINTMENT. The problems involved — fiscal policy, insurance, taxation, housing, teaching load, research assignment, campus development, and a host of others — in large part determine who are qualified to make the study, as well as the information they should have.

It is assumed that in almost all places a committee will be involved in the study. The decisions on the benefit program affect the whole institution to such a great extent that any committee studying the subject cannot be more than advisory to the faculty, to the administration, and to the governing board. However, the committee must be assured that its advice will be considered seriously.

The committee should be primarily a faculty committee, unless it is to study the benefits of the whole staff, in which case the non-faculty staff should be well represented. There should be administrative representation on the committee, for instance, a person from the business office and a dean. There should be one person with knowledge about taxes. (If no faculty or administrative member is so equipped, an alumnus lawyer might be willing to help.) Someone engaged in campus planning should be on the committee unless it is completely clear that housing will not be considered.

In spite of the fact that committees should usually be small, this one might well be larger than the average. A good deal of parceled-out work will be necessary. Except for a really small college, a committee of seven to ten persons would not scare me.

A very real problem arises as to whether the committee should be elected or appointed. An elected committee has already cleared a few hurdles. However, elections often fail to produce the balance and special knowledge that are needed on such a committee. If the faculty has an elected policy committee, it might well be that the faculty would ask this committee to work with the administration in selecting the committee to study benefits. I would recommend that the faculty decide how the committee is selected, but I believe that the faculty would be wise if it decided that the committee should be appointed. Clearly, the administrative members should be appointed.

The committee will be useless if it is not given a clear picture of the institution's financial status. It should understand what the present and probably future resources and obligations are. In particular, it must know the flexibilities and the inflexibilities in the budget. Many funds are limited by donors' stipulations or by legislation. In one place the cost of land for housing will compete with salary; in another, the land may be available, but inalienable. Gifts have at times been made for emergency funds, for the president's home, for travel for biologists, or for distinguished-service fellowships. The impact of federal and foundation support as well as the experience of administrative officers in acquiring and holding faculty should be described in detail. While the administration must realize that an uninformed committee is useless, the committee must realize that certain information is confidential and that, if given in confidence, it must not be divulged even if the "hush-hush" appears to be needless.

The committee must be devoted to the educational services of the institution. It should be expected to consider not merely the financial advantages to the faculty of a given program but also its educational effects. Thus, under certain circumstances, leaves might take precedence over salary increases and smaller quiz sections over either. A new classroom building might be built rather than houses for the faculty. Any programs should be assessed against all relevant options. I believe faculty benefits will easily survive such scrutiny.

The committee should be able to face questions and analysis such as the following:

We now have the faculty salary budget of $1,000,000 and our tuition is $900 a year. Tuition for faculty children is waived. There are, at present, 10 faculty children taking advantage of this. We estimate that one of these would have been awarded a tuition scholarship if we had no waiver plan. There are 15 faculty children going elsewhere to college. We are turning away qualified applicants for admission. Our present plan, therefore, costs us about $8,100 in tuition waivers. A grants plan for children to go elsewhere would cost another $13,500. The number of children of faculty members approaching college age is increasing. Thus a plan of grants would amount to $1\frac{1}{3}\%$ of salaries and would increase to nearly 2% in the near future.

We believe this is (is not) a program worth this lessening of faculty salaries. All this money should (should not) be used to decrease the size of freshman quiz sections by 10%. If our present waiver plan were abandoned, we could add .8% to all salaries at once and at least 1% in the near future. We believe this should not be done (should be done over a period of time).

Of course this example is oversimplified: Tax considerations, the competitive position of the college, and other questions will enter into the picture. It is given to emphasize how clearly alternatives should be faced.

Appendix IV indicates a few facts concerning a large list of benefits. To a greater degree, it indicates my reactions to these. Such a chart should be used to stimulate thought, not to dictate conclusions. However, I believe that a committee would find it useful to make a similar chart for their own institution. In the case of benefits where local circumstances control, there should be considerable variation among institutions and hence Appendix IV, of necessity, is lacking in definiteness. This fuzziness would disappear in a chart for a given institution. The importance of various items would get a firm rating rather than a wobbly one like "sometimes very important." Obligations already undertaken would in some instances be controlling. Relation of present and future status of a benefit would be considered. Although Appendix IV is by no means a model — even as to form, let alone content — the arriving at some abbreviated statement of conclusions, an outline of major factors in a form that compares various benefits is a head-clearing exercise, especially since (as was not the case in Appendix IV) a committee must reach a consensus. (I wish some committee would do this, first, as individuals at the start of a study, and then after some months as a committee, and let me see both results.)

The committee must not stop with generalities. It should make out an institutional list of priorities as to benefits both to be expanded or initiated, or even (is this a fatuous hope?) deleted. It should indicate not only their relative importance, but their importance in comparison with other uses of the same resources.

For those items that are to be expanded in the near future, much more detail should be given. For instance: If a housing program is to be undertaken, where will it be; how financed; how will rental rates compare with commercial rates; how will priority for space be determined; how long can people stay in the houses; who will manage it?

If it is a revision of a retirement plan that is under scrutiny, the study can well follow an outline such as that given in the brochure of TIAA on planning a retirement program.

The committee should not ask the faculty to pass on all details but only on general principles. Committee hearings could take the place of prolonged discussions in faculty meetings.

To do all this in a large or complex institution the committee should have secretarial help, a small budget, perhaps including some travel money, and some relief from other duties for the chairman. It is fair to ask the chairman to be two men, but not three.

A study, such as I have suggested, should improve the benefit program of an institution, but it may well yield an additional bonus. It should not only make the faculty members realize the genuine concern that the institution has in their welfare, but also reveal anew to the administration the genuine concern of the faculty for the welfare and educational integrity of the institution.

APPENDICES

QUESTIONNAIRE

IN this appendix the questionnaire used in this study is reproduced. Only two alterations have been made. Page numbers (for this volume) have been introduced and three blank pages of the questionnaire (pages 2, 28, and 32) have been omitted.

The tables of Appendices II and III and almost all of the quotes in the "'They' Say" sections in the chapters of this report were derived from replies to this questionnaire. In addition, these responses formed, along with visits and conversations, a major ingredient of the background upon which the descriptions and judgments of the text were based.

Commission on Faculty and Staff Benefits
of the Association of American Colleges

PLEASE RETURN THIS COPY

January 2, 1963

STUDY OF FACULTY BENEFITS (OTHER THAN RETIREMENT AND INSURANCE)

Association of American Colleges
Teachers Insurance and Annuity Association
730 Third Avenue   New York 17, N. Y.

Request for Information

This questionnaire seeks information on a variety of benefits, other than retirement and insurance, often provided to faculty members by colleges and universities.

Directions

(1) Please fill out and return the white copy of this questionnaire. A postpaid return envelope is enclosed. The blue copies are for your use as a worksheet and for your files.

(2) Since it is possible that no individual will be acquainted with all topics covered, the questionnaire is divided into sections which may be separated for distribution to those who are best equipped to give information. The twelve topics are:

   1. Faculty Housing
   2. Mortgage Loans
   3. Personal Loans
   4. Faculty Travel Expenses
   5. Leaves of Absence
   6. Faculty Club
   7. Faculty Family Education
   8. Faculty Parking
   9. General Campus Facilities
   10. Privileges of Retired Faculty and Faculty Widows
   11. Other Faculty Benefits
   12. Experience in Recruiting and Retaining Faculty

Please be sure that all twelve sections are assembled for return.

(3) This inquiry covers both factual information and opinions. Some of the factual information will be published institution by institution. Opinions and evaluations, however, will not be identified.

(4) Please note that the final section of the questionnaire deals with your college or university's experience with recruiting and retaining faculty. It should be answered by someone acquainted with the institution's experience as a whole, such as the president or the dean of the faculty.

(5) Each section asks for copies of printed or mimeographed material describing the benefits discussed. In addition, we urgently invite you to go beyond the questionnaire by adding as many comments as you like. Descriptions of unusual benefits will be particularly appreciated. (see Section 11).

General Questions

(1) Name of Institution:

1 _____ 6

(2) If your institution has NO BRANCHES, check here ☐

   If your institution HAS BRANCHES, please complete the following:

   a. This report INCLUDES branches as follows:

   b. This report EXCLUDES branches as follows:

(3) As used in the following sections, the term FACULTY comprises all professionally trained staff members engaged in instruction and/or research, and generally holding the ranks of professor, assoc. professor, ass't. professor, instructor, or comparable positions.

Please indicate the number of full-time faculty members (as defined above), not including "equivalents," at your institution:

Number of full-time faculty:

7 _____ 10

(Catholic institutions: Please indicate only full-time lay faculty. Questionnaire refers to lay faculty only.)

WE WOULD GREATLY APPRECIATE THE RETURN OF THE COMPLETED QUESTIONNAIRE WITHIN A MONTH OF ITS RECEIPT BY YOU

AAC/TIAA, 730 Third Ave.,
New York 17, New York

SECTION 1 - FACULTY HOUSING

(Excluding official residences maintained for the president and administrative officers)

Name of Institution: _____

Your Name and Position: _____

_____

Write the name and position of the person (if other than yourself) to whom any further questions on faculty housing should be addressed:

_____

1. Does your institution maintain an office which helps faculty members locate rental housing in the community?

   11 - 1 ☐ NO
      - 2 ☐ YES

2. Does your institution have any plan of furnishing, leasing, or securing land on which faculty members may build houses?

   12 - 1 ☐ NO
      - 2 ☐ YES | IF YES, we would appreciate your attaching a short description of the plan.

3. Does your institution own houses or apartments in which faculty live?

   13 - 1 ☐ NO | IF NO, *please skip to Section 2 after answering this question:* Are you considering initiating a faculty housing program?
                   - 3 ☐ YES
                   - 4 ☐ NO

      - 2 ☐ YES | IF YES, *please answer the remaining questions in this section.*

4. How many faculty members occupy college-owned *dwelling houses,* how many occupy college-owned *apartment units,* and how many occupy units in *student dormitories?*

College-owned	Number of Faculty Occupying
Dwelling houses	14 16
Apartment units	17 19
Student dormitory units	20 21
Total number of faculty occupying college-owned housing	_____

5. Does your institution use a priority system in assigning faculty housing?

   22 - 1 ☐ NO
      - 2 ☐ YES | IF YES, please check below the criteria used in giving priority for faculty housing. *(Check all applicable items.)*

By length of service	By rank	By need
- 3 ☐ New faculty members	- 5 ☐ Professors	- x ☐ According to special need (e.g., large family)
- 4 ☐ Faculty with at least _____ years' service	- 6 ☐ Assoc. Profs.	
	- 7 ☐ Ass't. Profs.	
	- 8 ☐ Instructors	

           - 9 ☐ Other than above *(describe):*

6. How long may the eligible faculty member occupy college-owned housing? *(Please check all that apply.)*

   23 - 1 ☐ Until completion of a stated length of time *(Please state length of time: _____ years)*
      - 2 ☐ Until retirement
      - 3 ☐ Throughout retirement
      - 4 ☐ No specified length of time
      - 5 ☐ Other limitations than above *(Please describe):*

7. Are rentals *above, at the same level,* or *below* rentals for privately owned units of similar housing quality?

   24 - 1 ☐ Above
      - 2 ☐ At the same level
      - 3 ☐ Below | IF BELOW, by approximately what percent on the average?
                 - 4 ☐ less than 10% below
                 - 5 ☐ 10 to 25% below
                 - 6 ☐ 25 to 50% below
                 - 7 ☐ over 50% below

8. To what degree do rents charged cover costs of providing faculty housing (including depreciation and interest on investment)? *(Check one.)*

   25 - 1 ☐ Rents cover substantially more than cost

   - 2 ☐ Rents approximately cover the cost

   - 3 ☐ Rents are substantially less than cost

   - 4 ☐ Rents vs. cost not calculated

9. Are any faculty housing units furnished as part of compensation (i.e., in lieu of monetary compensation)?

   26 - 1 ☐ NO

   - 2 ☐ YES

IF YES, how many faculty members receive housing as a part of compensation?
_____
(number)

10. During the next five years the number of your college-owned dwelling units for faculty occupancy will probably: *(Check the appropriate item.)*

    27 - 1 ☐ Be expanded more rapidly than the faculty

    - 2 ☐ Be expanded about the same as the faculty

    - 3 ☐ Be expanded less rapidly than the faculty

    - 4 ☐ Remain about the same as now

    - 5 ☐ Be contracted

11. Please check the phrase which best describes your view of the contribution your faculty housing program makes for *recruiting* and *retaining* faculty.

    Recruiting

    28 - 1 ☐ Substantial contribution

    - 2 ☐ Moderate contribution

    - 3 ☐ Negligible contribution

    Retaining

    - 4 ☐ Substantial contribution

    - 5 ☐ Moderate contribution

    - 6 ☐ Negligible contribution

12. Please indicate briefly (a) the general purposes of your faculty housing program, (b) any significant problems experienced in connection with it, and (c) any important features in your program not covered by other questions of this section. *(Attach additional sheets if needed.)*

    (a) General Purposes:

    (b) Significant Problems:

    (c) Important Special Features:

    If you have published material describing the faculty housing provisions at your institution, please send us a copy under separate cover and list below what is being sent.

AAC/TIAA, 730 Third Ave.,
New York 17, New York

SECTION 2 - MORTGAGE LOANS

Name of Institution: _____

Your Name and Position: _____

What is the name and position of the person (if other than yourself) to whom further questions on mortgage loans should be addressed?

_____

1. Does your institution make *first mortgage* loans on the homes of faculty members?

   29 - 1 ☐ YES

   - 2 ☐ NO | IF NO, are you considering initiating a first mortgage loan program?

       - 3 ☐ YES

       - 4 ☐ NO

2. Does your institution make *second mortgage* loans on the homes of faculty members?

   30 - 1 ☐ YES

   - 2 ☐ NO | IF NO, are you considering initiating a second mortgage loan program?

       - 3 ☐ YES

       - 4 ☐ NO

If you now have a first or second mortgage loan program, please answer the remaining questions in this section.

3. How many faculty members now have mortgage loans held by the college?

	Number of Faculty	
First mortgage loans	31	33
Second mortgage loans	34	36
Total faculty having mortgage loans		

4. What faculty members are eligible for mortgage loans? *(Please check as many as apply.)*

   37 - 1 ☐ Professors   - 4 ☐ Instructors

   - 2 ☐ Assoc. Profs.   - 5 ☐ Others *(describe)*:

   - 3 ☐ Ass't. Profs.

5. What is the maximum portion of a home's market value for which a *first mortgage* loan is made? *(Check the nearest figure.)*

   38 - 1 ☐ Less than 2/3 - 5 ☐ 85% - 9 ☐ no first mortgage loans made

   - 2 ☐ 2/3   - 6 ☐ 90%

   - 3 ☐ 75%   - 7 ☐ 95%

   - 4 ☐ 80%   - 8 ☐ 100%

6. If you make *second mortgage* loans on faculty homes, to what portion of a home's market value are the combined first and second mortgages limited? *(Check the nearest figure.)*

   39 - 1 ☐ Less than 2/3 - 5 ☐ 85% - 9 ☐ no second mortgage loans made

   - 2 ☐ 2/3   - 6 ☐ 90%

   - 3 ☐ 75%   - 7 ☐ 95%

   - 4 ☐ 80%   - 8 ☐ 100%

7. Is the maximum amount your institution will lend to a faculty member on a *first mortgage* related to the size of his salary?

   40 - 1 ☐ NO

   - 2 ☐ NO first mortgage loans made

   - 3 ☐ YES   IF YES, *please describe:*

8. Is the maximum amount your institution will lend to a faculty member on a *second mortgage* related to the size of his salary?

   41 - 1 ☐ NO

   - 2 ☐ NO second mortgage loans made

   - 3 ☐ YES   IF YES, *please describe:*

9. Is there a dollar limit on the mortgage loans made to faculty members?

   First Mortgages   Second Mortgages

   42 - 1 ☐ NO   - 3 ☐ NO

   - 2 ☐ YES | IF YES, please state limit: $_____   - 4 ☐ YES | IF YES, please state limit: $_____

10. Please state the interest rate that you now normally charge on mortgage loans:

	On first mortgages	On second mortgages
Interest Rate	_____% 43 44	_____% 45 46

11. Does your institution make a service charge on its mortgage loans to faculty members?

On first mortgages

47 - 1 ☐ NO

- 2 ☐ YES   IF YES, what is the charge?

On second mortgages

- 3 ☐ NO

- 4 ☐ YES   IF YES, what is the charge?

12. What is the normal period over which recent mortgage loans are to be fully amortized?

	Number of years
First mortgages	_____ 48 49
Second mortgages	_____ 50 51

13. Are there any restrictions on where the mortgaged property can be located?

52 - 1 ☐ NO

- 2 ☐ YES   IF YES, *please describe:*

14. What is the total amount of mortgage loans for faculty housing currently outstanding?

$ _____
53   59

15. During the next five years your institution's mortgage loan program on dwellings for faculty members will probably: *(Please check the appropriate item.)*

60 - 1 ☐ Be expanded more rapidly than the faculty

- 2 ☐ Be expanded about the same as the faculty

- 3 ☐ Be expanded less rapidly than the faculty

- 4 ☐ Remain about the same as now

- 5 ☐ Be contracted

16. Please check the phrase which best describes your view of the contribution your mortgage loan program makes to *recruiting* and *retaining* faculty.

Recruiting

61 - 1 ☐ Substantial contribution

- 2 ☐ Moderate contribution

- 3 ☐ Negligible contribution

Retaining

- 4 ☐ Substantial contribution

- 5 ☐ Moderate contribution

- 6 ☐ Negligible contribution

17. Please indicate briefly (a) the general purposes of your mortgage loan program, (b) any significant problems experienced in connection with it, and (c) any important features in your program not covered by other questions of this section. *(Attach additional sheets if needed.)*

(a) General Purposes:

(b) Significant Problems:

(c) Important Special Features:

If you have published materials describing the mortgage loan provisions at your institution, please send us a copy of each under separate cover, listing below what is being sent.

AAC/TIAA, 730 Third Ave.,
New York 17, New York

SECTION 3 - PERSONAL LOANS TO FACULTY MEMBERS

Name of Institution: _____

Your Name and Position: _____

Write the name and position of the person (if other than yourself) to whom any further questions concerning personal loans to faculty should be addressed?

_____

1. Is there a faculty credit union (serving college personnel only) at your institution?

   62 - 1 ☐ NO

     - 2 ☐ YES | IF YES, does your institution give aid to the faculty credit union?
           - 3 ☐ NO
           - 4 ☐ YES IF YES, *check kinds of aid given:*
                   - 5 ☐ Financial
                   - 6 ☐ Clerical help
                   - 7 ☐ Office space
                   - 8 ☐ Repayment by payroll deductions
                   - 9 ☐ Other *(describe):*

2. Is there an outside credit union serving your faculty?

   63 - 1 ☐ NO

     - 2 ☐ YES | IF YES, does your institution give aid to this credit union?
           - 3 ☐ NO
           - 4 ☐ YES IF YES, *check kinds of aid given:*
                   - 5 ☐ Financial
                   - 6 ☐ Clerical help
                   - 7 ☐ Office space
                   - 8 ☐ Repayment by payroll deductions
                   - 9 ☐ Other *(describe):*

3. Does your institution make personal loans to faculty members?

   64 - 1 ☐ NO | IF NO, this is the last question to answer in this section.

     - 2 ☐ YES | IF YES, *please answer the remaining questions in this section.*

4. How many personal loans were made during the 1962 calendar year?

        —————————————
        65 (number of loans made) 67

5. What was the total dollar amount of personal loans made during the 1962 calendar year?

      $ —————————————
        68   72

6. What was the amount of the largest single loan made during the 1962 calendar year?

      $ —————————————
        73   77

7. What faculty members are eligible for personal loans from your institution? *(Please check as many as apply.)*

   78 - 1 ☐ Professors   - 4 ☐ Instructors

     - 2 ☐ Assoc. Profs.   - 5 ☐ Others *(describe)*:

     - 3 ☐ Ass't. Profs.

8. Is there a limit to the amount of a personal loan a faculty member may have outstanding at any given time?

   79 - 1 ☐ NO

     - 2 ☐ YES IF YES, what is this limit? 80 - 1
                                        1 6

9. What is the typical interest rate (effective rate on outstanding balance) now being charged on personal loans?

      —————————————%
      7   8

10. What is the normal period of time for which personal loans are made?

     9 —————————————
           (length of time)

  (If related to size of loan, please attach schedule.)

11. Please check all the reasons below for which personal loans are made by your institution.

   10 - 1 ☐ Advanced study to complete a degree

     - 2 ☐ Research

     - 3 ☐ Children's education

     - 4 ☐ Family emergency

     - 5 ☐ Other *(describe):*

12. What types of security, if any, do you require for personal loans? *(Please check as many as apply.)*

11 - 1 ☐ No security required

- 2 ☐ Assignment of life insurance

- 3 ☐ Real estate

- 4 ☐ Other *(describe):*

13. Do you arrange for payroll deductions as a means of repayment of personal loans?

12 - 1 ☐ YES

- 2 ☐ NO

14. During the next five years your institution's personal loan program for faculty members will probably: *(Please check the appropriate item.)*

13 - 1 ☐ Be expanded more rapidly than the faculty

- 2 ☐ Be expanded about the same as the faculty

- 3 ☐ Be expanded less rapidly than the faculty

- 4 ☐ Remain about the same as now

- 5 ☐ Be contracted

15. Please check the phrase which best describes your view of the contribution your personal loan program makes for *recruiting* and *retaining* faculty.

Recruiting

14 - 1 ☐ Substantial contribution

- 2 ☐ Moderate contribution

- 3 ☐ Negligible contribution

Retaining

- 4 ☐ Substantial contribution

- 5 ☐ Moderate contribution

- 6 ☐ Negligible contribution

16. Please indicate briefly (a) the general purposes of your personal loan program, (b) any significant problems experienced in connection with it, and (c) any important feature in your program not covered by other questions in this section. *(Attach additional sheets if needed.)*

(a) General Purposes:

(b) Significant Problems:

(c) Important Special Features:

If you have published materials describing the personal loan program at your institution, please send us a copy of each under separate cover, listing below what is being sent.

AAC/TIAA, 730 Third Ave.,
New York 17, New York

SECTION 4 - FACULTY TRAVEL EXPENSES

Name of Institution: _____

Your Name and Position: _____

What is the name and position of the person (if other than yourself) to whom further questions concerning faculty travel expenses should be addressed?

1. Are there specified limits (cost, number of trips, distance, etc.) within which any one faculty member may be reimbursed for travel in a given year from university or college funds (i.e., funds not provided through special grants or contracts)?

   a. For professional meetings when not giving a paper.

      15 - 1 ☐ NO reimbursement

      - 2 ☐ Reimbursement with following limitations *(please describe):*

   b. For professional meetings when giving a paper.

      - 3 ☐ NO reimbursement

      - 4 ☐ Reimbursement with following limitations *(please describe):*

   c. For professional meetings when faculty member is an officer of the organization.

      - 5 ☐ NO reimbursement

      - 6 ☐ Reimbursement with following limitations *(please describe):*

   d. For scholarly conferences.

      - 7 ☐ NO reimbursement

      - 8 ☐ Reimbursement with following limitations *(please describe):*

   e. For travel in connection with research leaves.

      - 9 ☐ NO reimbursement

      - x ☐ Reimbursement with following limitations *(please describe):*

2. Does your policy differ as to reimbursement of (a) transportation expenses and (b) other expenses?

   16 - 1 ☐ NO

   - 2 ☐ YES   IF YES, *please describe:*

3. Which of the following faculty ranks are eligible for reimbursement for the expenses indicated in questions 1 and 2? *(Check as many as apply.)*

   17 - 1 ☐ Professor   - 4 ☐ Instructor

   - 2 ☐ Assoc. Prof.   - 5 ☐ Other *(describe):*

   - 3 ☐ Ass't. Prof.

4. Does your institution set any limits on transportation and other expenses which are chargeable to special grants or contracts for the following types of travel?

	Limit Set On Transportation Expenses?	Limit Set On Other Expenses?
a. Professional meetings	18 - 1 ☐ YES - 2 ☐ NO	- 3 ☐ YES - 4 ☐ NO
b. Scholarly conferences	19 - 1 ☐ YES - 2 ☐ NO	- 3 ☐ YES - 4 ☐ NO
c. Research travel	20 - 1 ☐ YES - 2 ☐ NO	- 3 ☐ YES - 4 ☐ NO

5. If the faculty member who is eligible to be reimbursed for transportation expenses uses his own automobile, what formula is used to determine the amount due him?

21

6. During the next five years, your institution's faculty travel expense program will probably: *(Please check the appropriate item.)*

    22 - 1 ☐ Be expanded more rapidly than the faculty

    - 2 ☐ Be expanded about the same as the faculty

    - 3 ☐ Be expanded less rapidly than the faculty

    - 4 ☐ Remain about the same as now

    - 5 ☐ Be contracted

7. Please check the phrase which best describes your view of the contribution your faculty travel expense program makes to *recruiting* and *retaining* faculty.

Recruiting

    23 - 1 ☐ Substantial contribution

    - 2 ☐ Moderate contribution

    - 3 ☐ Negligible contribution

Retaining

    - 4 ☐ Substantial contribution

    - 5 ☐ Moderate contribution

    - 6 ☐ Negligible contribution

8. Does your institution pay moving expenses of newly hired staff members?

    a. Tenure ranks?

        24 - 1 ☐ NO

        - 2 ☐ YES   IF YES, please indicate amounts, limits, etc:

                25   27

    b. Non-tenure ranks?

        28 - 1 ☐ NO

        - 2 ☐ YES   IF YES, please indicate amounts, limits, etc:

                29   31

9. Please indicate briefly (a) the general purposes of your faculty travel expense program, (b) any significant problems experienced in connection with it, and (c) any important features in your program not covered by other questions of this section. *(Attach additional sheets if needed.)*

(a) General Purposes:

(b) Significant Problems:

(c) Important Special Features:

If you have a published description of your faculty travel expense policy, please send us a copy and note below what is being sent.

AAC/TIAA, 730 Third Ave.,
New York 17, New York

SECTION 5 - LEAVES OF ABSENCE

Name of Institution: _____

Your Name and Position: _____

What is the name and position of the person (if other than yourself) to whom further questions on leaves of absence should be addressed?

_____

This section deals with three types of leaves:

A. **Sabbatical leaves.** Sabbatical leaves are defined as *leaves with pay* to which a faculty member becomes entitled primarily because of service through a given period of time.

B. **Other leaves with pay.** In addition to, or instead of, sabbatical leaves, many institutions make appointments on pay (frequently called leaves) which temporarily free faculty members from their regular teaching duties. These leaves may or may not involve absence from the campus. Examples of such leaves are research leaves or leaves for study.

C. **Leaves without pay.**

A. SABBATICAL LEAVES

1. Does your institution grant sabbatical leaves (as defined above)?

   32 - 1 ☐ NO | IF NO, *please skip to question 19 after answering this question:* Are you considering initiating a sabbatical leave program?

   - 3 ☐ YES
   - 4 ☐ NO

   - 2 ☐ YES | IF YES, *please answer the following questions.*

2. Which of the following faculty ranks are eligible for sabbatical leaves of absence? *(Please check as many as apply.)*

   33 - 1 ☐ Professors   - 4 ☐ Instructors
   - 2 ☐ Assoc. Profs.   - 5 ☐ Other *(describe):*
   - 3 ☐ Ass't. Profs.

3. Is *tenure* also a requirement for eligibility for sabbatical leave?

   34 - 1 ☐ YES
   - 2 ☐ NO

4. For persons of each rank, please indicate the number of years of service (a) in a given rank and (b) in the institution (either or both, whichever is applicable) that are required before the *first* sabbatical leave may be taken. *(Write in number of years in each space.)*

	Years of Service Required for First Sabbatical Leave	
	(a) In Rank Indicated	(b) In the Institution
Professor	35 yrs.	39 yrs.
Assoc. Prof.	36 yrs.	40 yrs.
Ass't. Prof.	37 yrs.	41 yrs.
Instructor	38 yrs.	42 yrs.

5. For each rank, how many years of service must be completed after one sabbatical leave before becoming eligible for another? *(Please write in the number of years opposite each rank.)*

Rank	Number of Years of Service
Professor	43 yrs.
Assoc. Prof.	44 yrs.
Ass't. Prof	45 yrs.
Instructor	46 yrs.

6. Are funds usually available so that a faculty member may go on sabbatical leave as soon as he becomes eligible?

   47 - 1 ☐ YES
   - 2 ☐ NO | IF NO, how many more years must he usually wait before taking sabbatical leave?

   48 _____
   (number of years)

7. Which of the following are required as conditions for receiving a sabbatical leave? *(Check as many as apply.)*

   49 - 1 ☐ Research project   - 5 ☐ Travel plan
   - 2 ☐ Writing project   - 6 ☐ Must leave campus
   - 3 ☐ Plan for study   - 7 ☐ No special requirement beyond service requirement
   - 4 ☐ Plan for teaching improvement

   - 8 ☐ Other *(describe):*

8. May the individual accept (a) full-time or (b) part-time teaching or (c) other paid employment during his sabbatical leave?

    a. Full-time teaching   50 - 1 ☐ YES   - 2 ☐ NO

    b. Part-time teaching   51 - 1 ☐ YES   - 2 ☐ NO

    c. Other paid employment   52 - 1 ☐ YES   - 2 ☐ NO

9. May the individual use sabbatical leave for study for an advanced degree?

    53 - 1 ☐ YES

       - 2 ☐ NO

10. What is the maximum length of time your institution will pay (a) full salary or (b) half salary to an individual on sabbatical leave? *(Check one space in each column.)*

	(a) Maximum Time on Full Salary	(b) Maximum Time on Half Salary
1 semester	54 - 1 ☐	55 - 1 ☐
2 semesters	- 2 ☐	- 2 ☐
1 quarter	- 3 ☐	- 3 ☐
2 quarters	- 4 ☐	- 4 ☐
3 quarters	- 5 ☐	- 5 ☐
4 quarters	- 6 ☐	- 6 ☐

11. If your institution's salary arrangements for faculty members on sabbatical leave do not fall in the categories in question 10, or if additional salary arrangements are available, *please describe:*

    56 - 1

12. When there is a choice between (a) and (b) below, which is the arrangement most frequently taken? *(Check one.)*

    a. 57 - 1 ☐ Full salary for the shorter period.

        About what percent choose this? ___%
                         58   59

    b. - 2 ☐ Half salary for the longer period.

        About what percent choose this? ___%
                         60   61

    c. - 3 ☐ No choice available

13. In any given year, about what proportion of the faculty who are eligible to take sabbatical leave *do not* do so? (E.g., 1 *out of 4, 10%, 1/3, etc.*)

          62   63

14. During sabbatical leave on *partial* pay, is the *employer* contribution to the retirement plan continued? *(Check one.)*

    64 - 1 ☐ On basis of full pay

       - 2 ☐ On basis of partial pay

       - 3 ☐ Employer contribution not continued

       - 4 ☐ Do not have retirement plan

15. Are the following group insurance coverages continued during sabbatical leaves? *(Check one box for each coverage.)*

	Yes	No	Do Not Have Plan
a. Basic Hospital Surgical (E.g., Blue Cross- Blue Shield)	65 - 1 ☐	- 2 ☐	- 3 ☐
b. Group Life Insurance	66 - 1 ☐	- 2 ☐	- 3 ☐
c. Group Major Medical	67 - 1 ☐	- 2 ☐	- 3 ☐
d. Group Disa- bility Income	68 - 1 ☐	- 2 ☐	- 3 ☐

16. Is the faculty member obligated to return to his position after taking a sabbatical leave?

    69 - 1 ☐ NO

       - 2 ☐ YES   IF YES, is there a specified length of time he must then stay?

                - 3 ☐ NO

                - 4 ☐ YES   IF YES, how long?

                         70 ___
                           (number of years)

17. Please describe any changes your institution plans to make in its sabbatical leave program in the next few years.

    71 - 1

18. Please check the phrase which best describes your view of the contribution your sabbatical leave program makes to *recruiting* and *retaining* faculty.

Recruiting

    72 - 1 ☐ Substantial contribution

       - 2 ☐ Moderate contribution

       - 3 ☐ Negligible contribution

Retaining

       - 4 ☐ Substantial contribution

       - 5 ☐ Moderate contribution

       - 6 ☐ Negligible contribution

B. OTHER LEAVES WITH PAY

Name of Institution: _____

19. For which of the following purposes does the institution grant leaves of absence with pay (other than sabbatical) when funds are from university or college resources (i.e., funds not provided through special grants or contracts)? *(Check as many as apply.)*

73 - 1 ☐ Research   - 7 ☐ NONE GRANTED

- 2 ☐ Teaching Improvement

- 3 ☐ Study

- 4 ☐ Travel

- 5 ☐ Writing

- 6 ☐ Other *(describe):*

20. For which of the following purposes does the institution grant leaves of absence with pay *in the summer? (Check as many as apply.)*

74 - 1 ☐ Research   - 7 ☐ NONE GRANTED

- 2 ☐ Teaching Improvement

- 3 ☐ Study

- 4 ☐ Travel

- 5 ☐ Writing

- 6 ☐ Other *(describe):*

21. For which of the following purposes does the institution grant leaves of absence with pay (other than sabbatical) when funds are from special grants or contracts? *(Check as many as apply.)*

75 - 1 ☐ Research   - 7 ☐ NONE GRANTED

- 2 ☐ Teaching Improvement

- 3 ☐ Study

- 4 ☐ Travel

- 5 ☐ Writing

- 6 ☐ Other *(describe):*

22. Does your institution supplement outside fellowships or other grants received by the individual to make it feasible for him to accept such grants?

76 - 1 ☐ NO

- 2 ☐ YES

23. Which of the following faculty ranks are eligible for leaves of absence with pay (other than sabbatical) when (a) funds are from university or college resources and (b) funds are from special grants or contracts? *(Check each eligible rank under (a) and (b).)*

	(a) When funds are from university or college resources	(b) When funds are from special grants or contracts
Professor	77 - 1 ☐	78 - 1 ☐
Assoc. Prof.	- 2 ☐	- 2 ☐
Ass't. Prof.	- 3 ☐	- 3 ☐
Instructor	- 4 ☐	- 4 ☐

24. Is the faculty member obligated to return after a leave of absence with pay (other than sabbatical)?

79 - 1 ☐ NO

- 2 ☐ YES   IF YES, is there a specified length of time he must then stay?

- 3 ☐ NO   80 - 2

- 4 ☐ YES   IF YES, how   1   6
long?

7 _____
(number of years)

25. Please describe any changes your institution plans to make in its program for leaves with pay other than sabbatical in the next five years.

8 - 1

26. Please check the phrase that best describes your view of the contribution your leave of absence with pay (other than sabbatical) program makes to *recruiting* and *retaining* faculty.

Recruiting

9 - 1 ☐ Substantial contribution

- 2 ☐ Moderate contribution

- 3 ☐ Negligible contribution

Retaining

- 4 ☐ Substantial contribution

- 5 ☐ Moderate contribution

- 6 ☐ Negligible contribution

C. LEAVES OF ABSENCE WITHOUT PAY

27. What purposes are recognized as (a) justifying leaves without pay and (b) what is the maximum period of time for which leave without pay is granted for each purpose? *(Please check as many as apply under (a) and circle the maximum period under (b).)*

(a) Purpose of Leave	(b) Maximum time granted Semesters or Quarters
10 - ☐ Study for degree	1 2 3 4 5 6 / 1 2 3 4 5 6 7 8 9 x
11 - ☐ Thesis writing or research	1 2 3 4 5 6 / 1 2 3 4 5 6 7 8 9 x
12 - ☐ Postdoctoral research	1 2 3 4 5 6 / 1 2 3 4 5 6 7 8 9 x
13 - ☐ Teaching elsewhere in U.S.	1 2 3 4 5 6 / 1 2 3 4 5 6 7 8 9 x
14 - ☐ Teaching outside U.S.	1 2 3 4 5 6 / 1 2 3 4 5 6 7 8 9 x
15 - ☐ Government Service in U.S.	1 2 3 4 5 6 / 1 2 3 4 5 6 7 8 9 x
16 - ☐ U.S. Government Service (other than teaching) outside U.S.	1 2 3 4 5 6 / 1 2 3 4 5 6 7 8 9 x
17 - ☐ International Service	1 2 3 4 5 6 / 1 2 3 4 5 6 7 8 9 x
18 - ☐ Private Employment	1 2 3 4 5 6 / 1 2 3 4 5 6 7 8 9 x
19 - ☐ Other *(describe)*:	1 2 3 4 5 6 / 1 2 3 4 5 6 7 8 9 x

28. What faculty members are eligible for leaves without pay? *(Check as many as apply.)*

20 - 1 ☐ Professor   - 4 ☐ Instructor
- 2 ☐ Assoc. Prof.   - 5 ☐ Other *(describe)*:
- 3 ☐ Ass't. Prof.

29. Is there a minimum period of service required before the first leave without pay may be granted?

21 - 1 ☐ NO
- 2 ☐ YES   IF YES, what is this period? _____
                                                    22

30. Is there a formal limit on the frequency with which leaves of absence without pay are granted?

23 - 1 ☐ NO
- 2 ☐ YES   IF YES, state limit: _____
                                                    24

31. Does a leave of absence without pay postpone the consideration of salary increases and promotion for an individual?

25 - 1 ☐ YES
- 2 ☐ NO
- 3 ☐ Sometimes

32. Is a faculty member obligated to return after a leave without pay?

26 - 1 ☐ NO
- 2 ☐ YES   IF YES, how long must he remain?

_____
        27

33. Are the *employer* contributions to the insured plans below made (a) for full-time faculty not on leave and (b) for faculty on leave without pay? *(If you have the plan, check under both of columns a and b; if you do not have the plan check under column c.)*

	If you have this plan:				
	(a) Does Employer Contribute to Plan for Faculty Not on Leave?		(b) Does Employer Contribute if Faculty Member is on Leave Without Pay?		(c) Do Not Have This Plan
Type of Plan	YES	NO	YES	NO	
Retirement	28 - 1 ☐	- 2 ☐	- 3 ☐	- 4 ☐	- 5 ☐
Group Life	29 - 1 ☐	- 2 ☐	- 3 ☐	- 4 ☐	- 5 ☐
Basic Hosp.-Surgical	30 - 1 ☐	- 2 ☐	- 3 ☐	- 4 ☐	- 5 ☐
Major Medical	31 - 1 ☐	- 2 ☐	- 3 ☐	- 4 ☐	- 5 ☐
Disability (temporary)	32 - 1 ☐	- 2 ☐	- 3 ☐	- 4 ☐	- 5 ☐
Disability (permanent)	33 - 1 ☐	- 2 ☐	- 3 ☐	- 4 ☐	- 5 ☐

34. Please describe any change your institution plans to make in its program for leaves without pay in the next five years.

34 - 1

35. Please check the phrase that best describes your view of the contribution your program of leaves without pay makes to *recruiting* and *retaining* faculty members.

Recruiting
35 - 1 ☐ Substantial contribution
- 2 ☐ Moderate contribution
- 3 ☐ Negligible contribution

Retaining
- 4 ☐ Substantial contribution
- 5 ☐ Moderate contribution
- 6 ☐ Negligible contribution

D. GENERAL QUESTIONS

36. For the 1962-63 academic year, how many faculty members do you estimate will have taken leave of absence? *(Write in the number of faculty members taking each type of leave.)*

Type of Leave	Number of Faculty
Sabbatical	36 ___ 38
Other leave with pay a. with college funds	39 ___ 41
b. with grant or contract funds	42 ___ 44
Without pay	45 ___ 47
Total number of faculty who took leave of absence	___

37. Previous questions have been asked about the frequency with which the several types of leaves may be taken. Do you have rules that govern the frequency of the various types of leaves combined?

    48 - 1 ☐ NO

    - 2 ☐ YES   IF YES, *please describe.*

38. Are limits placed on the number of persons who may be on leave from a given department at any one time?

    49 - 1 ☐ NO

    - 2 ☐ YES   IF YES, *describe the limits.*

39. When more persons desire to be away than can be allowed, what criteria are used in determining priorities? *(Describe.)*

40. Who reviews and decides upon requests for sabbatical and other leaves of absence?

Name of Institution: _____

41. If your institution has a fixed period within which tenure must be determined, does time on leave of absence count in this period?

    50 - 1 ☐ YES

    - 2 ☐ NO

    - 3 ☐ Question not applicable

42. What provisions are made for carrying on work of a department during the absence on leave of staff members? *(Check as many as apply.)*

    51 - 1 ☐ A temporary replacement is hired

    - 2 ☐ Extra work is assumed by remaining staff

    - 3 ☐ In some departments staff large enough to permit some to be away

    - 4 ☐ Department program is reduced

    - 5 ☐ Other *(describe):*

43. Please indicate briefly (a) the general purposes of your faculty leave of absence program (with and without pay), (b) any significant problems experienced in connection with it, and (c) any important features in your program not covered by other questions of this section. *(Attach additional sheets if necessary.)*

    (a) *General Purposes:*

    (b) *Significant Problems:*

(over)

(c) Important Special Features:

If you have published materials describing the leave of absence program at your institution, please send us a copy of each under separate cover, listing below what is being sent.

AAC/TIAA, 730 Third Ave.,
New York 17, New York

SECTION 6 - FACULTY CLUB

Name of Institution: _____

Your Name and Position: _____

What is the name and position of the person (if other than yourself) to whom further questions on the faculty club should be addressed?

1. Does your institution have a building or other space used as a club or as social rooms for the faculty or for faculty and other staff members?

   52 - 1 ☐ NO | IF NO, *please skip to question 13.*
   - 2 ☐ YES | IF YES, *please answer the following questions.*

2. What services does this facility provide? (*Please check as many as apply.*)

   53 - 1 ☐ Dining room (table service)
   - 2 ☐ Private dining rooms
   - 3 ☐ Cafeteria or lunch counter
   - 4 ☐ Coffee break facilities
   - 5 ☐ Bar for alcoholic beverages
   - 6 ☐ Reading room
   - 7 ☐ Lounge for members and guests
   - 8 ☐ Separate public rooms for men and women
   - 9 ☐ Billiard room
   54 - 1 ☐ Bowling alley
   - 2 ☐ Game room
   - 3 ☐ Gymnasium
   - 4 ☐ Tennis courts
   - 5 ☐ Swimming pool
   - 6 ☐ Library
   - 7 ☐ Conference rooms

3. Does this facility have sleeping quarters for guests?

   55 - 1 ☐ NO
   - 2 ☐ YES | IF YES, how many rooms are available?

   _____
   56 (number of rooms) 58

4. Does this facility have living quarters for single faculty members?

   59 - 1 ☐ NO
   - 2 ☐ YES | IF YES, how many rooms are available?

   _____
   60 (number of rooms) 62

5. Is this facility generally considered *adequate* or *inadequate* in the following respects? (*Check the appropriate response for each item.*)

Item	Adequate	Inadequate	Not considered important
Size	63 - 1 ☐	- 2 ☐	- 3 ☐
Location	64 - 1 ☐	- 2 ☐	- 3 ☐
Guest facilities	65 - 1 ☐	- 2 ☐	- 3 ☐
Dining facilities	66 - 1 ☐	- 2 ☐	- 3 ☐
Space for recreation	67 - 1 ☐	- 2 ☐	- 3 ☐
Space for meetings	68 - 1 ☐	- 2 ☐	- 3 ☐

6. Does the college or university make a financial contribution to the operation of this facility? (*Check as many as apply.*)

   69 - 1 ☐ Makes an annual dollar contribution.
   - 2 ☐ Provides building or rooms.
   - 3 ☐ Provides utilities.
   - 4 ☐ Provides operating personnel.
   - 5 ☐ Other (*describe*):

7. Is this facility organized as a faculty club?

   70 - 1 ☐ NO | IF NO, *please skip to question 13.*
   - 2 ☐ YES | IF YES, *please answer the following questions.*

8. Does the club admit both men and women as members? *(Check one.)*

71 - 1 ☐ Both men and women

- 2 ☐ Men only

- 3 ☐ Women only

9. Does the club accept as members persons who are not members of the faculty?

72 - 1 ☐ NO

- 2 ☐ YES   IF YES, what non-faculty groups are eligible? *(Describe)*

10. How many full-time faculty members belong to the faculty club?

73 (number of members) 75

11. What are the annual dues for faculty members? *(Give amount or formula in the space below.)*

76   78

12. Approximately what percent of the club's operating costs (including maintenance, interest, and depreciation) are covered by membership dues and operating receipts? *(Check the appropriate percentage category.)*

79 - 1 ☐ Below 50%

- 2 ☐ 50 - 79%

- 3 ☐ 80 - 99%

- 4 ☐ 100%

80 - 3
1   6

13. Does your institution have a "student union" facility?

7 - 1 ☐ NO

- 2 ☐ YES   IF YES, are its facilities used by the faculty in ways comparable to the use of a faculty club? *(Check one.)*

- 3 ☐ Not at all

- 4 ☐ Used to a small extent

- 5 ☐ Used quite a bit

- 6 ☐ Used a great deal

14. Please check the phrase which best describes your view of the contribution your faculty club makes to *recruiting* and *retaining* faculty.

Recruiting

8 - 1 ☐ Substantial contribution

- 2 ☐ Moderate contribution

- 3 ☐ Negligible contribution

Retaining

- 4 ☐ Substantial contribution

- 5 ☐ Moderate contribution

- 6 ☐ Negligible contribution

15. Please indicate briefly (a) the general purposes of your faculty club facility, (b) any significant problems experienced in connection with it, and (c) any important features not covered by other questions of this section. *(Attach additional sheets if necessary.)*

(a) General Purposes:

(b) Significant Problems:

(c) Important Special Features:

If you have published materials describing the faculty club facilities at your institution, please send us a copy of each under separate cover, listing below what is being sent.

AAC/TIAA, 730 Third Ave.,
New York 17, New York

SECTION 7 - FACULTY FAMILY EDUCATION

Name of Institution: _____

Your Name and Position: _____

_____

What is the name and position of the person (if other than yourself) to whom further questions on faculty children's education should be addressed?

_____

> *This section contains five parts:*
>
> A. Nursery School
> B. Elementary School
> C. Secondary School
> D. College Education
> E. Education of Adults
>
> *Please be sure to answer all five parts.*

A. NURSERY SCHOOL

1. Does your institution maintain a nursery school where faculty children receive preferential financial treatment?

   9 - 1 ☐ NO

   - 2 ☐ YES   ┌─────────────────────────────┐
   │ IF YES, (a) is there a tuition charge │
   │ for eligible faculty chil- │
   │ dren? │
   │ │
   │ - 3 ☐ YES │
   │ - 4 ☐ NO │
   │ │
   │ (b) approximately what percent │
   │ of nursery school age fac- │
   │ ulty children attend it? │
   │ │
   │   _____%   │
   │   10   11   │
   └─────────────────────────────┘

2. Does your institution make cash grants for tuition for nursery school for faculty children?

   12 - 1 ☐ YES

   - 2 ☐ NO

3. If you have any other preferential nursery school arrangements for faculty children, *please describe:*

   13 - 1

B. ELEMENTARY SCHOOL

4. Does your institution make cash grants for tuition for elementary school for faculty children?

   14 - 1 ☐ YES

   - 2 ☐ NO

5. If you have any other preferential elementary school arrangements for faculty children, *please describe:*

   15 - 1

C. SECONDARY SCHOOL

6. Does your institution make cash grants for tuition for secondary school for faculty children?

   16 - 1 ☐ YES

   - 2 ☐ NO

7. If you have any other preferential secondary school arrangements for faculty children, *please describe:*

   17 - 1

D. COLLEGE EDUCATION

8. Does your institution provide a waiver of tuition if a faculty child attends your own institution?

   18 - 1 ☐ NO

   - 2 ☐ YES   ┌─────────────────────────────┐
   │ IF YES, what amount and percent of │
   │ your *annual tuition* is waived for faculty │
   │ children? *(Answer both a and b.)* │
   │ │
   │ a. Amount of annual tuition waived │
   │ │
   │ $_____   │
   │   19   22   │
   │ │
   │ b. Percent of annual tuition waived │
   │ │
   │   _____%   │
   │   23   25   │
   └─────────────────────────────┘

9. Does your institution belong to the Tuition Exchange, Inc.?

   26 - 1 ☐ YES

   - 2 ☐ NO

10. Does your institution provide cash grants for undergraduate college tuition of faculty children?

27 - 1 ☐ NO

   - 2 ☐ YES   IF YES, is the amount of the grant: *(Check as many as apply.)*

    - 3 ☐ Less than your own annual tuition.

    - 4 ☐ Equal to the amount of tuition to be paid up to the amount of your own tuition, which is

$$\$\ \underline{\hphantom{28}}_{28}\ \underline{\hphantom{31}}_{31}.$$

    - 5 ☐ Greater than your own tuition if tuition to be paid is greater, but not more than

$$\$\ \underline{\hphantom{32}}_{32}\ \underline{\hphantom{35}}_{35}.$$

    - 6 ☐ A specified annual dollar amount. *(State amount.)*

$$\$\ \underline{\hphantom{36}}_{36}\ \underline{\hphantom{39}}_{39}$$

11. If you plan to change your program of aid for the education of faculty members' children during the next five years, *please describe the changes contemplated:*

40 - 1

12. Please check the phrase which best describes your view of the contribution your faculty children's education program makes to *recruiting* and *retaining* faculty.

Recruiting

41 - 1 ☐ Substantial contribution

  - 2 ☐ Moderate contribution

  - 3 ☐ Negligible contribution

Retaining

  - 4 ☐ Substantial contribution

  - 5 ☐ Moderate contribution

  - 6 ☐ Negligible contribution

E. EDUCATION OF ADULTS

13. May a member of the faculty attend your institution's classes without tuition charge? *(Check one.)*

42 - 1 ☐ NO

  - 2 ☐ YES, as auditor only

  - 3 ☐ YES, either as auditor or for credit

14. May the spouse of a faculty member attend your institution's classes without tuition charge? *(Check one.)*

43 - 1 ☐ NO

  - 2 ☐ YES, as auditor only

  - 3 ☐ YES, either as auditor or for credit

15. Please indicate briefly (a) the general objectives of your faculty children's education program, (b) any significant problems experienced in connection with it, and (c) any important features in your program not covered by other questions of this section.

(a) General Objectives:

(b) Significant Problems:

(c) Important Special Features:

If you have published materials describing the faculty children's education program at your institution, or the program for faculty members and spouses, please send us a copy of each under separate cover, listing below what is being sent.

AAC/TIAA, 730 Third Ave.,
New York 17, New York

SECTION 8 - FACULTY PARKING

Name of Institution: _____

Your Name and Position: _____

What is the name and position of the person (if other than yourself) to whom further questions on faculty parking should be addressed?

_____

1. What types of parking space, located on your institution's premises, are available to faculty members? *(Please check as many as apply. Indicate the monthly charges opposite the item. Write* free *if no charge is made. Also check whether facility is outdoor or garage.)*

Type	Range of Monthly Charge	Location Out-door	Garage
44 - 1 ☐ Space reserved for faculty	$ _____ 45 46	49 - 1 ☐	- 3 ☐
- 2 ☐ Space also open to public or students	$ _____ 47 48	- 2 ☐	- 4 ☐
- 3 ☐ No space provided	IF NO, *please skip to question 4.*		

2. If space is reserved for faculty, is it: *(Check one.)*

   50 - 1 ☐ Reserved by general area.

   - 2 ☐ Reserved by assigned stalls.

   If reserved by assignments, what criteria are used in determining priorities? *(Describe:)*

3. Approximately how many faculty automobiles can be accommodated by the spaces provided?

   _____
   51   (number of autos)   54

4. How many automobiles would be accommodated if faculty parking were to be adequate?

   _____
   55   (number of autos)   58

5. Are parking facilities available to persons visiting faculty members? *(Check as many as apply.)*

   59 - 1 ☐ In space open to general public

   - 2 ☐ In space reserved for visitors

   - 3 ☐ In space reserved for faculty

   - 4 ☐ No space provided

6. Is there an intra-campus bus service at your institution?

   60 - 1 ☐ NO

   - 2 ☐ YES | IF YES, is it provided free of charge?
   | | - 3 ☐ NO
   | | - 4 ☐ YES

7. During the next five years your institution's faculty parking facilities will probably: *(Please check the appropriate item)*

   61 - 1 ☐ Be expanded more rapidly than the faculty

   - 2 ☐ Be expanded about the same as the faculty

   - 3 ☐ Be expanded less rapidly than the faculty

   - 4 ☐ Remain about the same as now

   - 5 ☐ Be contracted

8. In general, do you now regard the parking facilities for your faculty as: *(Check one.)*

   62 - 1 ☐ Adequate

   - 2 ☐ Inadequate

9. Please indicate briefly (a) any significant problems with faculty parking and (b) any important features not covered by other questions in this section.

   (a) Significant Problems:

(over)

(b) Important Special Features:

If you have published material regarding the faculty parking facilities at your institution, please send a copy under separate cover, listing below what is being sent.

AAC/TIAA, 730 Third Ave.,
New York 17, New York

SECTION 9 - GENERAL CAMPUS FACILITIES AND EVENTS

Name of Institution: _____

Your Name and Position: _____

What is the name and position of the person (if other than yourself) to whom further questions on general campus facilities and events should be addressed?

1. Please check the following facilities as to (a) whether college has such a facility and, if so, (b) whether it is available to faculty and dependents, either free or charged for. *(Please check under the appropriate column or columns for each item listed at left.)*

A. RECREATION

	(a) Does College Have Facility	(b) Available to Faculty and Dependents		
		Faculty	Spouses	Children
1. Swimming Pool	63 -1 ☐ YES -2 ☐ NO	-3 ☐YES -4 ☐ Free ☐NO ☐ Chg.	-5 ☐ YES -6 ☐ Free ☐ NO ☐ Chg.	-7 ☐ YES -8☐ Free ☐ NO ☐ Chg.
2. Gymnasium	64 -1 ☐ YES -2 ☐ NO	-3 ☐YES -4 ☐ Free ☐NO ☐ Chg.	-5 ☐ YES -6 ☐ Free ☐ NO ☐ Chg.	-7 ☐ YES -8☐ Free ☐ NO ☐ Chg.
3. Tennis Courts	65 -1 ☐ YES -2 ☐ NO	-3 ☐YES -4 ☐ Free ☐NO ☐ Chg.	-5 ☐ YES -6 ☐ Free ☐ NO ☐ Chg.	-7 ☐ YES -8☐ Free ☐ NO ☐ Chg.
4. Handball Courts	66 -1 ☐ YES -2 ☐ NO	-3 ☐YES -4 ☐ Free ☐NO ☐ Chg.	-5 ☐ YES -6 ☐ Free ☐ NO ☐ Chg.	-7 ☐ YES -8☐ Free ☐ NO ☐ Chg.
5. Golf Course	67 -1 ☐ YES -2 ☐ NO	-3 ☐YES -4 ☐ Free ☐NO ☐ Chg.	-5 ☐ YES -6 ☐ Free ☐ NO ☐ Chg.	-7 ☐ YES -8☐ Free ☐ NO ☐ Chg.
6. Billiards	68 -1 ☐ YES -2 ☐ NO	-3 ☐YES -4 ☐ Free ☐NO ☐ Chg.	-5 ☐ YES -6 ☐ Free ☐ NO ☐ Chg.	-7 ☐ YES -8☐ Free ☐ NO ☐ Chg.
7. Bowling Alley	69 -1 ☐ YES -2 ☐ NO	-3 ☐YES -4 ☐ Free ☐NO ☐ Chg.	-5 ☐ YES -6 ☐ Free ☐ NO ☐ Chg.	-7 ☐ YES -8☐ Free ☐ NO ☐ Chg.
8. Other *(describe):*	70 -1	-3 ☐YES -4 ☐ Free ☐NO ☐ Chg.	-5 ☐ YES -6 ☐ Free ☐ NO ☐ Chg.	-7 ☐ YES -8☐ Free ☐ NO ☐ Chg.

B. SPECIAL EVENTS

It is assumed that the charge is the same as to the public unless the item under (b) is marked as Free or as Reduced Charge (R.C.).

	(a) Does College Have Event	(b) Available to Faculty and Dependents		
		Faculty	Spouses	Children
1. Athletic Events	71 -1 ☐ YES -2 ☐ NO	-3 ☐ YES -4 ☐ Free ☐ NO -5 ☐ R.C.	-6 ☐ YES -7 ☐ Free ☐ NO -8 ☐ R.C.	-9 ☐ YES -x☐ Free ☐ NO -y☐ R.C.
2. Student Drama	72 -1 ☐ YES -2 ☐ NO	-3 ☐ YES -4 ☐ Free ☐ NO -5 ☐ R.C.	-6 ☐ YES -7 ☐ Free ☐ NO -8 ☐ R.C.	-9 ☐ YES -x☐ Free ☐ NO -y☐ R.C.
3. Student Concerts	73 -1 ☐ YES -2 ☐ NO	-3 ☐ YES -4 ☐ Free ☐ NO -5 ☐ R.C.	-6 ☐ YES -7 ☐ Free ☐ NO -8 ☐ R.C.	-9 ☐ YES -x☐ Free ☐ NO -y☐ R.C.
4. Professional Drama	74 -1 ☐ YES -2 ☐ NO	-3 ☐ YES -4 ☐ Free ☐ NO -5 ☐ R.C.	-6 ☐ YES -7 ☐ Free ☐ NO -8 ☐ R.C.	-9 ☐ YES -x☐ Free ☐ NO -y☐ R.C.
5. Professional Concerts	75 -1 ☐ YES -2 ☐ NO	-3 ☐ YES -4 ☐ Free ☐ NO -5 ☐ R.C.	-6 ☐ YES -7 ☐ Free ☐ NO -8 ☐ R.C.	-9 ☐ YES -x☐ Free ☐ NO -y☐ R.C.
6. Special Lectures	76 -1 ☐ YES -2 ☐ NO	-3 ☐ YES -4 ☐ Free ☐ NO -5 ☐ R.C.	-6 ☐ YES -7 ☐ Free ☐ NO -8 ☐ R.C.	-9 ☐ YES -x☐ Free ☐ NO -y☐ R.C.
7. Other *(describe):*	77 -1	-3 ☐ YES -4 ☐ Free ☐ NO -5 ☐ R.C.	-6 ☐ YES -7 ☐ Free ☐ NO -8 ☐ R.C.	-9 ☐ YES -x☐ Free ☐ NO -y☐ R.C.

C. HEALTH SERVICES *(Please check under the appropriate column or columns for each item listed at left.)*

80 - 4
1   6

	(a) Does College Have Service	(b) Available to Faculty and Dependents		
		Faculty	Spouses	Children
1. Doctor's Consultation	7 -1 ☐ YES -2 ☐ NO	-3 ☐ YES -4 ☐ Free ☐ NO ☐ Chg.	-5 ☐ YES -6 ☐ Free ☐ NO ☐ Chg.	-7 ☐ YES -8 ☐ Free ☐ NO ☐ Chg.
2. Emergency Medical Treatment	8 -1 ☐ YES -2 ☐ NO	-3 ☐ YES -4 ☐ Free ☐ NO ☐ Chg.	-5 ☐ YES -6 ☐ Free ☐ NO ☐ Chg.	-7 ☐ YES -8 ☐ Free ☐ NO ☐ Chg.
3. Regular Medical Treatment	9 -1 ☐ YES -2 ☐ NO	-3 ☐ YES -4 ☐ Free ☐ NO ☐ Chg.	-5 ☐ YES -6 ☐ Free ☐ NO ☐ Chg.	-7 ☐ YES -8 ☐ Free ☐ NO ☐ Chg.
4. Annual Physical Exam	10 -1 ☐ YES -2 ☐ NO	-3 ☐ YES -4 ☐ Free ☐ NO ☐ Chg.	-5 ☐ YES -6 ☐ Free ☐ NO ☐ Chg.	-7 ☐ YES -8 ☐ Free ☐ NO ☐ Chg.
5. Infirmary or Hospital Bed	11 -1 ☐ YES -2 ☐ NO	-3 ☐ YES -4 ☐ Free ☐ NO ☐ Chg.	-5 ☐ YES -6 ☐ Free ☐ NO ☐ Chg.	-7 ☐ YES -8 ☐ Free ☐ NO ☐ Chg.

2. Discount Purchases

May faculty members make purchases through the institution at a discount rate?

12 - 1 ☐ NO

- 2 ☐ YES   IF YES, *please describe the arrangement:*

3. Please check the phrase that best describes your view of the contribution faculty use of facilities and events on your campus makes to *recruiting* and *retaining* faculty. *(Check one in each column.)*

Recruiting

13 - 1 ☐ Substantial contribution

- 2 ☐ Moderate contribution

- 3 ☐ Negligible contribution

Retaining

- 4 ☐ Substantial contribution

- 5 ☐ Moderate contribution

- 6 ☐ Negligible contribution

4. Please indicate (a) any significant problems experienced in connection with the provisions of facilities and events for faculty members and (b) any important features in your program not covered by other questions of this section.

(a) Significant Problems:

(b) Important Special Features:

If you have published materials describing the campus facilities and events available to faculty members and their dependents, please send us copies of each and list below what is being sent.

AAC/TIAA, 730 Third Ave.,
New York 17, New York

SECTION 10 - PRIVILEGES OF RETIRED FACULTY
AND FACULTY WIDOWS

Name of Institution: _____

Your Name and Position: _____

What is the name and position of the person (if other than
yourself) to whom further questions on privileges of retired faculty should be addressed?

_____

1. Please check the availability (and charges, if any) of the following privileges for retired faculty members:

				Charge, if Available		
	Available to Retired Faculty		Free	Same as Reg. Faculty	Lower Than Reg. Faculty	Higher Than Reg. Faculty
a. Faculty club membership	14 - 1 ☐ YES	- 2 ☐ NO	- 3 ☐	- 4 ☐	- 5 ☐	- 6 ☐
b. College gym facilities	15 - 1 ☐ YES	- 2 ☐ NO	- 3 ☐	- 4 ☐	- 5 ☐	- 6 ☐
c. Athletic events	16 - 1 ☐ YES	- 2 ☐ NO	- 3 ☐	- 4 ☐	- 5 ☐	- 6 ☐
d. Student dramatics	17 - 1 ☐ YES	- 2 ☐ NO	- 3 ☐	- 4 ☐	- 5 ☐	- 6 ☐
e. Student concerts	18 - 1 ☐ YES	- 2 ☐ NO	- 3 ☐	- 4 ☐	- 5 ☐	- 6 ☐
f. Professional dramatics	19 - 1 ☐ YES	- 2 ☐ NO	- 3 ☐	- 4 ☐	- 5 ☐	- 6 ☐
g. Professional concerts	20 - 1 ☐ YES	- 2 ☐ NO	- 3 ☐	- 4 ☐	- 5 ☐	- 6 ☐
h. Special lectures	21 - 1 ☐ YES	- 2 ☐ NO	- 3 ☐	- 4 ☐	- 5 ☐	- 6 ☐
i. Use of student union	22 - 1 ☐ YES	- 2 ☐ NO	- 3 ☐	- 4 ☐	- 5 ☐	- 6 ☐
j. Parking	23 - 1 ☐ YES	- 2 ☐ NO				
k. Library	24 - 1 ☐ YES	- 2 ☐ NO				
l. Other *(describe):*	25 - 1					

2. Please check the availability (and charges, if any) of the following health services of your institution for retired faculty members:

				Charge, if Available		
	Available to Retired Faculty		Free	Same as Reg. Faculty	Lower Than Reg. Faculty	Higher Than Reg. Faculty
a. Doctor's consultation	26 - 1 ☐ YES	- 2 ☐ NO	- 3 ☐	- 4 ☐	- 5 ☐	- 6 ☐
b. Emergency medical treatment	27 - 1 ☐ YES	- 2 ☐ NO	- 3 ☐	- 4 ☐	- 5 ☐	- 6 ☐
c. Regular medical treatment	28 - 1 ☐ YES	- 2 ☐ NO	- 3 ☐	- 4 ☐	- 5 ☐	- 6 ☐
d. Annual physical exam	29 - 1 ☐ YES	- 2 ☐ NO	- 3 ☐	- 4 ☐	- 5 ☐	- 6 ☐
e. Infirmary or hospital bed	30 - 1 ☐ YES	- 2 ☐ NO	- 3 ☐	- 4 ☐	- 5 ☐	- 6 ☐

3. Are the following facilities provided retired faculty members, if requested?

  a. Office facilities   31 - 1 ☐ YES   - 2 ☐ NO

  b. Laboratory facilities   32 - 1 ☐ YES   - 2 ☐ NO

  c. Research assistance   33 - 1 ☐ YES   - 2 ☐ NO

  d. Secretarial assistance   34 - 1 ☐ YES   - 2 ☐ NO

  e. Library desk space   35 - 1 ☐ YES   - 2 ☐ NO

4. Which available privileges and facilities listed in questions 1, 2, and 3, are *used most* by retired faculty members. *(Please list them by their identifying numbers, e.g., 1a, 1b, 2b, 3d, etc.)*

Items Used Most:

36 - 1

5. Please check the availability (and charges, if any) of the following privileges for *widows* of retired faculty members:

	Available to Widows of Retired Faculty	Free	Charge, if Available Same as Reg. Faculty	Lower Than Reg. Faculty	Higher Than Reg. Faculty
a. Faculty club membership	37 - 1 ☐ YES - 2 ☐ NO	- 3 ☐	- 4 ☐	- 5 ☐	- 6 ☐
b. College gym facilities	38 - 1 ☐ YES - 2 ☐ NO	- 3 ☐	- 4 ☐	- 5 ☐	- 6 ☐
c. Athletic events	39 - 1 ☐ YES - 2 ☐ NO	- 3 ☐	- 4 ☐	- 5 ☐	- 6 ☐
d. Student dramatics	40 - 1 ☐ YES - 2 ☐ NO	- 3 ☐	- 4 ☐	- 5 ☐	- 6 ☐
e. Student concerts	41 - 1 ☐ YES - 2 ☐ NO	- 3 ☐	- 4 ☐	- 5 ☐	- 6 ☐
f. Professional dramatics	42 - 1 ☐ YES - 2 ☐ NO	- 3 ☐	- 4 ☐	- 5 ☐	- 6 ☐
g. Professional concerts	43 - 1 ☐ YES - 2 ☐ NO	- 3 ☐	- 4 ☐	- 5 ☐	- 6 ☐
h. Special lectures	44 - 1 ☐ YES - 2 ☐ NO	- 3 ☐	- 4 ☐	- 5 ☐	- 6 ☐
i. Use of student union	45 - 1 ☐ YES - 2 ☐ NO	- 3 ☐	- 4 ☐	- 5 ☐	- 6 ☐
j. Parking	46 - 1 ☐ YES - 2 ☐ NO				
k. Library	47 - 1 ☐ YES - 2 ☐ NO				
l. Other *(describe):*	48 - 1				

6. Please check the availability (and charges, if any) of the following health services of your institution for *widows* of retired faculty members:

	Available to Widows of Retired Faculty	Free	Charge, if Available Same as Reg. Faculty	Lower Than Reg. Faculty	Higher Than Reg. Faculty
a. Doctor's consultation	49 - 1 ☐ YES - 2 ☐ NO	- 3 ☐	- 4 ☐	- 5 ☐	- 6 ☐
b. Emergency medical treatment	50 - 1 ☐ YES - 2 ☐ NO	- 3 ☐	- 4 ☐	- 5 ☐	- 6 ☐
c. Regular medical treatment	51 - 1 ☐ YES - 2 ☐ NO	- 3 ☐	- 4 ☐	- 5 ☐	- 6 ☐
d. Annual physical exam	52 - 1 ☐ YES - 2 ☐ NO	- 3 ☐	- 4 ☐	- 5 ☐	- 6 ☐
e. Infirmary or hospital bed	53 - 1 ☐ YES - 2 ☐ NO	- 3 ☐	- 4 ☐	- 5 ☐	- 6 ☐

7. Which available privileges and facilities listed in questions 5 and 6, (for retired faculty members' widows) are *used most* by retired faculty widows. *(Please list them by their identifying numbers, e.g., 5b, 6b, etc.)*

   Items Used Most:

   54 - 1

8. Is your institution planning to add any privileges and/or facilities for retired faculty and widows to those now offered?

   55 - 1 ☐ NO

   - 2 ☐ YES   IF YES, *please describe:*

9. Please indicate briefly (a) the general objectives of your program of providing privileges and facilities for retired faculty and widows, (b) any significant problems experienced in connection with this program, and (c) any important features in your program not covered by other questions of this section.   *(Attach additional sheets if needed.)*

   (a) General Objectives:

   (b) Significant Problems:

   (c) Important Special Features:

   If you have published materials describing the privileges of retired faculty and faculty widows at your institution, please send us a copy of each under separate cover, listing below what is being sent.

AAC/TIAA, 730 Third Ave.,
New York 17, New York

SECTION 11 - OTHER FACULTY BENEFITS

Name of Institution: _____

Your Name and Position: _____

A. Secretarial Help

1. Do you provide secretarial help for faculty members for the following purposes? *(Please check for each item.)*

	Yes	Some-times	No
a. Institutional business	56 - 1 ☐	- 2 ☐	- 3 ☐
Typing of: b. Research articles	57 - 1 ☐	- 2 ☐	- 3 ☐
c. Scholarly book mss.	58 - 1 ☐	- 2 ☐	- 3 ☐
d. Instructional material	59 - 1 ☐	- 2 ☐	- 3 ☐
e. Textbook mss.	60 - 1 ☐	- 2 ☐	- 3 ☐
f. Speeches and essays	61 - 1 ☐	- 2 ☐	- 3 ☐
g. Personal business	62 - 1 ☐	- 2 ☐	- 3 ☐
h. Other *(please describe):*	63 - 1 ☐		

B. Grants in Aid

2. Do you have a faculty "grants in aid" program not covered by the sections on travel, leaves of absence, or secretarial help?

   64 - 1 ☐ NO

   - 2 ☐ YES   IF YES, *please describe, giving purpose and type:*

C. Salary Continuation During Sickness

3. Are your institution's arrangements for continuation of salary during absence due to sickness or other disability (a) informal or (b) part of a stated institutional policy?

   65 - 1 ☐ Informal — Each case on its merits.

   > IF INFORMAL, *please skip to question 7.*

   - 2 ☐ Formal — Policy formally stated.

   > IF FORMAL, *please answer the following questions.*

4. When a faculty member is absent due to illness or other disability, what is the longest period of time during which your institution will continue salary or its equivalent? *(Please check the nearest applicable outside limit.)*

   66 - 1 ☐ 1 to 4 weeks

   - 2 ☐ 4 to 6 weeks

   - 3 ☐ 6 to 12 weeks

   - 4 ☐ 12 to 24 weeks

   - 5 ☐ Over 24 weeks

   - 6 ☐ To end of current semester

   - 7 ☐ To end of current academic year

   - 8 ☐ Other *(please describe):*

5. Does the length of time salary is continued during disability depend on the length of time the faculty member has been employed at your institution?

   67 - 1 ☐ NO

   - 2 ☐ YES   IF YES, please indicate below the service periods required for the prescribed duration of sick pay:

Years of Service	Duration of Sick Pay

6. Does your institution's salary continuation during disability include any arrangements for the tapering off of salary before salary finally terminates?

68 - 1 ☐ NO

  - 2 ☐ YES   IF YES, *please describe:*

7. Are the faculty members at your institution covered under state Workmen's Compensation laws?

69 - 1 ☐ YES

  - 2 ☐ NO

8. Please indicate briefly (a) any significant problems experienced in connection with salary continuation during sickness or other disability and (b) any important features in your program not covered by other questions in this section.

  (a) Significant Problems:

  (b) Important Special Features:

D. Additional Faculty Benefits

Please list below any faculty benefits provided by your institution (other than salary, retirement, and insurance) not previously mentioned in this questionnaire.

For each such benefit it would be helpful to have:

1. *General description of benefit.*

2. *Extent used by faculty members.*

3. *Cost to faculty member.*

4. *Objectives of the benefit and comments on your experience with it.*

70 - 1

80 - 5

If you have published materials describing the faculty benefits covered in this section, please send us a copy under separate cover, listing below what is being sent.

AAC/TIAA, 730 Third Ave.,
New York 17, New York

Name of Institution: _____

Your Name: _____

SECTION 12 - EXPERIENCE IN RECRUITING AND RETAINING FACULTY

To The President:

In summary, would you please comment on the following questions. Your observations will be most helpful in placing in proper perspective the benefits covered by this study.

(1) The ease or difficulty your institution has experienced during the last five years in recruiting and retaining staff members.

(2) The extent, if any, to which benefits covered by this questionnaire and available at your institution have been helpful in (a) recruiting and retaining staff members and (b) in attaining other institutional objectives.

(3) Which benefits you would consider developing or expanding for the future.

(Please attach additional sheets if necessary.)

I believe that this study will be of value to higher education in America and that your cooperation is of importance.

Sincerely,

Mark H. Ingraham, Director
Study for the AAC Commission on
Faculty and Staff Benefits

INSTITUTIONAL LISTINGS

THIS appendix gives in tabular form the replies, institution-by-institution, to some of the questions in the questionnaire as well as certain ratios based upon these replies. These are derived as follows:

Number of full-time faculty from first page of the questionnaire.

Ratio of faculty in college housing to full-time faculty from Section 1, Question 4. (Some of those listed may not have been full-time faculty members so the ratio is greater than the percentage of full-time faculty in such housing.)

First-mortgage home loans from Section 2, Question 1.

Second-mortgage home loans from Section 2, Question 2.

Ratio of faculty with college mortgage to full-time faculty from Section 2, Question 3. (Some of those listed may not have been full-time faculty members so the ratio is greater than the percentage of full-time faculty members having such mortgages.)

Personal loans from Section 3, Question 3.

% of faculty children tuition waivers from Section 7, Question 8.

Member Tuition Exchange, Inc. from Section 7, Question 9.

Cash grants for faculty children's tuitions from Section 7, Question 10.

Emergency medical treatment and *Annual physical examination* from Section 9, Subsection C.

Sabbatical leaves from Section 5, Question 1.

Maximum time sabbatical leave on full salary and *Maximum time sabbatical leave on half salary* from Section 5, Question 10.

Leaves with pay other than sabbatical from institution funds from Section 5, Question 19.

Ratio of faculty with leaves during year to full-time faculty from Section 5, Question 36. (Some of those listed may not have been full-time faculty members so the ratio is greater than the percentage of full-time faculty taking leaves; on the other hand, the denominator includes faculty members with research appointments for whom leaves often are not appropriate — hence at some universities this is decidedly an under-statement of the proportion of the teaching faculty which had leaves in 1962–63.)

Copies of the listings in this appendix were sent to the institutions and corrections have been incorporated. I trust this has increased the accuracy, though I fear that in a few cases it may have led to updating rather than correcting the data.

Name of Institution	No. of full-time faculty (Lay in Catholic insts.)	Ratio of faculty in college housing to full-time faculty	First-mortgage home loans	Second-mortgage home loans	Ratio of faculty with college mortgage to full-time faculty	Personal loans
ALABAMA						
1 Athens Col.	23	A	...	...	...	...
2 Auburn U.	622	...	...	...	...	...
3 Birmingham–Southern Col.	66	A	x	...	A	x
4 Florence St. Col.	90	B	...	...	...	...
5 Howard Col.	121	C	...	...	...	...
6 Judson Col.	23	Z	...	...	...	x
7 Livingston St. Col.	44	B	...	...	...	...
8 Oakwood Col.	27	Z	...	...	...	...
9 St. Bernard Col.	15	A	...	...	...	...
10 Spring Hill Col.	34	...	...	...	...	x
11 Stillman Col.	40	Z	x	...	C	x
12 Tuskegee Inst.	238	A	...	...	...	...
13 U. of Alabama	504	D	x	...	C	...
ALASKA						
1 U. of Alaska	226	A	...	...	...	...
ARIZONA						
1 Ariz. St. Col., Flagstaff	150	D	...	...	...	...
2 Ariz. St. U., Tempe	507	...	...	...	...	...
3 Grand Canyon Col.	24	...	...	...	...	x
4 U. of Arizona	1113	...	...	...	...	...
ARKANSAS						
1 Arkansas A & M Col.	60	A	...	...	...	...
2 Arkansas Col.	13	...	...	...	...	...
3 Arkansas Poly. Col.	69	A	...	...	...	...
4 Arkansas St. Col.	118	A	...	...	...	x
5 Col. of the Ozarks	30	Z	...	...	...	x
6 Harding Col.	76	A	...	...	...	...
7 Henderson S.T.C.	71	A	...	...	...	...
8 Hendrix Col.	41	C	...	...	...	...
9 Ouachita Baptist Col.	56	B	...	...	...	x
10 Southern St. Col.	62	A	...	...	...	...
11 U. of Arkansas	408	...	...	...	...	...
CALIFORNIA						
1 Calif. Inst. Tech.	250	D	...	...	...	...
2 Calif. St. Col. at Fullerton	126	...	...	...	...	...
3 Calif. St. Poly. Col.	327	D	...	...	...	...
4 Chapman Col.	46	C	...	...	...	...

x = Has program   B = 10% but < 20%   1S = 1 Semester, 2S = 2 Semesters
Z = 50% up   C = 5% but < 10%   1Q = 1 Quarter, etc.
A = 20% but < 50%   D = Some, but < 5%   ... = Either no program or no answer

Institution	% of fac. children tuition waivers	Member Tuition Exchange, Inc.	Cash grants for fac. children's tuitions	Emergency medical treatment	Annual physical examination	Sabbatical leaves	Max. time sab. leave on full salary	Max. time sab. leave on half salary	Leaves with pay other than sab. from inst. funds	Ratio of faculty with leaves during year to full-time faculty
ALA										
1	50	...	...	...	...	...	...	...	...	...
2	...	...	...	...	...	x	2Q	4Q	...	D
3	100	...	...	...	...	x	...	...	x	C
4	...	...	...	F	...	...	...	...	...	...
5	54	...	...	...	...	x	1S	2S	...	C
6	100	...	...	...	...	...	...	...	x	A
7	...	...	...	Fsc	...	...	...	...	...	...
8	...	...	x	Fscrw	...	x	2S	...	...	...
9	100	...	...	f	...	...	...	...	...	C
10	100	...	...	...	...	...	...	...	x	...
11	...	...	...	...	...	...	...	...	x	C
12	...	...	...	fscrw	fscrw	x	1S	2S	x	C
13	...	...	...	...	...	...	...	...	...	D
ALAS										
1	...	...	...	...	...	...	...	...	...	D
ARIZ										
1	...	...	...	F	...	x	1S	...	...	D
2	...	...	...	...	...	x	1S	...	...	C
3	100	...	...	Fscrw	...	...	...	...	x	D
4	68	...	...	..	...	x	1S	...	...	D
ARK										
1	...	..:	...	Fsc	...	...	...	...	...	D
2	96	...	...	Fsc	...	...	...	...	x	...
3	25	...	...	...	...	x	...	...	...	D
4	60	...	...	...	...	...	...	...	...	...
5	100	...	...	...	...	...	...	...	...	...
6	50	x	...	...	...	x	1S	2S	x	C
7	...	...	...	...	...	...	...	...	x	D
8	100	...	...	...	...	...	...	...	...	...
9	100	...	...	...	...	x	1S	2S	...	D
10	100	...	...	...	...	...	...	...	...	C
11	...	...	...	F	...	...	...	...	x	C
CAL										
1	100	...	...	f	f	...	...	...	x	C
2	...	...	...	F	...	x	1S	2S	...	D
3	...	...	...	F	...	x	2Q	4Q	...	D
4	50	...	...	fsc	...	x	1S	2S	...	C

F = Free to faculty
f = Available to faculty
s = Available to spouse

c = Available to children
r = Available to retired faculty
w = Available to widow

Name of Institution	No. of full-time faculty (Lay in Catholic insts.)	Ratio of faculty in college housing to full-time faculty	First-mortgage home loans	Second-mortgage home loans	Ratio of faculty with college mortgage to full-time faculty	Personal loans
CALIFORNIA						
5 Chico St. Col.	220	...	...	...	...	...
6 Claremont Men's Col.	44	B	...	...	...	...
7 Col. of the Holy Names	19	...	...	...	...	x
8 Col. of Notre Dame	12	...	...	...	...	...
9 Fresno St. Col.	327	...	...	...	...	...
10 Harvey Mudd Col.	43	B	...	...	...	...
11 Humboldt St. Col.	178	...	...	...	...	...
12 Immaculate Heart Col.	39	...	...	...	...	...
13 La Sierra Col.	62	B	...	...	...	x
14 La Verne Col.	31	...	x	...	B	x
15 Long Beach St. Col.	456	...	...	...	...	...
16 L.A. St. Col. App. Arts	580	...	...	...	...	...
17 Loyola U. of L.A.	58	...	x	x	C	x
18 Mills Col.	58	A	...	...	...	...
19 Mount St. Mary's Col.	39	...	...	...	...	x
20 Occidental Col.	90	C	x	...	...	x
21 Pacific Union Col.	78	A	...	...	...	...
22 Pasadena Col.	60	...	...	...	...	x
23 Pomona Col.	102	B	x	...	B	...
24 Sacramento St. Col.	293	...	...	...	...	...
25 St. Mary's Col. of Calif.	41	D	...	...	...	...
26 San Fernando Val. St. Col.	386	...	...	...	...	...
27 San Francisco Col. for Wo.	21	...	...	...	...	...
28 San Francisco St. Col.	616	...	...	...	...	...
29 San Jose St. Col.	797	...	...	...	...	...
30 Scripps Col.	24	C	...	...	...	...
31 Stanford U.	800	D	x	...	A	x
32 U. of California	5370	...	...	...	...	x
33 U. of the Pacific	135	...	...	...	...	...
34 U. of Redlands	91	...	...	...	...	x
35 U. of San Francisco	78	...	...	...	...	...
36 U. of Santa Clara	83	...	...	...	...	...
37 U. of Southern Calif.	858	...	...	...	...	...
38 Westmont Col.	30	...	...	...	...	...
39 Whittier Col.	102	...	...	...	...	...
COLORADO						
1 Adams St. Col.	96	B	...	...	...	...

x = Has program   B = 10% but < 20%   1S = 1 Semester, 2S = 2 Semesters
Z = 50% up   C = 5% but < 10%   1Q = 1 Quarter, etc.
A = 20% but < 50%   D = Some, but < 5%   ... = Either no program or no answer

Institution	% of fac. children tuition waivers	Member Tuition Exchange, Inc.	Cash grants for fac. children's tuitions	Emergency medical treatment	Annual physical examination	Sabbatical leaves	Max. time sab. leave on full salary	Max. time sab. leave on half salary	Leaves with pay other than sab. from inst. funds	Ratio of faculty with leaves during year to full-time faculty
CAL										
5	...	...	...	F	...	x	1S	2S	...	D
6	50	x	...	f	...	x	1S	2S	x	C
7	100	...	...	...	...	x	1S	2S	x	C
8	100	...	...	...	...	x	1S	2S	x	...
9	...	...	...	F	...	x	1S	2S	...	C
10	50	...	x	...	...	x	1S	2S	...	C
11	100	...	...	...	...	x	1S	2S	x	D
12	100	...	...	...	...	x	1S	...	...	C
13	25	...	x	f	...	x	1Q	...	x	B
14	100	...	...	...	...	x	...	2S	x	B
15	...	...	...	F	F	x	1S	2S	...	C
16	...	...	...	F	...	x	1S	2S	...	D
17	50	...	...	...	...	x	1S	2S	x	B
18	100	x	...	f	...	x	1S	2S	x	B
19	40	...	...	Fscrw	Fscrw	x	1S	2S	...	...
20	100	x	...	F	...	x	1S	2S	x	B
21	25	...	x	fscrw	...	x	1Q	...	x	B
22	60	...	...	...	...	...	...	...	x	...
23	50	...	x	...	...	x	1S	2S	...	C
24	...	...	...	...	..	x	1S	2S	...	D
25	100	...	...	F	...	x	1S	2S	...	...
26	...	...	...	Fsc	...	x	1S	2S	...	D
27	100	...	...	...	...	x	1S	2S	...	B
28	...	...	...	F	...	x	1S	2S	...	C
29	...	...	...	F	...	x	1S	2S	x	D
30	50	...	x	...	...	x	1S	2S	...	A
31	100	x	...	f	...	x	1Q	4Q	...	D
32	100	...	...	Fscrw	...	x	1S	...	x	C
33	90	x	...	...	...	x	1S	2S	...	D
34	100	x	...	F	...	x	1S	2S	...	D
35	50	...	...	Fr	f	x	1S	2S	...	C
36	100	...	...	...	...	x	1S	2S	x	D
37	100	x	...	f	...	x	1S	2S	...	D
38	100	...	...	F	...	x	1S	2S	...	B
39	100	...	x	fs	...	x	1S	2S	...	D
COLO										
1	...	...	...	Fsc	fsc	x	1Q	3Q	...	B

F = Free to faculty
f = Available to faculty
s = Available to spouse

c = Available to children
r = Available to retired faculty
w = Available to widow

Name of Institution	No. of full-time faculty (Lay in Catholic insts.)	Ratio of faculty in college housing to full-time faculty	First-mortgage home loans	Second-mortgage home loans	Ratio of faculty with college mortgage to full-time faculty	Personal loans
COLORADO						
2 Colorado Col.	89	C	...	...	...	...
3 Colorado Sch. of Mines	106	A	...	...	...	...
4 Colorado St. Col.	245	A	...	...	...	...
5 Colorado St. U.	490	C	...	...	...	...
6 Loretto Heights Col.	63	...	...	...	...	...
7 Regis Col.	26	...	x	x	...	x
8 U. of Colorado	569	C	x	...	D	...
9 U. of Denver	200	A	...	...	...	x
10 Western St. Col. of Colo.	70	A	...	...	...	...
CONNECTICUT						
1 Albertus Magnus Col.	9	...	...	...	...	...
2 Annhurst Col.	8	...	...	...	...	...
3 Connecticut Col.	102	Z	...	...	...	...
4 Fairfield U.	55	D	...	...	...	...
5 Quinnipiac Col.	48	D	...	...	...	...
6 St. Basil's Col.	5	A	...	...	...	x
7 St. Joseph Col.	30	...	...	...	...	...
8 Southern Conn. St. Col.	201	...	...	...	...	...
9 Trinity Col.	106	B	...	...	...	...
10 U. of Bridgeport	185	...	...	...	...	...
11 U. of Connecticut	727	A	...	...	...	...
12 Wesleyan U.	144	Z	x	...	B	...
13 Yale U.	1000	C	x	...	A	x
DELAWARE						
1 Delaware St. Col.	49	Z	...	...	...	...
2 U. of Delaware	214	B	x	...	Z	...
DISTRICT OF COLUMBIA						
1 American U.	239	...	...	...	...	...
2 Cath. U. of America	249	...	...	...	...	...
3 Dunbarton Col. of Holy Cross	18	...	...	...	...	...
4 Georgetown U.	483	...	...	...	D	x
5 George Washington U.	310	...	...	...	...	...
6 Howard U.	433	...	...	...	...	x
7 Trinity Col.	23	...	...	...	...	...
FLORIDA						
1 Barry Col.	11	...	...	...	...	...

x = Has program   B = 10% but < 20%   1S = 1 Semester, 2S = 2 Semesters
Z = 50% up   C = 5% but < 10%   1Q = 1 Quarter, etc.
A = 20% but < 50%   D = Some, but < 5%   ... = Either no program or no answer

Institution	% of fac. children tuition waivers	Member Tuition Exchange, Inc.	Cash grants for fac. children's tuitions	Emergency medical treatment	Annual physical examination	Sabbatical leaves	Max. time sab. leave on full salary	Max. time sab. leave on half salary	Leaves with pay other than sab. from inst. funds	Ratio of faculty with leaves during year to full-time faculty
COLO										
2	100	x	x	fscr	...	x	1S	2S	...	C
3	...	...	...	...	...	x	...	2S	...	...
4	...	...	...	F	F	x	...	...	...	B
5	...	...	...	...	...	x	...	...	...	C
6	50	...	...	F	...	x	1S	2S	...	D
7	90	...	...	F	...	...	...	...	x	D
8	...	...	...	F	...	...	...	...	x	B
9	70	...	...	fr	...	...	...	...	x	D
10	...	...	...	...	...	x	1Q	3Q	...	C
CONN										
1	50	...	...	F	...	...	...	...	x	B
2	100	...	...	F	...	...	...	...	...	...
3	100	...	x	Fscrw	...	...	...	...	x	B
4	100	...	...	Fsc	...	...	...	...	...	D
5	100	x	...	...	...	...	...	...	...	...
6	...	...	...	Fr	...	...	...	...	...	...
7	100	...	...	...	...	...	...	...	x	...
8	...	...	...	F	...	x	1S	2S	...	D
9	100	...	x	F	...	x	1S	2S	...	C
10	100	x	...	F	...	x	1S	2S	...	D
11	...	...	...	Fsc	F	x	1S	2S	x	C
12	...	...	x	Fscrw	...	x	1S	2S	...	B
13	...	...	x	F	F	x	...	...	...	B
DELA										
1	...	...	...	F	...	x	1S	2S	...	D
2	...	...	...	F	F	x	1S	2S	...	...
D C										
1	100	x	x	F	...	x	1S	2S	x	D
2	50	...	...	F	...	x	1S	2S	...	C
3	...	...	...	F	...	x	1S	2S	...	...
4	100	...	...	f	F	x	1S	2S	...	D
5	100	...	...	Fr	...	x	1S	2S	x	D
6	100	...	...	F	...	x	1S	2S	x	D
7	100	...	...	...	...	x	1S	2S	...	C
FLA										
1	100	...	...	F	...	...	...	...	...	...

F = Free to faculty
f = Available to faculty
s = Available to spouse

c = Available to children
r = Available to retired faculty
w = Available to widow

Name of Institution	No. of full-time faculty (Lay in Catholic insts.)	Ratio of faculty in college housing to full-time faculty	First-mortgage home loans	Second-mortgage home loans	Ratio of faculty with college mortgage to full-time faculty	Personal loans
FLORIDA						
2 Florida St. U.	591	...	...	...	...	...
3 Jacksonville U.	68	...	...	...	...	...
4 Rollins Col.	80	D	...	...	...	x
5 Stetson U.	97	C	...	...	...	...
6 U. of Florida	1057	...	...	...	...	...
7 U. of Miami	508	D	...	...	...	...
8 U. of South Florida	170	D	...	...	...	...
GEORGIA						
1 Atlanta U.	60	A	...	...	...	...
2 Berry Col.	46	Z	...	...	...	...
3 Brenau Col.	50	Z	...	...	...	...
4 Emory U.	482	C	...	...	...	...
5 Georgia Inst. Tech.	516	C	...	...	...	...
6 Mercer U.	86	Z	...	x	D	...
7 Morehouse Col.	52	A	...	...	...	...
8 North Georgia Col.	40	Z	...	...	...	...
9 Oglethorpe U.	24	Z	x	...	D	x
10 Savannah St. Col.	65	...	...	...	...	...
11 Shorter Col.	40	Z	...	...	...	...
12 Spelman Col.	45	A	...	...	...	x
13 U. of Georgia	692	D	...	...	...	...
14 Wesleyan Col.	46	C	...	...	...	...
15 Woman's Col. of Ga.	66	A	...	...	...	...
HAWAII						
1 Church Col. of Hawaii	52	A	...	...	...	x
2 U. of Hawaii	800	C	...	...	...	...
IDAHO						
1 Idaho St. Col.	235	D	...	...	...	...
2 Northwest Nazarene Col.	41	B	...	...	...	x
3 U. of Idaho	314	B	...	...	...	...
ILLINOIS						
1 Augustana Col.	86	B	x	...	B	...
2 Blackburn Col.	27	A	x	...	C	...
3 Bradley U.	199	D	x	...	C	...
4 Carthage Col.	42	Z	...	...	...	...
5 Col. of St. Francis	7	...	...	...	...	...
6 DePaul U.	187	...	...	...	...	x

x = Has program   B = 10% but < 20%   1S = 1 Semester, 2S = 2 Semesters
Z = 50% up   C = 5% but < 10%   1Q = 1 Quarter, etc.
A = 20% but < 50%   D = Some, but < 5%   ... = Either no program or no answer

Institution	% of fac. children tuition waivers	Member Tuition Exchange, Inc.	Cash grants for fac. children's tuitions	Emergency medical treatment	Annual physical examination	Sabbatical leaves	Max. time sab. leave on full salary	Max. time sab. leave on half salary	Leaves with pay other than sab. from inst. funds	Ratio of faculty with leaves during year to full-time faculty
FLA										
2	...	...	...	...	...	...	...	...	...	C
3	100	...	...	fsc	...	...	...	...	x	D
4	100	x	...	...	...	...	...	...	...	D
5	100	...	...	fscrw	...	...	...	...	x	D
6	...	x	...	...	...	...	...	...	...	C
7	75+	...	x	fsc	...	...	...	...	x	D
8	...	...	...	F	...	...	...	...	x	D
GA										
1	...	...	...	F	...	x	1S	2S	...	B
2	50	...	...	fsc	...	...	...	...	...	D
3	100	...	...	Fscrw	F	...	...	...	...	D
4	100	...	...	fscrw	...	...	...	...	x	D
5	...	...	...	F	...	...	...	...	x	D
6	94	...	x	fsc	...	x	...	3Q	x	C
7	100	...	...	fscrw	...	...	...	...	x	C
8	...	...	...	...	...	...	...	...	x	C
9	100	x	...	Fscr	...	...	...	...	...	...
10	...	...	...	...	F	...	...	...	...	D
11	100	x	...	Fsc	...	x	...	...	x	C
12	...	...	...	F	...	...	...	...	...	D
13	...	...	...	Fscr	...	...	...	...	x	D
14	100	x	...	Fr	...	...	...	...	x	...
15	...	...	...	...	...	...	...	...	x	D
HAW										
1	...	...	...	...	...	x	1S	2S	x	C
2	...	...	...	f	...	x	1S	2S	x	C
IDA										
1	...	...	...	...	...	x	...	2S	...	D
2	100	...	...	...	...	...	...	...	x	C
3	...	...	...	F	...	x	1S	2S	x	D
ILL										
1	100	x	...	Fscrw	...	x	1S	2S	x	D
2	100	...	x	...	...	x	1S	2S	...	C
3	100	x	...	...	...	x	1S	2S	...	C
4	100	...	...	...	...	...	...	...	x	D
5	100	...	...	F	...	...	...	...	...	...
6	100	...	...	f	...	...	...	...	x	D

F = Free to faculty
f = Available to faculty
s = Available to spouse

c = Available to children
r = Available to retired faculty
w = Available to widow

Name of Institution	No. of full-time faculty (Lay in Catholic insts.)	Ratio of faculty in college housing to full-time faculty	First-mortgage home loans	Second-mortgage home loans	Ratio of faculty with college mortgage to full-time faculty	Personal loans
ILLINOIS						
7 Eastern Illinois U.	267	D	...	...	...	...
8 Elmhurst Col.	58	A	...	...	...	...
9 Eureka Col.	24	C	...	x	D	x
10 George Williams Col.	37	...	...	...	...	x
11 Greenville Col.	27	B	...	...	...	...
12 Illinois Col.	32	C	...	...	...	...
13 Illinois Inst. Tech.	227	B	...	...	...	...
14 Illinois Wesleyan U.	81	B	...	x	D	...
15 Knox Col.	82	B	...	...	...	x
16 Lake Forest Col.	65	A	x	...	D	...
17 Loyola U.	310	...	...	x	D	x
18 McKendree Col.	17	...	...	...	...	...
19 Millikin U.	70	C	...	...	...	...
20 Monmouth Col.	52	B	...	...	...	...
21 Mundelein Col.	28	...	...	...	...	...
22 North Central Col.	55	B	x	...	...	...
23 Northern Illinois U.	527	...	...	...	...	...
24 Northwestern U.	730	B	x	x	A	x
25 Principia Col.	47	Z	...	x	B	x
26 Quincy Col.	28	A	x	x	B	x
27 Rockford Col.	43	A	...	...	...	...
28 Roosevelt U.	152	...	...	...	...	...
29 Rosary Col.	22	...	...	...	...	x
30 St. Procopius Col.	18	...	...	...	...	...
31 St. Xavier Col.	40	...	...	...	...	x
32 Shimer Col.	24	A	x	...	C	...
33 Southern Illinois U.	778	B	...	...	...	...
34 U. of Chicago	1167	A	...	x	B	x
35 U. of Illinois	2912	D	...	...	...	...
36 Western Illinois U.	256	...	...	...	...	...
37 Wheaton Col.	125	C	x	...	B	x
INDIANA						
1 Anderson Col.	62	B	...	x	D	x
2 Ball S.T.C.	287	D	...	...	...	...
3 Bethel Col., Inc.	19	...	...	...	...	...
4 Butler U.	124	...	...	x	C	...
5 Concordia Sr. Col.	36	Z	...	...	...	...
6 DePauw U.	159	A	x	...	C	...

x = Has program   B = 10% but < 20%   1S = 1 Semester, 2S = 2 Semesters
Z = 50% up   C = 5% but < 10%   1Q = 1 Quarter, etc.
A = 20% but < 50%   D = Some, but < 5%   ... = Either no program or no answer

Institution	% of fac. children tuition waivers	Member Tuition Exchange, Inc.	Cash grants for fac. children's tuitions	Emergency medical treatment	Annual physical examination	Sabbatical leaves	Max. time sab. leave on full salary	Max. time sab. leave on half salary	Leaves with pay other than sab. from inst. funds	Ratio of faculty with leaves during year to full-time faculty
ILL										
7	...	...	...	f	...	x	2Q	3Q	...	C
8	100	x	...	F	...	...	...	...	...	D
9	50	...	...	fscrw	...	x	1S	2S	...	D
10	50	...	...	...	...	x	...	3Q	...	C
11	100	...	...	...	...	x	1S	2S	...	B
12	100	x	...	...	...	x	1S	...	x	D
13	100	x	...	Fscr	...	...	...	...	...	D
14	100	...	x	F	Fs	x	1S	2S	x	C
15	100	x	...	Fscrw	...	x	1S	2S	...	D
16	100	x	x	F	...	x	1Q	3Q	x	C
17	100	...	...	F	...	...	...	...	x	...
18	50	...	...	F	...	...	...	...	...	C
19	100	...	...	...	...	...	...	...	...	...
20	100	x	...	...	...	x	1Q	3Q	...	C
21	...	...	...	...	...	x	1S	2S	...	...
22	50	...	...	f	...	x	1S	2S	x	D
23	...	...	...	...	...	x	1S	2S	...	...
24	50	...	...	...	...	...	...	...	x	C
25	20	...	...	...	...	x	1Q	3Q	x	C
26	67	...	...	...	...	...	...	...	...	...
27	100	x	...	F	...	x	1S	2S	...	D
28	100	x	...	F	f	...	...	...	x	C
29	100	...	x	...	...	...	...	...	...	...
30	50	...	...	F	...	...	...	...	...	...
31	100	...	...	Fr	...	...	...	...	...	...
32	100	x	...	...	...	x	...	...	...	C
33	...	...	...	...	...	x	$\frac{1}{2}$Q	3Q	x	C
34	50	...	x	fscrw	...	...	...	...	x	...
35	...	...	...	F	...	x	1S	2S	...	D
36	...	...	...	F	...	x	2Q	3Q	...	C
37	100	...	...	fscrw	...	...	...	...	x	C
IND										
1	100	...	...	f	...	x	1S	2S	x	C
2	...	...	...	f	...	x	1Q	3Q	...	B
3	15	...	...	fsc	...	x	1S	2S	x	B
4	...	x	...	Fscrw	...	x	1S	2S	...	D
5	100	...	...	Fsc	...	x	2Q	4Q	x	B
6	100	...	x	...	...	x	1S	2S	...	B

F = Free to faculty   c = Available to children
f = Available to faculty   r = Available to retired faculty
s = Available to spouse   w = Available to widow

Name of Institution	No. of full-time faculty (Lay in Catholic insts.)	Ratio of faculty in college housing to full-time faculty	First-mortgage home loans	Second-mortgage home loans	Ratio of faculty with college mortgage to full-time faculty	Personal loans
INDIANA						
7　Earlham Col.	72	B	...	x	A	...
8　Evansville Col.	97	...	...	...	...	x
9　Franklin Col. of Ind.	40	A	x	...	B	...
10　Grace Theol. Sem. & Col.	20	...	...	...	...	x
11　Hanover Col.	49	Z	...	x	C	x
12　Huntington Col.	33	A	...	...	...	x
13　Indiana Central Col.	50	C	...	...	...	...
14　Indiana St. Col.	256	C	...	...	...	...
15　Indiana U.	1495	C	...	...	...	...
16　Manchester Col.	64	A	...	...	...	...
17　Marion Col., Marion	27	D	...	...	...	x
18　Oakland City Col.	25	C	...	...	...	...
19　Purdue U.	1773	C	...	...	...	...
20　St. Mary-of-the-Woods Col.	13	Z	...	...	...	...
21　St. Mary's Col.	42	...	...	...	...	...
22　Taylor U.	56	A	...	...	...	...
23　U. of Notre Dame	398	D	...	...	...	x
24　Valparaiso U.	189	C	x	...	B	...
25　Wabash Col.	51	A	x	x	B	x
IOWA						
1　Briar Cliff Col.	7	...	...	...	...	x
2　Buena Vista Col.	36	...	...	...	...	...
3　Clarke Col.	9	...	...	...	...	...
4　Coe Col.	61	A	x	...	B	...
5　Cornell Col.	68	A	x	...	A	...
6　Drake U.	207	C	...	...	...	...
7　Grinnell Col.	100	B	...	x	B	...
8　Iowa St. U. Sci. & Tech.	682	B	...	...	...	...
9　Iowa Wesleyan Col.	42	Z	...	...	...	...
10　Loras Col.	46	B	...	...	...	x
11　Luther Col.	75	A	x	x	B	x
12　Marycrest Col.	20	...	...	...	...	x
13　Morningside Col.	52	A	...	...	...	...
14　Parsons Col.	68	C	...	x	A	x
15　Simpson Col.	48	Z	...	x	D	...
16　St. Col. of Iowa	261	...	...	...	...	...
17　State U. of Iowa	729	B	...	...	...	...

x = Has program　　　B = 10% but < 20%　　　1S = 1 Semester, 2S = 2 Semesters
Z = 50% up　　　　　　C = 5% but < 10%　　　1Q = 1 Quarter, etc.
A = 20% but < 50%　　D = Some, but < 5%　　... = Either no program or no answer

Institution	% of fac. children tuition waivers	Member Tuition Exchange, Inc.	Cash grants for fac. children's tuitions	Emergency medical treatment	Annual physical examination	Sabbatical leaves	Max. time sab. leave on full salary	Max. time sab. leave on half salary	Leaves with pay other than sab. from inst. funds	Ratio of faculty with leaves during year to full-time faculty
IND										
7	100	...	x	fscrw	...	x	...	...	x	B
8	100	...	...	F	...	...	...	...	x	D
9	100	x	...	...	...	x	1S	2S	x	C
10	100	...	...	...	...	x	1S	2S	...	C
11	100	x	x	fscrw	...	x	...	...	...	...
12	14	...	...	fsc	...	x	...	2S	...	...
13	100	x	...	F	...	x	1S	2S	...	C
14	...	...	...	F	...	x	1S	2S	x	C
15	...	...	...	...	...	x	1S	2S	...	C
16	100	...	...	fsc	...	x	1Q	2Q	x	C
17	...	...	...	fscr	...	x	1S	2S	x	D
18	100	...	...	...	...	x	2S	...	x	...
19	100	...	...	F	...	x	1S	2S	...	D
20	100	...	...	F	...	...	...	...	x	C
21	100	...	...	F	...	x	1S	2S	...	D
22	100	...	...	F	...	x	1S	2S	x	C
23	67	...	...	...	...	...	...	...	x	C
24	100	x	...	frw	...	x	1S	2S	x	C
25	100	x	x	...	...	x	1S	2S	...	B
IOWA										
1	100	...	...	F	...	x	1S	2S	...	...
2	100	...	...	...	...	...	...	...	...	...
3	...	...	...	F	...	x	1S	2S	x	A
4	100	...	...	...	...	x	3Q	3Q	...	D
5	100	x	...	fscrw	...	x	1S	2S	...	C
6	100	x	...	f	...	...	...	...	x	...
7	100	x	x	...	...	x	1S	2S	...	B
8	...	...	...	fscr	fscr	...	...	...	x	B
9	100	x	...	f	...	x	1S	2S	...	...
10	100	...	...	...	...	...	...	...	...	C
11	100	x	x	fscrw	...	...	...	...	x	C
12	100	...	...	f	...	x	1S	2S	...	B
13	100	...	...	...	...	x	1S	2S	x	C
14	100	x	...	F	...	x	1S	2S	x	Z
15	100	...	...	Fsc	...	x	1S	2S	x	C
16	...	...	...	f	...	...	...	...	...	D
17	...	...	...	...	...	...	...	...	x	D

F = Free to faculty
f = Available to faculty
s = Available to spouse

c = Available to children
r = Available to retired faculty
w = Available to widow

Name of Institution	No. of full-time faculty (Lay in Catholic insts.)	Ratio of faculty in college housing to full-time faculty	First-mortgage home loans	Second-mortgage home loans	Ratio of faculty with college mortgage to full-time faculty	Personal loans
IOWA						
18 U. of Dubuque	53	A	x	...	C	x
19 Upper Iowa U.	44	B	...	...	D	x
20 Wartburg Col.	60	...	...	...	...	...
21 Westmar Col.	47	B	...	...	...	x
22 William Penn Col.	40	B	...	...	...	...
KANSAS						
1 Bethany Col.	39	B	x	...	B	...
2 Bethel Col.	30	A	...	...	...	...
3 Col. of Emporia	42	...	...	...	...	...
4 Friends U.	32	C	x	...	...	x
5 Kan. St. Col., Pittsburg	229	...	...	...	...	...
6 Kan. S.T.C., Emporia	262	...	...	...	...	...
7 Kan. St. U. Agric. & App. Sci.	833	D	...	...	...	...
8 Kan. Wesleyan U.	36	A	x	...	D	x
9 Marymount Col.	14	...	...	...	...	...
10 McPherson Col.	28	...	...	...	...	x
11 Ottawa U.	36	...	...	x	D	x
12 Sacred Heart Col.	4	A	...	...	...	...
13 St. Benedict's Col.	23	C	...	...	...	x
14 St. Mary Col.	7	C	...	...	...	...
15 Southwestern Col.	41	B	...	...	...	...
16 Sterling Col.	29	A	...	...	...	x
17 Tabor Col.	27	...	...	...	...	...
18 U. of Kansas	630	D	...	...	...	x
19 U. of Wichita	213	...	...	...	...	...
20 Washburn U. of Topeka	86	D	...	...	...	...
KENTUCKY						
1 Bellarmine Col.	32	...	...	...	...	x
2 Berea Col.	98	Z	x	...	A	...
3 Brescia Col.	10	...	...	...	...	...
4 Catherine Spalding Col.	33	...	...	...	...	...
5 Centre Col. of Ky.	43	C	x	...	B	...
6 Eastern Ky. St. Col.	161	D	...	...	...	...
7 Georgetown Col.	52	B	...	...	...	...
8 Kentucky Wesleyan Col.	32	...	...	...	...	...
9 Murray St. Col.	175	C	...	...	...	...
10 Transylvania Col.	41	...	...	...	...	x
11 U. of Kentucky	874	C	...	...	...	...

x = Has program   B = 10% but < 20%   1S = 1 Semester, 2S = 2 Semesters
Z = 50% up   C = 5% but < 10%   1Q = 1 Quarter, etc.
A = 20% but < 50%   D = Some, but < 5%   ... = Either no program or no answer

Institution	% of fac. children tuition waivers	Member Tuition Exchange, Inc.	Cash grants for fac. children's tuitions	Emergency medical treatment	Annual physical examination	Sabbatical leaves	Max. time sab. leave on full salary	Max. time sab. leave on half salary	Leaves with pay other than sab. from inst. funds	Ratio of faculty with leaves during year to full-time faculty
IOWA										
18	100	...	...	F	...	x	1S	2S	x	...
19	100	...	...	...	...	x	1S	2S	x	B
20	100	x	...	f	f	...	...	...	x	...
21	100	...	...	fsc	...	x	1S	2S	x	B
22	50	...	...	f	...	x	1S	2S	x	C
KAN										
1	100	...	...	F	...	x	1S	2S	...	C
2	50	...	...	...	...	x	1Q	3Q	...	C
3	100	...	...	...	...	...	...	...	...	...
4	100	...	...	Fr	...	x	1S	2S	x	B
5	...	...	...	...	...	x	1S	2S	...	D
6	...	...	...	F	...	x	1S	2S	...	D
7	...	...	...	f	...	x	1S	2S	...	B
8	100	...	...	...	...	x	...	2S	x	B
9	100	...	...	...	...	x	...	...	...	...
10	100	x	...	...	...	x	1S	2S	...	B
11	100	x	...	F	...	x	1S	2S	...	...
12	...	...	...	...	...	...	...	...	...	...
13	100	...	...	...	...	...	...	...	x	...
14	100	...	...	f	...	x	1S	2S	...	C
15	100	...	...	fsc	...	x	1S	2S	x	C
16	100	...	...	Fsc	...	x	2S	...	...	...
17	50	...	...	F	...	x	1S	2S	x	D
18	...	...	...	Fscrw	...	x	1S	2S	...	C
19	50	...	...	F	...	...	...	...	x	D
20	...	...	...	F	...	...	...	...	...	D
KY										
1	100	...	...	F	...	...	...	...	x	D
2	...	x	...	Fscrw	Fscrw	x	1S	2S	x	C
3	...	...	...	...	...	...	...	...	...	...
4	100	...	...	F	...	...	...	...	x	D
5	100	x	...	F	...	...	...	...	...	D
6	...	...	...	fsc	...	x	1S	2S	...	D
7	90	...	...	...	...	...	...	...	x	C
8	100	...	...	F	...	...	...	...	...	C
9	...	...	...	F	...	x	1S	...	...	C
10	80	...	...	F	...	...	...	...	x	D
11	...	...	...	f	...	x	1S	2S	...	C

F = Free to faculty   c = Available to children
f = Available to faculty   r = Available to retired faculty
s = Available to spouse   w = Available to widow

Name of Institution	No. of full-time faculty (Lay in Catholic insts.)	Ratio of faculty in college housing to full-time faculty	First-mortgage home loans	Second-mortgage home loans	Ratio of faculty with college mortgage to full-time faculty	Personal loans
KENTUCKY						
12 U. of Louisville	319	...	...	...	...	...
13 Ursuline Col.	4	...	...	...	...	...
14 Villa Madonna Col.	22	...	...	...	...	...
15 Western Ky. St. Col.	197	C	...	...	...	...
LOUISIANA						
1 Centenary Col.	63	B	...	...	...	...
2 Francis T. Nicholls St. Col.	59	...	...	...	...	...
3 Louisiana Col.	46	B	...	...	...	...
4 Louisiana Poly. Inst.	203	...	...	...	...	...
5 Louisiana St. U.	1435	...	...	...	...	...
6 Loyola U.	108	...	...	...	...	x
7 Northeast La. St. Col.	167	...	...	...	...	...
8 Northwestern St. Col. of La.	192	...	...	...	...	...
9 Tulane U. of La.	649	C	...	x	B	x
10 U. of Southwestern La.	325	D	...	...	...	...
MAINE						
1 Bates Col.	54	B	...	...	...	...
2 Bowdoin Col.	65	A	x	...	A	...
3 Nasson Col.	30	C	...	...	...	...
4 St. Francis Col.	20	...	...	...	...	...
5 U. of Maine	348	C	...	...	...	...
MARYLAND						
1 Goucher Col.	60	B	...	...	...	x
2 Hood Col.	48	...	...	...	...	...
3 Morgan St. Col.	162	...	...	...	...	...
4 Mount St. Agnes Col.	13	A	...	...	...	...
5 St. John's Col.	38	...	x	...	A	x
6 St. Joseph Col.	17	A	...	x	C	...
7 S.T.C., Salisbury	38	...	...	...	...	...
8 U. of Maryland	1574	...	...	...	...	...
9 Washington Col.	41	A	...	...	...	x
MASSACHUSETTS						
1 American Internat. Col.	49	...	...	...	...	x
2 Amherst Col.	123	Z	...	x	B	x
3 Anna Maria Col. for Wo.	5	...	...	...	...	...
4 Assumption Col.	35	C	...	...	...	...
5 Boston Col.	321	...	x	...	D	x
6 Boston U.	721	C	...	...	...	...

x = Has program   B = 10% but < 20%   1S = 1 Semester, 2S = 2 Semesters
Z = 50% up   C = 5% but < 10%   1Q = 1 Quarter, etc.
A = 20% but < 50%   D = Some, but < 5%   ... = Either no program or no answer

Institution	% of fac. children tuition waivers	Member Tuition Exchange, Inc.	Cash grants for fac. children's tuitions	Emergency medical treatment	Annual physical examination	Sabbatical leaves	Max. time sab. leave on full salary	Max. time sab. leave on half salary	Leaves with pay other than sab. from inst. funds	Ratio of faculty with leaves during year to full-time faculty
KY										
12	100	x	...	F	...	x	1S	2S	x	C
13	100	...	...	...	...	...	...	...	...	...
14	100	...	...	...	...	...	...	...	...	B
15	...	...	...	Frw	...	...	...	...	x	C
LA										
1	100	...	...	...	...	...	...	...	...	D
2	...	...	...	...	...	x	...	...	x	B
3	50	...	...	Fsc	...	x	1S	2S	...	D
4	100	...	...	fscrw	w	x	...	...	x	D
5	...	...	...	...	...	x	1S	2S	...	D
6	86	...	...	Fs	...	...	...	...	x	D
7	...	...	...	...	...	x	...	...	...	C
8	...	...	...	F	...	x	...	2S	...	C
9	100	x	...	f	fscrw	...	...	...	x	C
10	...	...	...	...	...	x	...	...	...	D
ME										
1	60	...	x	Frw	...	x	1S	2S	...	C
2	100	...	x	f	...	x	1S	2S	...	C
3	50	...	x	F	...	x	1S	2S	...	D
4	100	...	...	F	...	...	...	...	...	B
5	...	...	...	...	...	x	1S	2S	...	D
MD										
1	100	...	...	F	...	...	...	...	x	C
2	100	...	x	F	...	...	...	...	x	D
3	...	...	...	F	...	x	...	2S	...	...
4	75	...	...	...	...	x	...	2S	...	...
5	100	x	...	...	...	x	4Q	...	...	B
6	100	...	...	Fsc	...	x	1S	2S	...	B
7	...	...	...	...	...	...	...	...	...	D
8	...	...	...	f	...	x	1S	2S	...	D
9	100	x	...	...	...	x	1S	2S	x	D
MASS										
1	100	...	...	fsc	...	x	1S	2S	...	D
2	100	...	x	r	...	x	1S	...	x	A
3	...	...	...	F	...	...	...	...	...	...
4	...	...	...	F	...	...	...	...	...	D
5	100	...	...	F	...	...	...	...	x	B
6	100	...	...	F	...	x	1S	2S	...	C

F = Free to faculty   c = Available to children
f = Available to faculty   r = Available to retired faculty
s = Available to spouse   w = Available to widow

Name of Institution	No. of full-time faculty (Lay in Catholic insts.)	Ratio of faculty in college housing to full-time faculty	First-mortgage home loans	Second-mortgage home loans	Ratio of faculty with college mortgage to full-time faculty	Personal loans
MASSACHUSETTS						
7 Brandeis U.	262	...	...	x	D	x
8 Cardinal Cushing Col.	12	...	...	...	...	...
9 Clark U.	80	B	...	...	...	...
10 Col. of the Holy Cross	70	...	...	...	...	x
11 Eastern Nazarene Col.	36	B	...	...	...	x
12 Gordon Col.	31	...	...	...	...	...
13 Harvard U.	569	A	...	x	B	...
14 Mass. Inst. Tech.	728	D	...	...	...	x
15 Merrimack Col.	64	...	...	...	...	x
16 Mount Holyoke Col.	128	Z	x	...	A	...
17 Northeastern U.	269	...	...	...	...	x
18 Simmons Col.	110	...	...	...	...	...
19 Smith Col.	231	Z	...	x	B	x
20 Springfield Col.	74	...	...	...	...	...
21 Stonehill Col.	27	...	...	...	...	...
22 Suffolk U.	54	...	...	...	...	...
23 Tufts U.	169	A	...	...	...	...
24 U. of Massachusetts	406	B	...	...	...	...
25 Wellesley Col.	145	Z	x	...	D	x
26 Wheaton Col.	76	A	...	...	...	...
27 Williams Col.	130	Z	x	x	A	...
28 Worcester Poly. Inst.	122	D	...	...	...	...
MICHIGAN						
1 Adrian Col.	46	...	...	...	...	...
2 Albion Col.	91	C	x	...	B	x
3 Alma Col.	53	B	...	...	...	x
4 Aquinas Col.	32	...	...	...	...	...
5 Calvin Col.	108	...	...	...	...	...
6 Central Michigan U.	258	D	...	...	...	x
7 Eastern Michigan U.	194	...	...	...	...	...
8 Ferris Inst.	231	...	...	...	...	...
9 Hillsdale Col.	41	C	...	...	...	...
10 Hope Col.	86	C	...	...	...	...
11 Marygrove Col.	23	...	...	...	...	x
12 Mich. St. U. Agric. & App. Sci.	1700	B	...	...	...	...
13 Nazareth Col.	8	...	...	...	...	...
14 Northern Michigan Col.	133	B	...	...	...	...

x = Has program   B = 10% but < 20%   1S = 1 Semester, 2S = 2 Semesters
Z = 50% up   C = 5% but < 10%   1Q = 1 Quarter, etc.
A = 20% but < 50%   D = Some, but < 5%   ... = Either no program or no answer

Institution	% of fac. children tuition waivers	Member Tuition Exchange, Inc.	Cash grants for fac. children's tuitions	Emergency medical treatment	Annual physical examination	Sabbatical leaves	Max. time sab. leave on full salary	Max. time sab. leave on half salary	Leaves with pay other than sab. from inst. funds	Ratio of faculty with leaves during year to full-time faculty
MASS										
7	100	...	...	Fsc	...	x	1S	2S	...	B
8	100	...	...	F	...	...	...	...	...	C
9	100	x	x	...	...	x	1S	2S	...	D
10	100	...	...	F	...	x	1S	2S	x	D
11	100	...	...	Fscrw	...	x	1S	2S	...	...
12	100	...	...	Fsc	...	x	...	...	x	C
13	...	...	...	Fr	Fr	x	1S	2S	x	B
14	100	...	x	Fscrw	Fr	...	...	...	x	...
15	50	...	...	Fr	...	...	...	...	x	C
16	100	...	x	Fr	...	x	1S	2S	...	C
17	100	...	...	Fr	...	x	...	...	x	D
18	100	x	...	F	...	x	1S	2S	...	C
19	100	...	x	fr	...	x	1S	2S	x	B
20	100	x	...	frw	...	x	...	...	...	D
21	100	...	...	F	...	x	...	...	x	...
22	100	...	...	...	...	...	...	...	x	D
23	100	...	x	fscrw	fsc	x	1S	2S	x	C
24	...	...	...	f	...	x	...	...	x	C
25	100	...	x	Fr	...	x	...	2S	x	B
26	100	...	x	f	...	x	1S	2S	...	D
27	95	x	x	...	...	x	1S	...	x	B
28	75	...	x	f	...	...	...	...	x	D
MICH										
1	100	x	...	F	...	x	1S	2S	...	D
2	...	...	...	...	...	x	1S	2S	x	C
3	100	...	...	F	...	...	...	...	x	...
4	100	...	...	F	...	x	...	2S	...	...
5	...	...	...	F	...	x	2S	1S	...	C
6	...	...	...	F	...	x	1S	2S	...	D
7	...	...	...	f	...	x	...	...	...	D
8	...	...	...	F	...	...	...	...	x	D
9	100	x	...	f	...	...	...	...	x	C
10	...	...	...	f	...	...	...	...	x	D
11	100	...	...	F	...	...	...	...	x	C
12	...	...	...	...	...	x	1Q	4Q	...	B
13	100	...	x	F	...	...	...	...	...	...
14	...	...	...	f	...	x	1S	2S	...	D

F = Free to faculty   c = Available to children
f = Available to faculty   r = Available to retired faculty
s = Available to spouse   w = Available to widow

Name of Institution	No. of full-time faculty (Lay in Catholic insts.)	Ratio of faculty in college housing to full-time faculty	First-mortgage home loans	Second-mortgage home loans	Ratio of faculty with college mortgage to full-time faculty	Personal loans
MICHIGAN						
15 Olivet Col.	40	C	...	...	...	...
16 Sacred Heart Sem.	2	...	...	...	...	...
17 U. of Detroit	282	D	...	...	...	...
18 U. of Michigan	2746	C	x	...	A	...
19 Wayne St. U.	819	D	...	...	...	...
20 Western Michigan U.	508	C	...	...	...	...
MINNESOTA						
1 Augsburg Col.	58	B	...	x	B	x
2 Bemidji St. Col.	113	...	...	...	...	...
3 Carleton Col.	100	A	...	x	A	...
4 Col. of St. Scholastica	14	...	...	...	...	...
5 Col. of St. Thomas	81	...	...	...	...	x
6 Concordia Col., Moorhead	110	C	...	...	...	...
7 Gustavus Adolphus Col.	88	...	x	...	B	...
8 Hamline U.	60	A	...	...	...	...
9 Macalester Col.	96	B	x	...	D	...
10 Mankato St. Col.	290	...	...	...	...	...
11 St. Cloud St. Col.	222	...	...	...	...	...
12 St. John's U.	40	B	x	x	A	x
13 St. Mary's Col.	28	B	...	x	D	x
14 St. Olaf Col.	130	C	x	x	B	x
15 U. of Minnesota	1676	...	x	...	D	x
16 Winona St. Col.	90	...	...	...	...	...
MISSISSIPPI						
1 Delta St. Col.	65	B	...	...	...	...
2 Jackson St. Col.	81	A	...	...	...	...
3 Millsaps Col.	55	A	...	...	...	...
4 Mississippi Col.	74	...	...	...	...	...
5 Miss. St. Col. for Wo.	105	A	...	...	...	...
6 Miss. St. U.	410	A	...	...	...	...
7 Miss. Vocational Col.	92	Z	...	...	...	...
8 Rust Col.	24	Z	...	...	...	...
9 Tougaloo So. Chris. Col.	34	Z	...	...	...	x
10 U. of Mississippi	262	A	...	...	...	...
11 U. of Southern Mississippi	191	B	...	...	...	...
12 William Carey Col.	44	...	...	...	...	...
MISSOURI						
1 Central Methodist Col.	51	C	x	...	C	...

x = Has program   B = 10% but < 20%   1S = 1 Semester, 2S = 2 Semesters
Z = 50% up   C = 5% but < 10%   1Q = 1 Quarter, etc.
A = 20% but < 50%   D = Some, but < 5%   ... = Either no program or no answer

Institution	% of fac. children tuition waivers	Member Tuition Exchange, Inc.	Cash grants for fac. children's tuitions	Emergency medical treatment	Annual physical examination	Sabbatical leaves	Max. time sab. leave on full salary	Max. time sab. leave on half salary	Leaves with pay other than sab. from inst. funds	Ratio of faculty with leaves during year to full-time faculty
MICH										
15	50	...	...	...	...	...	...	...	x	D
16	...	...	...	F	...	x	2S	...	...	...
17	100	...	...	F	...	...	...	...	x	D
18	...	...	...	fscrw	Fscrw	x	1S	2S	...	C
19	...	...	...	F	...	x	...	3Q	...	C
20	...	...	...	F	...	x	...	2S	...	D
MINN										
1	100	...	...	f	F	x	1S	2S	x	C
2	...	...	...	F	...	x	...	3Q	...	D
3	70	...	x	F	...	x	2Q	4Q	...	B
4	100	...	...	...	F	...	...	...	x	...
5	100	...	...	F	...	...	...	...	...	D
6	100	...	...	fscrw	...	...	...	...	...	C
7	100	...	...	...	...	...	...	...	x	C
8	100	x	...	F	...	x	1S	2S	...	...
9	100	...	...	Fr	...	x	1S	2S	...	C
10	...	...	...	...	...	x	...	3Q	...	D
11	...	...	...	F	...	x	...	3Q	...	D
12	87	...	x	fsc	...	x	...	...	x	C
13	100	...	...	Fsc	...	x	...	1S	...	B
14	100	...	x	...	...	x	1S	2S	x	C
15	...	...	...	fr	fr	x	...	3Q	x	C
16	...	...	...	...	...	x	...	3Q	...	D
MISS										
1	...	...	...	F	...	x	...	2S	...	...
2	...	...	...	fscr	fscr	x	2Q	3Q	x	C
3	100	x	...	rw	...	x	2S	1S	...	C
4	...	...	...	F	...	...	...	...	...	...
5	...	...	...	...	...	x	...	2S	...	D
6	...	...	...	fsc	fsc	x	...	2S	...	D
7	...	...	x	...	...	x	1S	1S	x	D
8	25	...	...	...	...	...	...	...	x	A
9	...	...	...	...	...	...	...	...	...	D
10	...	...	...	fsc	...	x	1S	2S	x	D
11	...	...	...	F	...	x	...	3Q	...	D
12	...	...	...	fsc	...	...	...	...	...	D
MO										
1	100	...	...	fscr	Fscr	x	...	...	...	D

F = Free to faculty
f = Available to faculty
s = Available to spouse

c = Available to children
r = Available to retired faculty
w = Available to widow

Name of Institution	No. of full-time faculty (Lay in Catholic insts.)	Ratio of faculty in college housing to full-time faculty	First-mortgage home loans	Second-mortgage home loans	Ratio of faculty with college mortgage to full-time faculty	Personal loans
MISSOURI						
2 Culver-Stockton Col.	30	A	...	...	...	...
3 Drury Col.	54	...	...	...	...	...
4 Evangel Col.	30	Z	...	...	...	...
5 Harris Tchrs. Col.	60	...	...	...	...	...
6 Maryville Col. of Sacred Heart	10	A	...	...	...	...
7 Missouri Val. Col.	34	A	...	...	...	...
8 National Col.	20	A	x	...	B	...
9 Northwest Mo. St. Col.	112	...	...	...	...	...
10 Park Col.	39	A	x	...	B	...
11 Rockhurst Col.	39	D	...	...	...	x
12 St. Louis U.	474	...	...	...	...	x
13 Southwest Mo. St. Col.	148	...	...	...	...	...
14 Tarkio Col.	27	...	...	...	...	...
15 U. of Missouri	1010	B	...	...	...	...
16 Washington U.	629	B	...	...	...	...
17 Webster Col.	25	A	...	...	...	...
18 Westminster Col.	52	...	...	...	...	...
MONTANA						
1 Col. of Great Falls	20	...	...	...	...	...
2 Eastern Mont. Col. Ed.	85	...	...	...	...	...
3 Montana St. Col.	332	C	...	...	...	...
4 Montana St. U.	266	C	...	...	...	...
5 Northern Montana Col.	46	B	...	...	...	...
6 Rocky Mountain Col.	30	A	x	x	D	x
NEBRASKA						
1 Creighton U.	128	...	...	...	...	x
2 Doane Col.	33	B	...	...	C	...
3 Midland Col.	39	B	...	...	...	...
4 Municipal U. of Omaha	156	...	...	...	...	...
5 Neb. S.T.C., Chadron	65	A	...	...	...	...
6 Neb. S.T.C., Kearney	128	B	...	...	...	...
7 Neb. S.T.C., Peru	58	B	...	...	...	...
8 Neb. S.T.C., Wayne	80	A	...	...	...	...
9 Neb. Wesleyan U.	64	...	...	...	...	...
10 U. of Nebraska	514	C	...	...	...	...
NEVADA						
1 U. of Nevada	389	...	...	...	...	...

x = Has program   B = 10% but < 20%   1S = 1 Semester, 2S = 2 Semesters
Z = 50% up   C = 5% but < 10%   1Q = 1 Quarter, etc.
A = 20% but < 50%   D = Some, but < 5%   ... = Either no program or no answer

Institution	% of fac. children tuition waivers	Member Tuition Exchange, Inc.	Cash grants for fac. children's tuitions	Emergency medical treatment	Annual physical examination	Sabbatical leaves	Max. time sab. leave on full salary	Max. time sab. leave on half salary	Leaves with pay other than sab. from inst. funds	Ratio of faculty with leaves during year to full-time faculty
MO										
2	100	x	...	...	...	...	...	...	...	...
3	80	...	...	f	...	...	...	...	x	B
4	100	...	...	fsc	...	x	...	2S	x	B
5	...	...	...	F	...	...	...	...	x	D
6	50	...	...	...	...	x	1S	2S	...	...
7	50	...	...	...	...	...	...	...	...	C
8	50	...	...	...	...	x	1S	2S	...	C
9	...	...	...	Frw	...	x	...	2S	...	D
10	100	x	x	fscrw	...	x	1S	2S	x	B
11	100	...	...	...	...	...	...	...	...	B
12	50	...	...	F	...	...	...	...	x	B
13	...	...	...	fscrw	fscrw	x	1S	2S	x	D
14	100	...	...	...	...	x	1S	2S	...	C
15	...	...	...	Fr	...	x	1S	2S	...	D
16	100	x	...	Fscrw	...	...	...	...	x	C
17	...	...	...	F	...	x	1S	2S	x	...
18	100	x	...	F	...	x	1S	2S	x	D
MONT										
1	100	...	...	F	...	x	...	2S	...	...
2	...	...	...	...	...	x	2Q	...	...	C
3	...	...	...	...	...	...	...	...	x	A
4	...	...	...	...	...	...	...	...	...	D
5	...	...	...	...	...	x	2Q	...	...	B
6	50	...	...	...	...	x	1S	2S	...	B
NEBR										
1	100	...	...	...	...	x	1S	2S	...	C
2	100	...	...	...	...	x	1S	2S	...	D
3	100	...	...	...	...	x	1S	2S	x	B
4	...	...	...	F	F	...	...	...	x	D
5	...	...	...	Fscrw	...	x	...	2S	...	D
6	...	...	...	F	...	...	...	...	x	D
7	...	...	...	Fsc	...	...	...	2S	x	D
8	...	...	...	...	...	x	...	3Q	...	D
9	33	...	...	Fsc	...	...	...	...	x	C
10	...	...	...	fr	fr	...	...	...	x	D
NEV										
1	100	...	...	F	...	x	1S	2S	...	D

F = Free to faculty   c = Available to children
f = Available to faculty   r = Available to retired faculty
s = Available to spouse   w = Available to widow

Name of Institution	No. of full-time faculty (Lay in Catholic insts.)	Ratio of faculty in college housing to full-time faculty	First-mortgage home loans	Second-mortgage home loans	Ratio of faculty with college mortgage to full-time faculty	Personal loans
NEW HAMPSHIRE						
1 Dartmouth Col.	211	A	x	...	A	x
2 New England Col.	20	B	...	...	...	...
3 Rivier Col.	4	...	...	...	...	...
4 U. of New Hampshire	301	D	...	...	...	x
NEW JERSEY						
1 Alma White Col.	10	Z	...	...	...	...
2 Bloomfield Col.	45	C	...	...	...	...
3 Drew U.	68	A	x	x	A	...
4 Monmouth Col.	93	...	...	...	...	...
5 Princeton U.	739	Z	x	...	B	x
6 Rutgers, The St. U.	1297	C	...	...	...	...
7 St. Peter's Col.	68	...	...	...	...	...
8 Seton Hall U.	266	D	...	...	...	x
9 Stevens Inst. Tech.	125	A	...	x	D	x
10 Upsala Col.	77	B	...	...	...	x
NEW MEXICO						
1 Col. of St. Jos. on Rio Grande	27	...	...	...	...	x
2 Eastern New Mexico U.	101	...	...	...	...	...
3 U. of New Mexico	303	...	x	...	C	...
NEW YORK						
1 Alfred U.	100	A	...	...	...	...
2 Bard Col.	35	Z	...	...	...	...
3 Brooklyn Col.	685	...	...	...	...	...
4 Canisius Col.	69	...	...	x	...	x
5 City Col. of N.Y.	841	...	...	...	...	...
6 Colgate U.	131	...	...	...	...	...
7 Col. of New Rochelle	39	C	...	...	...	x
8 Col. of St. Rose	35	D	...	...	...	x
9 Columbia U.	2012	A	x	x	D	x
10 Cornell U.	1300	...	...	...	...	...
11 D'Youville Col.	38	...	...	...	...	...
12 Elmira Col.	57	A	...	x	D	x
13 Fordham U.	265	...	...	...	...	x
14 Good Counsel Col.	9	...	...	...	...	...
15 Hamilton Col.	71	Z	x	...	C	...
16 Hartwick Col.	53	...	...	...	...	...
17 Hobart & Wm. Smith Cols.	89	C	...	...	...	...

x = Has program   B = 10% but < 20%   1S = 1 Semester, 2S = 2 Semesters
Z = 50% up   C = 5% but < 10%   1Q = 1 Quarter, etc.
A = 20% but < 50%   D = Some, but < 5%   ... = Either no program or no answer

Institution	% of fac. children tuition waivers	Member Tuition Exchange, Inc.	Cash grants for fac. children's tuitions	Emergency medical treatment	Annual physical examination	Sabbatical leaves	Max. time sab. leave on full salary	Max. time sab. leave on half salary	Leaves with pay other than sab. from inst. funds	Ratio of faculty with leaves during year to full-time faculty
N H										
1	100	...	x	...	...	x	2Q	3Q	x	B
2	100	...	...	F	...	x	2Q	3Q	x	...
3	100	...	...	...	...	...	...	...	...	...
4	50	...	...	F	...	x	1S	2S	...	C
N J										
1	93	...	x	Fscrw	...	...	...	...	...	...
2	100	...	...	Fsc	...	...	...	...	x	D
3	100	x	x	F	...	x	1S	2S	x	...
4	100	...	...	Fr	...	...	...	...	...	D
5	...	...	x	Fr	Fr	...	...	...	x	C
6	100	x	...	Fsc	...	...	...	...	x	D
7	100	...	x	...	...	...	...	...	x	C
8	100	...	...	F	...	x	1S	2S	x	D
9	100	x	...	Fscrw	...	...	...	...	x	D
10	100	x	...	...	...	...	...	...	x	C
N M										
1	80	...	...	f	...	x	...	...	...	C
2	...	...	...	...	...	x	1S	2S	...	B
3	...	...	...	...	...	x	1S	...	...	C
N Y										
1	100	x	...	...	...	...	...	...	x	C
2	100	x	...	fscrw	...	x	1S	2S	...	A
3	...	...	...	f	...	x	...	2S	x	C
4	50	...	...	...	...	x	1S	2S	...	B
5	...	...	...	F	...	x	...	2S	x	C
6	50	x	x	...	...	x	1S	2S	...	B
7	100	...	...	...	...	x	1S	2S	...	C
8	100	...	...	F	F	x	1S	2S	...	C
9	100	x	...	Fs	...	x	1S	2S	x	C
10	100	x	...	F	...	x	1S	2S	x	B
11	100	...	...	F	...	...	...	...	x	C
12	100	...	x	F	...	x	1S	2S	x	D
13	100	...	...	F	...	x	1S	2S	x	C
14	...	...	...	Fscr	...	...	...	...	...	...
15	100	x	...	...	...	...	...	...	x	C
16	100	x	x	F	...	x	1S	2S	...	D
17	100	x	x	...	...	x	1S	2S	...	B

F = Free to faculty   c = Available to children
f = Available to faculty   r = Available to retired faculty
s = Available to spouse   w = Available to widow

Name of Institution	No. of full-time faculty (Lay in Catholic insts.)	Ratio of faculty in college housing to full-time faculty	First-mortgage home loans	Second-mortgage home loans	Ratio of faculty with college mortgage to full-time faculty	Personal loans
NEW YORK						
18 Hofstra U.	296	...	...	...	...	x
19 Hunter Col.	443	...	...	...	...	...
20 Iona Col.	74	D	...	...	...	...
21 Ithaca Col.	97	...	...	...	...	...
22 Keuka Col.	48	Z	x	...	D	...
23 King's Col.	27	Z	...	...	...	x
24 LeMoyne Col.	46	...	...	...	...	x
25 Long Island U.	318	D	...	x	...	x
26 Manhattan Col.	128	...	...	...	...	...
27 Marist Col.	14	...	...	...	...	x
28 Molloy Cath. Col. for Wo.	7	...	...	...	...	...
29 Nazareth Col.	21	D	...	...	...	x
30 New Sch. Social Research	28	...	...	...	...	x
31 New York U.	1923	C	...	x	D	...
32 Notre Dame Col. of Staten I.	16	...	...	...	...	...
33 Poly. Inst. of Brooklyn	250	...	...	...	...	...
34 Queens Col. of C.U.N.Y.	404	...	...	...	...	x
35 Roberts Wesleyan Col.	33	A	...	...	...	...
36 Rochester Inst. Tech.	156	B	...	...	...	...
37 Rosary Hill Col.	31	...	...	...	...	...
38 Russell Sage Col.	75	C	...	x	C	...
39 St. Bernardine of Siena Col.	42	...	...	...	...	x
40 St. Bonaventure U.	51	...	...	x	D	x
41 St. Francis Col.	49	...	...	...	...	...
42 St. John Fisher Col., Inc.	26	...	...	x	B	...
43 St. John's U.	396	...	...	...	...	...
44 St. Joseph's Col. for Wo.	16	...	...	...	...	...
45 St. Lawrence U.	89	A	...	...	...	...
46 Sarah Lawrence Col.	66	C	...	...	...	x
47 Skidmore Col.	126	B	...	...	...	x
48 St. U. of N.Y. at Albany	295	...	...	...	...	...
49 St. U. of N.Y. at Buffalo	648	...	...	...	...	...
50 St. U. of N.Y. Harpur Col.	132	...	...	...	...	...
51 St. U. of N.Y. at Stony Brook	121	...	...	...	...	...
52 Syracuse U.	566	C	...	...	...	...
53 Union Col.	110	B	...	x	B	...
54 U. of Rochester	728	...	...	...	...	...

x = Has program   B = 10% but < 20%   1S = 1 Semester, 2S = 2 Semesters
Z = 50% up   C = 5% but < 10%   1Q = 1 Quarter, etc.
A = 20% but < 50%   D = Some, but < 5%   ... = Either no program or no answer

Institution	% of fac. children tuition waivers	Member Tuition Exchange, Inc.	Cash grants for fac. children's tuitions	Emergency medical treatment	Annual physical examination	Sabbatical leaves	Max. time sab. leave on full salary	Max. time sab. leave on half salary	Leaves with pay other than sab. from inst. funds	Ratio of faculty with leaves during year to full-time faculty
N Y										
18	100	...	x	Fsc	...	...	...	...	x	D
19	...	...	...	...	...	x	...	2S	...	C
20	50	...	...	Fr	...	x	...	...	...	...
21	100	x	...	...	...	x	1S	2S	...	D
22	100	...	...	f	...	x	2Q	4Q	...	D
23	100	...	...	...	...	...	...	...	...	...
24	100	...	...	...	...	...	...	...	x	...
25	100	...	...	Fscr	...	...	...	...	...	...
26	100	...	...	F	...	...	...	...	...	D
27	...	...	...	...	...	...	...	...	...	A
28	...	...	...	...	...	...	...	...	...	...
29	100	...	...	...	...	...	...	...	x	D
30	100	...	...	...	...	x	1S	...	...	A
31	100	...	...	Fr	fr	x	1S	...	...	D
32	100	...	...	F	...	...	...	...	x	C
33	100	...	...	F	...	x	...	2S	...	D
34	...	...	...	fscrw	...	x	...	2S	x	C
35	80	...	...	fsc	...	x	1S	2S	...	D
36	100	x	...	Fscrw	Fscrw	...	...	...	x	D
37	...	...	...	F	...	x	...	...	x	C
38	50	...	...	f	...	...	...	...	x	D
39	100	...	...	F	...	...	...	...	...	D
40	100	...	...	F	...	...	...	...	x	D
41	100	...	...	F	...	x	1S	2S	...	C
42	50	...	...	f	...	x	...	2S	...	...
43	100	...	...	F	...	x	1S	2S	x	D
44	100	...	x	...	...	x	1S	2S	...	C
45	100	x	x	...	...	...	...	...	...	C
46	100	...	x	F	...	x	1S	2S	...	B
47	100	...	x	F	...	x	1S	2S	x	D
48	...	...	...	F	...	x	1S	2S	...	...
49	...	...	...	F	...	x	1S	2S	...	D
50	...	...	...	F	...	x	1S	2S	...	C
51	...	...	...	...	...	x	1S	2S	x	D
52	100	x	...	F	fr	...	...	...	x	C
53	100	x	x	F	F	x	1S	2S	...	B
54	100	...	x	...	...	...	...	...	x	D

F = Free to faculty
f = Available to faculty
s = Available to spouse

c = Available to children
r = Available to retired faculty
w = Available to widow

Name of Institution	No. of full-time faculty (Lay in Catholic insts.)	Ratio of faculty in college housing to full-time faculty	First-mortgage home loans	Second-mortgage home loans	Ratio of faculty with college mortgage to full-time faculty	Personal loans
NEW YORK						
55 Vassar Col.	153	Z	x	...	D	x
56 Wagner Col.	93	C	...	...	...	...
57 Wells Col.	55	Z	...	...	...	...
58 Yeshiva U.	482	...	...	...	...	...
NORTH CAROLINA						
1 Appalachian S.T.C.	143	A	...	...	...	...
2 Atlantic Chris. Col.	56	D	...	...	...	x
3 Catawba Col.	58	A	...	...	...	...
4 Davidson Col.	75	A	x	...	A	...
5 Duke U.	702	D	...	x	B	...
6 East Carolina Col.	298	C	...	...	...	...
7 Elon Col.	48	A	...	...	...	x
8 Guilford Col.	59	A	x	...	B	...
9 Johnson C. Smith U.	55	A	...	...	...	...
10 Livingstone Col.	41	A	...	...	...	...
11 N.C. Col. at Durham	128	A	...	...	...	...
12 N.C. Wesleyan Col., Inc.	22	B	...	...	...	...
13 St. Andrews Presb. Col.	60	...	...	x	A	...
14 St. Augustine's Col.	46	A	...	...	...	...
15 Salem Col.	35	B	...	...	...	x
16 Shaw U.	41	...	...	...	...	...
17 U. of N.C., Chapel Hill	697	D	...	...	...	...
18 U.N.C. St. Col. Agric. & Eng.	726	...	...	...	...	...
19 U.N.C. Women's Col.	206	D	...	...	...	...
20 Wake Forest Col.	149	A	...	...	...	...
NORTH DAKOTA						
1 Jamestown Col.	31	A	...	...	...	...
2 N. Dakota St. U.	219	C	...	...	...	...
3 S.T.C., Minot	100	...	...	...	...	...
4 S.T.C., Valley City	58	C	...	...	...	...
5 U. of N. Dakota	350	B	...	...	...	x
OHIO						
1 Baldwin-Wallace Col.	94	A	x	...	A	...
2 Capital U.	81	B	x	...	D	...
3 Case Inst. Tech.	213	...	...	...	...	...
4 Central St. Col.	76	A	...	...	...	...
5 Col. of St. Mary of Springs	10	...	...	...	...	...
6 Col. of Wooster	110	...	...	...	...	...

x = Has program	B = 10% but < 20%	1S = 1 Semester, 2S = 2 Semesters
Z = 50% up	C = 5% but < 10%	1Q = 1 Quarter, etc.
A = 20% but < 50%	D = Some, but < 5%	... = Either no program or no answer

Institution	% of fac. children tuition waivers	Member Tuition Exchange, Inc.	Cash grants for fac. children's tuitions	Emergency medical treatment	Annual physical examination	Sabbatical leaves	Max. time sab. leave on full salary	Max. time sab. leave on half salary	Leaves with pay other than sab. from inst. funds	Ratio of faculty with leaves during year to full-time faculty
N Y										
55	100	...	x	Frw	f	...	...	...	x	C
56	50	x	...	Fsc	...	...	...	...	...	D
57	100	x	x	Fscrw	...	x	1S	2S	...	B
58	50	...	...	F	...	x	1S	2S	x	...
N C										
1	...	...	...	...	...	...	...	...	...	D
2	50	...	...	fr	...	...	...	...	x	D
3	100	x	...	Fscr	...	...	...	...	...	D
4	100	x	x	...	...	x	1S	2S	...	...
5	100	...	x	fscrw	fscrw	x	1S	2S	...	C
6	...	...	...	F	...	...	...	...	...	D
7	30	...	...	Fscw	fscrw	...	...	...	x	...
8	100	...	...	...	...	...	...	...	x	C
9	100	...	...	Fsc	Fsc	...	...	...	x	D
10	90	...	...	...	...	...	...	...	...	...
11	...	...	...	...	...	...	...	...	...	D
12	100	...	...	f	...	...	...	...	...	...
13	75	x	...	Fscrw	...	...	...	...	x	D
14	100	...	...	Fscrw	...	...	...	...	x	D
15	100	x	...	F	...	x	1S	2S	...	C
16	...	...	...	Fsc	Fsc	x	2S	...	...	...
17	...	...	...	...	...	...	...	...	x	D
18	...	...	...	...	...	...	...	...	...	D
19	...	...	...	f	...	x	1S	2S	...	...
20	43	...	...	Frw	...	...	...	...	...	D
N D										
1	100	...	...	...	...	...	...	...	x	C
2	...	...	...	f	...	x	...	3Q	...	D
3	...	...	...	F	...	x	...	4Q	...	C
4	...	...	...	f	...	x	...	...	...	C
5	...	...	...	r	r	x	1S	2S	x	D
OHIO										
1	100	x	...	F	...	x	1Q	3Q	...	B
2	100	...	...	F	...	...	...	...	x	D
3	100	...	x	F	...	...	...	...	x	D
4	40	...	...	fsc	...	...	...	...	x	...
5	50	...	...	F	...	...	...	...	...	A
6	100	...	x	F	...	x	2S	2S	x	C

F = Free to faculty
f = Available to faculty
s = Available to spouse

c = Available to children
r = Available to retired faculty
w = Available to widow

Name of Institution	No. of full-time faculty (Lay in Catholic insts.)	Ratio of faculty in college housing to full-time faculty	First-mortgage home loans	Second-mortgage home loans	Ratio of faculty with college mortgage to full-time faculty	Personal loans
OHIO						
7 Denison U.	115	Z	x	...	A	...
8 Fenn Col.	90	...	...	...	...	...
9 Findlay Col.	46	D	x	...	D	x
10 Heidelberg Col.	70	B	...	...	...	...
11 Hiram Col.	56	A	x	...	A	...
12 Kent St. U.	450	...	...	...	...	...
13 Kenyon Col.	80	Z	...	...	...	...
14 Malone Col.	26	...	...	x	B	x
15 Mary Manse Col.	20	...	...	...	...	...
16 Miami U.	474	D	...	...	...	...
17 Mount Union Col.	58	B	...	...	...	...
18 Muskingum Col.	81	A	...	x	C	x
19 Notre Dame Col.	7	...	...	...	...	...
20 Oberlin Col.	212	B	...	...	...	...
21 Ohio Northern U.	113	C	...	...	...	...
22 Ohio St. U.	1741	C	...	...	...	x
23 Ohio U.	463	C	...	...	...	...
24 Ohio Wesleyan U.	152	B	x	...	A	x
25 Otterbein Col.	62	D	x	x	B	...
26 Our Lady of Cincinnati Col.	38	...	...	...	...	...
27 Rio Grande Col.	20	A	...	...	...	...
28 U. of Akron	158	D	...	...	...	x
29 U. of Cincinnati	728	...	...	...	...	x
30 U. of Dayton	161	...	...	x	C	x
31 U. of Toledo	202	C	...	...	...	...
32 Walsh Col.	7	...	...	...	...	...
33 Western Col. for Wo.	43	A	x	...	...	x
34 Western Reserve U.	594	D	...	...	...	x
35 Wilmington Col.	40	A	...	...	...	...
36 Xavier U.	79	...	...	x	D	x
OKLAHOMA						
1 Bethany Nazarene Col.	48	C	...	...	...	...
2 Central St. Col.	182	...	...	...	...	...
3 Langston U.	50	Z	...	...	...	...
4 Northwestern St. Col.	57	...	...	...	...	...
5 Oklahoma Baptist U.	58	Z	...	...	...	x
6 Oklahoma Chris. Col.	31	...	...	...	...	...
7 Oklahoma City U.	88	...	...	...	...	...

x = Has program   B = 10% but < 20%   1S = 1 Semester, 2S = 2 Semesters
Z = 50% up   C = 5% but < 10%   1Q = 1 Quarter, etc.
A = 20% but < 50%   D = Some, but < 5%   ... = Either no program or no answer

Institution	% of fac. children tuition waivers	Member Tuition Exchange, Inc.	Cash grants for fac. children's tuitions	Emergency medical treatment	Annual physical examination	Sabbatical leaves	Max. time sab. leave on full salary	Max. time sab. leave on half salary	Leaves with pay other than sab. from inst. funds	Ratio of faculty with leaves during year to full-time faculty
OHIO										
7	100	x	x	F	...	x	1S	2S	...	B
8	100	x	...	Fscrw	...	...	...	...	x	D
9	50	...	...	f	...	x	1S	2S	...	C
10	100	...	x	f	...	x	1S	2S	x	D
11	100	...	x	fscrw	fscrw	x	...	...	x	C
12	...	...	...	Fsc	...	...	...	...	x	D
13	100	...	...	fr	...	x	1S	2S	x	C
14	50	...	...	F	...	x	1S	2S	...	D
15	...	...	...	...	...	...	...	...	...	...
16	100	...	...	...	...	...	...	...	x	D
17	100	...	x	Frw	...	x	1Q	3Q	x	D
18	100	...	x	f	...	x	1S	2S	...	C
19	...	...	...	...	...	...	...	...	...	...
20	100	...	x	...	...	x	1S	2S	x	C
21	100	...	...	...	...	x	1Q	3Q	...	D
22	...	...	...	...	...	...	...	...	...	D
23	....	...	...	...	...	...	...	...	x	D
24	90	...	x	fsc	...	...	...	...	x	C
25	100	x	...	Fr	F	x	1S	2S	...	D
26	...	...	...	F	...	x	1S	2S	x	C
27	100	...	...	Fscw	...	...	...	...	...	...
28	100	...	...	F	...	...	...	...	...	D
29	100	...	...	Fsc	...	x	1S	2S	x	D
30	100	...	...	F	...	...	...	...	x	B
31	100	...	...	Fsc	...	...	...	...	...	D
32	100	...	...	...	...	...	...	...	...	...
33	...	...	x	F	F	...	...	...	x	C
34	100	x	...	...	...	x	1S	2S	x	...
35	100	x	...	...	...	x	1S	2S	x	A
36	100	...	...	F	...	...	...	...	...	D
OKLA										
1	80	...	...	F	...	x	1S	2S	...	D
2	...	...	...	...	...	x	...	2S	x	D
3	...	...	...	Fscrw	...	x	1S	2S	x	B
4	...	...	...	F	...	x	...	2S	...	D
5	75	...	...	r	...	...	...	...	...	C
6	33	...	...	F	...	...	...	...	x	C
7	50	...	...	frw	...	...	...	...	x	D

F = Free to faculty   c = Available to children
f = Available to faculty   r = Available to retired faculty
s = Available to spouse   w = Available to widow

Name of Institution	No. of full-time faculty (Lay in Catholic insts.)	Ratio of faculty in college housing to full-time faculty	First-mortgage home loans	Second-mortgage home loans	Ratio of faculty with college mortgage to full-time faculty	Personal loans
OKLAHOMA						
8 Oklahoma Col. for Wo.	43	B	...	...	...	...
9 Okla. St. U. Agric. & App. Sci.	620	D	...	...	...	...
10 Panhandle A & M Col.	50	Z	...	...	...	...
11 Southwestern St. Col.	84	...	...	...	...	...
12 U. of Tulsa	139	D	x	...	C	...
OREGON						
1 Cascade Col.	21	A	...	...	...	x
2 Eastern Oregon Col.	79	C	...	...	...	...
3 Lewis & Clark Col.	71	...	...	...	...	...
4 Linfield Col.	57	A	x	...	A	x
5 Marylhurst Col.	6	B	...	...	...	...
6 Mount Angel Col.	11	...	...	...	...	...
7 Oregon Col. Ed.	113	C	...	...	...	...
8 Oregon St. U.	1167	...	...	...	...	...
9 Pacific U.	51	...	...	...	...	...
10 Portland St. Col.	263	...	...	...	...	...
11 Reed Col.	90	C	...	·x	D	...
12 Southern Oregon Col.	125	D	...	...	...	x
13 U. of Oregon	718	...	...	...	...	...
14 U. of Portland	85	D	...	...	...	...
15 Willamette U.	70	...	...	...	...	...
PENNSYLVANIA						
1 Albright Col.	56	...	...	...	...	...
2 Allegheny Col.	84	C	x	...	B	...
3 Beaver Col.	45	...	...	...	...	...
4 Bryn Mawr Col.	95	Z	x	...	A	...
5 Bucknell U.	156	B	x	...	A	x
6 Carnegie Inst. Tech.	305	C	...	x	D	...
7 Cedar Crest Col.	39	...	x	...	C	...
8 Chatham Col.	44	A	...	...	...	x
9 Chestnut Hill Col.	16	...	...	...	...	...
10 Dickinson Col.	82	B	...	...	...	x
11 Drexel Inst. Tech.	292	...	...	...	...	x
12 Duquesne U.	230	...	...	...	...	x
13 Eastern Baptist Col.	28	A	...	...	...	...
14 Elizabethtown Col.	47	B	x	...	D	...
15 Franklin & Marshall Col.	100	...	...	...	...	...
16 Gannon Col.	59	...	...	...	...	x

x = Has program   B = 10% but < 20%   1S = 1 Semester, 2S = 2 Semesters
Z = 50% up   C = 5% but < 10%   1Q = 1 Quarter, etc.
A = 20% but < 50%   D = Some, but < 5%   ... = Either no program or no answer

Institution	% of fac. children tuition waivers	Member Tuition Exchange, Inc.	Cash grants for fac. children's tuitions	Emergency medical treatment	Annual physical examination	Sabbatical leaves	Max. time sab. leave on full salary	Max. time sab. leave on half salary	Leaves with pay other than sab. from inst. funds	Ratio of faculty with leaves during year to full-time faculty
OKLA										
8	...	...	...	...	...	x	...	2S	...	D
9	...	...	...	f	...	x	1S	2S	x	D
10	...	...	...	frw	...	x	...	2S	...	C
11	...	...	...	f	...	x	...	2S	...	B
12	50	...	...	F	...	...	...	...	x	D
ORE										
1	100	...	...	Fsc	...	...	...	...	x	B
2	...	...	...	...	...	x	1Q	4Q	...	C
3	100	x	...	fw	...	...	...	...	...	C
4	90	x	...	...	...	...	...	...	...	D
5	100	...	...	F	...	...	...	...	...	B
6	100	...	...	Fsc	...	...	...	...	...	...
7	...	...	...	...	...	x	1Q	3Q	...	D
8	...	...	...	...	...	x	1Q	3Q	...	D
9	100	x	...	...	...	x	1S	2S	x	D
10	...	...	...	F	...	x	1Q	3Q	...	C
11	67	x	x	Fsc	...	x	1S	2S	...	B
12	...	...	...	...	...	x	1Q	3Q	...	D
13	...	...	...	...	...	x	1Q	3Q	...	C
14	100	...	...	...	...	x	...	2S	x	C
15	100	x	...	Frw	...	...	...	...	x	D
PA										
1	90	x	...	fsc	...	x	1S	2S	...	D
2	100	...	x	fsc	...	x	...	...	...	B
3	100	x	...	F	...	x	...	...	x	D
4	67	...	x	Fsc	...	x	...	2S	...	C
5	100	x	x	Fscrw	...	x	1S	2S	x	D
6	100	...	x	F	...	x	1S	2S	...	C
7	100	x	...	F	...	...	...	...	...	...
8	100	x	x	F	...	x	1S	2S	x	D
9	100	...	...	...	...	...	...	...	x	...
10	100	...	x	Frw	...	...	...	...	...	D
11	100	x	x	F	...	...	...	...	x	C
12	100	...	...	f	...	x	...	...	...	D
13	100	...	...	f	f	x	1S	2S	...	D
14	100	...	...	...	...	x	1S	2S	x	C
15	100	...	x	Fscrw	...	x	1S	2S	...	C
16	100	...	...	F	...	...	...	...	x	C

F = Free to faculty
f = Available to faculty
s = Available to spouse

c = Available to children
r = Available to retired faculty
w = Available to widow

Name of Institution	No. of full-time faculty (Lay in Catholic insts.)	Ratio of faculty in college housing to full-time faculty	First-mortgage home loans	Second-mortgage home loans	Ratio of faculty with college mortgage to full-time faculty	Personal loans
PENNSYLVANIA						
17 Geneva Col.	67	C	...	...	...	...
18 Gettysburg Col.	126	...	...	...	...	...
19 Haverford Col.	60	Z	x	...	B	x
20 Immaculata Col.	16	...	...	...	...	...
21 Juniata Col.	64	A	x	x	B	...
22 King's Col.	47	...	...	...	...	...
23 Lafayette Col.	131	A	...	...	...	...
24 Lebanon Val. Col.	50	D	...	...	...	...
25 Lehigh U.	226	...	...	...	...	...
26 Lincoln U.	27	Z	...	...	...	x
27 Lycoming Col.	75	C	...	...	...	x
28 Marywood Col.	30	...	...	...	...	...
29 Mercyhurst Col.	11	...	...	...	...	...
30 Moravian Col.	55	C	...	...	...	...
31 Muhlenberg Col.	86	...	x	...	A	...
32 Del. Val. Col. Sci. & Agric.	37	A	...	...	...	...
33 Pennsylvania Mil. Col.	64	...	...	...	...	...
34 Pennsylvania St. U.	1763	D	...	...	...	...
35 St. Francis Col.	47	...	...	...	...	x
36 St. Joseph's Col.	62	...	...	...	...	x
37 Seton Hill Col.	27	B	x	...	C	...
38 Susquehanna U.	69	A	...	...	...	...
39 Swarthmore Col.	105	A	x	...	A	...
40 Temple U.	1427	...	...	...	...	...
41 Thiel Col.	52	...	...	...	...	...
42 U. of Pennsylvania	1048	D	...	...	...	x
43 U. of Pittsburgh	994	...	...	x	D	...
44 U. of Scranton	56	C	...	...	...	x
45 Ursinus Col.	50	C	x	...	A	x
46 Villanova U.	294	...	...	...	...	...
47 Washington & Jefferson Col.	66	A	...	...	...	x
48 Waynesburg Col.	50	B	x	...	B	...
49 Westminster Col.	81	A	...	...	...	x
50 Wilkes Col.	77	...	...	...	...	x
51 Wilson Col.	56	A	x	...	D	...
PUERTO RICO						
1 Cath. U. of Puerto Rico	60	...	...	...	...	...

x = Has program   B = 10% but < 20%   1S = 1 Semester, 2S = 2 Semesters
Z = 50% up   C = 5% but < 10%   1Q = 1 Quarter, etc.
A = 20% but < 50%   D = Some, but < 5%   ... = Either no program or no answer

Institution	% of fac. children tuition waivers	Member Tuition Exchange, Inc.	Cash grants for fac. children's tuitions	Emergency medical treatment	Annual physical examination	Sabbatical leaves	Max. time sab. leave on full salary	Max. time sab. leave on half salary	Leaves with pay other than sab. from inst. funds	Ratio of faculty with leaves during year to full-time faculty
PA
17	100	x	...	...	...	...	...	...	x	C
18	90	x	x	F	...	x	1S	2S	...	C
19	...	...	x	...	...	x	1S	2S	x	B
20	100	...	...	F	...	x	...	...	x	D
21	...	...	x	f	...	x	1S	2S	...	D
22	100	...	...	...	...	x	1S	2S	...	D
23	100	x	x	...	...	x	1S	2S	...	D
24	100	x	x	F	...	x	1S	2S	...	C
25	100	x	...	F	F	...	...	...	x	D
26	100	...	...	fscrw	...	x	1S	2S	...	...
27	100	...	...	F	...	x	...	...	x	C
28	100	...	...	F	...	...	...	...	...	...
29	100	...	...	F	F	...	...	...	...	...
30	100	x	...	...	...	x	1S	2S	x	C
31	100	x	x	F	...	x	1S	2S	...	D
32	100	...	...	F	...	...	...	...	...	...
33	100	x	x	F	...	...	...	...	x	D
34	75	...	...	f	...	x	2Q	4Q	x	C
35	100	...	...	F	...	x	1S	2S	...	D
36	100	...	...	...	...	x	2S	...	x	D
37	100	...	...	...	...	x	1S	2S	...	C
38	100	x	...	...	...	x	1S	2S	...	D
39	50	...	x	fsc	...	x	1S	2S	x	C
40	100	...	...	f	...	...	...	...	x	D
41	100	x	x	Fscrw	...	x	1S	2S	x	B
42	100	...	x	fscrw	fscrw	x	1S	2S	x	C
43	100	x	x	f	F	x	...	...	...	D
44	100	...	x	...	...	...	...	...	x	D
45	100	x	x	F	...	x	...	2S	...	D
46	100	...	...	Fr	...	x	1S	2S	...	D
47	100	x	...	...	...	...	...	...	x	D
48	100	...	...	Fsc	...	x	...	2S	...	...
49	100	...	...	Fscrw	...	x	1S	2S	...	D
50	100	...	...	...	...	x	1S	2S	x	C
51	100	x	...	fsc	...	x	...	2S	...	C
P R
1	...	...	...	...	...	...	...	...	x	C

F = Free to faculty   c = Available to children
f = Available to faculty   r = Available to retired faculty
s = Available to spouse   w = Available to widow

Name of Institution	No. of full-time faculty (Lay in Catholic insts.)	Ratio of faculty in college housing to full-time faculty	First-mortgage home loans	Second-mortgage home loans	Ratio of faculty with college mortgage to full-time faculty	Personal loans
PUERTO RICO						
2 Col. of the Sacred Heart	13	...	...	...	...	...
3 U. of Puerto Rico	1643	C	x	...	B	x
RHODE ISLAND						
1 Brown U.	442	C	x	...	A	x
2 Providence Col.	75	...	...	...	...	x
3 Salve Regina Col.	14	...	...	...	...	...
4 U. of Rhode Island	329	C	...	...	...	...
SOUTH CAROLINA						
1 Allen U.	39	A	...	...	...	x
2 Clemson Agric. Col.	347	A	...	...	...	...
3 Columbia Col.	57	D	...	...	...	...
4 Converse Col.	65	...	...	...	...	...
5 Erskine Col.	42	B	...	...	...	x
6 Furman U.	96	C	...	...	...	...
7 Limestone Col.	30	Z	x	...	C	x
8 Newberry Col.	47	C	...	...	...	...
9 U. of S. Carolina	320	...	...	...	...	x
10 Winthrop Col.	139	B	...	...	...	...
11 Wofford Col.	45	...	...	...	...	...
SOUTH DAKOTA						
1 Augustana Col.	68	C	x	...	C	x
2 Black Hills Tchrs. Col.	55	D	...	...	...	...
3 Dakota Wesleyan U.	28	A	x	...	...	...
4 Huron Col.	28	A	...	...	...	x
5 Northern S.T.C.	91	...	...	...	...	...
6 Sioux Falls Col.	29	B	...	...	...	...
7 St. U. of S. Dakota	175	C	...	...	...	...
TENNESSEE						
1 Austin Peay St. Col.	84	A	...	...	...	...
2 Bethel Col.	25	...	...	...	...	...
3 Carson-Newman Col.	97	B	...	...	...	...
4 Chris. Brothers Col.	17	...	...	...	...	...
5 David Lipscomb Col.	74	...	...	...	...	...
6 Geo. Peabody Col. for Tchrs.	95	...	...	...	...	...
7 King Col.	25	A	x	...	A	x
8 Knoxville Col.	42	A	...	...	...	...
9 Lambuth Col.	26	...	...	...	...	...

x = Has program   B = 10% but < 20%   1S = 1 Semester, 2S = 2 Semesters
Z = 50% up   C = 5% but < 10%   1Q = 1 Quarter, etc.
A = 20% but < 50%   D = Some, but < 5%   ... = Either no program or no answer

Institution	% of fac. children tuition waivers	Member Tuition Exchange, Inc.	Cash grants for fac. children's tuitions	Emergency medical treatment	Annual physical examination	Sabbatical leaves	Max. time sab. leave on full salary	Max. time sab. leave on half salary	Leaves with pay other than sab. from inst. funds	Ratio of faculty with leaves during year to full-time faculty
P R										
2	...	...	..	f	...	...	...	...	...	...
3	...	...	...	...	...	x	2S	...	x	C
R I										
1	100	...	x	fr	...	x	1S	2S	...	C
2	100	...	...	F	...	x	1S	2S	...	D
3	100	...	...	fw	...	...	...	...	...	...
4	100	...	...	F	...	x	1S	2S	x	D
S C										
1	100	...	...	F scr	Fr	...	...	...	x	...
2	...	...	...	fscrw	...	x	...	...	x	C
3	100	x	...	...	...	x	1S	2S	...	D
4	...	x	...	...	...	...	...	...	...	D
5	100	...	...	f	...	...	...	...	x	C
6	100	x	...	Fsc	...	...	...	...	x	D
7	100	...	...	...	...	...	...	...	...	...
8	50	...	...	...	...	...	...	...	x	D
9	...	...	...	F	...	x	1S	2S	x	D
10	...	...	...	F	...	...	...	...	...	D
11	100	x	...	...	...	...	...	...	...	...
S D										
1	100	...	...	...	...	...	...	...	x	C
2	...	...	...	f	...	x	...	3Q	...	D
3	50	...	...	Fsc	...	x	...	2S	x	D
4	25	...	...	...	...	x	...	...	...	...
5	...	...	...	...	...	x	...	3Q	...	D
6	100	...	...	...	...	x	1S	2S	...	D
7	...	...	...	...	...	x	...	2S	x	D
TENN										
1	...	...	...	F	...	...	...	...	x	C
2	100	...	...	...	...	...	...	...	x	B
3	100	...	...	...	...	x	...	...	...	D
4	...	...	...	...	...	...	...	...	...	B
5	75	...	...	Fsc	fsc	...	...	...	x	B
6	100	...	...	...	...	x	1Q	...	...	C
7	100	...	...	...	...	...	...	...	...	...
8	50	...	...	frw	fr	...	...	...	x	C
9	25	...	...	...	...	...	...	...	...	...

F = Free to faculty
f = Available to faculty
s = Available to spouse

c = Available to children
r = Available to retired faculty
w = Available to widow

Name of Institution	No. of full-time faculty (Lay in Catholic insts.)	Ratio of faculty in college housing to full-time faculty	First-mortgage home loans	Second-mortgage home loans	Ratio of faculty with college mortgage to full-time faculty	Personal loans
TENNESSEE						
10 Lincoln Memorial U.	30	Z	...	...	...	...
11 Maryville Col.	58	B	...	...	...	x
12 Memphis St. U.	277	C	...	...	...	...
13 Middle Tenn. St. Col.	157	D	...	...	...	...
14 Southern Missionary Col.	61	A	...	...	...	...
15 Southwestern at Memphis	65	B	...	...	...	...
16 Tenn. Poly. Inst.	162	C	...	...	...	...
17 Tenn. Wesleyan Col.	30	A	...	...	...	...
18 Trevecca Nazarene Col.	18	...	...	...	...	...
19 Tusculum Col.	20	Z	...	...	...	...
20 Union U.	39	A	x	x	C	x
21 U. of Chattanooga	74	...	...	...	...	...
22 U. of the South	58	A	x	...	A	...
23 U. of Tennessee	463	C	...	...	...	...
24 Vanderbilt U.	450	D	x	...	A	...
25 William J. Bryan Col.	13	C	...	...	...	x
TEXAS						
1 Arlington St. Col.	260	D	...	...	...	...
2 Austin Col.	68	B	x	...	B	x
3 Baylor U.	245	D	...	...	...	...
4 Bishop Col.	44	A	...	...	...	x
5 East Texas Baptist Col.	31	...	...	...	...	...
6 Hardin-Simmons U.	116	C	...	...	...	x
7 Howard Payne Col.	77	C	...	...	...	x
8 Incarnate Word Col.	13	...	...	...	...	x
9 Lamar St. Col. Tech.	210	...	...	...	...	...
10 McMurry Col.	53	B	...	...	...	...
11 Midwestern U.	61	...	...	...	...	...
12 North Texas St. U.	374	...	...	...	...	...
13 Rice U.	178	...	x	...	A	...
14 Sacred Heart Dominican Col.	16	...	...	...	...	x
15 St. Mary's U. of San Antonio	47	...	...	...	...	...
16 Southern Methodist U.	330	...	x	...	C	...
17 Stephen F. Austin St. Col.	115	B	...	...	...	...
18 Sul Ross St. Col.	57	...	...	...	...	...
19 Tarleton St. Col.	60	...	...	...	...	...
20 Texas A&M U.	524	...	...	...	...	...
21 Texas Col.	29	Z	...	...	...	...

x = Has program   B = 10% but < 20%   1S = 1 Semester, 2S = 2 Semesters
Z = 50% up   C = 5% but < 10%   1Q = 1 Quarter, etc.
A = 20% but < 50%   D = Same, but < 5%   ... = Either no program or no answer

Institution	% of fac. children tuition waivers	Member Tuition Exchange, Inc.	Cash grants for fac. children's tuitions	Emergency medical treatment	Annual physical examination	Sabbatical leaves	Max. time sab. leave on full salary	Max. time sab. leave on half salary	Leaves with pay other than sab. from inst. funds	Ratio of faculty with leaves during year to full-time faculty
TENN										
10	100	...	...	fsc	...	...	...	...	...	...
11	50	...	...	...	...	x	1S	2S	...	C
12	...	...	...	Fr	...	...	...	...	x	D
13	...	...	...	...	...	...	...	...	x	D
14	25	...	...	Fscrw	...	x	4Q	...	x	A
15	100	...	...	Fsc	...	...	...	...	...	...
16	...	...	...	f	...	...	...	...	x	D
17	100	...	...	fsc	...	...	...	...	...	...
18	...	...	...	...	...	x	1Q	...	x	...
19	50	...	...	...	...	...	...	...	...	C
20	100	...	...	F	f	x	1S	...	...	A
21	90	...	...	...	...	x	...	1S	...	...
22	100	x	...	fscrw	fscrw	x	1S	2S	x	B
23	...	...	...	f	...	...	...	...	x	C
24	94	...	...	fsc	fsc	...	...	...	x	C
25	100	...	...	...	...	x	1S	2S	x	A
TEX										
1	...	...	...	...	...	...	...	...	...	D
2	90	...	...	F	...	x	1S	2S	...	D
3	100	x	...	rw	...	...	...	...	...	...
4	40	...	...	fscrw	...	x	1S	2S	x	D
5	100	...	...	...	...	...	...	...	...	B
6	50	...	...	...	...	...	...	...	x	C
7	50	...	x	rw	...	...	...	...	x	C
8	100	...	...	F	...	...	...	...	...	C
9	...	...	...	...	...	...	...	...	...	D
10	50	...	...	...	...	...	...	...	x	C
11	...	...	...	f	f	...	...	...	...	...
12	...	...	...	...	...	...	...	...	...	D
13	...	x	...	F	...	x	1S	2S	x	C
14	100	...	...	...	...	x	2S	1S	...	B
15	50	...	...	f	f	...	...	...	...	...
16	100	...	...	fscr	fscr	x	...	2S	...	D
17	...	...	...	...	...	...	...	...	x	C
18	...	...	...	...	...	...	...	...	...	C
19	...	...	...	...	...	...	...	...	x	B
20	...	...	...	...	...	...	...	...	...	D
21	...	...	...	...	fsc	...	...	...	x	C

F = Free to faculty   c = Available to children
f = Available to faculty   r = Available to retired faculty
s = Available to spouse   w = Available to widow

Name of Institution	No. of full-time faculty (Lay in Catholic insts.)	Ratio of faculty in college housing to full-time faculty	First-mortgage home loans	Second-mortgage home loans	Ratio of faculty with college mortgage to full-time faculty	Personal loans
TEXAS						
22 Texas Col. Arts & Ind.	151	...	...	...	...	...
23 Texas Lutheran Col.	50	C	...	...	...	x
24 Texas Southern U.	159	...	...	...	...	...
25 Texas Tech. Col.	406	...	...	...	...	...
26 Texas Wesleyan Col.	55	A	...	...	...	x
27 Texas Western Col.	185	...	...	...	...	...
28 Trinity U.	101	D	...	...	...	x
29 U. of Dallas	29	...	...	...	...	...
30 U. of Houston	404	...	...	...	...	...
31 U. of St. Thomas	12	...	...	...	...	...
32 U. of Texas	1675	...	...	...	...	...
33 Wayland Baptist Col.	39	A	...	...	...	x
34 West Texas St. Col.	127	C	...	...	...	...
UTAH						
1 Brigham Young U.	550	D	...	...	...	x
2 U. of Utah	511	...	...	...	...	...
3 Utah St. U. Agric. & App. Sci.	363	D	...	...	...	...
4 Westminster Col.	33	C	..	x	C	x
VERMONT						
1 Bennington Col.	46	Z	...	...	...	...
2 Marlboro Col.	16	B	...	...	...	...
3 Middlebury Col.	81	A	...	x	A	...
4 Norwich U.	71	Z	...	x	A	...
5 St. Michael's Col.	33	B	...	...	...	...
6 U. of Vermont	328	A	...	...	...	x
7 Windham Col.	19	B	...	...	...	x
VIRGINIA						
1 Eastern Mennonite Col.	60	...	x	...	C	x
2 Emory & Henry Col.	37	Z	x	...	...	...
3 Hampden-Sydney Col.	29	Z	x	...	D	...
4 Hampton Inst.	115	Z	...	...	...	...
5 Hollins Col.	68	A	...	...	...	...
6 Lynchburg Col.	53	A	...	...	...	...
7 Mary Baldwin Col.	33	...	x	...	B	...
8 Old Dominion Col.	189	...	...	...	...	...
9 Randolph-Macon Col.	54	A	x	x	...	x
10 R-M Woman's Col.	75	A	x	x	B	...

x = Has program   B = 10% but < 20%   1S = 1 Semester, 2S = 2 Semesters
Z = 50% up   C = 5% but < 10%   1Q = 1 Quarter, etc.
A = 20% but < 50% D = Some, but < 5%   ... = Either no program or no answer

Institution	% of fac. children tuition waivers	Member Tuition Exchange, Inc.	Cash grants for fac. children's tuitions	Emergency medical treatment	Annual physical examination	Sabbatical leaves	Max. time sab. leave on full salary	Max. time sab. leave on half salary	Leaves with pay other than sab. from inst. funds	Ratio of faculty with leaves during year to full-time faculty
TEX										
22	...	...	...	...	...	...	...	...	...	D
23	100	...	...	...	...	x	1S	2S	...	D
24	...	...	...	...	...	...	...	...	...	C
25	...	...	...	...	...	...	...	...	x	D
26	100	...	...	Fsc	...	...	...	...	x	...
27	...	...	...	F	...	...	...	...	...	...
28	100	x	...	f	...	...	...	...	x	D
29	100	...	...	f	...	x	1S	2S	...	C
30	75	...	...	Fscrw	...	...	...	...	...	D
31	75	...	...	f	...	...	...	...	...	...
32	...	...	...	...	...	...	...	...	x	C
33	100	...	...	...	...	...	...	...	x	C
34	...	...	...	...	...	...	...	...	...	C
UTAH										
1	...	...	...	...	f	x	1S	2S	x	B
2	...	...	...	...	...	x	...	...	x	C
3	...	...	...	...	...	x	2Q	4Q	...	D
4	80	x	...	Frw	...	x	...	1S	...	C
VT										
1	51	x	x	Fscrw	...	x	1S	2S	...	A
2	100	...	x	Fsc	...	...	...	...	...	...
3	100	x	x	...	...	x	1S	2S	...	C
4	100	x	x	Fr	...	...	...	...	x	B
5	100	...	...	F	...	...	...	...	x	D
6	100	x	...	F	...	x	1S	2S	...	D
7	100	...	...	r	...	...	...	...	...	...
VA										
1	50	...	...	fscrw	...	x	1S	2S	...	C
2	100	x	...	Fsc	...	...	...	...	...	...
3	100	x	x	...	...	...	...	...	...	...
4	100	...	...	...	...	x	1S	2S	...	D
5	100	...	x	Fscrw	...	x	1S	2S	x	C
6	100	x	...	f	...	x	1S	2S	...	B
7	100	x	...	F	...	...	...	...	...	...
8	50	...	...	...	...	x	...	2S	...	D
9	100	...	...	Frw	...	x	1S	...	x	C
10	100	x	x	Frw	...	x	1S	2S	...	C

F = Free to faculty   c = Available to children
f = Available to faculty   r = Available to retired faculty
s = Available to spouse   w = Available to widow

Name of Institution	No. of full-time faculty (Lay in Catholic insts.)	Ratio of faculty in college housing to full-time faculty	First-mortgage home loans	Second-mortgage home loans	Ratio of faculty with college mortgage to full-time faculty	Personal loans
VIRGINIA						
11 Sweet Briar Col.	56	A	...	...	...	...
12 U. of Richmond	125	C	x	...	B	...
13 U. of Virginia	496	B	x	...	A	x
14 U.V. Mary Wash. Col.	135	...	...	...	...	...
15 Virginia Mil. Inst.	98	Z	x	...	D	...
16 Va. Poly. Inst. Radford Col.	102	...	...	...	...	...
17 Washington & Lee U.	94	A	x	...	A	x
WASHINGTON						
1 Central Wash. St. Col.	153	D	...	...	...	...
2 Eastern Wash. St. Col.	125	B	...	...	...	...
3 Gonzaga U.	74	D	...	...	...	x
4 Holy Names College	2	Z	...	...	...	...
5 Seattle Pacific Col.	70	C	...	...	...	...
6 U. of Puget Sound	78	...	...	...	...	...
7 U. of Washington	1417	D	...	...	...	...
8 Washington St. U.	590	C	...	...	...	...
9 Western Wash. St. Col.	231	...	...	...	...	...
10 Whitman Col.	62	...	...	...	...	...
11 Whitworth Col.	60	...	...	...	...	...
WEST VIRGINIA						
1 Alderson-Broaddus Col.	32	A	...	...	...	...
2 Bluefield St. Col.	33	B	...	...	...	...
3 Concord Col.	76	C	...	...	...	...
4 Davis & Elkins Col.	43	D	...	...	...	...
5 Fairmont St. Col.	62	...	...	...	...	...
6 Glenville St. Col.	39	B	...	...	...	...
7 Marshall U.	202	D	...	...	...	...
8 Morris Harvey Col.	55	A	...	...	...	x
9 Shepherd Col.	41	C	...	...	...	...
10 West Liberty St. Col.	63	A	...	...	...	...
11 W. Virginia Inst. Tech.	64	A	...	...	...	...
12 W. Virginia St. Col.	89	A	...	...	...	...
13 W. Virginia U.	613	C	...	...	...	x
14 Wheeling Col.	19	...	...	...	...	...
WISCONSIN						
1 Beloit Col.	85	A	...	x	B	...
2 Cardinal Stritch Col.	3	...	...	...	...	...

x = Has program   B = 10% but < 20%   1S = 1 Semester, 2S = 2 Semesters
Z = 50% up   C = 5% but < 10%   1Q = 1 Quarter, etc.
A = 20% but < 50% D = Some, but < 5%   ... = Either no program or no answer

Institution	% of fac. children tuition waivers	Member Tuition Exchange, Inc.	Cash grants for fac. children's tuitions	Emergency medical treatment	Annual physical examination	Sabbatical leaves	Max. time sab. leave on full salary	Max. time sab. leave on half salary	Leaves with pay other than sab. from inst. funds	Ratio of faculty with leaves during year to full-time faculty
VA										
11	100	...	x	Fsc	F	x	1S	2S	x	C
12	100	x	...	F	...	x	1S	2S	x	D
13	...	...	...	fscrw	fscrw	...	...	...	x	D
14	...	...	...	...	...	...	...	...	x	C
15	100	x	...	fsc	...	...	...	...	x	A
16	...	...	...	...	...	...	...	...	x	D
17	100	...	x	...	...	...	...	...	...	...
WASH										
1	...	...	...	Frw	...	x	...	3Q	...	D
2	...	...	...	F	...	...	...	...	x	B
3	100	...	...	...	...	...	...	...	x	D
4	...	...	...	Fsc	...	x	1S	2S	...	Z
5	100	...	...	F	...	x	1Q	2Q	...	C
6	100	x	x	f	...	...	...	...	x	D
7	...	...	...	F	...	...	...	...	x	D
8	...	...	...	...	...	x	1S	2S	...	C
9	...	...	...	...	...	x	...	3Q	...	D
10	100	...	x	F	...	x	1S	...	...	C
11	100	x	...	fsc	...	x	1S	2S	...	...
W VA										
1	100	...	...	Frw	f	x	1S	2S	...	C
2	...	...	...	...	...	x	1S	2S	...	B
3	...	...	...	f	...	x	1S	2S	...	D
4	100	x	...	F	...	x	1S	2S	x	D
5	...	...	...	F	...	x	1S	2S	...	D
6	...	...	...	Fscr	...	x	1S	2S	...	D
7	...	...	...	...	...	x	1S	2S	x	D
8	100	...	...	...	...	...	...	...	x	D
9	...	x	...	...	...	x	1S	2S	...	...
10	...	...	...	Fsc	F	x	1S	2S	...	D
11	...	...	...	...	...	x	1S	...	...	...
12	...	...	...	f	...	x	1S	2S	...	C
13	...	...	...	fr	fr	...	...	...	x	D
14	100	...	...	f	...	x	1S	2S	...	...
WIS										
1	100	x	...	F	...	x	1S	2S	...	D
2	...	...	...	F	...	...	...	...	x	...

F = Free to faculty
f = Available to faculty
s = Available to spouse

c = Available to children
r = Available to retired faculty
w = Available

Name of Institution	No. of full-time faculty (Lay in Catholic insts.)	Ratio of faculty in college housing to full-time faculty	First-mortgage home loans	Second-mortgage home loans	Ratio of faculty with college mortgage to full-time faculty	Personal loans
WISCONSIN						
3 Carroll Col.	52	A	...	x	B	...
4 Dominican Col.	8	...	...	...	...	...
5 Holy Family Col.	1	...	...	...	...	...
6 Lawrence Col.	96	B	...	x	B	x
7 Marquette U.	442	...	...	...	...	x
8 Milton Col.	26	B	...	...	...	...
9 Milwaukee-Downer Col.	31	...	...	...	...	...
10 Mount Mary Col.	20	...	...	...	...	x
11 Ripon Col.	50	A	...	...	...	...
12 St. Norbert Col.	35	...	x	x	A	x
13 U. of Wisconsin	1403	B	x	...	D	...
14 U. of Wis., Milwaukee Campus	497	...	...	...	...	...
15 Wis. St. Col., Eau Claire	149	...	...	...	...	...
16 Wis. St. Col., La Crosse	135	...	...	...	...	...
17 Wis. St. Col., Oshkosh	183	...	...	...	...	...
18 Wis. St. Col., River Falls	116	...	...	...	...	...
19 Wis. St. Col., Stevens Point	140	...	...	...	...	...
20 Wis. St. Col., Superior	101	...	...	...	...	...
21 Wis. St. Col., Whitewater	178	...	...	...	...	...
22 Wis. St. Col. & Inst. Tech.	142	...	...	...	...	...
WYOMING						
1 U. of Wyoming	387	...	...	...	...	...

x = Has program   B = 10% but < 20%   1S = 1 Semester, 2S = 2 Semesters
Z = 50% up   C = 5% but < 10%   1Q = 1 Quarter, etc.
A = 20% but < 50%   D = Some, but < 5%   ... = Either no program or no answer

Institution	% of fac. children tuition waivers	Member Tuition Exchange, Inc.	Cash grants for fac. children's tuitions	Emergency medical treatment	Annual physical examination	Sabbatical leaves	Max. time sab. leave on full salary	Max. time sab. leave on half salary	Leaves with pay other than sab. from inst. funds	Ratio of faculty with leaves during year to full-time faculty
WIS										
3	100	x	...	...	...	x	1S	2S	...	D
4	100	...	...	...	...	...	...	...	...	...
5	...	...	...	...	...	x	1S	2S	...	...
6	100	x	x	Fr	...	...	...	...	x	B
7	50	...	...	f	...	...	...	...	x	C
8	91	...	...	...	...	x	1S	2S	...	B
9	100	x	...	F	...	...	...	...	...	...
10	100	...	...	F	...	...	...	...	...	...
11	100	...	...	fscrw	fscrw	...	...	...	...	D
12	100	...	...	...	...	x	1S	2S	...	D
13	...	...	...	...	...	...	...	...	x	C
14	...	...	...	...	...	...	...	...	x	...
15	...	...	...	F	...	...	...	...	...	D
16	...	...	...	F	F	...	...	...	...	D
17	...	...	...	F	...	...	...	...	...	D
18	...	...	...	...	...	...	...	...	...	D
19	...	...	...	F	...	...	...	...	...	D
20	...	...	...	f	f	...	...	...	...	D
21	...	...	...	...	...	...	...	...	...	D
22	...	...	...	...	...	...	...	...	...	D
WYO										
1	...	...	...	...	...	x	1S	2S	...	C

F = Free to faculty   c = Available to children
f = Available to faculty   r = Available to retired faculty
s = Available to spouse   w = Available to widow

APPENDIX III

SUMMARY TABLES

Caveat Lector!

THESE tables give summaries of the replies to most of the questions in the questionnaire which lend themselves to coding for machine computation. The headings are at times slightly elliptical but on each table the question (or questions) from which the table is derived is indicated and a perusal of the question should help give a clear idea of the nature of the information contained in the table.

Do not try to check these tables against that of Appendix II! Besides any coding errors we might have made (or counting and classifying errors you might make) there are two other reasons why this will not work: First, some institutions replied too late to be included in these summary tables, but were included in Appendix II. Second, institutions were given the opportunity to correct items in Appendix II; the tendency was to increase both the size of the faculty and the benefits reported. All these factors together do not affect the magnitude of the figures involved and hence the validity of this appendix as summary tables is unaltered.

TABLE 1: RESPONSE TO THE AAC/TIAA STUDY QUESTIONNAIRE
Questionnaire page 1

	All Institutions			Public Institutions			Private Institutions		
	Total	Univ.	Col.	Total	Univ.	Col.	Total	Univ.	Col.
1. Replies received	745	148	597	217	84	133	528	64	464
2. Replies not received	258	13	245	58	6	52	200	7	193
3. Replies received as percent of total mailed	74.3%	91.9%	70.9%	78.9%	93.3%	71.9%	72.5%	90.1%	70.6%
4. Full-time faculty in replying insts.	146,443	96,640	49,803	88,550	65,327	23,223	57,893	31,313	26,580
5. Full-time faculty in non-replying insts.	21,482	4,807	16,675	8,543	1,925	6,618	12,939	2,882	10,057
6. Ratio full-time fac. replying insts. to total full-time fac.	87.2%	95.3%	74.9%	91.2%	97.1%	77.8%	81.7%	91.6%	72.5%

The full-time faculty figures for non-replying institutions (column 5) were obtained from the 1962—63 College Facts Chart and January 12, 1963 issue of School and Society. These figures included both the lay and religious faculty in Catholic institutions. Since all questionnaire replies referred to lay faculty only and specifically excluded facilities for faculty belonging to religious orders, the ratio of full-time faculty in replying institutions to total full-time faculty to which the questionnaire applies (column 6) is therefore slightly understated.

Twelve institutions replied too late to be included in the summary tables of Appendix III but early enough to be included in the listing of Appendix II. Of these, 3 were public universities, 3 public colleges, 2 private universities, and 4 private colleges. The faculty in these institutions totaled about 9,900. Hence, we estimate that about 93 percent of the full-time faculty of the total number of institutions queried were covered by replies.

TABLE 2: PLAN OF FURNISHING, LEASING, OR SECURING LAND ON WHICH FACULTY MEMBERS MAY BUILD HOMES
Questionnaire Sect. 1 Q. 2

	All Institutions			Public Institutions			Private Institutions		
	Total	Univ.	Col.	Total	Univ.	Col.	Total	Univ.	Col.
Plan in Effect									
1. Number	81	11	70	5	4	1	76	7	69
2. Percent	10.9%	7.4%	11.7%	2.3%	4.8%	.8%	14.4%	10.9%	14.9%
No Plan in Effect									
3. Number	651	136	515	211	79	132	440	57	383
4. Percent	87.4%	91.9%	86.3%	97.2%	94.0%	99.2%	83.3%	89.1%	82.5%
No Response									
5. Number	13	1	12	1	1	...	12	...	12
6. Percent	1.7%	.7%	2.0%	.5%	1.2%	...	2.3%	...	2.6%
7. Total	745	148	597	217	84	133	528	64	464

224

Appendix III

TABLE 3: INSTITUTIONAL OWNERSHIP OF HOUSES OR APARTMENTS FOR FACULTY OCCUPANCY
Questionnaire Sect. 1 Q. 3

	All Institutions			Public Institutions			Private Institutions		
	Total	Univ.	Col.	Total	Univ.	Col.	Total	Univ.	Col.
Owned									
1. Number	452	94	358	127	58	69	325	36	289
2. Percent	60.7%	63.5%	60.0%	58.5%	69.0%	51.9%	61.6%	56.3%	62.3%
Not Owned									
3. Number	288	54	234	90	26	64	198	28	170
4. Percent	38.7%	36.5%	39.2%	41.5%	31.0%	48.1%	37.5%	43.7%	36.6%
No Response									
5. Number	5	...	5	...	...	...	5	...	5
6. Percent	.6%	...	.8%	...	...	...	.9%	...	1.1%
7. Total	745	148	597	217	84	133	528	64	464

TABLE 4: FACULTY OCCUPANCY OF INSTITUTIONALLY OWNED HOUSES, APARTMENTS, AND
DORMITORIES
Questionnaire Sect. 1 Q. 4

	All Institutions			Public Institutions			Private Institutions		
	Total	Univ.	Col.	Total	Univ.	Col.	Total	Univ.	Col.
1. Insts. reporting any occupants	440	93	347	123	57	66	317	36	281
2. Insts. reporting house occupants	365	71	294	90	40	50	275	31	244
3. Insts. reporting apt. occupants	336	78	258	102	50	52	234	28	206
4. Insts. reporting dormitory occupants	197	32	165	44	17	27	153	15	138
5. Number of faculty in houses	3,998	1,538	2,460	1,263	903	360	2,735	635	2,100
6. Number of faculty in apts.	7,273	4,433	2,840	3,135	2,430	705	4,138	2,003	2,135
7. Number of faculty in dormitories	1,076	360	716	278	137	141	798	223	575
8. Total faculty in inst.-owned housing	12,347	6,331	6,016	4,676	3,470	1,206	7,671	2,861	4,810
9. Total faculty of insts. reporting numbers of occupants	88,122	62,215	25,907	50,502	42,021	8,481	37,620	20,194	17,426
10. Percent of faculty in insts. with housing occupying inst.-owned housing	14.0%	10.2%	23.2%	9.3%	8.3%	14.3%	20.4%	14.2%	27.6%
11. Percent of faculty of all insts. occupying inst.-owned housing	8.4%	6.6%	12.1%	5.3%	5.3%	5.2%	13.3%	9.1%	18.1%

Since some of the faculty reported as occupying housing may not be full time, columns 10 and 11 may be overstatements.

TABLE 5: PRIORITY SYSTEM FOR ASSIGNMENT OF FACULTY HOUSING
Questionnaire Sect. 1 Q. 5

		All Institutions			Public Institutions			Private Institutions		
		Total	Univ.	Col.	Total	Univ.	Col.	Total	Univ.	Col.
1.	No priority system	215	34	181	45	15	30	170	19	151
2.	Priority system	236	60	176	81	43	38	155	17	138
3.	New faculty	120	40	80	51	31	20	69	9	60
4.	Faculty with service	15	2	13	1	1	...	14	1	13
5.	Profs.	28	12	16	9	7	2	19	5	14
6.	Assoc. profs.	22	11	11	8	7	1	14	4	10
7.	Asst. profs	22	10	12	6	5	1	16	5	11
8.	Instrs.	25	12	13	8	7	1	17	5	12
9.	Other	80	26	54	26	17	9	54	9	45
10.	Need	113	23	90	30	15	15	83	8	75

Columns 5 to 8 have little meaning except for the fact that the numbers are small. A given institution may have checked several of these categories.

TABLE 6: LENGTH OF OCCUPANCY PROVISIONS IN FACULTY HOUSING
Questionnaire Sect. 1 Q. 6

		All Institutions			Public Institutions			Private Institutions		
		Total	Univ.	Col.	Total	Univ.	Col.	Total	Univ.	Col.
1.	Insts. stating length of occupancy	444	93	351	124	57	67	320	36	284
2.	Stated length of time	81	36	45	51	31	20	30	5	25
3.	Until retirement	65	10	55	13	6	7	52	4	48
4.	Throughout retirement	7	2	5	...	...	...	7	2	5
5.	No specified time	287	44	243	52	16	36	235	28	207
6.	Other	32	12	20	15	9	6	17	3	14
7.	No response	8	1	7	3	1	2	5	...	5
8.	Total cards	452	94	358	127	58	69	325	36	289

TABLE 7: RENTAL LEVEL CHARGED FOR FACULTY HOUSING COMPARED WITH PRIVATELY OWNED
UNITS OF SIMILAR QUALITY, AND, IF BELOW, PERCENT BELOW
Questionnaire Sect. 1 Q. 7

		All Institutions			Public Institutions			Private Institutions		
		Total	Univ.	Col.	Total	Univ.	Col.	Total	Univ.	Col.
1.	Insts. responding	445	93	352	125	57	68	320	36	284
2.	Above similar quality	3	...	3	2	...	2	1	...	1
3.	Same as similar quality	119	30	89	35	18	17	84	12	72
4.	Below similar quality	323	63	260	88	39	49	235	24	211
5.	No response	7	1	6	2	1	1	5	...	5
6.	Less than 10% below	37	10	27	9	6	3	28	4	24
7.	10–25% below	178	39	139	57	26	31	121	13	108
8.	25–50% below	67	7	60	11	4	7	56	3	53
9.	More than 50% below	25	5	20	6	2	4	19	3	16
10.	No response	16	2	14	5	1	4	11	1	10

TABLE 8: DEGREE TO WHICH RENTS CHARGED COVER COST OF FACULTY HOUSING
Questionnaire Sect. 1 Q. 8

	All Institutions			Public Institutions			Private Institutions		
	Total	Univ.	Col.	Total	Univ.	Col.	Total	Univ.	Col.
1. Insts. reporting	434	94	340	123	58	65	311	36	275
2. Substantially more than cost	15	5	10	6	3	3	9	2	7
3. Approximately cover cost	269	64	205	81	39	42	188	25	163
4. Substantially less than cost	69	8	61	7	3	4	62	5	57
5. Not calculated	81	17	64	29	13	16	52	4	48
6. No response	18	...	18	4	...	4	14	...	14
7. Total	452	94	358	127	58	69	325	36	289

TABLE 9: PLANS FOR FUTURE OF FACULTY HOUSING PROGRAM (EXPANSION OF PROGRAM VS. EXPANSION OF FACULTY)
Questionnaire Sect. 1 Q. 10

	All Institutions			Public Institutions			Private Institutions		
	Total	Univ.	Col.	Total	Univ.	Col.	Total	Univ.	Col.
1. More rapidly	27	10	17	7	3	4	20	7	13
2. Same rate	59	10	49	10	6	4	49	4	45
3. Less rapidly	93	15	78	31	13	18	62	2	60
4. Remain as is	239	52	187	70	33	37	169	19	150
5. Contracted	28	7	21	8	3	5	20	4	16
6. No response	6	...	6	1	...	1	5	...	5
7. Total	452	94	358	127	58	69	325	36	289

TABLE 10: OCCUPANCY OF FACULTY HOUSING AS RELATED TO SIGNIFICANCE OF PROGRAM IN RECRUITING AND RETAINING FACULTY
Questionnaire p. 1 and Sect. 1 Q. 4, 11

	All Institutions			Public Institutions			Private Institutions		
	Total	Univ.	Col.	Total	Univ.	Col.	Total	Univ.	Col.
Percent Faculty in Inst.-Owned Housing									
1. Where housing makes substantial contribution	35.2%	28.2%	47.6%	23.8%	20.3%	42.6%	51.0%	54.0%	49.3%
2. Where housing makes moderate contribution	21.0%	17.8%	28.2%	10.7%	9.2%	18.7%	28.3%	26.5%	30.8%
3. Where housing makes negligible contribution	5.3%	3.6%	8.9%	4.1%	3.4%	6.3%	7.1%	4.0%	11.2%

TABLE 11: NUMBER OF INSTITUTIONS MAKING MORTGAGE LOANS TO FACULTY
Questionnaire Sect. 2 Q. 1, 2

	All Institutions			Public Institutions			Private Institutions		
	Total	Univ.	Col.	Total	Univ.	Col.	Total	Univ.	Col.
First Mortgage Loans Made									
1. Number	107	21	86	10	10	...	97	11	86
2. Percent	14.4%	14.2%	14.4%	4.6%	11.9%	...	18.4%	17.2%	18.5%
Second Mortgage Loans Made									
3. Number	65	...	65	...	...	...	65	14	51
4. Percent	8.7%	...	10.9%	...	...	...	12.3%	21.9%	11.0%
Both First & Second Mortgage Loans Made									
5. Number	18	2	16	...	...	...	18	2	16
6. Percent	2.4%	1.4%	2.7%	...	...	...	3.4%	3.1%	3.4%
7. Responding insts.	745	148	597	217	84	133	528	64	464

TABLE 12: FIRST AND SECOND MORTGAGE LOANS TO FACULTY MEMBERS
Questionnaire Sect. 2 Q. 3, 14

	All Institutions			Public Institutions			Private Institutions		
	Total	Univ.	Col.	Total	Univ.	Col.	Total	Univ.	Col.
Insts. Reporting Number of Outstanding First Mortgage Loans									
1. Number	99	21	78	10	10	...	89	11	78
2. Percent	13.3%	14.2%	13.1%	4.6%	11.9%	...	16.9%	17.9%	16.8%
3. Number of faculty having first mortgage loans	3,188	2,295	893	1,270	1,270	...	1,918	1,025	893
4. Total faculty at insts. with first mortgage loans outstanding	22,490	16,411	6,079	9,552	9,552	...	12,938	6,859	6,079
5. Percent of faculty holding first mortgage loans	14.2%	18.1%	14.7%	13.3%	13.3%	...	14.8%	14.9%	14.7%
Insts. Reporting Number of Outstanding Second Mortgage Loans									
6. Number	61	14	47	...	...	...	61	14	47
7. Percent	8.2%	9.5%	7.9%	...	...	...	11.6%	24.1%	10.1%
8. Number of faculty having second mortgage loans	946	552	394	...	...	...	946	552	394
9. Total faculty at insts. with second mortgage loans outstanding	13,684	10,203	3,481	...	...	...	13,684	10,203	3,481
10. Percent of faculty holding second mortgage loans	6.9%	5.4%	11.3%	...	...	...	6.9%	5.4%	11.3%
Insts. Reporting Both First and Second Mortgage Loans Outstanding									
11. Number	16	3	13	...	...	...	16	3	13
12. Percent	2.1%	2.0%	2.2%	...	...	...	3.0%	4.7%	2.8%
13. Total amount of mortgage loans outstanding (millions of dollars)	46	35	12	14	14	...	32	21	12

TABLE 13: FACULTY ELIGIBLE FOR MORTGAGE LOANS
Questionnaire Sect. 2 Q. 4

	All Institutions			Public Institutions			Private Institutions		
	Total	Univ.	Col.	Total	Univ.	Col.	Total	Univ.	Col.
1. Insts. reporting	149	32	117	10	10	...	139	22	117
2. Profs.	138	31	107	10	10	...	128	21	107
3. Assoc. profs.	138	31	107	10	10	...	128	21	107
4. Asst. profs.	126	28	98	9	9	...	117	19	98
5. Instrs.	92	20	72	6	6	...	86	14	72
6. Others	49	11	38	4	4	...	45	7	38
7. No response	5	1	4	...	...	...	5	1	4

TABLE 14: MAXIMUM FIRST MORTGAGE LOAN AS PERCENTAGE OF PROPERTY MARKET VALUE
Questionnaire Sect. 2 Q. 5

	All Institutions			Public Institutions			Private Institutions		
	Total	Univ.	Col.	Total	Univ.	Col.	Total	Univ.	Col.
1. Less than 2/3	8	...	8	...	...	...	8	...	8
2. 2/3	13	3	10	1	1	...	12	2	10
3. 75%	20	5	15	4	4	...	16	1	15
4. 80%	15	6	9	3	3	...	12	3	9
5. 85%	6	1	5	1	1	...	5	...	5
6. 90%	25	2	23	1	1	...	24	1	23
7. 95%	3	1	2	...	...	...	3	1	2
8. 100%	11	1	10	...	...	...	11	1	10
9. No response	6	2	4	...	...	...	6	2	4
10. Total	107	21	86	10	10	...	97	11	86

TABLE 15: SECOND MORTGAGES: MAXIMUM PERCENT PROPERTY MARKET VALUE FOR COMBINED
FIRST AND SECOND MORTGAGE LOANS
Questionnaire Sect. 2 Q. 6

	All Institutions			Public Institutions			Private Institutions		
	Total	Univ.	Col.	Total	Univ.	Col.	Total	Univ.	Col.
1. Less than 2/3	9	1	8	...	...	...	9	1	8
2. 2/3	...	...	...	...	...	...	...	...	...
3. 75%	2	...	2	...	...	...	2	...	2
4. 80%	3	...	3	...	...	...	3	...	3
5. 85%	1	1	...	...	...	...	1	1	...
6. 90%	14	3	11	...	...	...	14	3	11
7. 95%	10	1	9	...	...	...	10	1	9
8. 100%	11	5	6	...	...	...	11	5	6
9. No response	15	3	12	...	...	...	15	3	12
10. Total	65	14	51	...	...	...	65	14	51

Often the first-mortgage loan is not with the institution.

TABLE 16: DOLLAR LIMIT ON MORTGAGE LOANS TO FACULTY
Questionnaire Sect. 2 Q. 9

	All Institutions			Public Institutions			Private Institutions		
	Total	Univ.	Col.	Total	Univ.	Col.	Total	Univ.	Col.
First Mortgages
1. No limit	66	12	54	4	4	...	62	8	54
2. Limit	38	9	29	6	6	...	32	3	29
3. No response	3	...	3	...	...	...	3	...	3
4. Total	107	21	86	10	10	...	97	11	86
Second Mortgage
5. No limit	31	6	25	...	...	...	31	6	25
6. Limit	28	8	20	...	...	...	28	8	20
7. No response	6	...	6	...	...	...	6	...	6
8. Total	65	14	51	...	...	...	65	14	51

The number of institutions with limitations based on salary is close to but slightly less than the number with dollar limits shown above.

TABLE 17: INTEREST RATE CHARGED ON MORTGAGE LOANS
Questionnaire Sect. 2 Q. 10

	All Institutions			Public Institutions			Private Institutions		
	Total	Univ.	Col.	Total	Univ.	Col.	Total	Univ.	Col.
First Mortgage Rates									
1. No response	3	1	2	...	...	...	3	1	2
2. 0—2%	5	2	3	1	1	...	4	1	3
3. 2.1—4%	14	3	11	2	2	...	12	1	11
4. 4.1—5%	51	6	45	3	3	...	48	3	45
5. 5.1—6%	34	9	25	4	4	...	30	5	25
6. Above 6%	...	...	...	...	...	...	...	...	...
Second Mortgage Rates									
7. No response	3	...	3	...	...	...	3	...	3
8. 0—2%	7	...	7	...	...	...	7	...	7
9. 2.1—4%	10	4	6	...	...	...	10	4	6
10. 4.1—5%	26	4	22	...	...	...	26	4	22
11. 5.1—6%	18	6	12	...	...	...	18	6	12
12. Above 6%	1	...	1	...	...	...	1	...	1

There are almost no institutions which make service charges on mortgage loans.

TABLE 18: AMORTIZATION PERIOD FOR MORTGAGE LOANS
Questionnaire Sect. 2 Q. 12

	All Institutions			Public Institutions			Private Institutions		
	Total	Univ.	Col.	Total	Univ.	Col.	Total	Univ.	Col.
First Mortgages									
1. No response	8	1	7	...	...	...	8	1	7
2. Under 6 years	6	1	5	1	1	...	5	...	5
3. 6—10 years	6	...	6	...	...	...	6	...	6
4. 11—15 years	22	4	18	1	1	...	21	3	18
5. 16—20 years	50	11	39	7	7	...	43	4	39
6. 21 years and above	15	4	11	1	1	...	14	3	11
Second Mortgages									
7. No response	9	2	7	...	...	...	9	2	7
8. Under 6 years	19	3	16	...	...	...	19	3	16
9. 6—10 years	12	4	8	...	...	...	12	4	8
10. 11—15 years	11	3	8	...	...	...	11	3	8
11. 16—20 years	10	1	9	...	...	...	10	1	9
12. 21 years and above	4	1	3	...	...	...	4	1	3

TABLE 19: FUTURE PLANS FOR MORTGAGE LENDING PROGRAM (EXPANSION OF PROGRAM VS.
EXPANSION OF FACULTY)
Questionnaire Sect. 2 Q. 15

	All Institutions			Public Institutions			Private Institutions		
	Total	Univ.	Col.	Total	Univ.	Col.	Total	Univ.	Col.
1. More rapidly	14	4	10	1	1	...	13	3	10
2. Same rate	60	12	48	3	3	...	57	9	48
3. Less rapidly	19	5	14	1	1	...	18	4	14
4. Remain same	47	12	35	5	5	...	42	7	35
5. Be contracted	9	...	9	...	...	...	9	...	9
6. No response	5	...	5	...	...	...	5	...	5
7. Total	154	33	121	10	10	...	144	23	121

TABLE 20: CONTRIBUTION OF MORTGAGE LOAN PROGRAM TO RECRUITING AND RETAINING
FACULTY
Questionnaire Sect. 2 Q. 3, 16

	All Institutions			Public Institutions			Private Institutions		
	Total	Univ.	Col.	Total	Univ.	Col.	Total	Univ.	Col.
Recruiting									
1. Substantial	30	11	19	4	4	...	26	7	19
2. Moderate	62	8	54	1	1	...	61	7	54
3. Negligible	54	13	41	5	5	...	49	8	41
4. No response	8	1	7	...	...	...	8	1	7
5. Total	154	33	121	10	10	...	144	23	121
Retaining									
6. Substantial	46	8	38	3	3	...	43	5	38
7. Moderate	69	16	53	4	4	...	65	12	53
8. Negligible	30	8	22	3	3	...	27	5	22
9. No response	9	1	8	...	...	...	9	1	8
10. Total	154	33	121	10	10	...	144	23	121
11. Percent of faculty with mortgage loans from inst. where these make substantial contribution to recruiting and retaining	14.9%	14.3%	18.9%	21.6%	21.6%	...	10.9%	8.7%	18.9%

TABLE 21: FACULTY CREDIT UNION SERVING COLLEGE PERSONNEL ONLY
Questionnaire Sect. 3 Q. 1

	All Institutions			Public Institutions			Private Institutions		
	Total	Univ.	Col.	Total	Univ.	Col.	Total	Univ.	Col.
Faculty Credit Union in Operation									
1. Number	115	60	55	73	41	32	42	19	23
2. Percent	15.4%	40.5%	9.2%	33.7%	48.8%	24.0%	8.0%	29.7%	5.0%
No Faculty Credit Union									
3. Number	614	84	530	137	39	98	477	45	432
4. Percent	82.4%	56.8%	88.8%	63.1%	46.4%	73.7%	90.3%	70.3%	93.1%
No Response									
5. Number	16	4	12	7	4	3	9	...	9
6. Percent	2.2%	2.7%	2.0%	3.2%	4.8%	2.3%	1.7%	...	1.9%
7. Total	745	148	597	217	84	133	528	64	464

TABLE 22: TYPES OF INSTITUTIONAL AID GIVEN TO FACULTY CREDIT UNION SERVING COLLEGE
PERSONNEL ONLY
Questionnaire Sect. 3 Q. 1

	All Institutions			Public Institutions			Private Institutions		
	Total	Univ.	Col.	Total	Univ.	Col.	Total	Univ.	Col.
1. No faculty credit union	614	84	530	137	39	98	477	45	432
2. Faculty credit union	115	60	55	73	41	32	42	19	23
3. No aid given to credit union	35	16	19	25	13	12	10	3	7
4. Aid given	78	43	35	46	27	19	32	16	16
5. Percent giving aid where there is faculty credit union	67.8%	71.7%	63.6%	63.0%	65.9%	59.4%	76.2%	84.2%	69.6%
6. No response as to aid	2	1	1	2	1	1	...	...	...
Type of Aid									
7. Financial aid	1	...	1	...	...	...	1	...	1
8. Clerical help	17	6	11	9	3	6	8	3	5
9. Office space	69	38	31	39	22	17	30	16	14
10. Repayment by payroll deductions	50	29	21	23	15	8	27	14	13
11. Other	8	3	5	4	...	4	4	3	1

TABLE 23: PERSONAL LOANS TO FACULTY MEMBERS
Questionnaire Sect. 3 Q. 3

	All Institutions			Public Institutions			Private Institutions		
	Total	Univ.	Col.	Total	Univ.	Col.	Total	Univ.	Col.
Inst. Makes Personal Loans									
1. Number	193	41	152	17	14	3	176	27	149
2. Percent	25.9%	27.7%	25.5%	7.8%	16.7%	3.0%	33.3%	42.2%	32.1%
Inst. Does Not Make Personal Loans									
3. Number	535	103	432	192	66	126	343	37	306
4. Percent	71.9%	69.6%	72.4%	88.5%	78.6%	94.7%	65.0%	57.8%	66.0%
No Response									
5. Number	17	4	13	8	4	4	9	...	9
6. Percent	2.2%	2.7%	2.1%	3.7%	4.7%	2.3%	1.7%	...	1.9%
7. Total	745	148	597	217	84	133	528	64	464

TABLE 24: PERSONAL LOANS MADE IN 1962—NUMBER AND AMOUNT
Questionnaire Sect. 3 Q. 4, 5

	All Institutions			Public Institutions			Private Institutions		
	Total	Univ.	Col.	Total	Univ.	Col.	Total	Univ.	Col.
1. Number of insts. reporting loans made in 1962	172	39	133	16	13	3	156	26	130
2. Number of loans in 1962	6,110	4,939	1,171	4,116	4,039	77	1,994	900	1,094
3. Total amount of loans (thousands of dollars)	4,007	3,364	643	2,873	2,854	20	1,134	510	624
4. Average loan	656	681	550	698	707	256	569	567	570

Faculty rank is seldom used as a criterion for loan eligibility.

TABLE 25: LIMIT TO AMOUNT OF PERSONAL LOANS OUTSTANDING
Questionnaire Sect. 3 Q. 8

	All Institutions			Public Institutions			Private Institutions		
	Total	Univ.	Col.	Total	Univ.	Col.	Total	Univ.	Col.
No Limit Set									
1. Number	82	15	67	5	4	1	77	11	66
2. Percent	42.5%	36.6%	44.0%	29.4%	28.6%	33.3%	43.8%	40.7%	44.3%
Limit Set									
3. Number	103	26	77	12	10	2	91	16	75
4. Percent	53.4%	63.4%	50.7%	70.6%	71.4%	66.7%	51.7%	59.3%	50.3%
No Response									
5. Number	8	...	8	...	...	...	8	...	8
6. Percent	4.1%	...	5.3%	...	...	...	4.5%	...	5.4%
7. Total	193	41	152	17	14	3	176	27	149

TABLE 26: INTEREST RATE ON PERSONAL LOANS
Questionnaire Sect. 3 Q. 9

	All Institutions			Public Institutions			Private Institutions		
	Total	Univ.	Col.	Total	Univ.	Col.	Total	Univ.	Col.
1. 0%	78	15	63	8	7	1	70	8	62
2. .1—2%	8	2	6	...	...	...	8	2	6
3. 2.1—4%	41	9	32	2	1	1	39	8	31
4. 4.1—5%	30	11	19	6	5	1	24	6	18
5. 5.1—6%	26	3	23	1	1	...	25	2	23
6. Above 6%	...	...	...	...	...	...	...	...	...
7. No response	10	1	9	...	...	...	10	1	9
8. Total	193	41	152	17	14	3	176	27	149

Sometimes rate is higher if loan is long term.

TABLE 27: PERIOD OF TIME (YEARS) FOR WHICH LOANS ARE NORMALLY MADE
Questionnaire Sect. 3 Q. 10

	All Institutions			Public Institutions			Private Institutions		
	Total	Univ.	Col.	Total	Univ.	Col.	Total	Univ.	Col.
1. 1 year	123	24	99	12	10	2	111	14	97
2. 2 years	17	4	13	2	2	...	15	2	13
3. 3 years	12	4	8	1	1	...	11	3	8
4. 4 years	3	1	2	...	...	...	3	1	2
5. 5 years	8	3	5	1	1	...	7	2	5
6. 6 years	...	...	...	...	...	...	...	...	...
7. 7 years	...	...	...	...	...	...	...	...	...
8. 8 years	1	1	...	...	...	...	1	1	...
9. 9 years	...	...	...	...	...	...	...	...	...
10. No response	29	4	25	1	...	1	28	4	24

    The answers appear to report maximum periods rather than average periods. Many loans are made for very short periods, for instance until the next payday.

TABLE 28: REASONS FOR WHICH PERSONAL LOANS ARE MADE
Questionnaire Sect. 3 Q. 11

	All Institutions			Public Institutions			Private Institutions		
	Total	Univ.	Col.	Total	Univ.	Col.	Total	Univ.	Col.
1. Insts. reporting	181	41	140	16	14	2	165	27	138
2. Study for degree	98	16	82	8	6	2	90	10	80
3. Research	46	10	36	3	3	...	43	7	36
4. Children's education	38	13	25	4	4	...	34	9	25
5. Family emergency	157	37	120	14	12	2	143	25	118
6. Other	52	15	37	8	7	1	44	8	36
7. No response	12	...	12	1	...	1	11	...	11

    To "consolidate debt" is sometimes mentioned. Some institutions report that it is their policy not to ask the reason for borrowing.

TABLE 29: PAYROLL DEDUCTIONS FOR REPAYMENT OF PERSONAL LOANS
Questionnaire Sect. 3 Q. 13

	All Institutions			Public Institutions			Private Institutions		
	Total	Univ.	Col.	Total	Univ.	Col.	Total	Univ.	Col.
Payroll Deductions Made									
1. Number	152	29	123	7	6	1	145	23	122
2. Percent	78.8%	70.7%	80.9%	41.2%	42.9%	33.3%	82.4%	85.2%	81.9%
Deductions Not Made									
3. Number	37	12	25	10	8	2	27	4	23
4. Percent	19.2%	29.3%	16.5%	58.8%	57.1%	66.7%	15.4%	14.8%	15.4%
No Response									
5. Number	4	...	4	...	...	...	4	...	4
6. Percent	2.0%	...	2.6%	...	...	...	2.2%	...	2.7%
7. Total	193	41	152	17	14	3	176	27	149

TABLE 30: CONTRIBUTION OF PERSONAL LOAN PROGRAM TO RECRUITING AND RETAINING
FACULTY
Questionnaire Sect. 3 Q. 15

	All Institutions			Public Institutions			Private Institutions		
	Total	Univ.	Col.	Total	Univ.	Col.	Total	Univ.	Col.
Recruiting									
1. Substantial	3	1	2	1	1	...	2	...	2
2. Moderate	32	10	22	4	3	1	28	7	21
3. Negligible	150	29	121	12	10	2	138	19	119
4. No response	8	1	7						
Retaining									
5. Substantial	9	2	7	...	...	...	9	2	7
6. Moderate	64	16	48	6	5	1	58	11	47
7. Negligible	111	21	90	'10	8	2	101	13	88
8. No response	9	2	7	1	1	...	8	1	7

TABLE 31: REIMBURSEMENT FOR FACULTY TRAVEL
Questionnaire Sect. 4 Q. 1

	All Institutions			Public Institutions			Private Institutions		
	Total	Univ.	Col.	Total	Univ.	Col.	Total	Univ.	Col.
1. Insts. responding	732	145	587	212	83	129	520	62	458
2. No response	13	3	10	5	1	4	8	2	6
Professional Meetings									
Not giving paper									
3. No reimbursement	50	14	36	13	4	9	37	10	27
4. Reimbursement	672	130	542	196	78	118	476	52	424
Giving paper									
5. No reimbursement	16	2	14	5	...	5	11	2	9
6. Reimbursement	696	138	558	199	80	119	497	58	439
Society officer									
7. No reimbursement	27	5	22	9	2	7	18	3	15
8. Reimbursement	674	133	541	195	76	119	479	57	422
Scholarly Conferences									
9. No reimbursement	54	10	44	12	3	9	42	7	35
10. Reimbursement	633	124	509	192	74	118	441	50	391
Research Leaves									
11. No reimbursement	471	76	395	143	49	94	328	27	301
12. Reimbursement	180	57	123	58	30	28	122	27	95

Partial reimbursement is listed as reimbursement. This table is misleading in that the
reimbursement when giving a paper is often greater than when not giving a paper. Though
there may be partial reimbursement in the latter case, the difference will not show up in the
table.

TABLE 32: DIFFERENCE IN REIMBURSEMENT POLICY FOR TRANSPORTATION EXPENSES AS
COMPARED WITH OTHER EXPENSES
Questionnaire Sect. 4 Q. 2

	All Institutions			Public Institutions			Private Institutions		
	Total	Univ.	Col.	Total	Univ.	Col.	Total	Univ.	Col.
1. No difference	480	73	407	132	42	90	348	31	317
2. Different policy	216	66	150	76	39	37	140	27	113
3. No response	49	9	40	9	3	6	40	6	34
4. Total	745	148	597	217	84	133	528	64	464

The transportation costs are the more frequently reimbursed.

TABLE 33: LIMITS ON TRANSPORTATION AND OTHER EXPENSES CHARGEABLE TO SPECIAL GRANTS
OR CONTRACTS
Questionnaire Sect. 4 Q. 4

	All Institutions			Public Institutions			Private Institutions		
	Total	Univ.	Col.	Total	Univ.	Col.	Total	Univ.	Col.
1. Limits on both	154	38	116	54	22	32	100	16	84
2. No limits on either	256	50	206	74	27	47	182	23	159
3. Limits in certain categories but not in all	60	21	39	23	14	9	37	7	30
4. Incomplete answers	275	39	236	66	21	45	209	18	191

TABLE 34: REIMBURSEMENT FOR FACULTY AUTOMOBILE TRAVEL
Questionnaire Sect. 4 Q. 5

	All Institutions			Public Institutions			Private Institutions		
	Total	Univ.	Col.	Total	Univ.	Col.	Total	Univ.	Col.
1. Other	103	23	80	42	19	23	61	4	57
Cents Per Mile									
2. 4¢	3	1	2	1	1	...	2	...	2
3. 5¢	16	1	15	1	...	1	15	1	14
4. 6¢	28	3	25	5	2	3	23	1	22
5. 7¢	199	30	169	72	22	50	127	8	119
6. 8¢	258	54	204	64	23	41	194	31	163
7. 9¢	37	14	23	12	8	4	25	6	19
8. 10¢	52	16	36	9	5	4	43	11	32
9. 11¢	1	1	...	1	1	...	...	...	...
10. No response	48	5	43	10	3	7	38	2	36
11. Total	745	148	597	217	84	133	528	64	464

No reimbursements of less than 4¢ per mile were reported.
Frequently the rates vary according to some formula, e.g., 1) less beyond a certain number
of miles; 2) greater if more than one person going; 3) different in-state and out-of-state;
4) less if institution owned car was available but not used.

TABLE 35: FUTURE PLANS FOR FACULTY TRAVEL EXPENSE PROGRAM (EXPANSION OF PROGRAM; EXPANSION OF FACULTY)
Questionnaire Sect. 4 Q. 6

	All Institutions			Public Institutions			Private Institutions		
	Total	Univ.	Col.	Total	Univ.	Col.	Total	Univ.	Col.
1. More rapidly	145	21	124	36	9	27	109	12	97
2. Same rate	355	78	277	110	44	66	245	34	211
3. Less rapidly	43	13	30	25	12	13	18	1	17
4. Remain as is	171	32	139	41	16	25	130	16	114
5. Contracted	4	1	3	1	...	1	3	1	2
6. No response	27	3	24	4	3	1	23	...	23
7. Total	745	148	597	217	84	133	528	64	464

TABLE 36: EFFECT OF FACULTY TRAVEL PROGRAM IN RECRUITING AND RETAINING FACULTY
Questionnaire Sect. 4 Q. 7

	All Institutions			Public Institutions			Private Institutions		
	Total	Univ.	Col.	Total	Univ.	Col.	Total	Univ.	Col.
Recruiting									
1. Substantial	88	22	66	33	16	17	55	6	49
2. Moderate	348	82	266	107	49	58	241	33	208
3. Negligible	277	42	235	71	17	54	206	25	181
4. No response	32	2	30	6	2	4	26	...	26
5. Total	745	148	597	217	84	133	528	64	464
Retaining									
6. Substantial	96	24	72	35	17	18	61	7	54
7. Moderate	391	82	309	109	46	63	282	36	246
8. Negligible	200	34	166	59	16	43	141	18	123
9. No response	58	8	50	14	5	9	44	3	41
10. Total	745	148	597	217	84	133	528	64	464

TABLE 37: PAYMENT OF MOVING EXPENSES FOR NEWLY HIRED STAFF MEMBERS—TENURE RANKS
Questionnaire Sect. 4 Q. 8a

	All Institutions			Public Institutions			Private Institutions		
	Total	Univ.	Col.	Total	Univ.	Col.	Total	Univ.	Col.
Expenses Paid									
1. Number	335	68	267	24	18	6	311	50	261
2. Percent	45.0%	45.9%	44.7%	11.1%	21.4%	4.5%	58.9%	78.1%	56.3%
Expenses Not Paid									
3. Number	367	73	294	189	63	126	178	10	168
4. Percent	49.3%	49.3%	49.2%	87.1%	75.0%	94.7%	33.7%	15.6%	36.2%
No Response									
5. Number	43	7	36	4	3	1	39	4	35
6. Percent	5.8%	4.7%	6.0%	1.8%	3.6%	.8%	7.4%	6.3%	7.5%
7. Total	745	148	597	217	84	133	528	64	464

The fact that an institution is included in column 1 does not mean that total expenses are paid or even that some expenses are always paid. Upper limits are frequent and conditions of eligibility or ad hoc decisions not uncommon. See next table.

TABLE 38: PAYMENT LIMITS OF MOVING EXPENSES FOR NEWLY HIRED STAFF MEMBERS—
           TENURE RANKS
Questionnaire Sect. 4 Q. 8a

	All Institutions			Public Institutions			Private Institutions		
	Total	Univ.	Col.	Total	Univ.	Col.	Total	Univ.	Col.
1. Insts. reporting	217	41	176	16	13	3	201	28	173
Percentage Responses									
2. 100%	32	5	27	1	1	...	31	4	27
3. Less than 100%									
(usually 50%)	52	8	44	3	3	...	49	5	44
Dollar Responses									
4. 0—$300	58	7	51	4	2	2	54	5	49
5. $301—600	61	13	48	5	4	1	56	9	47
6. $600—up	14	8	6	3	3	...	11	5	6

TABLE 39: PAYMENT OF MOVING EXPENSES FOR NEWLY HIRED STAFF MEMBERS—NON-TENURE
           RANKS
Questionnaire Sect. 4 Q. 8b

	All Institutions			Public Institutions			Private Institutions		
	Total	Univ.	Col.	Total	Univ.	Col.	Total	Univ.	Col.
Expenses Paid									
1. Number	299	57	242	18	13	5	281	44	237
2. Percent	40.1%	38.5%	40.5%	8.3%	15.5%	3.8%	53.2%	68.8%	51.1%
Expenses Not Paid									
3. Number	400	86	314	190	68	122	210	18	192
4. Percent	53.7%	58.1%	52.6%	87.6%	81.0%	91.7%	39.8%	28.1%	41.4%
No Response									
5. Number	46	5	41	9	3	6	37	2	35
6. Percent	6.2%	3.4%	6.9%	4.1%	3.6%	4.5%	7.0%	3.1%	7.5%
7. Total	745	148	597	217	84	133	528	64	464

See note on Table 37 and see next table.

TABLE 40: PAYMENT LIMITS OF MOVING EXPENSES FOR NEWLY HIRED STAFF MEMBERS—
           NON-TENURE RANKS
Questionnaire Sect. 4 Q. 8b

	All Institutions			Public Institutions			Private Institutions		
	Total	Univ.	Col.	Total	Univ.	Col.	Total	Univ.	Col.
1. Insts. reporting	187	35	152	12	10	2	175	25	150
Percentage Responses									
2. 100%	25	4	21	...	...	...	25	4	21
3. Less than 100%									
(usually 50%)	47	8	39	3	3	...	44	5	39
Dollar Responses									
4. 0—$300	56	8	48	4	2	2	52	6	46
5. $300—600	55	13	42	5	5	...	50	8	42
6. $600—up	4	2	2	...	...	...	4	2	2

TABLE 41: SABBATICAL LEAVES
Questionnaire Sect. 5 Q. 1

	All Institutions			Public Institutions			Private Institutions		
	Total	Univ.	Col.	Total	Univ.	Col.	Total	Univ.	Col.
Sabbatical Leaves Granted									
1. Number	425	87	338	136	54	82	289	33	256
2. Percent	57.0%	58.8%	56.6%	62.7%	64.3%	61.7%	54.7%	51.6%	55.2%
Sabbatical Leaves Not Granted									
3. Number	309	61	248	80	30	50	229	31	198
4. Percent	41.5%	41.2%	41.5%	36.9%	35.7%	37.6%	43.4%	48.4%	42.7%
No Response									
5. Number	11	...	11	1	...	1	10	...	10
6. Percent	1.5%	...	1.8%	.5%	...	.8%	1.9%	...	2.2%
7. Total	745	148	597	217	84	133	528	64	464

The questionnaire defines sabbatical leaves as "leaves with pay to which a faculty member becomes entitled primarily because of service through a given length of time." Many answers clearly did not follow this definition but applied the term to leaves restricted chiefly by conditions other than length of service, length of service in some cases being almost inconsequential.

TABLE 42: PLANS TO INITIATE A SABBATICAL LEAVE PROGRAM BY INSTITUTIONS CURRENTLY HAVING NO PLAN
Questionnaire Sect. 5 Q. 1

	All Institutions			Public Institutions			Private Institutions		
	Total	Univ.	Col.	Total	Univ.	Col.	Total	Univ.	Col.
Program Being Considered									
1. Number	68	6	62	15	2	13	53	4	49
2. Percent	22.0%	9.8%	25.0%	18.8%	6.7%	26.0%	23.1%	12.9%	24.7%
Program Not Being Considered									
3. Number	90	31	59	28	13	15	62	18	44
4. Percent	29.1%	50.8%	23.8%	35.0%	43.3%	30.0%	27.1%	58.1%	22.2%
No Response									
5. Number	151	24	127	37	15	22	114	9	105
6. Percent	48.9%	39.3%	51.2%	46.3%	50.0%	44.0%	49.8%	29.0%	53.0%
7. Total	309	61	248	80	30	50	229	31	198

TABLE 43: FACULTY RANKS ELIGIBLE FOR SABBATICAL LEAVE
Questionnaire Sect. 5 Q. 2

	All Institutions			Public Institutions			Private Institutions		
	Total	Univ.	Col.	Total	Univ.	Col.	Total	Univ.	Col.
1. Insts. responding	421	87	334	135	54	81	286	33	253
2. Prof.	415	86	329	132	53	79	283	33	250
3. Assoc. prof.	410	85	325	132	52	80	278	33	245
4. Asst. prof.	355	75	280	130	51	79	225	24	201
5. Instr.	142	27	115	71	19	52	71	8	63
6. Other	38	12	26	27	10	17	11	2	9
7. No response	4	...	4	1	...	1	3	...	3
8. Total	425	87	338	136	54	82	289	33	256

Although in many cases tenure is not required, in substance it almost always is because the length of service required for a sabbatical leave is greater than the period in which tenure is determined.

TABLE 44: YEARS OF SERVICE IN INSTITUTION REQUIRED BEFORE FIRST SABBATICAL MAY BE
TAKEN FOR RANK OF PROFESSOR
Questionnaire Sect. 5 Q. 4

	All Institutions			Public Institutions			Private Institutions		
	Total	Univ.	Col.	Total	Univ.	Col.	Total	Univ.	Col.
1. 2 years	8	1	7	6	...	6	2	1	1
2. 3 years	19	4	15	10	2	8	9	2	7
3. 4 years	12	...	12	3	...	3	9	...	9
4. 5 years	21	3	18	11	2	9	10	1	9
5. 6 years	211	61	150	83	40	43	128	21	107
6. 7 years	94	10	84	11	5	6	83	5	78
7. 8 years	...	...	...	...	...	...	...	...	...
8. 9 years	4	...	4	...	...	...	4	...	4
9. 10 years and over	10	...	10	...	...	...	10	...	10
10. Not applicable	46	8	38	12	5	7	34	3	31
11. Total	425	87	338	136	54	82	289	33	256

In my judgment many of those that answered "7" really meant 6, but replied "7" because it is in the 7th year that a person becomes eligible for sabbatical leave.

The figures for the rank of associate professor are almost identical with those above.

TABLE 45: YEARS OF SERVICE IN INSTITUTION REQUIRED BEFORE FIRST SABBATICAL MAY BE TAKEN FOR RANK OF ASSISTANT PROFESSOR

Questionnaire Sect. 5 Q. 4

		All Institutions			Public Institutions			Private Institutions		
		Total	Univ.	Col.	Total	Univ.	Col.	Total	Univ.	Col.
1.	2 years	7	...	7	6	...	6	1	...	1
2.	3 years	16	3	13	10	2	8	6	1	5
3.	4 years	10	1	9	4	1	3	6	...	6
4.	5 years	21	3	18	11	2	9	10	1	9
5.	6 years	188	57	131	81	39	42	107	18	89
6.	7 years	80	6	74	9	3	6	71	3	68
7.	8 years	1	...	1	...	...	...	1	...	1
8.	9 years	5	...	5	...	...	...	5	...	5
9.	10 years and over	9	...	9	...	...	...	9	...	9
10.	Not applicable	88	17	71	15	7	8	73	10	63
11.	Total	425	87	338	136	54	82	289	33	256

See note preceding table re answer "7 years."

TABLE 46: YEARS OF SERVICE IN INSTITUTION REQUIRED BEFORE FIRST SABBATICAL MAY BE TAKEN FOR RANK OF INSTRUCTOR

Questionnaire Sect. 5 Q. 4

		All Institutions			Public Institutions			Private Institutions		
		Total	Univ.	Col.	Total	Univ.	Col.	Total	Univ.	Col.
1.	0 years	2	1	1	...	...	...	2	1	1
2.	1 year	...	...	...	...	...	...	...*	...	...
3.	2 years	6	...	6	6	...	6	...	...	...
4.	3 years	12	1	11	8	1	7	4	...	4
5.	4 years	6	...	6	3	...	3	3	...	3
6.	5 years	10	...	10	7	...	7	3	...	3
7.	6 years	71	19	52	40	14	26	31	5	26
8.	7 years	32	1	31	4	...	4	28	1	27
9.	8 years	...	...	...	...	...	...	...	...	...
10.	9 years	3	1	2	1	1	...	2	...	2
11.	10 years and over	5	...	5	...	...	...	5	...	5
12.	Not applicable	278	64	214	67	38	29	211	26	185
13.	Total	425	87	338	136	54	82	289	33	256

See note Table 44 re answer "7 years."

TABLE 47: SERVICE REQUIRED BETWEEN COMPLETION OF ONE SABBATICAL AND ELIGIBILITY FOR
ANOTHER FOR RANK OF PROFESSOR
Questionnaire Sect. 5 Q. 5

	All Institutions			Public Institutions			Private Institutions		
	Total	Univ.	Col.	Total	Univ.	Col.	Total	Univ.	Col.
1. 1 year	1	...	1	...	...	...	1	...	1
2. 2 years	5	...	5	4	...	4	1	...	1
3. 3 years	15	3	12	8	2	6	7	1	6
4. 4 years	12	2	10	2	...	2	10	2	8
5. 5 years	14	2	12	8	2	6	6	...	6
6. 6 years	209	62	147	79	39	40	130	23	107
7. 7 years	86	7	79	15	6	9	71	1	70
8. 8 years	1	...	1	1	...	1	...	...	...
9. 9 years	1	...	1	...	...	...	1	...	1
10. 10 years and over	8	...	8	...	...	...	8	...	8
11. Not applicable	73	11	62	` 19	5	14	54	6	48
12. Total	425	87	338	136	54	82	289	33	256

See note Table 44 re answer "7 years."
Figures for rank of associate professor are almost identical with the above.

TABLE 48: SERVICE REQUIRED BETWEEN COMPLETION OF ONE SABBATICAL AND ELIGIBILITY FOR
ANOTHER FOR RANK OF ASSISTANT PROFESSOR
Questionnaire Sect. 5 Q. 5

	All Institutions			Public Institutions			Private Institutions		
	Total	Univ.	Col.	Total	Univ.	Col.	Total	Univ.	Col.
1. 1 year	1	...	1	...	...	...	1	...	1
2. 2 years	5	...	5	4	...	4	1	...	1
3. 3 years	13	2	11	8	2	6	5	...	5
4. 4 years	9	1	8	2	...	2	7	1	6
5. 5 years	14	2	12	8	2	6	6	...	6
6. 6 years	186	54	132	77	38	39	109	16	93
7. 7 years	68	6	62	13	4	9	55	2	53
8. 8 years	1	...	1	1	...	1	...	...	...
9. 9 years	1	...	1	...	...	...	1	...	1
10. 10 years and over	6	...	6	...	...	...	6	...	6
11. Not applicable	121	22	99	23	8	15	98	14	84
12. Total	425	87	338	136	54	82	289	33	256

See note Table 44 re answer "7 years."

TABLE 49: SERVICE REQUIRED BETWEEN COMPLETION OF ONE SABBATICAL AND ELIGIBILITY FOR ANOTHER FOR RANK OF INSTRUCTOR
Questionnaire Sect. 5 Q. 5

	All Institutions			Public Institutions			Private Institutions		
	Total	Univ.	Col.	Total	Univ.	Col.	Total	Univ.	Col.
1. 1 year	1	...	1	...	...	...	1	...	1
2. 2 years	4	...	4	4	...	4	...	...	...
3. 3 years	8	1	7	6	1	5	2	...	2
4. 4 years	5	...	5	2	...	2	3	...	3
5. 5 years	6	...	6	6	...	6	...	...	...
6. 6 years	67	19	48	36	14	22	31	5	26
7. 7 years	31	2	29	6	1	5	25	1	24
8. 8 years	1	...	1	1	...	1	...	...	...
9. 9 years	...	...	...	...	...	...	...	...	...
10. 10 years and over	4	...	4	...	...	...	4	...	4
11. Not applicable	298	65	233	75	38	37	223	27	196
12. Total	425	87	338	136	54	82	289	33	256

See note Table 44 re answer "7 years."

TABLE 50: AVAILABILITY OF FUNDS TO PERMIT SABBATICAL LEAVES WHEN ELIGIBLE
Questionnaire Sect. 5 Q. 6

	All Institutions			Public Institutions			Private Institutions		
	Total	Univ.	Col.	Total	Univ.	Col.	Total	Univ.	Col.
Funds Usually Available									
1. Number	337	69	268	97	42	55	240	27	213
2. Percent	79.3%	79.3%	79.3%	71.3%	77.8%	67.1%	83.0%	81.8%	83.2%
Funds Not Usually Available									
3. Number	68	15	53	34	10	24	34	5	29
4. Percent	16.0%	17.2%	15.7%	25.0%	18.5%	29.3%	11.8%	15.2%	11.3%
No Response									
5. Number	20	3	17	5	2	3	15	1	14
6. Percent	4.7%	3.4%	5.0%	3.7%	3.7%	3.7%	5.2%	3.0%	5.5%
7. Total	425	87	338	136	54	82	289	33	256

TABLE 51: PURPOSES FOR WHICH SABBATICAL LEAVE MAY BE TAKEN
Questionnaire Sect. 5 Q. 7

		All Institutions			Public Institutions			Private Institutions		
		Total	Univ.	Col.	Total	Univ.	Col.	Total	Univ.	Col.
1.	Insts. responding	415	87	328	134	54	80	281	33	248
2.	Research project	280	63	217	91	39	52	189	24	165
3.	Writing project	245	58	187	81	38	43	164	20	144
4.	Plan for study	335	66	269	111	43	68	224	23	201
5.	Teaching improvement	280	58	222	92	39	53	188	19	169
6.	Any of first four	216	52	164	71	35	36	145	17	128
7.	Travel plan	171	34	137	58	22	36	113	12	101
8.	Must leave campus	65	10	55	26	8	18	39	2	37
9.	No special requirement	48	9	39	7	3	4	41	6	35
10.	Other	58	24	34	31	14	17	27	10	17
11.	No response	10	...	10	2	...	2	8	...	8

TABLE 52: PERMISSION FOR TEACHING, EMPLOYMENT, OR STUDY FOR DEGREE DURING
SABBATICAL LEAVE
Questionnaire Sect. 5 Q. 8, 9

	All Institutions			Public Institutions			Private Institutions		
	Total	Univ.	Col.	Total	Univ.	Col.	Total	Univ.	Col.
Full-Time Teaching Permitted									
1. Yes	54	12	42	11	4	7	43	8	35
2. No	312	65	247	106	41	65	206	24	182
3. No response	59	10	49	19	9	10	40	1	39
4. Total	425	87	338	136	54	82	289	33	256
Part-Time Teaching Permitted									
5. Yes	181	41	140	59	26	33	122	15	107
6. No	200	39	161	61	23	38	139	16	123
7. No response	44	7	37	16	5	11	28	2	26
8. Total	425	87	338	136	54	82	289	33	256
Other Employment Permitted									
9. Yes	156	34	122	53	22	31	103	12	91
10. No	197	42	155	68	27	41	129	15	114
11. No response	72	11	61	15	5	10	57	6	51
12. Total	425	87	338	136	54	82	289	33	256
Study for Advanced Degree Permitted									
13. Yes	337	57	280	105	37	68	232	20	212
14. No	52	23	29	21	13	8	31	10	21
15. No response	36	7	29	10	4	6	26	3	23
16. Total	425	87	338	136	54	82	289	33	256

In some cases prior consent for teaching or other employment is required.
In many institutions study for an advanced degree is the primary purpose of leaves.

TABLE 53: MAXIMUM LENGTH OF SABBATICAL LEAVE ON FULL SALARY
(QUARTERS OR SEMESTERS)
Questionnaire Sect. 5 Q. 10

	All Institutions			Public Institutions			Private Institutions		
	Total	Univ.	Col.	Total	Univ.	Col.	Total	Univ.	Col.
1. 1 semester	289	59	230	70	34	36	219	25	194
2. 2 semesters	8	1	7	1	1	...	7	...	7
3. 1 quarter	22	4	18	9	3	6	13	1	12
4. 2 quarters	14	5	9	9	4	5	5	1	4
5. 3 quarters	...	...	...	...	...	...	...	...	...
6. 4 quarters	2	...	2	...	...	...	2	...	2
7. No response	90	18	72	47	12	35	43	6	37
8. Total	425	87	338	136	54	82	289	33	256

TABLE 54: MAXIMUM LENGTH OF SABBATICAL LEAVE ON HALF SALARY
(QUARTERS OR SEMESTERS)
Questionnaire Sect. 5 Q. 10

	All Institutions			Public Institutions			Private Institutions		
	Total	Univ.	Col.	Total	Univ.	Col.	Total	Univ.	Col.
1. 1 semester	5	...	5	1	...	1	4	...	4
2. 2 semesters	315	61	254	88	35	53	227	26	201
3. 1 quarter	...	...	...	...	...	...	...	...	...
4. 2 quarters	2	...	2	...	...	...	2	...	2
5. 3 quarters	33	8	25	23	7	16	10	1	9
6. 4 quarters	8	5	3	4	4	...	4	1	3
7. No response	62	13	49	20	8	12	42	5	37
8. Total	425	87	338	136	54	82	289	33	256

272 institutions reported as their basic plan: "One semester on full pay or two semesters on half pay."

TABLE 55: CHOICES MORE FREQUENTLY TAKEN BETWEEN FULL SALARY FOR SHORTER PERIOD OR HALF SALARY FOR LONGER PERIOD
Questionnaire Sect. 5 Q. 12

	All Institutions			Public Institutions			Private Institutions		
	Total	Univ.	Col.	Total	Univ.	Col.	Total	Univ.	Col.
Full Salary Shorter Period									
1. Number	141	28	113	36	15	21	105	13	92
2. Percent	33.2%	32.2%	33.4%	26.5%	27.8%	25.6%	36.3%	39.4%	35.9%
Half Salary Longer Period									
3. Number	138	36	102	40	22	18	98	14	84
4. Percent	32.5%	41.4%	30.2%	29.4%	40.7%	22.0%	33.9%	42.4%	32.8%
No Choice Available									
5. Number	68	11	57	39	8	31	29	3	26
6. Percent	16.0%	12.6%	16.9%	28.7%	14.8%	37.8%	10.0%	9.1%	10.2%
No Response									
7. Number	78	12	66	21	9	12	57	3	54
8. Percent	18.4%	13.8%	19.5%	15.4%	16.7%	14.6%	19.7%	9.1%	21.1%
9. Total	425	87	338	136	54	82	289	33	256

TABLE 56: PERCENTAGES OF FACULTY CHOOSING FULL SALARY FOR SHORTER SABBATICAL LEAVE PERIOD
Questionnaire Sect. 5 Q. 12

	All Institutions			Public Institutions			Private Institutions		
	Total	Univ.	Col.	Total	Univ.	Col.	Total	Univ.	Col.
1. 25% or less	61	16	45	20	11	9	41	5	36
2. 26—50%	80	21	59	19	11	8	61	10	51
3. 51—75%	59	15	44	19	11	8	40	4	36
4. 76—100%	55	10	45	13	3	10	42	7	35
5. No response	170	25	145	65	18	47	105	7	98

TABLE 57: PERCENTAGES OF FACULTY ELIGIBLE FOR SABBATICAL LEAVE WHO DO NOT TAKE IT IN ANY GIVEN YEAR
Questionnaire Sect. 5 Q. 13

	All Institutions			Public Institutions			Private Institutions		
	Total	Univ.	Col.	Total	Univ.	Col.	Total	Univ.	Col.
1. 25% or less	90	17	73	25	8	17	65	9	56
2. 26—50%	81	19	62	18	11	7	63	8	55
3. 51—75%	42	17	25	15	9	6	27	8	19
4. 76—100%	41	9	32	13	8	5	28	1	27
5. No response	171	25	146	65	18	47	106	7	99

TABLE 58: CONTINUATION OF EMPLOYEE'S RETIREMENT PLAN CONTRIBUTION DURING
SABBATICAL LEAVE ON PARTIAL PAY
Questionnaire Sect. 5 Q. 14

	All Institutions			Public Institutions			Private Institutions		
	Total	Univ.	Col.	Total	Univ.	Col.	Total	Univ.	Col.
Basis of Full Pay									
1. Number	166	38	128	35	16	19	131	22	109
2. Percent	39.0%	43.7%	37.9%	25.7%	29.6%	23.2%	45.3%	66.7%	42.6%
Basis of Partial Pay									
3. Number	193	42	151	82	31	51	111	11	100
4. Percent	45.4%	48.3%	44.7%	60.3%	57.4%	62.2%	38.4%	33.3%	39.1%
Not Continued									
5. Number	10	1	9	5	1	4	5	...	5
6. Percent	2.4%	1.1%	2.7%	3.7%	1.9%	4.9%	1.7%	...	2.0%
No Retirement Plan									
7. Number	12	...	12	...	...	...	12	...	12
8. Percent	2.8%	...	3.6%	...	...	...	4.2%	...	4.7%
No Response									
9. Number	44	6	38	14	6	8	30	...	30
10. Percent	10.4%	6.9%	11.2%	10.3%	11.1%	9.8%	10.4%	...	11.7%
11. Total	425	87	338	136	54	82	289	33	256

TABLE 59: CONTINUATION OF BASIC HOSPITAL-SURGICAL GROUP INSURANCE DURING
SABBATICAL LEAVE
Questionnaire Sect. 5 Q. 15

	All Institutions			Public Institutions			Private Institutions		
	Total	Univ.	Col.	Total	Univ.	Col.	Total	Univ.	Col.
Continued									
1. Number	322	67	255	102	39	63	220	28	192
2. Percent	75.8%	77.0%	75.4%	75.0%	72.2%	76.8%	76.1%	84.8%	75.0%
Not Continued									
3. Number	12	5	7	4	2	2	8	3	5
4. Percent	2.8%	5.7%	2.1%	2.9%	3.7%	2.4%	2.8%	9.1%	2.0%
No Such Plan									
5. Number	45	6	39	18	5	13	27	1	26
6. Percent	10.6%	6.9%	11.5%	13.2%	9.3%	15.9%	9.3%	3.0%	10.2%
No Response									
7. Number	46	9	37	12	8	4	34	1	33
8. Percent	10.8%	10.3%	10.9%	8.8%	14.8%	4.9%	11.8%	3.0%	12.9%
9. Total	425	87	338	136	54	82	289	33	256

TABLE 60: CONTINUATION OF LIFE INSURANCE COVERAGE DURING SABBATICAL LEAVE
Questionnaire Sect. 5 Q. 15

	All Institutions			Public Institutions			Private Institutions		
	Total	Univ.	Col.	Total	Univ.	Col.	Total	Univ.	Col.
Continued									
1. Number	285	72	213	83	40	43	202	32	170
2. Percent	67.1%	82.8%	63.0%	61.0%	74.1%	52.4%	69.9%	97.0%	66.4%
Not Continued									
3. Number	4	1	3	2	1	1	2	...	2
4. Percent	.9%	1.1%	.9%	1.5%	1.9%	1.2%	.7%	...	.8%
No Such Plan									
5. Number	88	9	79	39	8	31	49	1	48
6. Percent	20.7%	10.3%	23.4%	28.7%	14.8%	37.8%	17.0%	3.0%	18.8%
No Response									
7. Number	48	5	43	12	5	7	36	...	36
8. Percent	11.3%	5.7%	12.7%	8.8%	9.3%	8.5%	12.5%	...	14.1%
9. Total	425	87	338	136	54	82	289	33	256

TABLE 61: CONTINUATION OF GROUP MAJOR MEDICAL INSURANCE DURING SABBATICAL LEAVE
Questionnaire Sect. 5 Q. 15

	All Institutions			Public Institutions			Private Institutions		
	Total	Univ.	Col.	Total	Univ.	Col.	Total	Univ.	Col.
Continued									
1. Number	254	62	192	74	36	38	180	26	154
2. Percent	59.8%	71.3%	56.8%	54.4%	66.7%	46.3%	62.3%	78.8%	60.2%
Not Continued									
3. Number	6	2	4	1	...	1	5	2	3
4. Percent	1.4%	2.3%	1.2%	.7%	...	1.2%	1.7%	6.1%	1.2%
No Such Plan									
5. Number	109	12	97	41	9	32	68	3	65
6. Percent	25.6%	13.8%	28.7%	30.1%	16.7%	39.0%	23.5%	9.1%	25.4%
No Response									
7. Number	56	11	45	20	9	11	36	2	34
8. Percent	13.2%	12.6%	13.3%	14.7%	16.7%	13.4%	12.5%	6.1%	13.3%
9. Total	425	87	338	136	54	82	289	33	256

TABLE 62: CONTINUATION OF GROUP DISABILITY INCOME INSURANCE DURING SABBATICAL
LEAVE
Questionnaire Sect. 5 Q. 15

	All Institutions			Public Institutions			Private Institutions		
	Total	Univ.	Col.	Total	Univ.	Col.	Total	Univ.	Col.
Continued									
1. Number	104	26	78	37	18	19	67	8	59
2. Percent	24.5%	29.9%	23.1%	27.2%	33.3%	23.2%	23.2%	24.2%	23.0%
Not Continued									
3. Number	5	...	5	2	...	2	3	...	3
4. Percent	1.2%	...	1.5%	1.5%	...	2.4%	1.0%	...	1.2%
No Such Plan									
5. Number	211	45	166	66	24	42	145	21	124
6. Percent	49.6%	51.7%	49.1%	48.5%	44.4%	51.2%	50.2%	63.6%	48.4%
No Response									
7. Number	105	16	89	31	12	19	74	4	70
8. Percent	24.7%	18.4%	26.3%	22.8%	22.2%	23.2%	25.6%	12.1%	27.3%
9. Total	425	87	338	136	54	82	289	33	256

TABLE 63: OBLIGATION TO RETURN AFTER TAKING SABBATICAL LEAVE AND DURATION OF PERIOD
REQUIRED TO STAY, IF ANY
Questionnaire Sect. 5 Q. 16

	All Institutions			Public Institutions			Private Institutions		
	Total	Univ.	Col.	Total	Univ.	Col.	Total	Univ.	Col.
Not Obliged to Return									
1. Number	66	14	52	6	3	3	60	11	49
2. Percent	15.5%	16.1%	15.4%	4.4%	5.6%	3.7%	20.8%	33.3%	19.1%
Obliged to Return									
3. Number	344	70	274	127	49	78	217	21	196
4. Percent	80.9%	80.5%	81.1%	93.4%	90.7%	95.1%	75.1%	63.6%	76.6%
No Response									
5. Number	15	3	12	3	2	1	12	1	11
6. Percent	3.5%	3.4%	3.6%	2.2%	3.7%	1.2%	4.2%	3.0%	4.3%
7. Total	425	87	338	136	54	82	289	33	256
Years Faculty Member Must Stay									
8. 1 year	154	42	112	74	32	42	80	10	70
9. 2 years	70	11	59	28	8	20	42	3	39
10. 3 years	26	1	25	11	1	10	15	...	15
11. 4 years	6	...	6	...	...	...	6	...	6
12. 5 years	4	...	4	...	...	...	4	...	4
13. 6 years	1	...	1	...	...	...	1	...	1
14. Unspecified	65	12	53	8	4	4	57	8	49

Some institutions indicate "moral obligation only." In these cases some answered "not
obligated to return" and some answered "obligated to return."

TABLE 64: CONTRIBUTION OF SABBATICAL LEAVE PROGRAM TO RECRUITING AND RETAINING
FACULTY
Questionnaire Sect. 5 Q. 18

	All Institutions			Public Institutions			Private Institutions		
	Total	Univ.	Col.	Total	Univ.	Col.	Total	Univ.	Col.
Recruiting									
1. Substantial	122	27	95	33	16	17	89	11	78
2. Moderate	213	44	169	73	27	46	140	17	123
3. Negligible	65	9	56	20	5	15	45	4	41
4. No response	25	7	18	10	6	4	15	1	14
5. Total	425	87	338	136	54	82	289	33	256
Retaining									
6. Substantial	151	30	121	38	18	20	113	12	101
7. Moderate	211	45	166	75	27	48	136	18	118
8. Negligible	39	5	34	13	3	10	26	2	24
9. No response	24	7	17	10	6	4	14	1	13
10. Total	425	87	338	136	54	82	289	33	256

TABLE 65: PURPOSES RECOGNIZED FOR LEAVE OF ABSENCE WITH PAY (OTHER THAN
SABBATICAL) FROM FUNDS FROM UNIVERSITY OR COLLEGE SOURCES
Questionnaire Sect. 5 Q. 19

	All Institutions			Public Institutions			Private Institutions		
	Total	Univ.	Col.	Total	Univ.	Col.	Total	Univ.	Col.
1. Insts. stating purposes	317	88	229	78	43	35	239	45	194
2. Research	167	57	110	38	24	14	129	33	96
3. Teaching improvement	150	43	107	32	21	11	118	22	96
4. Study	221	53	168	41	23	18	180	30	150
5. Travel	56	15	41	13	7	6	43	8	35
6. Writing	114	41	73	26	16	10	88	25	63
7. Other	57	25	32	26	15	11	31	10	21
8. None granted	394	57	337	133	38	95	261	19	242
9. No response	34	3	31	6	3	3	28	...	28

TABLE 66: PURPOSES RECOGNIZED FOR LEAVE OF ABSENCE WITH PAY FROM FUNDS DERIVED
FROM SPECIAL GRANTS OR CONTRACTS
Questionnaire Sect. 5 Q. 21

	All Institutions			Public Institutions			Private Institutions		
	Total	Univ.	Col.	Total	Univ.	Col.	Total	Univ.	Col.
1. Insts. stating purposes	362	110	252	95	60	35	267	50	217
2. Research	307	102	205	77	52	25	230	50	180
3. Teaching improvement	243	71	172	56	38	18	187	33	154
4. Study	274	78	196	55	35	20	219	43	176
5. Travel	145	51	94	38	26	12	107	25	82
6. Writing	210	79	131	47	34	13	163	45	118
7. Other	29	14	15	15	9	6	14	5	9
8. None granted	297	29	268	107	19	88	190	10	180
9. No response	86	9	77	15	5	10	71	4	67

TABLE 67: SUPPLEMENTATION BY THE INSTITUTION OF OUTSIDE GRANTS OR FELLOWSHIPS
RECEIVED BY FACULTY MEMBER
Questionnaire Sect. 5 Q. 22

	All Institutions			Public Institutions			Private Institutions		
	Total	Univ.	Col.	Total	Univ.	Col.	Total	Univ.	Col.
Supplementations Not Made									
1. Number	339	55	284	134	41	93	205	14	191
2. Percent	45.5%	37.2%	47.6%	61.8%	48.8%	69.9%	38.8%	21.9%	41.2%
Supplementations Made									
3. Number	310	84	226	63	38	25	247	46	201
4. Percent	41.6%	56.8%	37.9%	29.0%	45.2%	18.8%	46.8%	71.9%	43.3%
No Response									
5. Number	96	9	87	20	5	15	76	4	72
6. Percent	12.9%	6.1%	14.6%	9.2%	6.0%	11.3%	14.4%	6.3%	15.5%
7. Total	745	148	597	217	84	133	528	64	464

TABLE 68: OBLIGATION TO RETURN AFTER TAKING LEAVE OF ABSENCE (OTHER THAN SABBATICAL)
Questionnaire Sect. 5 Q. 24

	All Institutions			Public Institutions			Private Institutions		
	Total	Univ.	Col.	Total	Univ.	Col.	Total	Univ.	Col.
Not Obliged to Return									
1. Number	178	62	116	62	33	29	116	29	87
2. Percent	23.9%	41.9%	19.4%	28.6%	39.3%	21.8%	22.0%	45.3%	18.8%
Obliged to Return									
3. Number	295	63	232	61	35	26	234	28	206
4. Percent	39.6%	42.6%	38.9%	28.1%	41.7%	19.5%	44.3%	43.8%	44.4%
No Response									
5. Number	272	23	249	94	16	78	178	7	171
6. Percent	36.5%	15.5%	41.7%	43.3%	19.0%	58.6%	33.7%	10.9%	36.9%
7. Total	745	148	597	217	84	133	528	64	464
Years Faculty Member Must Stay									
8. 1 year	103	28	75	34	19	15	69	9	60
9. 2 years	43	9	34	6	4	2	37	5	32
10. 3 years	31	3	28	3	1	2	28	2	26
11. 4 years	6	...	6	...	...	...	6	...	6
12. 5 years	3	...	3	...	...	...	3	...	3
13. Unspecified	79	15	64	8	6	2	71	9	62

See note Table 63.

TABLE 69: CONTRIBUTION OF LEAVE WITH PAY PROGRAM TO RECRUITING AND RETAINING FACULTY

Questionnaire Sect. 5 Q. 26

	All Institutions			Public Institutions			Private Institutions		
	Total	Univ.	Col.	Total	Univ.	Col.	Total	Univ.	Col.
Recruiting									
1. Substantial	77	18	59	11	8	3	66	10	56
2. Moderate	179	50	129	45	25	20	134	25	109
3. Negligible	191	50	141	57	30	27	134	20	114
4. No response	112	14	98	29	9	20	83	5	78
5. Total	559	132	427	142	72	70	417	60	357
Retaining									
6. Substantial	104	29	75	19	13	6	85	16	69
7. Moderate	206	57	149	52	28	24	154	29	125
8. Negligible	139	32	107	42	22	20	97	10	87
9. No response	110	14	96	29	9	20	81	5	76
10. Total	559	132	427	142	72	70	417	60	357

TABLE 70: MINIMUM PERIOD OF SERVICE BEFORE FIRST LEAVE WITHOUT PAY MAY BE GRANTED

Questionnaire Sect. 5 Q. 29

	All Institutions			Public Institutions			Private Institutions		
	Total	Univ.	Col.	Total	Univ.	Col.	Total	Univ.	Col.
1. No minimum period required	428	115	313	136	64	72	292	51	241
2. Minimum period required	232	29	203	72	16	56	160	13	147
Minimum Period of Service Required									
3. 1 year	62	10	52	27	6	21	35	4	31
4. 2 years	53	7	46	7	2	5	46	5	41
5. 3 years	74	8	66	21	4	17	53	4	49
6. 4 years	12	...	12	5	...	5	7	...	7
7. 5 years	15	1	14	3	1	2	12	...	12
8. 6 years	2	...	2	...	...	...	2	...	2
9. 7 years	2	...	2	...	...	...	2	...	2
10. 8 years	...	...	...	...	...	...	...	...	...
11. 9 years	...	...	...	...	...	...	...	...	...
12. 10 years and over	1	...	1	...	...	...	1	...	1

A few instances of leaves granted before coming to new institutions have been reported. These are by way of taking over promises of the old institutions. Also, institutions inviting men currently on leave of absence from other institutions have sometimes agreed to pay for those leaves if their offers are accepted.

TABLE 71: EFFECT OF LEAVE OF ABSENCE WITHOUT PAY ON CONSIDERATION OF SALARY
INCREASES AND PROMOTION (AMONG THE 572 INSTITUTIONS STATING THE
PURPOSES RECOGNIZED IN GRANTING LEAVES WITHOUT PAY)
Questionnaire Sect. 5 Q. 31

	All Institutions			Public Institutions			Private Institutions		
	Total	Univ.	Col.	Total	Univ.	Col.	Total	Univ.	Col.
Postpones Consideration									
1. Number	56	8	48	19	5	14	37	3	34
2. Percent	9.8%	6.5%	10.7%	10.6%	7.5%	12.5%	9.4%	5.4%	10.1%
Does Not Have Effect									
3. Number	292	68	224	91	37	54	201	31	170
4. Percent	51.0%	55.3%	49.9%	50.8%	55.2%	48.2%	51.1%	55.4%	50.4%
Sometimes Postpones Consideration									
5. Number	214	46	168	68	25	43	146	21	125
6. Percent	37.4%	37.4%	37.4%	38.0%	37.3%	38.4%	37.2%	37.5%	37.1%
No Response									
7. Number	10	1	9	1	...	1	9	1	8
8. Percent	1.7%	.8%	2.0%	.6%	...	.9%	2.3%	1.8%	2.4%
9. Total	572	123	449	179	67	112	393	56	337

TABLE 72: OBLIGATION TO RETURN AFTER LEAVE WITHOUT PAY (AMONG THE 572 INSTITUTIONS
STATING THE PURPOSES RECOGNIZED IN GRANTING LEAVES WITHOUT PAY)
Questionnaire Sect. 5 Q. 32

	All Institutions			Public Institutions			Private Institutions		
	Total	Univ.	Col.	Total	Univ.	Col.	Total	Univ.	Col.
Not Obliged to Return									
1. Number	436	99	337	143	55	88	293	44	249
2. Percent	76.2%	80.5%	75.1%	79.9%	82.1%	78.6%	74.6%	78.6%	73.9%
Obligated to Return									
3. Number	125	24	101	32	12	20	93	12	81
4. Percent	21.9%	19.5%	22.5%	17.9%	17.9%	17.9%	23.7%	21.4%	24.0%
No Response									
5. Number	11	...	11	4	...	4	7	...	7
6. Percent	1.9%	...	2.4%	2.2%	...	3.6%	1.8%	...	2.1%
7. Total	572	123	449	179	67	112	393	56	337
Years Faculty Member Must Return									
8. 1 year	73	12	61	22	7	15	51	5	46
9. 2 years	8	1	7	1	...	1	7	1	6
10. 3 years	2	...	2	...	...	...	2	...	2

TABLE 73: EMPLOYER CONTRIBUTIONS TO RETIREMENT PLAN DURING LEAVES OF ABSENCE WITHOUT PAY (AMONG THE 572 INSTITUTIONS STATING THE PURPOSES RECOGNIZED IN GRANTING LEAVES WITHOUT PAY)

Questionnaire Sect. 5 Q. 33

	All Institutions			Public Institutions			Private Institutions		
	Total	Univ.	Col.	Total	Univ.	Col.	Total	Univ.	Col.
1. Employer contributes normally (for faculty not on leave)	493	116	377	153	63	90	340	53	287
2. Employer contributes normally and for faculty on leave without pay	115	25	90	21	8	13	94	17	77
3. Employer contributes normally, but not for faculty on leave without pay	334	84	250	124	52	72	210	32	178
4. No employer contribution under normal operation of plan	18	1	17	9	...	9	9	1	8
5. No plan	18	2	16	5	2	3	13	...	13
6. No response	43	4	39	12	2	10	31	2	29
7. Total	572	123	449	179	67	112	393	56	337

TABLE 74: EMPLOYER CONTRIBUTIONS TO GROUP LIFE PLAN DURING LEAVES OF ABSENCE WITHOUT PAY (AMONG THE 572 INSTITUTIONS STATING THE PURPOSES RECOGNIZED IN GRANTING LEAVES WITHOUT PAY)

Questionnaire Sect. 5 Q. 33

	All Institutions			Public Institutions			Private Institutions		
	Total	Univ.	Col.	Total	Univ.	Col.	Total	Univ.	Col.
1. Employer contributes normally (for faculty not on leave)	325	88	237	71	36	35	254	52	202
2. Employer contributes normally and for faculty on leave without pay	138	39	99	20	11	9	118	28	90
3. Employer contributes normally but not for faculty on leave without pay	153	40	113	43	21	22	110	19	91
4. No employer contribution under normal operation of plan	57	14	43	38	12	26	19	2	17
5. No plan	116	16	100	51	16	35	65	...	65
6. No response	74	5	69	19	3	16	55	2	53
7. Total	572	123	449	179	67	112	393	56	337

TABLE 75: EMPLOYER CONTRIBUTIONS TO BASIC HOSPITAL-SURGICAL PLAN DURING
LEAVES OF ABSENCE WITHOUT PAY (AMONG THE 572 INSTITUTIONS
STATING THE PURPOSES RECOGNIZED IN GRANTING LEAVES WITHOUT PAY)
Questionnaire Sect. 5 Q. 33

	All Institutions			Public Institutions			Private Institutions		
	Total	Univ.	Col.	Total	Univ.	Col.	Total	Univ.	Col.
1. Employer contributes normally (for faculty not on leave)	226	37	189	68	23	45	158	14	144
2. Employer contributes normally and for faculty on leave without pay	72	9	63	12	5	7	60	4	56
3. Employer contributes normally, but not for faculty on leave without pay	126	23	103	49	15	34	77	8	69
4. No employer contribution under normal operation of plan	152	56	96	54	26	28	98	30	68
5. No plan	97	19	78	36	13	23	61	6	55
6. No response	97	11	86	21	5	16	76	6	70
7. Total	572	123	449	179	67	112	393	56	337

TABLE 76: EMPLOYER CONTRIBUTIONS TO MAJOR MEDICAL PLAN DURING LEAVES OF ABSENCE
WITHOUT PAY (AMONG THE 572 INSTITUTIONS STATING THE PURPOSES
RECOGNIZED IN GRANTING LEAVES WITHOUT PAY)
Questionnaire Sect. 5 Q. 33

	All Institutions			Public Institutions			Private Institutions		
	Total	Univ.	Col.	Total	Univ.	Col.	Total	Univ.	Col.
1. Employer contributes normally (for faculty not on leave)	282	63	219	56	28	28	226	35	191
2. Employer contributes normally and for faculty on leave without pay	112	29	83	17	10	7	95	19	76
3. Employer contributes normally but not for faculty on leave without pay	140	27	113	33	15	18	107	12	95
4. No employer contribution under normal operation of plan	84	29	55	52	19	33	32	10	22
5. No plan	128	24	104	47	16	31	81	8	73
6. No response	78	7	71	24	4	20	54	3	51
7. Total	572	123	449	179	67	112	393	56	337

TABLE 77: EMPLOYER CONTRIBUTIONS TO TEMPORARY DISABILITY PLAN DURING LEAVES
OF ABSENCE WITHOUT PAY (AMONG THE 572 INSTITUTIONS STATING THE
PURPOSES RECOGNIZED IN GRANTING LEAVES WITHOUT PAY)
Questionnaire Sect. 5 Q. 33

	All Institutions			Public Institutions			Private Institutions		
	Total	Univ.	Col.	Total	Univ.	Col.	Total	Univ.	Col.
1. Employer contributes normally (for faculty not on leave)	128	27	101	44	19	25	84	8	76
2. Employer contributes normally and for faculty on leave without pay	37	8	29	11	5	6	26	3	23
3. Employer contributes normally, but not for faculty on leave without pay	74	16	58	25	11	14	49	5	44
4. No employer contribution under normal operation of plan	52	11	41	30	9	21	22	2	20
5. No plan	272	75	197	75	33	42	197	42	155
6. No response	120	10	110	30	6	24	90	4	86
7. Total	572	123	449	179	67	112	393	56	337

TABLE 78: EMPLOYER CONTRIBUTIONS TO PERMANENT DISABILITY PLAN DURING LEAVES
OF ABSENCE WITHOUT PAY (AMONG THE 572 INSTITUTIONS STATING THE
PURPOSES RECOGNIZED IN GRANTING LEAVES WITHOUT PAY)
Questionnaire Sect. 5 Q. 33

	All Institutions			Public Institutions			Private Institutions		
	Total	Univ.	Col.	Total	Univ.	Col.	Total	Univ.	Col.
1. Employer contributes normally (for faculty not on leave)	119	33	86	44	22	22	75	11	64
2. Employer contributes normally and for faculty on leave without pay	33	12	21	11	6	5	22	6	16
3. Employer contributes normally, but not for faculty on leave without pay	70	19	51	27	14	13	43	5	38
4. No employer contribution under normal operation of plan	49	9	40	27	5	22	22	4	18
5. No plan	272	68	204	75	32	43	197	36	161
6. No response	132	13	119	33	8	25	99	5	94
7. Total	572	123	449	179	67	112	393	56	337

TABLE 79: CONTRIBUTION OF LEAVE WITHOUT PAY PROGRAM TO RECRUITING AND RETAINING
FACULTY (AMONG THE 572 INSTITUTIONS STATING THE PURPOSES RECOGNIZED
IN GRANTING LEAVES WITHOUT PAY)
Questionnaire Sect. 5 Q. 35

	All Institutions			Public Institutions			Private Institutions		
	Total	Univ.	Col.	Total	Univ.	Col.	Total	Univ.	Col.
Recruiting									
1. Substantial	48	12	36	11	3	8	37	9	28
2. Moderate	201	54	147	69	35	34	132	19	113
3. Negligible	296	52	244	90	25	65	206	27	179
4. No response	27	5	22	9	4	5	18	1	17
5. Total	572	123	449	179	67	112	393	56	337
Retaining									
6. Substantial	73	20	53	19	8	11	54	12	42
7. Moderate	251	61	190	81	37	44	170	24	146
8. Negligible	224	38	186	71	19	52	153	19	134
9. No response	24	4	20	8	3	5	16	1	15
10. Total	572	123	449	179	67	112	393	56	337

TABLE 80: NUMBER OF FACULTY TAKING SABBATICAL LEAVE OF ABSENCE, 1962—63
Questionnaire Sect. 5 Q. 36

	All Institutions			Public Institutions			Private Institutions		
	Total	Univ.	Col.	Total	Univ.	Col.	Total	Univ.	Col.
1. Insts. reporting	324	82	242	114	49	65	210	33	177
2. Total faculty reported on sabbatical leave	3,057	2,072	985	1,783	1,394	389	1,274	678	596
3. Total faculty in reporting insts.	89,967	63,636	26,331	57,848	44,588	13,260	32,119	19,048	13,071
4. Percent of faculty on sabbatical leave	3.4%	3.3%	3.7%	3.1%	3.1%	2.9%	4.0%	3.6%	4.6%

TABLE 81: NUMBER OF FACULTY TAKING LEAVE WITH PAY OTHER THAN SABBATICAL
(FUNDS FROM COLLEGE OR UNIVERSITY SOURCES)
Questionnaire Sect. 5 Q. 36

	All Institutions			Public Institutions			Private Institutions		
	Total	Univ.	Col.	Total	Univ.	Col.	Total	Univ.	Col.
1. Insts. reporting	207	61	146	59	35	24	148	26	122
2. Total faculty reported on such leave	1,136	709	427	487	417	70	649	292	357
3. Total faculty in reporting insts.	49,857	36,509	13,348	28,126	23,604	4,522	21,731	12,905	8,826
4. Percent of faculty on such leave	2.3%	1.9%	3.2%	1.7%	1.8%	1.5%	3.0%	2.3%	4.0%

TABLE 82: NUMBER OF FACULTY TAKING LEAVE WITH PAY OTHER THAN SABBATICAL (FUNDS FROM GRANTS OR CONTRACTS)

Questionnaire Sect. 5 Q. 36

	All Institutions			Public Institutions			Private Institutions		
	Total	Univ.	Col.	Total	Univ.	Col.	Total	Univ.	Col.
1. Insts. reporting	211	67	144	71	39	32	140	28	112
2. Total faculty reported on such leave	734	432	302	356	264	92	378	168	210
3. Total faculty in reporting insts.	56,785	42,721	14,064	33,519	27,762	5,757	23,266	14,959	8,307
4. Percent of faculty on such leave	1.3%	1.0%	2.1%	1.1%	1.0%	1.6%	1.6%	1.1%	2.5%

TABLE 83: NUMBER OF FACULTY TAKING LEAVE OF ABSENCE WITHOUT PAY

Questionnaire Sect. 5 Q. 36

	All Institutions			Public Institutions			Private Institutions		
	Total	Univ.	Col.	Total	Univ.	Col.	Total	Univ.	Col.
1. Insts. reporting	451	132	319	170	77	93	281	55	226
2. Total faculty reported on leave without pay	2,858	1,956	902	1,852	1,454	398	1,006	502	504
3. Total faculty in reporting insts.	118,499	85,081	33,418	74,981	57,566	17,415	43,518	27,515	16,003
4. Percent of faculty on leave without pay	2.4%	2.3%	2.7%	2.5%	2.5%	2.3%	2.3%	1.8%	3.1%

TABLE 84: TOTAL OF ALL TYPES OF LEAVES OF ABSENCE TAKEN, 1962—63

Questionnaire Sect. 5 Q. 36

	All Institutions			Public Institutions			Private Institutions		
	Total	Univ.	Col.	Total	Univ.	Col.	Total	Univ.	Col.
1. Insts. reporting	606	140	466	200	81	119	406	59	347
2. Total faculty reported on leave	7,785	5,169	2,616	4,478	3,529	949	3,307	1,640	1,667
3. Total faculty in reporting insts.	136,512	93,334	43,178	85,330	64,544	20,786	51,182	28,790	22,392
4. Percent of faculty on leave	5.7%	5.5%	6.1%	5.2%	5.5%	4.6%	6.5%	5.7%	7.4%

TABLE 85: LIMITS ON NUMBER OF PERSONS WHO MAY BE ON LEAVE AT ANY ONE TIME
Questionnaire Sect. 5 Q. 38

	All Institutions			Public Institutions			Private Institutions		
	Total	Univ.	Col.	Total	Univ.	Col.	Total	Univ.	Col.
No Limit Made									
1. Number	354	82	272	122	42	80	232	40	192
2. Percent	47.5%	55.4%	45.6%	56.2%	50.0%	60.2%	43.9%	62.5%	41.4%
Limit Made									
3. Number	320	61	259	86	37	49	234	24	210
4. Percent	43.0%	41.2%	43.4%	39.6%	44.0%	36.8%	44.3%	37.5%	45.3%
No Response									
5. Number	71	5	66	9	5	4	62	...	62
6. Percent	9.5%	3.4%	11.1%	4.1%	6.0%	3.0%	11.7%	...	13.4%
7. Total	745	148	597	217	84	133	528	64	464

Actual limits are operative in most institutions but frequently on the departmental or divisional level.

TABLE 86: EFFECT OF LEAVE OF ABSENCE ON DETERMINATION OF TIME WITHIN WHICH
TENURE IS TO BE DETERMINED
Questionnaire Sect. 5 Q. 41

	All Institutions			Public Institutions			Private Institutions		
	Total	Univ.	Col.	Total	Univ.	Col.	Total	Univ.	Col.
Leave of Absence Counts Toward Tenure									
1. Number	214	47	167	55	19	36	159	28	131
2. Percent	28.7%	31.7%	28.0%	25.3%	22.6%	27.1%	30.1%	43.7%	28.2%
Leave of Absence Not Counted Toward Tenure									
3. Number	284	59	225	104	40	64	180	19	161
4. Percent	38.1%	39.9%	37.7%	47.9%	47.6%	48.1%	34.1%	29.7%	34.7%
Question Not Applicable									
5. Number	168	34	134	49	20	29	119	14	105
6. Percent	22.6%	23.0%	22.4%	22.6%	23.8%	21.8%	22.5%	21.9%	22.6%
No Reponse									
7. Number	79	8	71	9	5	4	70	3	67
8. Percent	10.6%	5.4%	11.9%	4.1%	6.0%	3.0%	13.3%	4.7%	14.4%
9. Total	745	148	597	217	84	133	528	64	464

TABLE 87: PROVISIONS FOR CONTINUATION OF DEPARTMENTAL WORK DURING LEAVE OF
           ABSENCE
Questionnaire Sect. 5 Q. 42

	All Institutions			Public Institutions			Private Institutions		
	Total	Univ.	Col.	Total	Univ.	Col.	Total	Univ.	Col.
1. Insts. responding	688	144	544	211	81	130	477	63	414
2. Temporary replace-ment	643	135	508	201	78	123	442	57	385
3. Extra work by re-maining staff	406	105	301	125	61	64	281	44	237
4. Staff large enough to permit some leaves	257	89	168	83	45	38	174	44	130
5. Department pro-gram reduced	208	50	158	52	23	29	156	27	129
6. Other	12	4	8	2	1	1	10	3	7
7. No response	57	4	53	6	3	3	51	1	50
8. Total	745	148	597	217	84	133	528	64	464

TABLE 88: PROVISIONS FOR LEAVE OF ABSENCE WITH PAY AMONG INSTITUTIONS NOT GRANTING
           SABBATICAL LEAVES
Questionnaire Sect. 5 Q. 1, 19, 21

	All Institutions			Public Institutions			Private Institutions		
	Total	Univ.	Col.	Total	Univ.	Col.	Total	Univ.	Col.
1. Insts. granting leave with pay	170	49	121	43	21	22	127	28	99
Leave With Pay Granted For									
2. Research	99	41	58	26	17	9	73	24	49
3. Teaching improve-ment	88	32	56	20	15	5	68	17	51
4. Study	132	37	95	28	15	13	104	22	82
5. Travel	31	11	20	8	5	3	23	6	17
6. Writing	73	31	42	21	13	8	52	18	34
7. Other	23	7	16	10	4	6	13	3	10
8. Leave with pay not granted	127	12	115	36	9	27	91	3	88
9. No response	12	...	12	1	...	1	11	...	11
10. Total insts. not granting sabbatical	309	61	248	80	30	50	229	31	198

TABLE 89: BUILDING OR OTHER SPACE USED AS CLUB OR SOCIAL ROOMS BY FACULTY OR
BY FACULTY AND OTHER STAFF
Questionnaire Sect. 6 Q. 1

	All Institutions			Public Institutions			Private Institutions		
	Total	Univ.	Col.	Total	Univ.	Col.	Total	Univ.	Col.
Inst. Has Bldg. or Space									
1. Number	341	100	241	110	57	53	231	43	188
2. Percent	45.8%	67.6%	40.4%	50.7%	67.9%	39.8%	43.8%	67.2%	40.5%
Inst. Does Not Have Bldg. or Space									
3. Number	392	48	344	103	27	76	289	21	268
4. Percent	52.6%	32.4%	57.6%	47.5%	32.1%	57.1%	54.7%	32.8%	57.8%
No Response									
5. Number	12	...	12	4	...	4	8	...	8
6. Percent	1.6%	...	2.0%	1.8%	...	3.0%	1.5%	...	1.7%
7. Total	745	148	597	217	84	133	528	64	464

TABLE 90: SERVICES PROVIDED BY FACULTY CLUB OR SOCIAL FACILITIES
Questionnaire Sect. 6 Q. 2

	All Institutions			Public Institutions			Private Institutions		
	Total	Univ.	Col.	Total	Univ.	Col.	Total	Univ.	Col.
1. Dining room	109	53	56	34	23	11	75	30	45
2. Private dining rooms	123	57	66	44	26	18	79	31	48
3. Cafeteria or lunch counter	106	44	62	40	25	15	66	19	47
4. Coffee break service	250	63	187	78	33	45	172	30	142
5. Bar (alcoholic beverages)	20	15	5	3	3	...	17	12	5
6. Reading room	162	66	96	57	37	20	105	29	76
7. Lounge	284	91	193	92	52	40	192	39	153
8. Separate public rooms for men and women	71	22	49	23	12	11	48	10	38
9. Billiard room	56	37	19	27	23	4	29	14	15
10. Bowling alley	15	6	9	6	3	3	9	3	6
11. Game room	51	36	15	25	21	4	26	15	11
12. Gymnasium	28	9	19	8	4	4	20	5	15
13. Tennis courts	27	9	18	5	3	2	22	6	16
14. Swimming pool	23	7	16	6	3	3	17	4	13
15. Library	51	22	29	12	10	2	39	12	27
16. Conference rooms	122	39	83	36	21	15	86	18	68
17. Total with club or social facility	341	100	241	110	57	53	231	43	188

Practically all institutions reporting club or social facilities responded to this question.

TABLE 91: SLEEPING QUARTERS FOR FACULTY CLUB GUESTS AND SINGLE FACULTY MEMBERS
Questionnaire Sect. 6 Q. 3, 4

	All Institutions			Public Institutions			Private Institutions		
	Total	Univ.	Col.	Total	Univ.	Col.	Total	Univ.	Col.
1. Sleeping quarters available	52	19	33	15	9	6	37	10	27
2. Number of rooms for guests	284	143	141	88	51	37	196	92	104
3. Living quarters for single faculty members	30	12	18	11	7	4	19	5	14
4. Number of rooms for single faculty members	354	222	132	236	154	82	118	68	50

Some institutions reported guest-rooms available not in faculty club.

TABLE 92: ADEQUACY EVALUATION OF FACULTY CLUB FACILITIES
Questionnaire Sect. 6 Q. 5

	All Institutions			Public Institutions			Private Institutions		
	Total	Univ.	Col.	Total	Univ.	Col.	Total	Univ.	Col.
Size									
1. Adequate	181	53	128	54	26	28	127	27	100
2. Inadequate	112	42	70	47	28	19	65	14	51
3. Not important	17	1	16	2	...	2	15	1	14
4. No response	31	4	27	7	3	4	24	1	23
Location									
5. Adequate	250	82	168	84	48	36	166	34	132
6. Inadequate	44	10	34	15	5	10	29	5	24
7. Not important	10	2	8	2	...	2	8	2	6
8. No response	37	6	31	9	4	5	28	2	26
Guest Facilities									
9. Adequate	44	16	28	12	6	6	32	10	22
10. Inadequate	121	43	78	45	28	17	76	15	61
11. Not important	112	29	83	34	14	20	78	15	63
12. No response	64	12	52	19	9	10	45	3	42
Dining Facilities									
13. Adequate	130	45	85	42	21	21	88	24	64
14. Inadequate	95	43	52	42	29	13	53	14	39
15. Not important	66	6	60	15	3	12	51	3	48
16. No response	50	6	44	11	4	7	39	2	37
Space for Recreation									
17. Adequate	80	34	46	26	17	9	54	17	37
18. Inadequate	114	40	74	45	25	20	69	15	54
19. Not important	91	19	72	26	10	16	65	9	56
20. No response	56	7	49	13	5	8	43	2	41
Space for Meetings									
21. Adequate	152	38	114	40	19	21	112	19	93
22. Inadequate	101	43	58	46	29	17	55	14	41
23. Not important	40	12	28	10	4	6	30	8	22
24. No response	48	7	41	14	5	9	34	2	32
25. Total	341	100	241	110	57	53	231	43	188

TABLE 93: INSTITUTIONAL CONTRIBUTION TO OPERATION OF FACULTY CLUB
Questionnaire Sect. 6 Q. 6

	All Institutions			Public Institutions			Private Institutions		
	Total	Univ.	Col.	Total	Univ.	Col.	Total	Univ.	Col.
1. Insts. reporting	321	95	226	102	52	50	219	43	176
2. Dollar contribution	26	12	14	5	4	1	21	8	13
3. Buildings or rooms	288	74	214	84	39	45	204	35	169
4. Utilities	245	69	176	75	38	37	170	31	139
5. Operating personnel	148	38	110	42	18	24	106	20	86
6. Other	45	27	18	22	17	5	23	10	13
7. No response	20	5	15	8	5	3	12	...	12
8. Total	341	100	241	110	57	53	231	43	188

TABLE 94: FACILITY ORGANIZED AS A FACULTY CLUB
Questionnaire Sect. 6 Q. 7, 9

	All Institutions			Public Institutions			Private Institutions		
	Total	Univ.	Col.	Total	Univ.	Col.	Total	Univ.	Col.
1. Organized as faculty club	140	75	65	62	48	14	78	27	51
2. Not organized as faculty club	195	25	170	47	9	38	148	16	132
3. No response	6	...	6	1	...	1	5	...	5
4. Total	341	100	241	110	57	53	231	43	188
5. Non-faculty accepted as members	37	16	21	22	13	9	15	3	12
6. Non-faculty not ac- cepted as members	97	58	39	37	34	3	60	24	36
7. No response	6	1	5	3	1	2	3	...	3

TABLE 95: NUMBER OF FULL-TIME FACULTY MEMBERS BELONGING TO FACULTY CLUB
Questionnaire Sect. 6 Q. 10

	All Institutions			Public Institutions			Private Institutions		
	Total	Univ.	Col.	Total	Univ.	Col.	Total	Univ.	Col.
1. Insts. reporting faculty club membership	126	71	55	55	46	9	71	25	46
2. Faculty club members reported	33,981	28,885	5,096	18,714	17,483	1,231	15,267	11,402	3,865
3. Total full-time faculty in reporting insts.	68,158	61,974	6,184	46,770	44,922	1,848	21,388	17,052	4,336
4. Percent of faculty belonging to faculty club	49.9%	46.6%	82.4%	40.0%	38.9%	66.6%	71.4%	66.9%	89.1%

TABLE 96: PROPORTION OF FACULTY CLUB OPERATING EXPENSES COVERED BY DUES AND OPERATING RECEIPTS
Questionnaire Sect. 6 Q. 12

	All Institutions			Public Institutions			Private Institutions		
	Total	Univ.	Col.	Total	Univ.	Col.	Total	Univ.	Col.
Below 50%									
1. Number	36	15	21	11	6	5	25	9	16
2. Percent	28.6%	21.1%	38.2%	20.0%	13.0%	55.6%	35.2%	36.0%	34.8%
50—79%									
3. Number	12	9	3	5	5	...	7	4	3
4. Percent	9.5%	12.7%	5.5%	9.1%	10.9%	...	9.9%	16.0%	6.5%
80—99%									
5. Number	23	15	8	11	10	1	12	5	7
6. Percent	18.3%	21.1%	14.5%	20.0%	21.7%	11.1%	16.9%	20.0%	15.2%
100%									
7. Number	37	24	13	21	19	2	16	5	11
8. Percent	29.4%	33.8%	23.6%	38.2%	41.3%	22.2%	22.5%	20.0%	23.9%
No Response									
9. Number	18	8	10	7	6	1	11	2	9
10. Percent	14.3%	11.3%	18.2%	12.7%	13.0%	11.1%	15.5%	8.0%	19.6%
11. Total	126	71	55	55	46	9	71	25	46

TABLE 97: STUDENT UNION USE BY FACULTY
Questionnaire Sect. 6 Q. 13

	All Institutions			Public Institutions			Private Institutions		
	Total	Univ.	Col.	Total	Univ.	Col.	Total	Univ.	Col.
Inst. Has Student Union									
1. Number	473	116	357	171	72	99	302	44	258
2. Percent	63.5%	78.4%	59.8%	78.8%	85.7%	74.4%	57.2%	68.8%	55.6%
Use by Faculty									
3. Not at all	57	10	47	11	3	8	46	7	39
4. Small extent	190	45	145	70	27	43	120	18	102
5. Quite a bit	143	34	109	52	24	28	91	10	81
6. Great deal	50	19	31	24	13	11	26	6	20
7. No response	33	8	25	14	5	9	19	3	16

TABLE 98: EFFECT OF FACULTY CLUB FACILITIES ON RECRUITING AND RETAINING FACULTY
Questionnaire Sect. 6 Q. 14

	All Institutions			Public Institutions			Private Institutions		
	Total	Univ.	Col.	Total	Univ.	Col.	Total	Univ.	Col.
Recruiting									
1. Substantial	15	6	9	5	4	1	10	2	8
2. Moderate	81	33	48	30	17	13	51	16	35
3. Negligible	188	52	136	59	31	28	129	21	108
4. No response	57	9	48	16	5	11	41	4	37
5. Total	341	100	241	110	57	53	231	43	188
Retaining									
6. Substantial	10	3	7	2	1	1	8	2	6
7. Moderate	104	43	61	36	23	13	68	20	48
8. Negligible	169	45	124	55	28	27	114	17	97
9. No response	58	9	49	17	5	12	41	4	37
10. Total	341	100	241	110	57	53	231	43	188

TABLE 99: WAIVER OF COLLEGE TUITION FOR FACULTY CHILDREN
Questionnaire Sect. 7 Q. 8

	All Institutions			Public Institutions			Private Institutions		
	Total	Univ.	Col.	Total	Univ.	Col.	Total	Univ.	Col.
Tuition Waived at Least in Part									
1. Number	519	77	442	28	18	10	491	59	432
2. Percent	69.7%	52.0%	74.0%	12.9%	21.4%	7.5%	93.0%	92.2%	93.1%
Tuition Not Waived									
3. Number	212	67	145	182	62	120	30	5	25
4. Percent	28.5%	45.3%	24.3%	83.9%	73.8%	90.2%	5.7%	7.8%	5.4%
No Response									
5. Number	14	4	10	7	4	3	7	...	7
6. Percent	1.9%	2.7%	1.7%	3.2%	4.8%	2.3%	1.3%	...	1.5%
7. Total	745	148	597	217	84	133	528	64	464

TABLE 100: PERCENTAGE OF TUITION WAIVED FOR FACULTY CHILDREN
Questionnaire Sect. 7 Q. 8

	All Institutions			Public Institutions			Private Institutions		
	Total	Univ.	Col.	Total	Univ.	Col.	Total	Univ.	Col.
1. Insts. reporting	498	74	424	25	17	8	473	57	416
Percentage of Tuition Waived									
2. 1—24%	3	...	3	...	...	...	3	...	3
3. 25—49%	14	...	14	2	...	2	12	...	12
4. 50%	61	9	52	4	3	1	57	6	51
5. 51—74%	11	3	8	2	1	1	9	2	7
6. 75—99%	31	5	26	2	2	...	29	3	26
7. 100%	378	57	321	15	11	4	363	46	317

In some cases the per cent was worked out from ambiguous answers. For example, institutions with fixed dollar waiver, but tuition varying from college to college.

TABLE 101: PARTICIPATION IN TUITION EXCHANGE, INC.
Questionnaire Sect. 7 Q. 9

	All Institutions			Public Institutions			Private Institutions		
	Total	Univ.	Col.	Total	Univ.	Col.	Total	Univ.	Col.
Inst. Participates									
1. Number	144	27	117	6	5	1	138	22	116
2. Percent	19.3%	18.2%	19.6%	2.8%	6.0%	.8%	26.1%	34.4%	25.0%
Inst. Does Not Participate									
3. Number	568	117	451	202	76	126	366	41	325
4. Percent	76.2%	79.1%	75.5%	93.1%	90.5%	94.7%	69.3%	64.1%	70.0%
No Response									
5. Number	33	4	29	9	3	6	24	1	23
6. Percent	4.4%	2.7%	4.9%	4.1%	3.6%	4.5%	4.5%	1.6%	5.0%
7. Total	745	148	597	217	84	133	528	64	464

This table is already out of date because of recent withdrawals. In 1962, 220 institutions (some of them not represented by replies to this questionnaire) belonged to the Tuition Exchange and at that time or since more than 40 institutions have withdrawn or expressed their intention of doing so.

TABLE 102: CASH GRANTS FOR UNDERGRADUATE TUITION OF FACULTY CHILDREN
Questionnaire Sect. 7 Q. 10

	All Institutions			Public Institutions			Private Institutions		
	Total	Univ.	Col.	Total	Univ.	Col.	Total	Univ.	Col.
Cash Grants Provided									
1. Number	109	15	94	1	...	1	108	15	93
2. Percent	14.6%	10.1%	15.7%	.5%	...	.8%	20.5%	23.4%	20.0%
No Cash Grants									
3. Number	617	132	485	213	83	130	404	49	355
4. Percent	82.8%	89.2%	81.2%	98.2%	98.8%	97.7%	76.5%	76.6%	76.5%
No Response									
5. Number	19	1	18	3	1	2	16	...	16
6. Percent	2.6%	.7%	3.0%	1.4%	1.2%	1.5%	3.0%	...	3.4%
7. Total	745	148	597	217	84	133	528	64	464

TABLE 103: LEVELS OF CASH TUITION GRANTS FOR FACULTY CHILDREN
Questionnaire Sect. 7 Q. 10

	All Institutions			Public Institutions			Private Institutions		
	Total	Univ.	Col.	Total	Univ.	Col.	Total	Univ.	Col.
1. Insts. reporting	105	15	90	...	...	...	105	15	90
2. Less than annual tuition at granting inst.	60	11	49	...	...	...	60	11	49
3. Equal to tuition charged up to total of tuition at granting inst.	42	4	38	...	...	...	42	4	38
4. Greater than tuition at granting inst., if charged by receiving inst.	2	...	2	...	...	...	2	...	2
5. Specified dollar amount	40	7	33	...	...	...	40	7	33

TABLE 104: EFFECT OF FACULTY CHILDREN'S EDUCATION PROGRAM ON RECRUITING AND
RETAINING FACULTY
Questionnaire Sect. 7 Q. 12

	All Institutions			Public Institutions			Private Institutions		
	Total	Univ.	Col.	Total	Univ.	Col.	Total	Univ.	Col.
Recruiting									
1. Substantial	159	30	129	8	5	3	151	25	126
2. Moderate	242	38	204	16	8	8	226	30	196
3. Negligible	103	13	90	18	8	10	85	5	80
4. No response	45	7	38	10	6	4	35	1	34
5. Total	549	88	461	52	27	25	497	61	436
Retaining									
6. Substantial	198	36	162	7	5	2	191	31	160
7. Moderate	215	32	183	15	8	7	200	24	176
8. Negligible	86	13	73	19	8	11	67	5	62
9. No response	50	7	43	11	6	5	39	1	38
10. Total	549	88	461	52	27	25	497	61	436

Of the institutions providing cash grants nearly 60% report that their children's education program helps substantially in retaining faculty.

TABLE 105: FACULTY ATTENDANCE OF CLASSES WITHOUT TUITION CHARGE
Questionnaire Sect. 7 Q. 13

	All Institutions			Public Institutions			Private Institutions		
	Total	Univ.	Col.	Total	Univ.	Col.	Total	Univ.	Col.
1. Attends without charge as auditor only	132	29	103	53	21	32	79	8	71
2. Attends without charge as auditor or for credit	436	80	356	61	34	27	375	46	329
3. Cannot attend without charge	152	36	116	97	28	69	55	8	47
4. No response	25	3	22	6	1	5	19	2	17
5. Total	745	148	597	217	84	133	528	64	464

If there is a charge, it is sometimes at reduced rate.

TABLE 106: FACULTY SPOUSE ATTENDANCE OF CLASSES WITHOUT TUITION CHARGE
Questionnaire Sect. 7 Q. 14

	All Institutions			Public Institutions			Private Institutions		
	Total	Univ.	Col.	Total	Univ.	Col.	Total	Univ.	Col.
1. Attends without charge as auditor only	55	14	41	15	9	6	40	5	35
2. Attends without charge as auditor or for credit	348	40	308	20	10	10	328	30	298
3. Cannot attend without charge	309	91	218	176	64	112	133	27	106
4. No response	33	3	30	6	1	5	27	2	25
5. Total	745	148	597	217	84	133	528	64	464

If there is a charge, it is sometimes at reduced rate.

TABLE 107: TYPE OF PARKING SPACE FOR FACULTY
Questionnaire Sect. 8 Q. 1

	All Institutions			Public Institutions			Private Institutions		
	Total	Univ.	Col.	Total	Univ.	Col.	Total	Univ.	Col.
1. In space reserved for faculty	584	133	451	173	75	98	411	58	353
2. In reserved space and also in space open to public	256	72	184	78	40	38	178	32	146
3. In space also open to public or students	384	86	298	115	48	67	269	38	231
4. No space provided	26	...	26	3	...	3	23	...	23
5. No response	7	1	6	4	1	3	3	...	3
6. Total	745	148	597	217	84	133	528	64	464

TABLE 108: MONTHLY PARKING CHARGES TO FACULTY
Questionnaire Sect. 8 Q. 1

	All Institutions			Public Institutions			Private Institutions		
	Total	Univ.	Col.	Total	Univ.	Col.	Total	Univ.	Col.
In Space Reserved for Faculty									
1. Insts. reporting	513	120	393	151	66	85	362	54	308
2. Free parking	452	89	363	110	49	61	342	40	302
3. Charge made	61	31	30	41	17	24	20	14	6
In Space Also Open to Public									
4. Insts. reporting	310	73	237	92	42	50	218	31	187
5. Free parking	263	49	214	63	28	35	200	21	179
6. Charge made	47	24	23	29	14	15	18	10	8

TABLE 109: RESERVATION OF SPACE FOR FACULTY
Questionnaire Sect. 8 Q. 2

	All Institutions			Public Institutions			Private Institutions		
	Total	Univ.	Col.	Total	Univ.	Col.	Total	Univ.	Col.
Reserved by General Area									
1. Number	459	118	341	155	71	84	304	47	257
2. Percent	78.6%	88.7%	75.6%	89.6%	94.7%	85.7%	74.0%	81.0%	72.8%
Reserved by Assigned Stalls									
3. Number	94	12	82	7	4	3	87	8	79
4. Percent	16.1%	9.0%	18.2%	4.0%	5.3%	3.1%	21.2%	13.8%	22.4%
No Response									
5. Number	31	3	28	11	...	11	20	3	17
6. Percent	5.3%	2.3%	6.2%	6.4%	...	11.2%	4.9%	5.2%	4.8%
7. Total	584	133	451	173	75	98	411	58	353

A mixture of these systems is sometimes used.

TABLE 110: NUMBER OF FACULTY AUTOMOBILES ACCOMMODATED AND THAT WOULD BE
ACCOMMODATED UNDER ADEQUATE PARKING
Questionnaire Sect 8 Q. 3, 4

	All Institutions			Public Institutions			Private Institutions		
	Total	Univ.	Col.	Total	Univ.	Col.	Total	Univ.	Col.
1. Insts. reporting	611	130	481	182	72	110	429	58	371
2. Autos accommodated	163,945	120,225	43,720	109,142	87,166	21,976	54,803	33,059	21,744
3. Autos that would be accommodated with adequate parking	189,185	140,704	48,481	126,151	101,199	24,952	63,034	39,505	23,529

This table has only moderate validity, since the coders evidently believed that in case of insufficient reply one space per full-time faculty member is needed. This yardstick is considered inadequate in some places and more than needed in others.

TABLE 111: PARKING SPACE FOR PERSONS VISITING FACULTY MEMBERS
Questionnaire Sect. 8 Q. 5

	All Institutions			Public Institutions			Private Institutions		
	Total	Univ.	Col.	Total	Univ.	Col.	Total	Univ.	Col.
Space Provided In 1. Area for general public	457	81	376	120	46	74	337	35	302
2. Area reserved for visitors	351	90	261	120	53	67	231	37	194
3. Area reserved for faculty	113	37	76	41	21	20	72	16	56
4. No space provided	39	6	33	9	3	6	30	3	27
5. No response	24	3	21	9	3	6	15	...	15
6. Total	745	148	597	217	84	133	528	64	464

TABLE 112: INTRA-CAMPUS BUS SERVICE
Questionnaire Sect. 8 Q. 6

	All Institutions			Public Institutions			Private Institutions		
	Total	Univ.	Col.	Total	Univ.	Col.	Total	Univ.	Col.
Bus Service									
1. Provided	45	21	24	20	13	7	25	8	17
2. Not provided	676	125	551	189	69	120	487	56	431
3. No response	24	2	22	8	2	6	16	...	16
4. Total	745	148	597	217	84	133	528	64	464
Charge									
5. Insts. reporting	43	21	22	19	13	6	24	8	16
6. Service free	30	12	18	12	7	5	18	5	13
7. Service charged for	13	9	4	7	6	1	6	3	3

Sometimes the bus service is within one large campus, e.g., the University of Wisconsin
or between two campuses, e.g., the University of Minnesota.
The charge is sometimes included in the parking fee.

TABLE 113: FUTURE PLANS FOR FACULTY PARKING FACILITIES ACCORDING TO EVALUATION
OF ADEQUACY OF PRESENT FACILITIES (EXPANSION OF FACILITIES VS.
EXPANSION OF FACULTY)
Questionnaire Sect. 8 Q. 7, 8

	All Institutions			Public Institutions			Private Institutions		
	Total	Univ.	Col.	Total	Univ.	Col.	Total	Univ.	Col.
Adequate at Present									
1. More rapidly	33	8	25	7	4	3	26	4	22
2. Same rate	300	47	253	89	28	61	211	19	192
3. Less rapidly	35	10	25	15	9	6	20	1	19
4. Remain as is	120	18	102	17	8	9	103	10	93
5. Contracted	3	1	2	...	...	...	3	1	2
6. No response	16	1	15	4	1	3	12	...	12
7. Total	507	85	422	132	50	82	375	35	340
Inadequate at Present									
8. More rapidly	67	24	43	23	11	12	44	13	31
9. Same rate	82	17	65	28	10	18	54	7	47
10. Less rapidly	37	11	26	16	4	12	21	7	14
11. Remain as is	27	8	19	13	7	6	14	1	13
12. Contracted	2	1	1	1	1	...	1	...	1
13. No response	6	1	5	2	...	2	4	1	3
14. Total	221	62	159	83	33	50	138	29	109
15. No adequacy evaluation	17	1	16	2	1	1	15	...	15

TABLE 114: FACULTY RECREATION—SWIMMING POOL
Questionnaire Sect. 9 Q. 1A

	All Institutions			Public Institutions			Private Institutions		
	Total	Univ.	Col.	Total	Univ.	Col.	Total	Univ.	Col.
1. Total	745	148	597	217	84	133	528	64	464
2. College has swim-									
ming pool	424	120	304	176	72	104	248	48	200
Available to Faculty									
3. Yes	410	116	294	173	70	103	237	46	191
4. No	14	4	10	3	2	1	11	2	9
5. Free	349	88	261	135	47	88	214	41	173
6. Charge	61	28	33	38	23	15	23	5	18
Available to Spouse									
7. Yes	380	103	277	165	63	102	215	40	175
8. No	44	17	27	11	9	2	33	8	25
9. Free	310	70	240	125	39	86	185	31	154
10. Charge	70	33	37	40	24	16	30	9	21
Available to Children									
11. Yes	364	98	266	157	59	98	207	39	168
12. No	60	22	38	19	13	6	41	9	32
13. Free	291	65	226	118	36	82	173	29	144
14. Charge	73	33	40	39	23	16	34	10	24

TABLE 115: FACULTY RECREATION—GYMNASIUM
Questionnaire Sect. 9 Q. 1A

	All Institutions			Public Institutions			Private Institutions		
	Total	Univ.	Col.	Total	Univ.	Col.	Total	Univ.	Col.
1. Total	745	148	597	217	84	133	528	64	464
2. College has									
gymnasium	683	144	539	211	82	129	472	62	410
Available to Faculty									
3. Yes	633	138	495	198	78	120	435	60	375
4. No	50	6	44	13	4	9	37	2	35
5. Free	593	122	471	183	67	116	410	55	355
6. Charge	40	16	24	15	11	4	25	5	20
Available to Spouse									
7. Yes	417	68	349	134	40	94	283	28	255
8. No	266	76	190	77	42	35	189	34	155
9. Free	389	61	328	122	34	88	267	27	240
10. Charge	28	7	21	12	6	6	16	1	15
Available to Children									
11. Yes	370	61	309	118	35	83	252	26	226
12. No	313	83	230	93	47	46	220	36	184
13. Free	343	55	288	110	32	78	233	23	210
14. Charge	27	6	21	8	3	5	19	3	16

TABLE 116: FACULTY RECREATION—TENNIS COURTS
Questionnaire Sect. 9 Q. 1A

	All Institutions			Public Institutions			Private Institutions		
	Total	Univ.	Col.	Total	Univ.	Col.	Total	Univ.	Col.
1. Total	745	148	597	217	84	133	528	64	464
2. College has tennis courts	647	131	516	203	79	124	444	52	392
Available to Faculty									
3. Yes	640	129	511	203	79	124	437	50	387
4. No	7	2	5	...	...	...	7	2	5
5. Free	603	117	486	194	74	120	409	43	366
6. Charge	37	12	25	9	5	4	28	7	21
Available to Spouse									
7. Yes	584	111	473	187	70	117	397	41	356
8. No	63	20	43	16	9	7	47	11	36
9. Free	542	97	445	175	64	111	367	33	334
10. Charge	42	14	28	12	6	6	30	8	22
Available to Children									
11. Yes	551	103	448	177	64	113	374	39	335
12. No	96	28	68	26	15	11	70	13	57
13. Free	514	91	423	170	60	110	344	31	313
14. Charge	37	12	25	7	4	3	30	8	22

TABLE 117: FACULTY RECREATION—HANDBALL COURTS
Questionnaire Sect. 9 Q. 1A

	All Institutions			Public Institutions			Private Institutions		
	Total	Univ.	Col.	Total	Univ.	Col.	Total	Univ.	Col.
1. Total	745	148	597	217	84	133	528	64	464
2. College has handball courts	303	101	202	118	59	59	185	42	143
Available to Faculty									
3. Yes	295	98	197	114	57	57	181	41	140
4. No	8	3	5	4	2	2	4	1	3
5. Free	274	86	188	107	50	57	167	36	131
6. Charge	21	12	9	7	7	...	14	5	9
Available to Spouse									
7. Yes	177	50	127	78	30	48	99	20	79
8. No	126	51	75	40	29	11	86	22	64
9. Free	168	45	123	73	26	47	95	19	76
10. Charge	9	5	4	5	4	1	4	1	3
Available to Children									
11. Yes	167	50	117	67	29	38	100	21	79
12. No	136	51	85	51	30	21	85	21	64
13. Free	155	46	109	64	27	37	91	19	72
14. Charge	12	4	8	3	2	1	9	2	7

TABLE 118: FACULTY RECREATION—GOLF COURSE
Questionnaire Sect. 9 Q. 1A

	All Institutions			Public Institutions			Private Institutions		
	Total	Univ.	Col.	Total	Univ.	Col.	Total	Univ.	Col.
1. Total	745	148	597	217	84	133	528	64	464
2. College has golf course	97	38	59	46	31	15	51	7	44
Available to Faculty									
3. Yes	96	38	58	46	31	15	50	7	43
4. No	1	...	1	...	...	...	1	...	1
5. Free	38	3	35	15	3	12	23	...	23
6. Charge	58	35	23	31	28	3	27	7	20
Available to Spouse									
7. Yes	90	36	54	44	30	14	46	6	40
8. No	7	2	5	2	1	1	5	1	4
9. Free	32	2	30	12	2	10	20	...	20
10. Charge	58	34	24	32	28	4	26	6	20
Available to Children									
11. Yes	84	34	50	39	27	12	45	7	38
12. No	13	4	9	7	4	3	6	...	6
13. Free	29	2	27	10	2	8	19	...	19
14. Charge	55	32	23	29	25	4	26	7	19

TABLE 119: FACULTY RECREATION—BILLIARDS
Questionnaire Sect. 9 Q. 1A

	All Institutions			Public Institutions			Private Institutions		
	Total	Univ.	Col.	Total	Univ.	Col.	Total	Univ.	Col.
1. Total	745	148	597	217	84	133	528	64	464
2. College has billiards	247	88	159	116	61	55	131	27	104
Available to Faculty									
3. Yes	229	85	144	113	60	53	116	25	91
4. No	18	3	15	3	1	2	15	2	13
5. Free	75	23	52	23	9	14	52	14	38
6. Charge	154	62	92	90	51	39	64	11	53
Available to Spouse									
7. Yes	168	64	104	89	46	43	79	18	61
8. No	79	24	55	27	15	12	52	9	43
9. Free	45	11	34	16	4	12	29	7	22
10. Charge	123	53	70	73	42	31	50	11	39
Available to Children									
11. Yes	138	57	81	76	42	34	62	15	47
12. No	109	31	78	40	19	21	69	12	57
13. Free	36	10	26	12	5	7	24	5	19
14. Charge	102	47	55	64	37	27	38	10	28

TABLE 120: FACULTY RECREATION—BOWLING ALLEY
Questionnaire Sect. 9 Q. 1A

	All Institutions			Public Institutions			Private Institutions		
	Total	Univ.	Col.	Total	Univ.	Col.	Total	Univ.	Col.
1. Total	745	148	597	217	84	133	528	64	464
2. College has bowling alley	161	72	89	79	53	26	82	19	63
Available to Faculty									
3. Yes	156	68	88	77	51	26	79	17	62
4. No	5	4	1	2	2	...	3	2	1
5. Free	28	1	27	3	...	3	25	1	24
6. Charge	128	67	61	74	51	23	54	16	38
Available to Spouse									
7. Yes	140	64	76	71	48	23	69	16	53
8. No	21	8	13	8	5	3	13	3	10
9. Free	21	1	20	2	...	2	19	1	18
10. Charge	119	63	56	69	48	21	50	15	35
Available to Children									
11. Yes	120	58	62	62	43	19	58	15	43
12. No	41	14	27	17	10	7	24	4	20
13. Free	12	1	11	...	...	...	12	1	11
14. Charge	108	57	51	62	43	19	46	14	32

TABLE 121: FACULTY RECREATION—ATHLETIC EVENTS
Questionnaire Sect. 9 Q. 1B

	All Institutions			Public Institutions			Private Institutions		
	Total	Univ.	Col.	Total	Univ.	Col.	Total	Univ.	Col.
1. Total	745	148	597	217	84	133	528	64	464
2. College has athletic events	674	146	528	211	82	129	463	64	399
Available to Faculty									
3. Yes	663	145	518	208	81	127	455	64	391
4. No	11	1	10	3	1	2	8	...	8
5. Free	397	29	368	50	4	46	347	25	322
6. Reduced charge	217	107	110	140	73	67	77	34	43
7. Regular charge	49	9	40	18	4	14	31	5	26
Available to Spouse									
8. Yes	650	144	506	206	81	125	444	63	381
9. No	24	2	22	5	1	4	19	1	18
10. Free	362	21	341	45	2	43	317	19	298
11. Reduced charge	224	107	117	138	72	66	86	35	51
12. Regular charge	64	16	48	23	7	16	41	9	32
Available to Children									
13. Yes	624	137	487	199	77	122	425	60	365
14. No	50	9	41	12	5	7	38	4	34
15. Free	326	16	310	42	1	41	284	15	269
16. Reduced charge	214	93	121	122	60	62	92	33	59
17. Regular charge	84	28	56	35	16	19	49	12	37

TABLE 122: FACULTY RECREATION—STUDENT DRAMA
Questionnaire Sect. 9 Q. 1 B

	All Institutions			Public Institutions			Private Institutions		
	Total	Univ.	Col.	Total	Univ.	Col.	Total	Univ.	Col.
1. Total	745	148	597	217	84	133	528	64	464
2. College has student drama	716	142	574	211	80	131	505	62	443
Available to Faculty									
3. Yes	700	142	558	207	80	127	493	62	431
4. No	16	...	16	4	...	4	12	...	12
5. Free	326	23	303	53	4	49	273	19	254
6. Reduced charge	194	63	131	80	37	43	114	26	88
7. Regular charge	180	56	124	74	39	35	106	17	89
Available to Spouse									
8. Yes	686	139	547	203	80	123	483	59	424
9. No	30	3	27	8	...	8	22	3	19
10. Free	307	21	286	50	4	46	257	17	240
11. Reduced charge	192	61	131	77	36	41	115	25	90
12. Regular charge	187	57	130	76	40	36	111	17	94
Available to Children									
13. Yes	653	135	518	199	79	120	454	56	398
14. No	63	7	56	12	1	11	51	6	45
15. Free	260	18	242	43	4	39	217	14	203
16. Reduced charge	196	55	141	75	31	44	121	24	97
17. Regular charge	197	62	135	81	44	37	116	18	98

TABLE 123: FACULTY RECREATION—STUDENT CONCERTS
Questionnaire Sect. 9 Q. 1 B

	All Institutions			Public Institutions			Private Institutions		
	Total	Univ.	Col.	Total	Univ.	Col.	Total	Univ.	Col.
1. Total	745	148	597	217	84	133	528	64	464
2. College has student concerts	704	144	560	213	82	131	491	62	429
Available to Faculty									
3. Yes	694	144	550	210	82	128	484	62	422
4. No	10	...	10	3	...	3	7	...	7
5. Free	544	89	455	145	49	96	399	40	359
6. Reduced charge	66	26	40	30	15	15	36	11	25
7. Regular charge	84	29	55	35	18	17	49	11	38
Available to Spouse									
8. Yes	683	143	540	206	82	124	477	61	416
9. No	21	1	20	7	...	7	14	1	13
10. Free	527	85	442	141	48	93	386	37	349
11. Reduced charge	64	27	37	27	15	12	37	12	25
12. Regular charge	92	31	61	38	19	19	54	12	42
Available to Children									
13. Yes	664	139	525	205	80	125	459	59	400
14. No	40	5	35	8	2	6	32	3	29
15. Free	503	83	420	138	47	91	365	36	329
16. Reduced charge	68	25	43	29	14	15	39	11	28
17. Regular charge	93	31	62	38	19	19	55	12	43

TABLE 124: FACULTY RECREATION—PROFESSIONAL DRAMA
Questionnaire Sect. 9 Q. 1B

	All Institutions			Public Institutions			Private Institutions		
	Total	Univ.	Col.	Total	Univ.	Col.	Total	Univ.	Col.
1. Total	745	148	597	217	84	133	528	64	464
2. College has pro-									
fessional drama	415	83	332	160	59	101	255	24	231
Available to Faculty									
3. Yes	406	83	323	157	59	98	249	24	225
4. No	9	...	9	3	...	3	6	...	6
5. Free	152	7	145	32	2	30	120	5	115
6. Reduced charge	138	40	98	69	29	40	69	11	58
7. Regular charge	116	36	80	56	28	28	60	8	52
Available to Spouse									
8. Yes	395	83	312	152	59	93	243	24	219
9. No	20	...	20	8	...	8	12	...	12
10. Free	141	6	135	31	2	29	110	4	106
11. Reduced charge	138	40	98	64	29	35	74	11	63
12. Regular charge	116	37	79	57	28	29	59	9	50
Available to Children									
13. Yes	382	80	302	149	57	92	233	23	210
14. No	33	3	30	11	2	9	22	1	21
15. Free	115	5	110	25	2	23	90	3	87
16. Reduced charge	145	35	110	63	24	39	82	11	71
17. Regular charge	122	40	82	61	31	30	61	9	52

TABLE 125: FACULTY RECREATION—PROFESSIONAL CONCERTS
Questionnaire Sect. 9 Q. 1B

	All Institutions			Public Institutions			Private Institutions		
	Total	Univ.	Col.	Total	Univ.	Col.	Total	Univ.	Col.
1. Total	745	148	597	217	84	133	528	64	464
2. College has pro-									
fessional concerts	611	124	487	197	77	120	414	47	367
Available to Faculty									
3. Yes	599	124	475	192	77	115	407	47	360
4. No	12	...	12	5	...	5	7	...	7
5. Free	258	22	236	43	6	37	215	16	199
6. Reduced charge	185	56	129	84	38	46	101	18	83
7. Regular charge	156	46	110	65	33	32	91	13	78
Available to Spouse									
8. Yes	593	124	469	189	77	112	404	47	357
9. No	18	...	18	8	...	8	10	...	10
10. Free	239	20	219	42	7	35	197	13	184
11. Reduced charge	189	54	135	80	37	43	109	17	92
12. Regular charge	165	50	115	67	33	34	98	17	81
Available to Children									
13. Yes	570	120	450	182	75	107	388	45	343
14. No	41	4	37	15	2	13	26	2	24
15. Free	206	17	189	33	5	28	173	12	161
16. Reduced charge	194	50	144	79	34	45	115	16	99
17. Regular charge	170	53	117	70	36	34	100	17	83

TABLE 126: FACULTY RECREATION—SPECIAL LECTURES
Questionnaire Sect. 9 Q. 1B

	All Institutions			Public Institutions			Private Institutions		
	Total	Univ.	Col.	Total	Univ.	Col.	Total	Univ.	Col.
1. Total	-745	148	597	217	84	133	528	64	464
2. College has special lectures	715	143	572	209	82	127	506	61	445
Available to Faculty									
3. Yes	705	142	563	206	82	124	499	60	439
4. No	10	1	9	3	...	3	7	1	6
5. Free	553	91	462	140	48	92	413	43	370
6. Reduced charge	71	25	46	35	17	18	36	8	28
7. Regular charge	81	26	55	31	17	14	50	9	41
Available to Spouse									
8. Yes	693	142	551	205	82	123	488	60	428
9. No	22	1	21	4	...	4	18	1	17
10. Free	531	88	443	137	47	90	394	41	353
11. Reduced charge	72	24	48	34	17	17	38	7	31
12. Regular charge	90	30	60	34	18	16	56	12	44
Available to Children									
13. Yes	660	138	522	197	79	118	463	59	404
14. No	55	5	50	12	3	9	43	2	41
15. Free	495	85	410	129	44	85	366	41	325
16. Reduced charge	76	21	55	33	15	18	43	6	37
17. Regular charge	89	32	57	35	20	15	54	12	42

TABLE 127: COLLEGE HEALTH SERVICE—DOCTOR'S CONSULTATION
Questionnaire Sect. 9 Q. 1C

	All Institutions			Public Institutions			Private Institutions		
	Total	Univ.	Col.	Total	Univ.	Col.	Total	Univ.	Col.
1. Total	745	148	597	217	84	133	528	64	464
2. College has service	496	104	392	150	58	92	346	46	300
Available to Faculty									
3. Yes	214	42	172	39	11	28	175	31	144
4. No	282	62	220	111	47	64	171	15	156
5. Free	110	21	89	21	4	17	89	17	72
6. Charge	104	21	83	18	7	11	86	14	72
Available to Spouse									
7. Yes	86	18	68	16	7	9	70	11	59
8. No	410	86	324	134	51	83	276	35	241
9. Free	19	3	16	4	1	3	15	2	13
10. Charge	67	15	52	12	6	6	55	9	46
Available to Children									
11. Yes	82	16	66	16	7	9	66	9	57
12. No	414	88	326	134	51	83	280	37	243
13. Free	17	1	16	4	1	3	13	...	13
14. Charge	65	15	50	12	6	6	53	9	44

TABLE 128: COLLEGE HEALTH SERVICE—EMERGENCY MEDICAL TREATMENT
Questionnaire Sect. 9 Q. 1C

	All Institutions			Public Institutions			Private Institutions		
	Total	Univ.	Col.	Total	Univ.	Col.	Total	Univ.	Col.
1. Total	745	148	597	217	84	133	528	64	464
2. College has emergency treatment	577	124	453	168	66	102	409	58	351
Available to Faculty									
3. Yes	471	100	371	126	47	79	345	53	292
4. No	106	24	82	42	19	23	64	5	59
5. Free	324	64	260	85	28	57	239	36	203
6. Charge	147	36	111	41	19	22	106	17	89
Available to Spouse									
7. Yes	148	30	118	31	15	16	117	15	102
8. No	429	94	335	137	51	86	292	43	249
9. Free	72	13	59	13	6	7	59	7	52
10. Charge	76	17	59	18	9	9	58	8	50
Available to Children									
11. Yes	146	28	118	32	15	17	114	13	101
12. No	431	96	335	136	51	85	295	45	250
13. Free	69	11	58	14	6	8	55	5	50
14. Charge	77	17	60	18	9	9	59	8	51

TABLE 129: COLLEGE HEALTH SERVICE—REGULAR MEDICAL TREATMENT
Questionnaire Sect. 9 Q. 1C

	All Institutions			Public Institutions			Private Institutions		
	Total	Univ.	Col.	Total	Univ.	Col.	Total	Univ.	Col.
1. Total	745	148	597	217	84	133	528	64	464
2. College has regular treatment	310	73	237	88	43	45	222	30	192
Available to Faculty									
3. Yes	89	18	71	14	8	6	75	10	65
4. No	221	55	166	74	35	39	147	20	127
5. Free	30	5	25	2	1	1	28	4	24
6. Charge	59	13	46	12	7	5	47	6	41
Available to Spouse									
7. Yes	49	12	37	10	6	4	39	6	33
8. No	261	61	200	78	37	41	183	24	159
9. Free	8	1	7	1	1	...	7	...	7
10. Charge	41	11	30	9	5	4	32	6	26
Available to Children									
11. Yes	50	12	38	11	6	5	39	6	33
12. No	260	61	199	77	37	40	183	24	159
13. Free	9	1	8	2	1	1	7	...	7
14. Charge	41	11	30	9	5	4	32	6	26

TABLE 130: COLLEGE HEALTH SERVICE—ANNUAL PHYSICAL EXAMINATION
Questionnaire Sect. 9 Q. 1C

	All Institutions			Public Institutions			Private Institutions		
	Total	Univ.	Col.	Total	Univ.	Col.	Total	Univ.	Col.
1. Total	745	148	597	217	84	133	528	64	464
2. College has annual physical	183	39	144	60	19	41	123	20	103
Available to Faculty									
3. Yes	69	27	42	21	10	11	48	17	31
4. No	114	12	102	39	9	30	75	3	72
5. Free	33	12	21	10	4	6	23	8	15
6. Charge	36	15	21	11	6	5	25	9	16
Available to Spouse									
7. Yes	26	10	16	7	4	3	19	6	13
8. No	157	29	128	53	15	38	104	14	90
9. Free	5	...	5	...	...	...	5	...	5
10. Charge	21	10	11	7	4	3	14	6	8
Available to Children									
11. Yes	25	10	15	7	4	3	18	6	12
12. No	158	29	129	53	15	38	105	14	91
13. Free	4	...	4	...	...	...	4	...	4
14. Charge	21	10	11	7	4	3	14	6	8

TABLE 131: COLLEGE HEALTH SERVICE—INFIRMARY OR HOSPITAL BED
Questionnaire Sect. 9 Q. 1C

	All Institutions			Public Institutions			Private Institutions		
	Total	Univ.	Col.	Total	Univ.	Col.	Total	Univ.	Col.
1. Total	745	148	597	217	84	133	528	64	464
2. College has infirmary or hospital bed	397	92	305	120	56	64	277	36	241
Available to Faculty									
3. Yes	83	23	60	19	10	9	64	13	51
4. No	314	69	245	101	46	55	213	23	190
5. Free	24	1	23	6	...	6	18	1	17
6. Charge	59	22	37	13	10	3	46	12	34
Available to Spouse									
7. Yes	39	19	20	13	9	4	26	10	16
8. No	358	73	285	107	47	60	251	26	225
9. Free	4	...	4	1	...	1	3	...	3
10. Charge	35	19	16	12	9	3	23	10	13
Available to Children									
11. Yes	38	19	19	14	9	5	24	10	14
12. No	359	73	286	106	47	59	253	26	227
13. Free	5	...	5	2	...	2	3	...	3
14. Charge	33	19	14	12	9	3	21	10	11

TABLE 132: EFFECT OF CAMPUS FACILITIES AND EVENTS ON RECRUITING AND RETAINING
FACULTY
Questionnaire Sect. 9 Q. 3

	All Institutions			Public Institutions			Private Institutions		
	Total	Univ.	Col.	Total	Univ.	Col.	Total	Univ.	Col.
Recruiting									
1. Substantial	34	8	26	12	5	7	22	3	19
2. Moderate	237	50	187	72	30	42	165	20	145
3. Negligible	399	80	319	116	41	75	283	39	244
4. No response	75	10	65	17	8	9	58	2	56
5. Total	745	148	597	217	84	133	528	64	464
Retaining									
6. Substantial	37	8	29	11	5	6	26	3	23
7. Moderate	272	59	213	83	35	48	189	24	165
8. Negligible	360	70	290	105	36	69	255	34	221
9. No response	76	11	65	18	8	10	58	3	55
10. Total	745	148	597	217	84	133	528	64	464

In spite of the wording of this question, referring to all facilities, I believe the answers
of "substantial" or "moderate" to this question are based on the health program.

TABLE 133: HEALTH SERVICES FOR RETIRED FACULTY—DOCTOR'S CONSULTATION
Questionnaire Sect. 10 Q. 2

	All Institutions			Public Institutions			Private Institutions		
	Total	Univ.	Col.	Total	Univ.	Col.	Total.	Univ.	Col.
Doctor's Consultation									
1. Yes	68	16	52	13	7	6	55	9	46
2. No	544	123	421	184	73	111	360	50	310
3. No response	133	9	124	20	4	16	113	5	108
4. Total	745	148	597	217	84	133	528	64	464
Charge, If Available									
5. Free	20	4	16	1	1	...	19	3	16
6. Same as faculty	42	9	33	9	4	5	33	5	28
7. Higher	4	2	2	2	1	1	2	1	1
8. No response	2	1	1	1	1	...	1	...	1

There were no instances of a lower charge for retired faculty than for regular faculty.

TABLE 134: HEALTH SERVICES FOR RETIRED FACULTY—EMERGENCY MEDICAL TREATMENT
Questionnaire Sect. 10 Q. 2

	All Institutions			Public Institutions			Private Institutions		
	Total	Univ.	Col.	Total	Univ.	Col.	Total	Univ.	Col.
Emergency Medical Treatment									
1. Yes	134	35	99	28	15	13	106	20	86
2. No	486	108	378	169	65	104	317	43	274
3. No response	125	5	120	20	4	16	105	1	104
4. Total	745	148	597	217	84	133	528	64	464
Charge, If Available									
5. Free	60	15	45	10	5	5	50	10	40
6. Same as faculty	63	17	46	15	8	7	48	9	39
7. Higher	4	2	2	2	1	1	2	1	1
8. No response	7	1	6	1	1	...	6	...	6

There were no instances of a lower charge for retired faculty than for regular faculty.

TABLE 135: HEALTH SERVICES FOR RETIRED FACULTY—REGULAR MEDICAL TREATMENT
Questionnaire Sect. 10 Q. 2

	All Institutions			Public Institutions			Private Institutions		
	Total	Univ.	Col.	Total	Univ.	Col.	Total	Univ.	Col.
Regular Medical Treatment									
1. Yes	37	13	24	11	7	4	26	6	20
2. No	570	126	444	186	73	113	384	53	331
3. No response	138	9	129	20	4	16	118	5	113
4. Total	745	148	597	217	84	133	528	64	464
Charge, If Available									
5. Free	6	2	4	1	1	...	5	1	4
6. Same as faculty	25	8	17	7	4	3	18	4	14
7. Higher	4	2	2	2	1	1	2	1	1
8. No response	2	1	1	1	1	...	1	...	1

There were no instances of a lower charge for retired faculty than for regular faculty.

TABLE 136: HEALTH SERVICES FOR RETIRED FACULTY—ANNUAL PHYSICAL EXAMINATION
Questionnaire Sect. 10 Q. 2

	All Institutions			Public Institutions			Private Institutions		
	Total	Univ.	Col.	Total	Univ.	Col.	Total	Univ.	Col.
Annual Physical Examination									
1. Yes	29	16	13	10	7	3	19	9	10
2. No	577	123	454	187	73	114	390	50	340
3. No response	139	9	130	20	4	16	119	5	114
4. Total	745	148	597	217	84	133	528	64	464
Charge, If Available									
5. Free	5	3	2	1	1	...	4	2	2
6. Same as faculty	22	12	10	7	5	2	15	7	8
7. Higher	1	...	1	1	...	1	...	...	...
8. No response	1	1	...	1	1	...	...	...	...

There were no instances of a lower charge for retired faculty than for regular faculty.

TABLE 137: HEALTH SERVICES FOR RETIRED FACULTY—INFIRMARY OR HOSPITAL BED
Questionnaire Sect. 10 Q. 2

	All Institutions			Public Institutions			Private Institutions		
	Total	Univ.	Col.	Total	Univ.	Col.	Total	Univ.	Col.
Infirmary or hospital bed									
1. Yes	34	17	17	12	8	4	22	9	13
2. No	566	121	445	181	70	111	385	51	334
3. No response	145	10	135	24	6	18	121	4	117
4. Total	745	148	597	217	84	133	528	64	464
Charge, If Available									
5. Free	3	1	2	...	...	...	3	1	2
6. Same as faculty	26	13	13	9	6	3	17	7	10
7. Higher	3	2	1	2	1	1	1	1	...
8. No response	2	1	1	1	1	...	1	...	1

There were no instances of a lower charge for retired faculty than for regular faculty.

TABLE 138: PROVISION OF WORK FACILITIES FOR RETIRED FACULTY, IF REQUESTED
Questionnaire Sect. 10 Q. 3

	All Institutions			Public Institutions			Private Institutions		
	Total	Univ.	Col.	Total	Univ.	Col.	Total	Univ.	Col.
Office Facilities									
1. Provided	182	75	107	65	47	18	117	28	89
2. Not provided	426	61	365	129	30	99	297	31	266
3. No response	137	12	125	23	7	16	114	5	109
Laboratory Facilities									
4. Provided	187	64	123	52	35	17	135	29	106
5. Not provided	413	71	342	139	41	98	274	30	244
6. No response	145	13	132	26	8	18	119	5	114
Research Assistance									
7. Provided	71	32	39	24	19	5	47	13	34
8. Not provided	520	99	421	166	55	111	354	44	310
9. No response	154	17	137	27	10	17	127	7	120
Secretarial Assistance									
10. Provided	80	32	48	24	18	6	56	14	42
11. Not provided	512	98	414	165	55	110	347	43	304
12. No response	153	18	135	28	11	17	125	7	118
Library Desk Space									
13. Provided	255	76	179	75	39	36	180	37	143
14. Not provided	335	55	280	115	36	79	220	19	201
15. No response	155	17	138	27	9	18	128	8	120
16. Total	745	148	597	217	84	133	528	64	464

TABLE 139: HEALTH SERVICES FOR WIDOWS OF RETIRED FACULTY—DOCTOR'S CONSULTATION
Questionnaire Sect. 10 Q. 6

	All Institutions			Public Institutions			Private Institutions		
	Total	Univ.	Col.	Total	Univ.	Col.	Total	Univ.	Col.
Doctor's Consultation									
1. Yes	43	7	36	6	3	3	37	4	33
2. No	541	129	412	188	76	112	353	53	300
3. No response	161	12	149	23	5	18	138	7	131
4. Total	745	148	597	217	84	133	528	64	464
Charge, If Available									
5. Free	11	1	10	1	1	...	10	...	10
6. Same as faculty	29	4	25	4	1	3	25	3	22
7. Higher	3	2	1	1	1	...	2	1	1
8. No response	...	...	...	...	...	...	...	...	...

There were no instances of a lower charge for faculty widows than for regular faculty.

TABLE 140: HEALTH SERVICES FOR WIDOWS OF RETIRED FACULTY—EMERGENCY MEDICAL
TREATMENT
Questionnaire Sect. 10 Q. 6

	All Institutions			Public Institutions			Private Institutions		
	Total	Univ.	Col.	Total	Univ.	Col.	Total	Univ.	Col.
Emergency Medical Treatment									
1. Yes	91	19	72	17	8	9	74	11	63
2. No	501	121	380	177	71	106	324	50	274
3. No response	153	8	145	23	5	18	130	3	127
4. Total	745	148	597	217	84	133	528	64	464
Charge, If Available									
5. Free	37	6	31	7	3	4	30	3	27
6. Same as faculty	47	11	36	9	4	5	38	7	31
7. Higher	3	2	1	1	1	...	2	1	1
8. No response	4	...	4	...	...	...	4	...	4

There were no instances of a lower charge for faculty widows than for regular faculty.

TABLE 141: HEALTH SERVICES FOR WIDOWS OF RETIRED FACULTY—REGULAR MEDICAL
TREATMENT
Questionnaire Sect. 10 Q. 6

	All Institutions			Public Institutions			Private Institutions		
	Total	Univ.	Col.	Total	Univ.	Col.	Total	Univ.	Col.
Regular Medical Treatment									
1. Yes	26	7	19	5	3	2	21	4	17
2. No	554	129	425	189	76	113	365	53	312
3. No response	165	12	153	23	5	18	142	7	135
4. Total	745	148	597	217	84	133	528	64	464
Charge, If Available									
5. Free	3	1	2	1	1	...	2	...	2
6. Same as faculty	20	4	16	3	1	2	17	3	14
7. Higher	3	2	1	1	1	...	2	1	1
8. No response	...	...	...	...	...	...	...	...	...

There were no instances of a lower charge for faculty widows than for regular faculty.

TABLE 142: HEALTH SERVICES FOR WIDOWS OF RETIRED FACULTY—ANNUAL PHYSICAL
            EXAMINATION
Questionnaire Sect. 10 Q. 6

	All Institutions			Public Institutions			Private Institutions		
	Total	Univ.	Col.	Total	Univ.	Col.	Total	Univ.	Col.
Annual Physical Examination									
1. Yes	15	6	9	4	2	2	11	4	7
2. No	565	130	435	190	77	113	375	53	322
3. No response	165	12	153	23	5	18	142	7	135
4. Total	745	148	597	217	84	133	528	64	464
Charge, If Available									
5. Free	1	...	1	...	...	...	1	...	1
6. Same as faculty	12	5	7	3	1	2	9	4	5
7. Higher	2	1	1	1	1	...	1	...	1
8. No response	...	...	...	...	...	...	...	...	...

There were no instances of a lower charge for faculty widows than for regular faculty.

TABLE 143: HEALTH SERVICES FOR WIDOWS OF RETIRED FACULTY—INFIRMARY OR HOSPITAL BED
Questionnaire Sect. 10 Q. 6

	All Institutions			Public Institutions			Private Institutions		
	Total	Univ.	Col.	Total	Univ.	Col.	Total	Univ.	Col.
Infirmary or Hospital Bed									
1. Yes	21	11	10	7	5	2	14	6	8
2. No	557	126	431	186	74	112	371	52	319
3. No response	167	11	156	24	5	19	143	6	137
4. Total	745	148	597	217	84	133	528	64	464
Charge, If Available									
5. Free	2	...	2	...	...	...	2	...	2
6. Same as faculty	17	9	8	6	4	2	11	5	6
7. Higher	2	2	...	1	1	...	1	1	...
8. No response	...	...	...	...	...	...	...	...	...

There were no instances of a lower charge for faculty widows than for regular faculty.

TABLE 144: FACULTY SECRETARIAL HELP FOR INSTITUTIONAL BUSINESS
Questionnaire Sect. 11 Q. 1

	All Institutions			Public Institutions			Private Institutions		
	Total	Univ.	Col.	Total	Univ.	Col.	Total	Univ.	Col.
Provided									
1. Number	619	133	486	187	77	110	432	56	376
2. Percent	83.1%	89.9%	81.4%	86.2%	91.7%	82.7%	81.8%	87.5%	81.0%
Sometimes Provided									
3. Number	91	11	80	22	5	17	69	6	63
4. Percent	12.2%	7.4%	13.4%	10.1%	6.0%	12.8%	13.1%	9.4%	13.6%
Not Provided									
5. Number	9	1	8	2	...	2	7	1	6
6. Percent	1.2%	.7%	1.3%	.9%	...	1.5%	1.3%	1.6%	1.3%
No Response									
7. Number	26	3	23	6	2	4	20	1	19
8. Percent	3.5%	2.0%	3.9%	2.8%	2.4%	3.0%	3.8%	1.6%	4.1%
9. Total	745	148	597	217	84	133	528	64	464

TABLE 145: FACULTY SECRETARIAL HELP FOR TYPING RESEARCH ARTICLES
Questionnaire Sect. 11 Q. 1

	All Institutions			Public Institutions			Private Institutions		
	Total	Univ.	Col.	Total	Univ.	Col.	Total	Univ.	Col.
Provided									
1. Number	292	78	214	93	46	47	199	32	167
2. Percent	39.2%	52.7%	35.8%	42.9%	54.8%	35.3%	37.7%	50.0%	36.0%
Sometimes Provided									
3. Number	296	60	236	91	35	56	205	25	180
4. Percent	39.7%	40.5%	39.5%	41.9%	41.7%	42.1%	38.8%	39.1%	38.8%
Not Provided									
5. Number	106	5	101	23	1	22	83	4	79
6. Percent	14.2%	3.4%	16.9%	10.6%	1.2%	16.5%	15.7%	6.3%	17.0%
No Response									
7. Number	51	5	46	10	2	8	41	3	38
8. Percent	6.8%	3.4%	7.7%	4.6%	2.4%	6.0%	7.8%	4.7%	8.2%
9. Total	745	148	597	217	84	133	528	64	464

TABLE 146: FACULTY SECRETARIAL HELP FOR TYPING SCHOLARLY BOOK MSS.
Questionnaire Sect. 11 Q. 1

	All Institutions			Public Institutions			Private Institutions		
	Total	Univ.	Col.	Total	Univ.	Col.	Total	Univ.	Col.
Provided									
1. Number	166	45	121	43	19	24	123	26	97
2. Percent	22.3%	30.4%	20.3%	19.8%	22.6%	18.0%	23.3%	40.6%	20.9%
Sometimes Provided									
3. Number	295	75	220	96	51	45	199	24	175
4. Percent	39.6%	50.7%	36.9%	44.2%	60.7%	33.8%	37.7%	37.5%	37.7%
Not Provided									
5. Number	200	18	182	59	9	50	141	9	132
6. Percent	26.8%	12.2%	30.5%	27.2%	10.7%	37.6%	26.7%	14.1%	28.4%
No Response									
7. Number	84	10	74	19	5	14	65	5	60
8. Percent	11.3%	6.8%	12.4%	8.8%	6.0%	10.5%	12.3%	7.8%	12.9%
9. Total	745	148	597	217	84	133	528	64	464

TABLE 147: FACULTY SECRETARIAL HELP FOR TYPING INSTRUCTIONAL MATERIAL
Questionnaire Sect. 11 Q. 1

	All Institutions			Public Institutions			Private Institutions		
	Total	Univ.	Col.	Total	Univ.	Col.	Total	Univ.	Col.
Provided									
1. Number	581	123	458	183	73	110	398	50	348
2. Percent	78.0%	83.1%	76.7%	84.3%	86.9%	82.7%	75.4%	78.1%	75.0%
Sometimes Provided									
3. Number	111	18	93	24	8	16	87	10	77
4. Percent	14.9%	12.2%	15.6%	11.1%	9.5%	12.0%	16.5%	15.6%	16.6%
Not Provided									
5. Number	19	2	17	1	...	1	18	2	16
6. Percent	2.6%	1.4%	2.8%	.5%	...	.8%	3.4%	3.1%	3.4%
No Response									
7. Number	34	5	29	9	3	6	25	2	23
8. Percent	4.6%	3.4%	4.9%	4.1%	3.6%	4.5%	4.7%	3.1%	5.0%
9. Total	745	148	597	217	84	133	528	64	464

TABLE 148: FACULTY SECRETARIAL HELP FOR TYPING TEXTBOOK MSS.
Questionnaire Sect. 11 Q. 1

	All Institutions			Public Institutions			Private Institutions		
	Total	Univ.	Col.	Total	Univ.	Col.	Total	Univ.	Col.
Provided									
1. Number	161	35	126	34	13	21	127	22	105
2. Percent	21.6%	23.6%	21.1%	15.7%	15.5%	15.8%	24.1%	34.4%	22.6%
Sometimes Provided									
3. Number	248	68	180	86	45	41	162	23	139
4. Percent	33.3%	45.9%	30.2%	39.6%	53.6%	30.8%	30.7%	35.9%	30.0%
Not Provided									
5. Number	241	33	208	75	20	55	166	13	153
6. Percent	32.3%	22.3%	34.8%	34.6%	23.8%	41.4%	31.4%	20.3%	33.0%
No Response									
7. Number	95	12	83	22	6	16	73	6	67
8. Percent	12.8%	8.1%	13.9%	10.1%	7.1%	12.0%	13.8%	9.4%	14.4%
9. Total	745	148	597	217	84	133	528	64	464

TABLE 149: FACULTY SECRETARIAL HELP ON TYPING SPEECHES AND ESSAYS
Questionnaire Sect. 11 Q. 1

	All Institutions			Public Institutions			Private Institutions		
	Total	Univ.	Col.	Total	Univ.	Col.	Total	Univ.	Col.
Provided									
1. Number	274	70	204	89	39	50	185	31	154
2. Percent	36.8%	47.3%	34.2%	41.0%	46.4%	37.6%	35.0%	48.4%	33.2%
Sometimes Provided									
3. Number	315	65	250	99	42	57	216	23	193
4. Percent	42.3%	43.9%	41.9%	45.6%	50.0%	42.9%	40.9%	35.9%	41.6%
Not Provided									
5. Number	93	8	85	17	1	16	76	7	69
6. Percent	12.5%	5.4%	14.2%	7.8%	1.2%	12.0%	14.4%	10.9%	14.9%
No Response									
7. Number	63	5	58	12	2	10	51	3	48
8. Percent	8.5%	3.4%	9.7%	5.5%	2.4%	7.5%	9.7%	4.7%	10.3%
9. Total	745	148	597	217	84	133	528	64	464

TABLE 150: FACULTY SECRETARIAL HELP FOR PERSONAL BUSINESS
Questionnaire Sect. 11 Q. 1

	All Institutions			Public Institutions			Private Institutions		
	Total	Univ.	Col.	Total	Univ.	Col.	Total	Univ.	Col.
Provided									
1. Number	18	4	14	1	1	...	17	3	14
2. Percent	2.4%	2.7%	2.3%	.5%	1.2%	...	3.2%	4.7%	3.0%
Sometimes Provided									
3. Number	128	28	100	27	12	15	101	16	85
4. Percent	17.2%	18.9%	16.8%	12.4%	14.3%	11.3%	19.1%	25.0%	18.3%
Not Provided									
5. Number	516	106	410	175	68	107	341	38	303
6. Percent	69.3%	71.6%	68.7%	80.6%	81.0%	80.5%	64.6%	59.4%	65.3%
No Response									
7. Number	83	10	73	14	3	11	69	7	62
8. Percent	11.1%	6.8%	12.2%	6.5%	3.6%	8.3%	13.1%	10.9%	13.4%
9. Total	745	148	597	217	84	133	528	64	464

TABLE 151: SALARY CONTINUATION PROGRAM DURING SICKNESS OR DISABILITY OF FACULTY
Questionnaire Sect. 11 Q. 3

	All Institutions			Public Institutions			Private Institutions		
	Total	Univ.	Col.	Total	Univ.	Col.	Total	Univ.	Col.
Informal Program									
1. Number	442	91	351	83	40	43	359	51	308
2. Percent	59.3%	61.5%	58.8%	38.2%	47.6%	32.3%	68.0%	79.7%	66.4%
Formal Program									
3. Number	285	55	230	130	42	88	155	13	142
4. Percent	38.3%	37.2%	38.5%	59.9%	50.0%	66.2%	29.4%	20.3%	30.6%
No Response									
5. Number	18	2	16	4	2	2	14	...	14
6. Percent	2.4%	1.4%	2.7%	1.8%	2.4%	1.5%	2.7%	...	3.0%
7. Total	745	148	597	217	84	133	528	64	464

TABLE 152: LONGEST PERIOD OF SALARY CONTINUATION UNDER FORMAL SICKNESS OR
DISABILITY POLICY
Questionnaire Sect. 11 Q. 4

	All Institutions			Public Institutions			Private Institutions		
	Total	Univ.	Col.	Total	Univ.	Col.	Total	Univ.	Col.
1. 1—4 weeks	36	5	31	13	3	10	23	2	21
2. 4—6 weeks	18	1	17	6	1	5	12	...	12
3. 6—12 weeks	35	5	30	20	5	15	15	...	15
4. 12—24 weeks	31	5	26	16	4	12	15	1	14
5. Over 24 weeks	19	4	15	6	4	2	13	...	13
6. End of semester	12	2	10	3	1	2	9	1	8
7. End of academic year	18	5	13	5	3	2	13	2	11
8. Other	91	25	66	48	19	29	43	6	37
9. No response	25	3	22	13	2	11	12	1	11
10. Total with formal program	285	55	230	130	42	88	155	13	142

TABLE 153: DEPENDENCE OF SALARY CONTINUATION DURING SICKNESS ON LENGTH OF
EMPLOYMENT AT INSTITUTION
Questionnaire Sect. 11 Q. 5

	All Institutions			Public Institutions			Private Institutions		
	Total	Univ.	Col.	Total	Univ.	Col.	Total	Univ.	Col.
Does Not Depend on Length									
1. Number	111	20	91	31	14	17	80	6	74
2. Percent	38.9%	36.4%	39.6%	23.8%	33.3%	19.3%	51.6%	46.2%	52.1%
Depends on Length									
3. Number	165	34	131	96	28	68	69	6	63
4. Percent	57.9%	61.8%	57.0%	73.8%	66.7%	77.3%	44.5%	46.2%	44.4%
No Response									
5. Number	9	1	8	3	...	3	6	1	5
6. Percent	3.2%	1.8%	3.5%	2.3%	...	3.4%	3.9%	7.7%	3.5%
7. Total	285	55	230	130	42	88	155	13	142

TABLE 154: TAPERING OFF OF SALARY CONTINUATION DURING SICKNESS BEFORE TERMINATION OF SALARY
Questionnaire Sect. 11 Q. 6

	All Institutions			Public Institutions			Private Institutions		
	Total	Univ.	Col.	Total	Univ.	Col.	Total	Univ.	Col.
1. No tapering arrange-ment	223	45	178	110	35	75	113	10	103
2. Tapering arrange-ment	38	9	29	14	6	8	24	3	21
3. No response	24	1	23	6	1	5	18	...	18
4. Total	285	55	230	130	42	88	155	13	142

TABLE 155: FACULTY COVERAGE UNDER STATE WORKMEN'S COMPENSATION LAWS
Questionnaire Sect. 11 Q. 7

	All Institutions			Public Institutions			Private Institutions		
	Total	Univ.	Col.	Total	Univ.	Col.	Total	Univ.	Col.
Faculty Covered									
1. Number	203	43	160	91	36	55	112	7	105
2. Percent	71.2%	78.2%	69.6%	70.0%	85.7%	62.5%	72.3%	53.8%	73.9%
Faculty Not Covered									
3. Number	64	10	54	35	5	30	29	5	24
4. Percent	22.5%	18.2%	23.5%	26.9%	11.9%	34.1%	18.7%	38.5%	16.9%
No Response									
5. Number	18	2	16	4	1	3	14	1	13
6. Percent	6.3%	3.6%	7.0%	3.1%	2.4%	3.4%	9.0%	7.7%	9.2%
7. Total	285	55	230	130	42	88	155	13	142

EVALUATION CHART

Both facts and author's opinions are involved.

IN order to help the reader remember certain salient facts and to make clear my own conclusions this table is included. No such abbreviated statement, even when generally valid, can apply to every institution. Moreover, my judgment on some items may be questioned by many, and on many items be questioned by some. If it has both a provocative and mnemonic effect, this chart will serve its purpose.

Although annuities and insurance are not discussed in detail in this report, they are included in this chart because in any balanced program of benefits they play a major role. A description and analysis of retirement and insurance plans are given in Greenough and King, *Retirement and Insurance Plans in American Colleges.*

Benefit	Financial benefit to individual	Other advantages
1. Salary	Total.	. . . .

ANNUITIES, INSURANCE, HEALTH (see introduction to this appendix)

2. O.A.S.I. (Social Security)	Substantial retirement annuities. Survivorship and disability benefits.	Generally a bargain for those who qualify and are now retired or near retirement. No federal tax on benefits.
3. Contribution to retirement annuity	Annuity after retirement.	To both individual and institution in protecting the retired and in making possible retirement at proper age. Taxes on institutional contribution deferred.
4. Formula retirement benefits (per cent of final salary, etc.)	Annuity after retirement.	May help keep up with pre-retirement inflation.
5. Life insurance	Protection for dependents.	Group rates and coverage of "poor risks." Protects institution against pressure based on sympathy.
6. Disability insurance	Protection against long-time disability.	Group rates and coverage of whole group.
7. Salary continuation during disability (sick leaves)	Total.	Sense of security.
8. Hospital and surgical insurance (Blue Cross, Blue Shield, etc.)	In case of surgery or hospitalization.	Group rates. Individual's contribution currently counts as medical expense for federal tax purposes.
9. Major medical insurance	Protects against catastrophic medical expenses.	Group rates. This is the true insurance, not just ironing out of minor fluctuations in expenses. Individual's contribution currently counts as medical expense for federal tax purposes.
10. Local medical services through institutional clinic	Less expensive than private individual service.	Prompt. Sometimes most expert available. May help keep local charges reasonable. Annual physical exam is help to both individual and institution.

Item	Cost to institution	Remarks	Recommendations
1.	Total.	. . . .	. . . .
2.	Institutional contribution.	Very important.	Have.
3.	Individual contribution is part of salary. Institutional contribution is additional cost.	This is an essential benefit. (If proportion of institutional contribution is increased, tax on annuity is increased and hence increase in total contribution should be considered.)	1/2–3/4 by institution, rest by individual; total, 12%–16% of salary. Immediate participation for full-time faculty and immediate vesting.
4.	Deferred, but very large.	No variable annuity for post-retirement inflation. Vesting is usually delayed.	Usually void. (Sometimes can be used advantageously in starting system to help those near or past retirement or as supplement after a period of sharp inflation.)
5.	Cost of contribution.	Important.	Some basic insurance, e.g., several units of TIAA collective term decreasing insurance or similar plan. Both individual and institution to contribute.
6.	Not high.	Important. Should be handled in coordination with sick leave and retirement provisions.	TIAA or similar plan.
7.	Depends on cost of substitutes.	Adequate provision whether formal or informal is important. Informal sick-leave plan often more generous than formal policy. Hard on staff if substitute is not secured.	Do not push for formal policy unless faculty demands it; if there is one, make it generous and dovetail with disability insurance.
8.	Institutional contribution.	Important, but less important than major medical insurance. Administration costs are high if minor ailments covered. Generally does not cover out-of-hospital expenses.	Have.
9.	Institutional contribution.	Among most important benefit provisions. Not very expensive on top of basic insurance.	Have with large "deductible" (corridor) and moderate co-insurance. Go as high as TIAA or similar plan will permit.
10.	Not great if student service already available.	Importance depends on local circumstances. Where other medical facilities are meager this may be very valuable. Sometimes creates bad relations with local medical group.	Include at least emergency service and medical exam, free to faculty, and available to emeriti and faculty widows. Beyond this, depends on local conditions.

Benefit	Financial benefit to individual	Other advantages
HOUSING		
11. Rental housing for faculty	Usually less expensive than commercial.	Easier to assure places to new faculty members. Controls environment. Affects local rates. Nearness of faculty to institution. Availability to visitors. Some places, advantage on local real estate taxes.
12. Mortgage loan plans on land with control of sales or repurchase agreement (sometimes lifetime leases)	Low land cost and below commercial mortgage rates.	Control environment. Nearness of faculty to institution. High coverage as compared to value. Some places, advantage on local real estate taxes.
13. Straight mortgage loans	Below commercial mortgage rates.	Higher upper limit of borrowing.
FAMILY EDUCATION		
14. Tuition waiver for faculty children	Direct benefit.	. . . .
15. Tuition exchange plan	Direct benefit.	Helps children go away to college. Special use for non-coeducational institutions.
16. Tuition grant to go elsewhere	Direct benefit.	Helps children go away to college. Appropriate plan for institutions with tuition waiver especially if non-coeducational or if with high entrance standards.
17. Tuition waiver for faculty member and spouse (especially for part-time programs)	Direct benefit.	Helps institution as well as individual.

Item	Cost to institution	Remarks	Recommendations
11.	Ranges from subsidy to smaller earning on investments.	Importance depends chiefly on local circumstances. Space for new arrivals often of major importance. In some places this is a good way to use houses already in expansion area until the area is needed for academic purposes. Problems: (1) Reaction of local real estate interests. (2) Relation of landlord to tenant. (3) Sometimes increases internal friction. (4) Unless assignment is by rule, may lead to charges of discrimination.	Try to have enough to cover certain well-defined categories. Usually new faculty members would have priority.
12.	Land cost in some cases. Loss of income slight.	Importance depends on local circumstances. May round out a rental plan. Repayments are usually by payroll deductions. Problems: (1) Sometimes bad relations with banks and realtors. (2) Unless widely available, discriminatory. (3) Often too-expensive homes.	Depends on local circumstances. In many cases very wise.
13.	At times some loss of income.	Importance depends on local circumstances. Problem: Bad relation with banks. (Banks are reported to like institutions to make a second-mortgage loan above the limits of the bank's first-mortgage loan.)	Second-mortgage loans in many cases. Where there is limited rental space used for new faculty, low rate first or second mortgage loans may help make it easier to have turnover.
14.	Varies from slight to total depending on whether institution is otherwise full or not. (Offset by certain fellowships.)	An important item to consider no matter what the conclusion may be. I do not like plan but recognize that it is highly considered by many wise educators and that it would be hard to abolish in "leagues" where it is established. Discriminatory between faculty members (most serious in coeducational institutions). Masks from faculty social effect of high tuition.	Private: Do not use, or use with grant plan. Public: Avoid, but might give new faculty in-state privileges at once.
15.	Unpredictable and inequitable between institutions.	Because of esteem for certain institutions, export-import balance is difficult to maintain. Tends to limit choice. System is breaking down.	Avoid or, if in, phase out.
16.	Direct cost.	For importance, see remarks under tuition waiver (item 14). Problem: How to handle cases where students would otherwise get scholarships.	Use if there is local tuition waiver. Otherwise not. Set limit equal to local tuition.
17.	Hard to assess, but not great.	Useful, but usually not of major importance.	Grant.

Benefit	Financial benefit to individual	Other advantages
LEAVES		
18. Leaves with pay (sabbatical or otherwise; also research assignments which are frequently considered as leaves)	Amount paid, except that expenses on leave usually greater than at home.	Improving quality of faculty member. Sometimes helps restore or maintain health. Research results.
19. Leaves (without pay)	Generally none, and expenses on leave usually greater than at home.	Often gives valuable varied experience. Often faculty members can serve public interest in this way.
OTHER		
20. Loans to faculty	Low rates.	Help in emergency.
21. "President's emergency fund"	Total, to a few individuals.	Meets dire emergency. May make it possible to avoid loans.
22. Moving expense	Direct benefit.	Individual makes decision more nearly on the merits of the position.
23. Discount privileges	Slight.	In very small communities, quality and variety of purchase may be enhanced.
24. Travel reimbursement for professional meetings, etc.	Total.	Encourages participation in professional activities. Increases effectiveness of faculty member. Can be used to equalize opportunities among departments.
25. Faculty club	(Usually a cost.)	Chiefly as a unifying and stimulating force.

Item	Cost to institution	Remarks	Recommendations
18.	Varies with cost of substitute, if any, or cost of staffing to permit leaves.	The total leaves and research assignment program is of major importance. In research-oriented institution, outside support for leaves is readily available in many fields and hard to get in others. Equalization is needed. Sabbatical leave inadequate method of securing doctorate. Problems: (1) Disruption of teaching program. (2) Disruption of work of graduate students. (3) Sometimes burden on colleagues.	In institution with research function, develop research assignments as basic program. Especially care for younger scholars. In other institutions, stress sabbatical leaves. Do not require return.
19.	Slight (sometimes a saving).	See leaves with pay (item 18). This is part of total leave program.	Grant unless clearly unreasonable to do so.
20.	Slight.	If such a program is deemed necessary, credit union is probably better. Some institutions favor educational loans for faculty member or his children. (This should be considered with family education.) Problems: (1) May encourage financial irresponsibility. (2) Lender-borrower relations not easy.	Avoid except possibly for family education.
21.	Not great. (Often a gift to college.)	Useful, but not a major item. Decisions should be made by individual, not committee. Problem: Arbitrary and possibly embarrassing decisions.	Establish, if possible.
22.	Total.	Great help to young man without backlog. Change in federal tax law (1964) permits deducting moving expenses under many circumstances.	Formalize. (Many use on ad hoc basis now.)
23.	Administration only.	Policy of doing this but hiding fact is bad. Sometimes administrative charge is made. Problems: (1) Bad relations with local businessmen. (2) Hard to get purchases serviced.	Do not do this except where local purchase is difficult. (Bookstore often desirable.)
24.	Total.	Some places, perhaps with stimulus to local scholarship but certainly to the detriment of meetings, pay more if paper is given. Some faculty members are away to an excessive extent (usually not at institutional expense).	Equalize opportunities between areas. Pay for official travel. Do not go all out. Same payment whether or not giving paper.
25.	Depends on subsidy (often substantial).	Facilities vary, and generalizations difficult.	Largely depends on local conditions. Meeting over food is an asset. I would push this, but in terms of local needs.

Benefit	Financial benefit to individual	Other advantages
26. Parking	(Often a cost.)	Convenience and morale.
27. Athletic facilities	Slight.	Good for health, morale and student contact.
28. Special events	Slight.	Cultural value, morale, and student contact.
29. Secretarial help	. . . .	. . . .
30. Payment of travel expenses for employment interview	. . . .	. . . .

PROGRAMS FOR RETIRED FACULTY AND WIDOWS (other than retirement annuities & insurance)*

Benefit	Financial benefit to individual	Other advantages
31. Work conditions for retired faculty	Slight.	Very great effect on morale, even before retirement. Often excellent work is done.
32. Health services for retired faculty	Substantial in some cases.	. . . .
33. Club, parking, athletic facilities, special events, etc., for retired faculty and widows	Slight.	Important to morale.
34. Housing for retired faculty members and widows; rental; restricted mortgage loans	May be substantial if rates below commercial.	Gives faculty sense of security, even before retirement. Some places, local real estate tax advantage.

*Medical insurance, of course, should be continuable.

Item	Cost to institution	Remarks	Recommendations
26.	To extent of subsidy.	Weather conditions may be major factor (consider our two largest states). Problems: (1) Ugliness. (2) Lack of exercise.	Entirely dependent on local conditions. Protect campus beauty. Since this is often a morale problem, work out with faculty.
27.	Slight in addition to facilities.	Family should be included when possible.	Meet student needs and treat faculty generously within these facilities.
28.	Slight. Depends on program for students.	Family should be included when possible.	Develop program to meet student need and then treat faculty generously within this program.
29.	. . . .	I consider this a condition of work except where help is given for personal business or thesis typing, etc.	Make as nearly adequate as possible.
30.	. . . .	I consider this a normal operating charge.	Pay, and include travel expenses of wife for visit in cases of tenure appointments.
31.	Can be considerable.	I consider this of real importance and insufficient attention has been given to it. Some items that are often needed: (1) Library use. (2) Office space. (3) Laboratory space. (4) Research assistance and equipment. (5) Secretarial help. Problem: Where needs are growing this takes much-needed facilities.	Make available on generous scale for those that actually use them (judge on activities rather than results). Do not hold space for person who does not use it.
32.	Not great unless program for faculty is elaborate.	Continuity of health services is important, especially where individual relationship has been established between doctor and patient.	Make available to emeriti and widows same health services that faculty have. Make it possible to continue all medical insurance policies.
33.	Slight.	. . . .	Be generous, and as generous to widows as to emeriti.
34.	Can be considerable, but usually slight loss of income.	Warrants more attention than has been given to it. Some places have plan by which elderly persons may move from large to smaller rental dwelling. Problem: Continued use of space that is larger than needed after family has flown.	Try to develop a reasonable program that avoids evictions in latter part of life. This depends on local conditions and on housing program for younger persons.

INDEX

THIS index does not cover the appendices. References are given at the end of each chapter to the relevant portions of the appendices.

Nursery school, 41

Papers, professional, 98
Parking: 5, 107–11, 139; diversity of
  needs, 4; affected by new buildings,
  107; for student cars, 108; charge for,
  108; policing of, 108; priorities, 108;
  bus service, 109; "they" say, 109–11;
  for retired faculty, 115
Personal loans. *See* Loans, personal
President's emergency funds, 56–57, 60–
  61
President's job: comments on, 122
Princeton plan, 14–17
Professional journals, 67
Professional papers, 98
Promotion: effect of leaves on, 80, 88

Quality of service: factors affecting, 135–
  36
Questionnaire: as basis for study, vi, viii,
  6

Real estate offices, 26
Recreational facilities: 5, 139; for faculty, 65; for retired faculty and
  widows, 117
Recruiting and retaining faculty: 134–
  35; related to type of institution, 119;
  "they" say, 123–29
Rental housing. *See* Housing, rental
Research: and policy of leaves, 83–86;
  related to recruitment of staff, 119–20,
  136
Retired faculty and widows: 114–18,
  138; lack of policy concerning, 114;
  health provisions for, 115; work space,
  115; housing for, 116; recreational
  facilities for, 117; "they" say, 117
Retirement: plans for, 4, 127, 137; contributions during leaves, 77
Retreats, 68
Robbins, Rainard B., 4

Sabbatical leaves. *See* Leaves, sabbatical

Salary: *vs.* other benefits, 3, 124
Secretarial help: 112–13; "they" say
  113; for retired faculty, 115
Sick leave, 49–52
Smoking in classrooms, 69
Special events: 5, 139; and faculty, 65
  and retired faculty and widows, 117

"Tax-deferred" annuities, 122
Tax regulations: 69, 137; effect on benefit programs, 4
Teachers' agency fees, 68
Teachers Insurance and Annuity Association of America, v, vi, vii, 4, 81, 122–
  32 *passim*
Tenure: related to leaves, 80, 88
"They," 123
Travel: 94–102; diversity of needs for,
  4; value to faculty member, 95; value
  to institution, 95; problems created by
  96, 101; purpose of, 100; "they" say
  100–102
—reimbursement for: 5, 136, 139; related to purpose, 94; basis of, 94; allotment, 95, 100–102; reasonable expenses, 96–98; inequities caused by
  grants, 96, 101; when giving papers,
  98; regulations in public institutions,
  98; for "prospects," 99
Travel fund: special recreational or cultural, 69
Tuition Exchange, Inc., 36, 38, 43–44
Tuition waiver, 128, 137. *See also* Educational privileges

Unemployment insurance, 121
U.S. Steel Foundation, v
University of Wisconsin, v, vii

Waiver of tuition, 128, 137. *See also*
  Educational privileges
Widows. *See* Retired faculty and widows
Working conditions, 136

X-ray examinations, 48